D0377532

PENGUIN BOOKS

THE PATRIOT CHIEFS

Alvin M. Josephy, Jr., is the author of many award-winning books on Indians and the American West, including *The Indian Heritage of America*, *The Nez Percé Indians and the Opening of the Northwest*, *Now That the Buffalo's Gone*, and *The Civil War in the American West*. He is a former Editor in Chief of *American Heritage* and was Founding Chairman of the Smithsonian's National Museum of the American Indian.

Also by Alvin M. Josephy, Jr.

The Nez Percé Indians and the Opening of the Northwest
The Indian Heritage of America
Red Power
The Long and the Short and the Tall
The Artist Was a Young Man
Black Hills—White Sky
On the Hill: A History of the United States Congress
Now That the Buffalo's Gone
The Civil War in the American West
America in 1492 (ed.)

THE PATRIOT CHIEFS

A Chronicle of American Indian Resistance

by ALVIN M. JOSEPHY, JR.

PENGUIN BOOKS

PENGUIN BOOKS
Published by the Penguin Group
Penguin Books USA Inc., 375 Hudson Street,
New York, New York 10014, U.S.A.
Penguin Books Ltd, 27 Wrights Lane, London W8 5TZ, England
Penguin Books Australia Ltd, Ringwood, Victoria, Australia
Penguin Books Canada Ltd, 10 Alcorn Avenue,
Toronto, Ontario, Canada M4V 3B2
Penguin Books (N.Z.) Ltd, 182–190 Wairau Road, Auckland 10, New Zealand

Penguin Books Ltd, Registered Offices:
Harmondsworth, Middlesex, England

First published in the United States of America by The Viking Press 1961
Viking Compass Edition published 1969
Published in Penguin Books 1976
This revised edition published in Penguin Books 1993

5 7 9 10 8 6

Portions of this book first appeared in *American Heritage*.

(CIP data available)
ISBN 0 14 02.3463 2

Printed in the United States of America
Set in Janson
Maps by Daniel Brownstein

To Betty, strong, patient,
and understanding,
a friend to people
who believe and
are unafraid.

CONTENTS

		PAGE
Acknowledgments		xi
Foreword		xiii
CHAPTER		
I:	The Real Hiawatha	1
II:	The Betrayal of King Philip	31
III:	Popé and the Great Pueblo Uprising	63
IV:	The Wilderness War of Pontiac	95
V:	Tecumseh, the Greatest Indian	129
VI:	The Death of Osceola	175
VII:	The Rivalry of Black Hawk and Keokuk	209
VIII:	Crazy Horse, Patriot of the Plains	255
IX:	The Last Stand of Chief Joseph	311
	Epilogue	341
	Bibliography	349
	Index	357

ACKNOWLEDGMENTS

THESE CHAPTERS could not have been written without the hard, pioneering work of numerous scholars and specialists who have provided the foundations of knowledge and understanding of the various Indian tribes. All serious writing about Indians must rest firmly on their studies, and I have listed in the bibliography with gratitude some that were most helpful and relevant to the preparation of this book.

In addition, save for two chapters where I pruned extensive bibliographies to appropriate lengths, I have mentioned most of the primary and secondary sources that I consulted. But I must particularly point out that in the case of many of the subjects of the chapters, a single author and book deserve more than passing acknowledgment. They are the basic biographies of people or the studies of tribes or historical occurrences already in print, whose fundamental, and sometimes monumental, research I could not have hoped to duplicate. Among them are the following which, while also listing them in the bibliography, I underscore here both to acknowledge my debt and to bring them to the attention of readers who might like to go on to their fuller treatments. They are: *Flintlock and Tomahawk*, Douglas Edward Leach's fine study of the King Philip War; Paul Horgan's beautiful narratives of the Pueblos and Popé's Revolt in *Great River*; Howard H. Peckham's brilliant work, *Pontiac and the Indian Uprising*; the sympathetic biography, *Tecumseh, Vision of Glory*, by Glenn Tucker; and the classic *Crazy Horse*, by Mari Sandoz.

I would also like to thank Miss Sandoz for additional material on Crazy Horse, and *American Heritage* magazine for permission to reprint "The Last Stand of Chief Joseph," which has been expanded for this book.

FOREWORD

THE AMERICAN INDIANS were many different peoples, often as different among themselves as the different peoples of Europe. Their great leaders also, when thought of as humans rather than "Indians," were like men anywhere who differed, one from another, in many ways. Some were military leaders of outstanding ability, if not genius. Others were gentle wise men with deep, philosophical understanding of human nature, both white and Indian. Still others were statesmen, remarkable orators or astute politicians. Most if not all of them might well have risen to leadership in a white world had they been whites.

From the first coming of the Europeans to America, the Indians were faced by the gravest threats that men face: challenges to freedom, right of conscience, personal security, the means of existence, and life itself. In each crisis the people and their leaders acted and reacted as other persons under similar circumstances would behave anywhere in the world. There were some cowards, some weaklings, some bargainers, some appeasers and compromisers; some were confused and frightened, some confused and very brave, and many were strong and unwavering patriots.

Some of the Indians' greatest patriots died unsung by white men, and because their peoples also were obliterated, or almost so, their very names are forgotten. But these are the stories of some of the greatest we know about—military men, philosophers, and statesmen. They were big men, as much a part of our heritage as any of our other heroes, and they belong to all Americans now, not just to the Indians.

Fairness and a balanced judgment demand further words of

explanation. In the first place, there were many other Indian leaders of heroic stature—Logan, Joseph Brant, John Ross, Cochise, and others—who might have been included here, and perhaps some readers will miss them. But they did not fit well into the scheme for this book. While this is not a history of American Indians, the subjects chosen were selected to provide variety in Indian backgrounds and cultures, geographic areas and historic periods, and particular large-scale problems that led to crises and conflicts. Arranged chronologically, they help to convey in ordered sense a narrative outline of much of Indian history.

Secondly, I trust that my motives will be understood in confining this book to the stories of Indian patriots. These men were, to the Indians, "good and brave men," their Nathan Hales, George Washingtons, and Benjamin Franklins. During their lifetimes, their white opponents considered them "bad Indians" and fastened their favor on others, less hostile or even friendly, whom they called "good Indians." Some of those so-called "good Indians" of the whites—Pushmataha, Washakie, Ouray, and others—were, in a way, patriots too, in that they recognized the inevitabilities of historic situations and tried peacefully to find paths to security for their peoples. They deserve understanding and appreciation also, but they are not the greatest heroes of the Indian peoples of today, and this book is not about them. Nor is it about truly trouble-making and ill-intentioned Indians, who were as plentiful in some situations as were unprincipled whites. The reader will understand, I am sure, that evil was never all on one side, and that the purpose of this book is not to imply that all Indians were "good" and all white men "bad."

In telling each story I have tried to be objective. If there is a fault, it is that this is a book only about the "good and brave men" of the American Indian people, and that the facts show that the sins did fall heavy against many of them.

—ALVIN M. JOSEPHY, JR.

THE PATRIOT CHIEFS

I

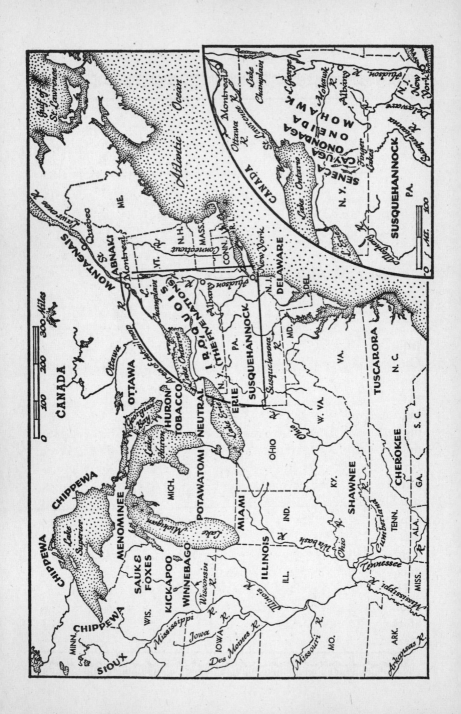

I

THE REAL HIAWATHA

Ye whose hearts are fresh and simple,
Who have faith in God and Nature
Who believe, that in all ages
Every human heart is human,
That in even savage bosoms
There are longings, yearnings, strivings
For the good they comprehend not . . .

Longfellow's *Hiawatha*

AT SUNRISE on March 16, 1649, an army of one thousand hideously-painted Iroquois Indians, far from their homeland in what is now New York State, war-whooped out of the Canadian woods to attack a quiet village of Hurons near the shore of Ontario's Georgian Bay. Behind a barrage of blazing firebrands the Iroquois scrambled over the walls of the stockade, butchering the settlement's panic-stricken inhabitants and seizing two French Jesuit missionaries from Quebec, Fathers Jean de Brébeuf and Gabriel Lalemant, who had been saying Mass for Huron converts in the village. A few of the Hurons, presumably after waiting long enough to observe the priests' fate, managed to escape the massacre and carry the news of what had happened to a nearby Jesuit mission station, which at that time was in charge of a French lay helper, Cristophe Regnault. In trembling hand Regnault recorded the details of what the Iroquois had done to the two priests.

His lurid narrative gave the world a horrifying report of Iroquois sadism, cannibalism, and blood rites. Yet it referred to one of the most intellectually advanced bodies of Indians north of Mexico, a great and powerful confederation of peoples that, even more incongruously, venerated as one of their most influ-

3

ential teachers a wise and gentle man named Hiawatha who years before had preached to them of universal peace, the brotherhood and equality of all mankind, and the end of torture and killing. What was more, in the structure of their political organization and the customs and institutions of their daily lives, they still followed the ideals of brotherhood and equality that Hiawatha had established among them, and based many of their tribal affairs on the peaceful standards of moral conduct that he had taught them. But to the world of his enemies, native or white, little of this showed. Unaware of Hiawatha or his philosophy, their antagonists knew only the sudden shriek of the war whoop and the ghastly, distorted face of the Iroquois at war.

Regnault's account of the deaths of the two priests was one of the earliest and most terrible tales of the fiendishness of the Iroquois to come from New France and, spread abroad in the Jesuit *Relations*, the annual reports of the missionaries in Canada, it helped to establish in white men's minds the reputation of the Iroquois for barbarism and cruelty that lasted until the nineteenth century. Many of the first whites in the Northeast, like Regnault, were undoubtedly influenced in their expectations of Indian savagery by Spanish narratives of tortures and horrors that had occurred in the Caribbean and the Mexican and South American areas during the ruthless conquests of the sixteenth century, and in his lonely and perilous surroundings the shocked French mission assistant might have loosed his imagination to exaggerate some of the details brought to him by the Hurons. But his gruesome recital was typical of a stream of bloodcurdling tales of other Iroquois atrocities that poured from the gloomy and war-torn colonial frontier for another century and a half. Despite the nobly humanitarian Hiawathan philosophy of brotherhood and peace that permeated their civilization, there was no doubt that aroused Iroquois warriors were capable of the worst. Long before the white men came, their enemies knew them as a fierce and merciless people who raided tirelessly for prisoners, practiced cannibalism, and indulged in torture and cruelty which to the Indians, as white men of a much later period came to recognize, was less a form of sadistic enjoyment than an honorable opportunity for their victims to demonstrate their courage and manhood while they were slowly and painfully done to death. Around the Iroquois, from as far back as legend and tradition could probe, there was an atmosphere of terror, and their name in the lore of surrounding tribes was a symbol of everything in the northern woodlands that was dreaded and hated.

From their first arrival on the borders of the Iroquois country, white men heard of them only in the most fearful terms. In 1609 Samuel de Champlain, the French explorer, established friendly trade relations with Algonquian Montagnais Indians around the site of present-day Quebec and Huron Indians who came from villages farther inland. Both peoples told him of fierce, man-eating demons called Iriakoiw, meaning rattlesnakes, who dwelled deep in the forests south of the St. Lawrence River. Later that same year, Champlain and some of his French fol-lowers, armed with heavy harquebuses, accompanied a war party of Montagnais and Hurons in search of the Iroquois. They found a large party of them on the eastern shore of the lake that now bears Champlain's name, and a battle ensued between the two groups. During the fighting, the French fired their harque-buses at the Iroquois, killing some of their leaders and startling the rest of them into flight. The Iroquois were stunned at first by the new "thunderhorn" weapons, and for a time were forced on the defensive by their ancient enemies, who now invaded their lands with French guns received in trade. But the Iroquois' anger mounted steadily against the French, and soon afterward, when the Dutch appeared at the site of present-day Albany and agreed to arm the Iroquois in return for furs, the rattlesnake people struck back with a vengeance against both their old native enemies and the French colonists who had been settling on the St. Lawrence. Fierce Iroquois war parties attacked Frenchmen everywhere and almost drove them from the continent. Though peace was established from time to time, the Dutch and later the English in New York held the Iroquois in tight alliance to themselves, and the French were never able to win to their side the tribesmen who refused to forget the first use of guns against them on Lake Champlain.

Though bound to the Iroquois by covenants of friendship, the Dutch, the British, and the American colonial leaders were always uneasily aware of their native allies' fanatic cruelty. The Iroquois war bands were, as the historian Francis Parkman later called them, "Tigers of America," who burned peaceful villages and cornfields, tomahawked, scalped, and bashed in the brains of women and children, and massacred soldiers and noncombatants alike. By the time of the American Revolution the colonists regarded the Iroquois with deep dread, and when most of the New York warriors chose to remain loyal to their traditional British allies the worst fears of the settlers along the border were realized by the bloody massacres of the Wyoming and Cherry Valleys.

Throughout the long colonial period, from the first explorers' meetings with the Iroquois until the end of the Revolution, few white men were able or willing to see more to the Iroquois than this surface barbarism of their war parties. Farther south, in Middle and South America, the Spaniards had long before found the advanced and admirable civilizations of the Aztecs and Incas which in many marvelous ways had even rivaled contemporary cultures of Europe. But everywhere else, in the generations of discoveries that had followed, the Indians had turned out to be Stone Age savages, considered so far below the intellectual level of white men as to deserve only extermination or the patronization and contempt of a superior race for an inferior one. The Iroquois had appeared to be no different. Their great numbers, military prowess, and ferocity had deterred the encroachments of whites on their lands, but the latter, while acknowledging grudging respect for their power, had continued to class them as unthinking savages, incapable of intellectual accomplishment.

And yet, to a few of the more perceptive and curious white men, unaware of the Indians' Hiawathan heritage, there were remarkably interesting things about the Iroquois, most of them all but obscured by their savage veneer, and many of them strangely incongruous when contrasted with their ferocious conduct in war. Among them were qualities first noticed by men who dealt with them in peace, by traders who received hospitable welcomes to their villages on the streams and wooded lake shores of central New York, and by colonial authorities who counciled with their leaders in solemn treaty meetings in Canada and at Albany. The sachems, as their principal chiefs were called, were often sage and impressive men, capable of deep and imaginative thinking, profound logic, intelligence, and soaring and persuasive oratory. Many whites, who observed the same intellectual qualities among lesser chiefs and villagers during peaceful visits to their settlements, called them "powerful reasoners," and described them as being considerably more intelligent and thoughtful than popular opinion held them to be.

Sometimes hints of such minority verdicts found their way into print. An early French historian of North America, Bacqueville de la Potherie, drawing on accounts of French officials who had met in peaceful councils with some of the Iroquois leaders, noted,

When one talks of the Five Nations (the Iroquois) in France, they are thought, by a common Mistake, to be meer Barbarians, always thirsting after Human Blood; but their true Character is very different; They are the Fiercest and most Formidable People in North America, and at the same time as Politick and Judicious as well can be conceiv'd.

Another writer, Cadwallader Colden, who wrote a history of the Iroquois in New York in 1727 based on the minutes and records of treaty meetings in Albany between the British and the Iroquois, praised the Indians as gifted orators and pointed out to his readers that "The Five Nations are a poor Barbarous

People, under the darkest Ignorance, and yet a bright and noble Genius shines thro' these black clouds."

Those who made serious efforts to observe the Iroquois found their intellectual abilities reflected most notably in certain highly developed customs and institutions of their daily lives, two of which in particular indicated an intelligence far above that of primitive barbarians. Though they had no written language, the Iroquois like other eastern Indians, had worked out an efficient substitute in the form of colored beads, called "wampum," which were fashioned from shells and strung together in strands or belts of various designs and symbols that had specific meanings. White traders and officials first found the Iroquois making and presenting the wampum belts to signify the binding of alliances and treaties or to record important decisions and events. But both strings and belts, some of which were made up of thousands of beads, were also used by the Iroquois as "memory aids," and were kept in the care of a Keeper of the Wampum, who was able to "read" from them and remind the people whenever necessary of the past occurrences which the different shells denoted.

Even more significant was a remarkably advanced moral and political system that seemed to run through all of Iroquois life, and could neither have been designed nor maintained by an uncomprehending people. The Iroquois, the whites early discovered, were in reality five separate tribes or nations, the Mohawks, Oneidas, Onondagas, Cayugas, and Senecas, united in a league or confederation that operated according to a constitution of laws. In an age of European monarchies and absolutism, the Indians' constitution, moreover, was based on principles of individual freedom and government by consent of the governed that white men themselves did not enjoy. "Each Nation," Colden wrote in 1727, "is an absolute Republick by its self, govern'd in all Publick Affairs of War and Peace by the Sachems or Old Men, whose Authority and Power is gain'd by and consists wholly in the Opinion the rest of the Nation have of their Wisdom and

Integrity. They never execute their Resolutions by Compulsion or Force upon any of their people. Honour and Esteem are their Principal Rewards, as Shame & being Despised are their Punishments."

So unique a native organization, resting on high-minded principles of republicanism and democracy, eventually quickened the interest of many colonial leaders, including Benjamin Franklin, but the gap between the two races was too wide and dangerous in the eighteenth century to permit serious study of the Iroquois system or its origins. A few traders and officials who gained the friendship and trust of the Indians did manage to provide eyewitness details of how the League worked. They talked of sachems sent from each nation to federal councils that met solemnly in a long, bark-covered house in the country of the Onondagas and, after long discussions in which each nation had equal voice, came to decisions that were binding on all the Iroquois. In addition, they furnished reports that described intricate divisions of each nation into family groups and clans that rose, pyramid-like, and conveyed authority and power from the bottom to the top, and other descriptions that hinted at an unusually powerful political role played by women. But it was not until after the American Revolution, when the Iroquois' war power was finally broken and white men, having conquered and subjugated them, could live and move safely among them, that more than superficial heed was paid to the backgrounds and intricacies of the Iroquoian civilization.

As information was then gathered and men began to recognize a marvelously sophisticated philosophical base on which the Iroquois' political system rested, their attention turned increasingly to the most intriguing question of all: When and how had this aboriginal people formed their League, a development that had apparently taken them farther along the road of political organization than any Indians north of the Aztecs? Had it been a gradual evolvement, or had it somehow occurred all at once?

For many years during the first part of the nineteenth century young Iroquois Indians who were receiving education at white men's schools tried to help supply an answer to the question. Traditional Iroquois teachings had been passed down to them from generation to generation, and they seemed confidently to possess the information the white men wanted. But when they tried to communicate, the white mind could not understand them. The Indians talked in English about the long ago, about the Iroquoian world and Iroquoian life of the past, but they told about it in the only way they could, the way in which it had come down to them from their fathers, wrapped in the imagery and metaphors of the Indian. In terms almost of myth they told of something called a Great Peace and of a period when great idealism had been brought to the Indians by the good and wise man, Hiawatha. White men who had been among the Iroquois had already begun to hear of Hiawatha during the previous century, but it had been difficult for them to understand what the Indians were saying about him. The Iroquois' imaginative way of recounting or singing their past had made him appear sometimes to have been a religious god or symbol, sometimes a legendary hero and sometimes a real man. Now, for the first time, he was linked to the founding of the League, but again in such a metaphorical manner that most of the white questioners became convinced that Hiawatha was simply a legendary hero used as a symbol for the real men who had founded the League.

In the second quarter of the nineteenth century Henry R. Schoolcraft, an early American ethnologist, collected some of the Iroquois legends and published them in such a way as to identify Hiawatha as the greatest of all the Iroquoian gods, the "Master of Life," whom the Indians actually called Teharonhiawagon, which Schoolcraft apparently assumed was just another way of spelling Hiawatha. At the same time he went on to identify the same god also as the chief deity of the Chippewa Indians, an Algonquian-speaking people who lived farther west in the Great Lakes region, and he ended by indiscriminately referring to the Chippewa deity as Hiawatha in a series of Chippewa myths which he published. The error was compounded by Henry Wadsworth Longfellow, who, fascinated by Schoolcraft's Chippewa legends, based his famous Indian poem on them, and in 1855 sent the name Hiawatha around the world to literary immortality as a fictionalized Chippewa hero.

To the Indians who knew better, nothing could have been more ridiculous. It was like making an ancient French leader into a mythical folk hero of the Germans. But no white man knew the difference, and many years were to pass before the true Iroquoian leader, Hiawatha, would emerge from the legendary mists of the past. Finally, late in the nineteenth century, J. N. B. Hewitt, a talented ethnologist associated with the Smithsonian Institution's Bureau of American Ethnology in Washington, and himself a Tuscarora Indian of the Iroquoian family, turned to the problem of making clear the history of the Iroquois League. Able to think with the mind of an Iroquois and "translate" the imagery of the Indian tongue into a factual narrative that white men could understand, Hewitt gathered the centuries-old Iroquois accounts of Hiawatha and the founding of the League, and in a series of important publications separated historical occurrences from the legendary material in which they were clothed, and for the first time revealed the scope and stature of the real man, Hiawatha.

Since no white man was present in Hiawatha's day to provide in white men's terms a contemporary account of his life, the telling of his story today rests greatly on an acceptance of Hewitt's work in determining where Indian imagery shrouded fact, and where it was simply myth. Happily, an even better understanding of the Iroquois past has been achieved since Hewitt's day, and more recent work by authorities such as Dr. William N. Fenton, a foremost specialist on the Iroquois, has uncovered in Indian institutions and traditions additional evidence of the real-life Hiawatha, and corroborated the main outline of Hewitt's version of his life.

Known to millions of school children and adults throughout the world as the very image of the "noble red man," the real Hiawatha was probably in the first years of his life a cannibal. He was born either a Mohawk or an Onondaga Indian in present-day upper New York State in the first or second quarter of the sixteenth century. Little is known about his early life except that, according to the traditions about him, he married the daughter of a chief, became an influential medicine man or magician, noted for his oratorical powers, and had either three or seven daughters—the story varies. The time he became important in Iroquois history has been established as about 1570, and the forces that came to a climax to make him important had been gathering about the Iroquois for many years.

At the time the Spaniards, fresh from their conquests of the Aztecs and Incas, were pushing northward from the Gulf Coast and through the deserts of the Southwest, but no known white man had yet been in the interior of the Northeast, and the settlements of Plymouth and New Amsterdam were still almost half a century in the future. Spread through the Appalachian forests of the eastern part of North America were two great divisions of Iroquoian-speaking people, still in barbarous state and entirely ignorant of the white invaders. The southern branch, made up of Cherokees or "cave people" and Tuscaroras or "hemp gatherers," occupied what are now North Carolina and Tennessee. The northerners were scattered in perhaps two hundred different villages from the St. Lawrence River to Ohio and Pennsylvania. There is speculation concerning the origin of all the Iroquoian people; some persons suggest that they migrated from a southern region sometime after the start of the Christian era, and others that they spread southward from near the mouth of the St. Lawrence. Recent evidence, however, indicates that they probably came from the Mississippi and Ohio River Valleys, and were descendants of mound-building Indians of the ancient Midwest.

By the middle of the sixteenth century the northerners were well established in semi-permanent, stockaded villages in the

northeastern wilderness, each village made up of a number
of long bark houses that resembled the shape of World War
II Quonset huts, in which up to ten families lived side by side
around their own fires. The men hunted, fished, and warred,
and the women cared for the affairs of home and tended the
cornfields that surrounded each village. Altogether, the northern
Iroquois numbered no more than forty thousand people. There
were Hurons, so-called Neutrals and Tobacco People in Canada,
Eries or "long tails," Honniasonts and Conestogas or Susquehannocks in Ohio and Pennsylvania, and five closely related tribes,
who called themselves Ongwanonsionni, or "people of the extended lodge," and lived in the New York lake and river valleys
between present-day Albany and Buffalo. The most numerous
and westerly of them were Senecas, grouped around the lake of
the same name. To their east were Cayugas, a small but cruel
tribe, and east of them were Onondagas, "Dwellers on hilltops,"
and Oneidas, spread along Oneida Lake. The most easterly of
the tribes were Hiawatha's people, who called themselves "the
flint people" but were known to their Algonquian enemies as
Mohawks, "eaters of men." They ranged west of Lake Champlain
and the Hudson River from the St. Lawrence to the upper waters
of the Delaware. The five tribes combined, it is believed, numbered about five thousand people.

Generally, the Iroquois were strong and athletic, with long
heads and a slender build, physically agile and trained from child-
hood to develop stamina and endure pain. In their political life
women held a special and important position. The basis of all
organization was the "fireside," consisting of the mother and all
her children. But each fireside, in turn, was part of a larger
group called an *ohwachira*, comprising all the descendants of a
particular woman—her children, grandchildren, great-grandchildren, and so on. The nature of the ohwachira, which was a
particularly complex unit, long defied the understanding of white
men, who could not fathom the unfamiliar way in which its
strands ran through Iroquois society, separating husbands from

wives, and fathers from their children, and binding together, instead, in large, sprawling, uterine families people who lived far
distant from one another. Thus, all of a woman's children were
members of the ohwachira to which she and her brothers and
sisters belonged, but their father belonged to his mother's
ohwachira, along with his brothers and sisters and all the children
of his sisters. Fathers were therefore not bound to their own
children (who called their mother's brothers "father") and were
responsible for nephews (whom they called "sons").

The system had originated far back in antiquity and, uniting
all the descendants in the female line of a particular woman, had
established uniquely cohesive political groups that had nothing
to do with where the members lived or what villages the individual firesides belonged to. From one generation to the next,
the head of an ohwachira was succeeded by her oldest daughter
who, upon elevation, assumed the unusual power and authority
that accompanied the position. Two or more ohwachiras made
up a clan, and the various clans within a tribe composed the
nation, but all basic authority up to the top stemmed from the
ohwachiras and the women who headed them. They appointed
the male delegates and deputies who represented the ohwachiras
in the clan and tribal councils, and in consultation with the other
women of marriageable age within their ohwachiras originated
the questions that would be discussed or acted upon in the men's
councils, and recommended to their male delegates what views
to present.

The religious, or philosophic, ideas of the Iroquois were
equally complex, and were based on a concept in which all life
was fused spiritually with the natural objects and forces around
the Indians. Many of those forces, including ones they could not
see—dangers in war and traveling, hunger, illness, and evil spirits
—constantly threatened them, and against those forces they believed they were armed to varying degrees with an inner
spiritual power called *orenda*, which helped them resist the ma-
levolent forces. One man's orenda was necessarily small, but it

contributed to the combined, and therefore greater, orendas of the firesides, ohwachiras, and clans. The sum of all the orendas within a tribe helped to make the nation strong, but whenever a person died or was killed the total orendas of the different social groups to which his had been added were reduced. To overcome such losses and maintain a group's sum orenda, prisoners had to be taken and adopted into the ohwachiras and tribes. The custom explained many of the Iroquoian raiding parties for prisoners, and though many captives who were not needed were killed, others eventually came to fill the ranks of the different nations, particularly of the Oneidas, two-thirds of whose members at the time of the arrival of the first whites were reported to be adopted Hurons and Algonquians who had been captured in war.

In addition, the Iroquois believed in a Master of Life, who had been the first being on earth and who had commanded men to love one another and live in peace. He was opposed, in their mythology, by an evil brother who led the Indians in wrongdoing, but the Master, Teharonhiawagon, had promised to send an ambassador to the tribes to help them fight evil when their need became great. By the time of Hiawatha that day seemed long overdue. The Iroquois had gone far down the road from Teharonhiawagon's noble teachings and were almost irretrievably in the hands of the Master's evil brother. Everywhere the Iroquois were at constant war. Even among the five tribes of New York there were no friendly bonds. They fought, tortured, and hated one another, sometimes over hunting and fishing rights and the infringements of tribal territories, but more often because of the custom of blood revenge. Every time a man was killed, his slaying had to be avenged by the murder of the man who had killed him. It meant a never-ending warfare and a state that approached anarchy among the different tribes. By the era of Hiawatha, "the men," according to an Onondaga legend translated by J. N. B. Hewitt, "were ragged with sacrifice and the women scarred with flints, so everywhere there was misery."

In the war-weary atmosphere of Iroquoian self-destruction,

there were leaders who again remembered the teachings of Teharonhiawagon, and wondered what could be done to return the
people to the road of his commandments. Some began to look
for the coming of the promised messiah, but others, trying to
find a way to end the bloody custom of revenge killings, proposed a council of all the leaders who were worried about the
future of the Iroquois. Among them was Hiawatha, who was apparently living among the Onondagas and was particularly
looked up to by the others because of his abilities as an orator
and worker of magic.

There are many versions, most of them still clothed in Iroquois idiom and subtlety, of what now occurred. Prominent in all
the accounts is the symbolic figure of a fierce and crafty Onondaga chief, named Atotarho, who was opposed to Hiawatha and
the council of reformers, and who used every method of witchcraft and wizardry to frustrate their plans. In his legendary guise
Atotarho is a fiendish and evil-minded character, possibly
thought of as the Master of Life's evil brother, still working hard
to keep control of the Iroquois. But despite the imagery that de-
scribes his body as being distorted by seven crooks, his hands
awry like those of a turtle, and his hair a mass of writhing, hissing serpents, he was an actual Onondaga leader (some versions
make him the half-brother of Hiawatha), who had established
something of a tyranny in the wilderness, complete with spies
and assassins, and who was hated and feared above all others by
the Iroquoian people.

Again and again Atotarho's informers brought him news of the
secret plans for the meetings of the council, and each time he appeared in his terrible wrath to confound and disperse the peace-
minded chiefs. From the beginning his worst venom was directed
at Hiawatha, whom he considered the principal moving force
of the reformers, and by working magic—a symbol, perhaps, for
accidents and actual murders—he killed Hiawatha's daughters,
one by one. The last one met her death in typical fashion. After
all the rest had been slain by the designs of the monstrous wiz-

ard, the grieving Hiawatha made one final attempt to hold a secret meeting. The other chiefs and their followers assembled
around him in the woods and built temporary cabins and lodges
near his. Then, suddenly, they learned that Atotarho had again
heard of the council from his spies, and was once more present
among them. Their fear increased, but, as nothing happened,
they waited uneasily for Hiawatha to call the meeting. Then one
day, when Hiawatha's last remaining daughter, who was heavy
with child, was in the forest gathering fagots for the fire, Atotarho rose to his feet and pointed to the sky, shouting, "Look ye
up! Some living thing is falling. What is it?" The people all
looked up and, following his gaze, saw a beautiful creature plum-
meting through the sky toward the woods where Hiawatha's
daughter was. Impelled by curiosity, the people started forward
in a great rush and, before they could stop, knocked down Hiawatha's daughter and trampled her to death. Again the evil
genius had triumphed, and the grief-stricken Hiawatha, admitting defeat, decided to abandon the Onondagas and carry his
cause into the lands of the other Iroquoian tribes.

As an exile he wandered far and long, moving from village to
village and pleading with the leaders of the Mohawks, Oneidas,
and Cayugas to renounce war and murder and restore peace and
brotherhood among the Iroquois. Everywhere, he was given shelter and a sympathetic hearing, but converts came to him slowly.
The woods were full of ancient hatreds and suspicions, and the
different tribes feared one another too deeply to drop their
guard. Finally, according to one version, the Oneidas tentatively
agreed to accept his teachings if the Mohawks would do the
same. The Mohawks, followed by the Cayugas, at last fell in line
too, but only on one condition, and that a seemingly impossible
one—that Hiawatha persuade the man most feared of all, Atotarho, to end his tyrannical ways and bring the Onondagas into
peaceful relations with the others.

The condition was too much for Hiawatha, and once again he
seemed defeated. At this point, a remarkable man named Dega-

nawidah entered his life, a wanderer whose extraordinary vision and purpose made him in many ways an even greater figure in Iroquois lore than Hiawatha. As a shining symbol endowed with the supernatural, Deganawidah has come down through the ages more a legend than a real man, but most students today believe that he was an actual Indian prophet, philosopher, or mystic who appeared from the wilderness at a critical moment in Iroquois history to guide and direct Hiawatha, and who, like Buddha and Zoroaster, was elevated after his death to the status of a demigod.

Deganawidah had come from the lands of the Hurons, the Iroquoian "crooked tongues" who lived along the lakes in eastern Ontario. Nothing for sure is known about his birth or early life, but tradition has woven a marvelous tale that might reflect influences sown among the Iroquois in later days by Christians. According to this story Deganawidah was the son of an unmarried virgin named Djigosasee, who lived alone with her mother, too poor and despised to belong to a clan, on the outskirts of a Huron village. No man paid Djigosasee attention, but when she began to show that she was carrying a child her mother grew furious and upbraided her for bringing scandal upon them by not having married the father. The poor, confused daughter protested tearfully, but her mother kept up her angry assaults until one night in a dream she learned that her daughter had been telling the truth, and that a male child would be born whom they should name Deganawidah, meaning "he the thinker." The boy, she also learned to her horror, would be destined indirectly to cause the ruin of the Huron people.

The next day the mother told the daughter of her dream and apologized for not having believed her, but, fearing the evil destiny of the child, the two women decided to destroy it when it was born. After its birth they took it to a frozen stream, cut a hole in the ice, pushed the child into the water, and returned to their lodge. The next morning when they awoke, the baby was lying unharmed and asleep between them. The bewildered women tried twice more to kill the infant, but each time it was returned to them unhurt, and they finally decided that it was the will of the Master of Life that they raise it.

With the name Deganawidah, the fatherless youth grew to manhood, a lonely, brooding figure, ignored and persecuted by the other Hurons. His only companion was his mother, who taught him tolerance and love and made him aware that he had been given a divine mission in the world. He stammered terribly and could scarcely talk, but he had a handsome face that came gradually to reflect the soul of a mystic. One day he had a powerful vision that swept over and transformed him. He saw a great spruce tree, reaching up to the sky and growing strong from soil composed of three sets of double principles of life. They were sanity of mind and health of body—peace between individuals and groups; righteousness in conduct, thought, and speech —equity and justice among peoples; physical strength and civil authority—power of the orenda. The tree was anchored in the ground by five roots, and from its base stretched a snow-white carpet that covered the rocky countryside. Atop the tree sat an eagle. In the symbolism of the vision, Deganawidah recognized the tree as humanity, growing from the basic principles of virtuous relations among men. The carpet protected the lands of tribes that adopted the three double principles, but it could be extended to the ends of the earth to provide the shelter of brotherhood and peace to every nation and race of mankind. The five roots were five tribes that gave the tree its firm support, and the eagle was humanity's lookout against any enemies that might try to disturb the peace.

Deganawidah now understood his mission. The vision had been a directive to him from the Master of Life to set out and unite the human race in a single family founded on the three double principles. It was impossible for him to begin his task among the Hurons, where he was an outcast and had no standing. So, after saying good-by to his mother, he left the country of the "crooked tongues" and traveled to the lands of other Iroquois, looking for converts and disciples. Because he belonged to no tribe he was allowed to move freely through the countries of strangers, but when he preached he stammered, and his words were not well received.

There are various versions regarding exactly when and under what conditions Deganawidah met Hiawatha. Some traditions that make Deganawidah more important than Hiawatha in the events leading to the founding of the Iroquois League relate that it was Deganawidah who first got all the tribes except the Onondagas to agree to unity, and that he finally met Hiawatha and used him to convert the evil Atotarho. Another version, more popularly accepted, has Deganawidah coming on the melancholy Hiawatha while the latter was an exile from the Onondagas after the death of his last daughter. In this story, Deganawidah, who was already embarked on his mission to bring peace to the world, heard of Hiawatha, but was distressed to learn that he followed the custom of eating humans. Here was a convert, he thought, but he must first cure him of the unvirtuous practice of cannibalism. Deganawidah went to Hiawatha's lodge and, finding him away, climbed to the roof and lay flat on his stomach, looking down through the smoke hole. Soon Hiawatha returned with the dead body of an Indian, which he cut up and threw into a kettle to boil. When it was cooked he prepared to eat it, but as he reached into the kettle he saw the face of Deganawidah reflected in the water from the smoke hole, and thought it was his own. He paused and began to think, coming finally to the conclusion that so beautiful a face did not agree with the hideousness of what he was doing. From then on he decided that he would give up cannibalism. He went outside to empty the kettle in a stream, and there met Deganawidah to whom he admitted the sudden change in his habits. Deganawidah congratulated him, and enlisted him in his cause.

However the two men actually met, they soon managed to complement each other in a common crusade. To Hiawatha's vague appeals for an end of Iroquois blood-letting, Deganawidah added a practical plan of unified government among the Indians, based on a set of specific principles or laws. But Deganawidah could not speak well, and Hiawatha became his messenger to the tribes, using his powers of statesmanship and oratory to win acceptance of what was to become known as the Great Peace. One nation after another, among the five, agreed to it, but again Atotarho and his Onondagas were the stumbling block to its final achievement. This time, with Deganawidah's guidance, Hiawatha succeeded in converting the evil wizard.

Iroquois legends tell of the great event with the usual imagery. According to one of the stories, Deganawidah held a great council with Hiawatha and the other chiefs who had already agreed to the peace, and they decided to visit Atotarho together. To help them straighten out his twisted mind and body, they fashioned thirteen strings of wampum and sang the Six Songs, which were part of the rites of the Dead Feast. Then they sent two spies to discover where Atotarho was. The spies found him and soon returned with terrifying stories of his ghastly physical appearance. Bolstering their courage, Deganawidah announced that it was their duty now to reconstruct the evil one's mind, and the chiefs started off on their mission, singing. Eventually, they reached Atotarho's village and, amid the frightened whispers of his followers, were ushered into his presence. The dreadful, twisted shape of the monster horrified them, but they unwrapped the thirteen strings of wampum and began to sing the Six Songs. Atotarho became entranced, and soon Deganawidah said to him, "Now we will reconstruct and straighten out your mind." The visitors continued singing, and as they handed Atotarho one of the strings of wampum, Deganawidah said, "This song hereafter shall belong to you alone. It is called 'I use it to beautify the earth.'" As Atotarho's mind began to change, Deganawidah passed his hands over the wizard's feet which had claws like a bear's and were shaped like those of a tortoise. They too instantly changed into the normal feet of a man. Next, Deganawidah restored his deformed hands and brushed the hissing snakes from his hair, saying, "Thy head shall now be like that of a human being." Finally, he straightened his twisted, misshapen body, and announced, "We have now redeemed Atotarho. Everything will now prosper in a natural and peaceful manner. It is now our duty to work, first, to secure to the nations peace and tranquillity."

In this version of Atotarho's redemption it is probable that Iroquois imagery had fused Deganawidah, the messiah, and Hiawatha, his instrument, into one symbolic person, for most of the other traditions credit Hiawatha as the man who actually combed the serpents of evil thoughts out of Atotarho's hair, and Hiawatha's name means just that—"he, the comber." The true story, quite possibly, was that Hiawatha was sent by Deganawidah to work on the real-life tyrant, and, by a combination of astute statesmanship and political bargaining, finally persuaded Atotarho to adopt Deganawidah's philosophy and join the new League of the Great Peace that the Iroquois were fashioning. How he accomplished it is not known, but significant precedents of other great conversions, such as that of Constantine to Christianity, abound in history. Probably Hiawatha made many appeals to Atotarho's vanity, for it is known that in the end he promised to name the Onondaga chief as the "firekeeper," or most important member of the new confederacy, and proclaimed to all the tribes that the great council fire of the League would burn perpetually in the land of the Onondagas. At any rate, Atotarho was completely converted and in his new, benign character agreed to join the League as soon as the Senecas were also enrolled, which occurred soon afterward.

The clan leaders of the five happily united tribes now gathered around council fires,. under the guidance of Deganawidah and Hiawatha, to fashion the government and laws of their new confederation. "We must now work on that which is the guarantee of our welfare . . . so that the nations of Natural Man may dwell in peace and tranquillity, undisturbed by the shedding of blood," said the mythically fused Deganawidah-Hiawatha figure. "Into our bundle have we gathered the causes of war, and have cast this bundle away. Yea, we even uprooted a tall pine tree, making a very deep hole in the earth, and at the bottom of this hole runs a swift water current. Into this current have we thrown the causes of wars and strife. Our great-grandchildren shall not see them, for we have set back in its former place the great tall pine tree."

Ignorant of the white man's long search for political freedom, and without previous experience of their own in self-government, the delegates of the five tribes gradually erected a new federal council by extending the traditional structures of their firesides, ohwachiras, and clans. To the new council, which could be called into session whenever necessary but which was obliged to meet at least every five years, would be sent fifty sachems, appointed by the female leaders of the tribal ohwachiras. The sachems would serve for life, but could be removed by the matrons of their own ohwachiras for infirmity, misconduct, or certain other specified reasons. Atotarho's Onondagas were privileged to send the largest number of delegates, fourteen, to the federal meetings. The Cayugas could send ten, the Oneidas and Mohawks nine each, and the Senecas eight. None of the federal sachems could be warriors, since warriors might be disposed to take warlike stands. Nor were their positions made hereditary. When a sachem died, the leader of his ohwachira appointed his successor, who adopted the name and federal functions of the man he succeeded. Thus the names and prescribed duties of the members of the first council were perpetuated. An Onondaga named Atotarho was always firekeeper and moderator, and in later times he appeared to the whites as the greatest of the living sachems. The places of Deganawidah and Hiawatha were the only ones that were never to be filled. After their deaths the places remained empty, though the originals were always considered present.

Without the knowledge of writing, the League's founders worked out a constitution that prescribed how the council would function. During its meetings the sachems, who would wear antlers on their heads to signify their positions, would be the supreme voice and law of all the tribes. Though the female ohwachira leaders could watch them closely, they could neither control nor advise the sachems in their discussions. The sachems voted as tribes rather than as individuals, and each tribe had one vote. The Mohawks and Senecas sat on one side of the fire, the Oneidas and Cayugas on the other, and the Onondagas, as fire-keepers and moderators, sat between them, at their head. The Mohawks had the privilege of opening proceedings by raising the question to be considered. After they and the Senecas had reached agreement on it, they "threw it across the fire" for discussion by the Oneidas and Cayugas. If they agreed with the Mohawks and Senecas, the issue was considered settled. If they did not agree, the Onondagas took it up for settlement. Sometimes they favored one side rather than the other, and sometimes they provided a compromise. Again the matter would be discussed, first by the Mohawks and Senecas, and then by the Oneidas and Cayugas. If agreement was still not reached, the Onondagas again rendered a decision, and this time it was final and binding on all.

The "capital" of the Iroquois League was established on the lands of the centrally located Onondagas, and at the time of the arrival of the first English it was situated in a lake-shore village near the present town of Cazenovia, New York, south of Syracuse. From time to time it was moved to different sites within the Onondaga country, but each time its federal fire was rekindled in a special Extended House, to which the delegates of the tribes periodically traveled for solemn meetings of the League.

In addition to establishing the forms of a federal government, the united tribes accepted Hiawatha's persuasive pleadings for laws based on Deganawidah's three double principles that were necessary to ensure the Great Peace and protect the lives and liberties of humanity. Cannibalism was outlawed, save as a symbolic act in war against enemies of the Great Peace (eating an enemy's heart to acquire his courage), and the rights of individuals to safety and justice were ensured. The most important reform ended the terrible custom of the blood feud. Thereafter when an Indian took the life of another one, the bereaved family no longer had the right to seek revenge by killing the murderer, but had to accept twenty strings of wampum from the family of the slayer, which included ten for the dead man and ten for the life of the murderer himself. If a woman was slain, the price of satisfaction was thirty strings of wampum.

In the council fire and new laws of the five tribes, Deganawidah saw the start of the realization of his great vision of universal peace and brotherhood. The new order and its wonderful guarantees of a world without strife and war applied only to the tribes that adopted his three double principles and allowed the great white, protecting carpet of his vision to be spread across their lands. But Deganawidah had faith now that it would spread to the ends of the earth. "A council fire for all nations shall be kindled," he had said. "It shall be lighted for the Cherokees and for the Wyandots. We will kindle it also for the seven nations living toward the sunrising, and these nations shall light such fires for the peoples living still further toward the sunrising. And we will kindle the fire also for the nations that dwell toward the sunsetting. All shall receive the Great Law and labor together for the welfare of man." There was no doubt in his mind that his work, so well begun, would now be embraced by all men, and one day, according to legend, he gathered the people and told them, "Now I shall be seen no more of men and I go whither none can follow me." Then he entered a canoe of luminously white stone, paddled out on Lake Onondaga, and disappeared forever into the sunset.

Hiawatha remained behind, a real man among the Iroquois, and as a wilderness apostle and missionary carried the League's message far and wide to other Iroquoian tribes. At first, among Eries, Hurons, and Neutrals, there were tentative acceptances, and Hiawatha and his messengers then went farther, in long, daring trips along the paths and waterways of the northeastern forests, to Shawnees, Delawares, Miamis, Sauk, and other alien and distant tribes as far away as Lake Superior and the waters of the Mississippi River. From all of them he returned with strings of wampum shells, bearing designs that told of men and nations that had agreed, after listening to him, to "put their minds" in the long house of the five tribes. As a result of his trips Hiawatha's reputation increased among his people, and the Iroquois viewed him as a great and wise man whose powers could bring all the nations of the earth to the Great Peace.

According to one tradition Hiawatha finally followed Deganawidah into the unknown, setting off one day in a mystical, white bark canoe and drifting into the mists of Lake Champlain. Another version says that he spent his old age among the Mohawks as a revered and beloved elder statesman. By the time he died he was accepted by the Iroquois as a man who had been close to the Master of Life himself, and after his death his name was rapidly clothed in mystery and legend. Soon his reputation eclipsed that of Deganawidah, and by the time white men began to interview the Iroquois about their myths and traditions, the memory of Deganawidah had grown dim, while that of Hiawatha was strong and moving.

Hiawatha's early successes in gaining acceptance for the Great Peace among other tribes proved illusionary almost from the beginning. There is no evidence that any of the nations which he is supposed to have visited ever understood the revolutionary nature of the newly created council fire that blazed in the country of the Onondagas. Deganawidah had provided for treating with such peoples who refused to join the Great Peace, and the League's constitution said specifically that when the five united nations failed peacefully to convince war-minded tribes to come onto the great white carpet of peace and brotherhood "the war captain shall let a string of white lake shells fall from his outstretched hands. War shall thereby be declared and the war captain shall have his men at his back to support him."

White shells were soon falling like snow, and Iroquois war

parties set off in all directions, like inspired Moslems of the Old World, to fight fanatically against peoples who resisted the ambassadors of the League and Deganawidah's principles. When the first French arrived, the Iroquois crusade against the Hurons and the Algonquian tribes of the St. Lawrence River was well under way, but the newcomers to the continent regarded it as little more than a purposeless warfare of savages. At the same time the introduction of the white men's tempting offer of trade goods for furs aroused new and unprecedentedly bitter rivalries among tribes and added a strong economic motive to the war aims of the Iroquois. Though the Hiawathan crusade continued as the spiritual core of their drives, the Iroquois' efforts to dominate the Indian fur trade and the cruelty and blood lust with which they pursued their objectives tended to obscure the philosophic basis of their wars. Gradually they conquered and dispersed all the tribes that resisted them, including the Hurons, Neutrals, Tobacco People, Eries, and Susquehannocks. The theoretical unity of the League did not always find the Five Nations arrayed together in battle, but generally it provided a mainspring and strength to their cause, enabling them to combine war parties of the five individual tribes into Confederation armies of more than a thousand men, which no single native people could oppose. In time the triumphant Iroquoian warriors ranged against tribes far beyond their homelands, and spread terror among Potawatomis, Mascoutens, Illinois, and Sauk on the Great Lakes and the Mississippi River, and against Algonquin tribes as far south as Virginia and the Carolinas. Victories swelled the power of their orendas with prisoners from a dozen different nations, and the dominion over which they were virtually uncontested stretched at one time across thousands of square miles, from the Atlantic to Lake Superior, and from Canada to the Tennessee River.

Despite their conquests, they never lost sight of the ideals of the white carpet, and over the tribes they subdued they often exercised paternal supervision. They discouraged internal strife, and, whenever one of the conquered nations got into trouble, sent them a delegation of chiefs to restore tranquillity and suggest methods for avoiding future difficulties. Eventually, as the advancing white men overran countries of the Indians, various tribes, including some that had originally resisted the Iroquois warriors, voluntarily asked for, and received, sanctuary on the lands of the Five Nations. From Long Island, Manhattan, New Jersey, Delaware, and Pennsylvania distraught Leni-Lenapes, or Delawares, trekked to the country of Hiawatha, seeking shelter and protection under the laws of Deganawidah's three sets of double principles. They were followed by Piscataways from the Potomac River, Nanticokes from Maryland's eastern shore, Saponis and Tutelos from Virginia, and finally by the once-powerful Iroquoian Tuscaroras who came up from the Carolinas after suffering disastrous defeats by the whites and joined the Iroquois League as a Sixth Nation, in equality with the original Five, about 1715.

Through two strife-torn centuries, the unity of Hiawatha's confederation maintained the power and strength of the Five Nations against all enemies, native and white. And when military defeat during the American Revolution finally ended the League's ability to resist further, its marvelous political institutions lived on, in part, in the new governments that civilized white men were establishing for themselves. Throughout the eighteenth century the republican and democratic principles that lay at the heart of the Five Nations' system of self-government had been included among the studies of the enlightened philosophers of Europe and America who were seeking more just and humane ways for men to be governed. The political organization of the League was also eyed by colonial leaders, dreaming of unity among the English settlements, and on several occasions Iroquois leaders are known to have chided the colonists for not forming a union modeled on the League of the Five Nations.

In 1754 Benjamin Franklin's proposed Albany Plan of Union

for the colonies drew direct inspiration from Hiawatha's League, and Franklin was not hesitant in reminding his fellow colonists that "It would be a strange thing if Six Nations of ignorant savages should be capable of forming a scheme for such an union and be able to execute it in such a manner as that it has subsisted ages and appears indissoluble; and yet that a like union should be impracticable for ten or a dozen English colonies, to whom it is more necessary and must be more advantageous, and who cannot be supposed to want an equal understanding of their interests."

It would be impossible to trace more than an indirect influence of the Iroquois League, via the liberal philosophers of the eighteenth century, on the United States government as it was constituted in 1789. But in such forms as the methods by which Congressional Senate and House conferees work out bills in compromise sessions, one may recognize striking similarities to the institutions of the great council fire of the League which, despite the corrosive surroundings of the white man's civilization, the Iroquois people still faithfully maintain at their present-day "capital" near Brantford, Ontario. Even more genius, however, can be credited to the humanitarian Iroquoian conceptions of brotherhood and peace, for they were devised and achieved by Deganawidah and Hiawatha for Stone Age savages before the coming of the white man, and they are still earnestly yearned for by the parliaments and United Nations of twentieth-century humanity.

II

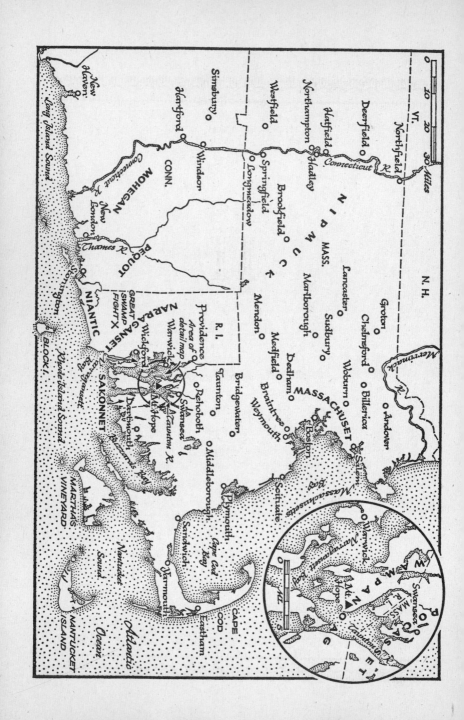

II

THE BETRAYAL OF KING PHILIP

To the observer who stands far enough back, the history of the Americas can be viewed as a narrative of intrusions by many different peoples. The last major group of newcomers, the white men of Europe, were the most thorough in their effect; they seized all the land and, with minor exceptions, conquered or exterminated everyone already on the continents.

The first people in America came probably more than twenty thousand years ago, drifting after wild game across a land bridge that existed between Siberia and present-day Alaska, and not recognizing as they pushed ahead that they were entering a new, uninhabited world. The Ice Age glaciers still covered much of the northern land, and the migrants moved gradually south, following the ice-free, protected valleys of the Yukon and Mackenzie River basins and the deep trenches of the Rocky Mountains in search of warmer regions. In time these people were followed by others, and through the dim ages of prehistory new bands continued to come, probably from central and northern and southeastern Asia, from the outer islands of that continent and from its heartland, from Malaya, Mongolia, Siberia, and the Kuriles. As they entered the new land they ran into groups that had arrived ahead of them, and because they were different peoples, they in a way were invaders who either conquered or were conquered. But there was no finality, no lasting decision in the multitude of isolated conflicts. Bands and tribes pushed into each other, fought, merged, quarreled, and split apart. Some were more warlike and powerful than others, and their arrivals led to dispersals of weaker peoples, whose scatterings acted like chain reactions that drove tribal elements up and down and back and forth across the continents. The last waves of conquerors prior to the arrival of the whites probably reached North America only a few centuries before Columbus. They may have been the fierce Athapascans who settled in the northwest of Canada and later, just a few decades before the coming of the Spaniards, sent a wandering offshoot down to the southwest plains and deserts, where they are known today as Navahos and Apaches.

It took the white men generations to realize that the Indians were not all one people. They recognized differences in tribal names, customs, and languages, but they persisted in thinking that the natives had a common heritage, and speculated fancifully concerning their origin, suggesting among other romantic notions that they were descendants of a lost tribe of Israel or quite possibly survivors from the sunken continent of Atlantis.

But if they failed to understand the anthropological differences among the peoples they lumped together as "Indians," the whites readily recognized the hostilities that existed among the various tribes they met, and from the beginning they were quick to turn native rivalries, jealousies, enmities, and ambitions to their own advantage, following the "divide and conquer" policy and playing ancient foes against one another for the benefit of themselves. It was a one-sided maneuver that worked devastatingly against the Indians, for whether the white man realized it or not the long war of conquest that wrested the continents from the earlier inhabitants was fought by the new invader from beginning to end as a racial conflict that pitted the "superior" white race of Europe against all Indians, who were regarded as "savages," unworthy of freedom, the right of ownership, or even life itself.

With this attitude, which stemmed in part from the Aristotelian theory that some persons were by nature meant to be masters and others slaves, the white man's conquest began in the Caribbean where Columbus and his heirs set native against native and annihilated them all. It went on to Mexico, as Cortes used Tlaxcalans against Aztecs, and finally it spread overwhelmingly north and south across both continents until the last pockets of aboriginal resistance collapsed. Time and again the struggles of the Indians, usually desperate, patriotic attempts to maintain life and freedom, were undermined and defeated by ancient animosities within their own ranks, and, though the whites found it difficult, if not impossible, to agree that Indians were not all from one mold, they were delighted temporarily to make use of the divisive forces among the natives, and not to wonder why they existed.

In what is now the United States the first great wars of colonial history saw the struggling white settlers inevitably using native allies against Indians who opposed their spreading grasp for land. A scant fifteen years after the establishment of Jamestown, Christianized natives helped the colonists fight to secure all of tidewater Virginia from the fiercely resisting Powhatans, while farther north other Indians sided enthusiastically with Connecticut Puritans who in 1637 used fire and sword to drive the Pequots from coveted harbors on Long Island Sound. But of all the early conflicts, none more sharply demonstrated the decisive role of the whites' Indian allies than that known as King Philip's War in New England, and, similarly, no Indian leader who ever fought his heart out for the right as he saw it was more opposed and deceived by his own people than the Wampanoag sachem, Philip. For the United States that savage and almost forgotten colonial war of 1675-1676 set a cruel pattern of racial conflict that was to continue along a westward-moving frontier for two centuries, but its bitter theme, also to be repeated on other borders, was disunity on the Indian side and betrayal by distraught natives of their own racial cause and leadership.

To the God-fearing Puritans of New England, Philip was a satanic agent, "a hellhound, fiend, serpent, caitiff, and dog."

Somehow, in their panic and wrath, they conceived of him as a rebel, leading a conspiracy and an uprising against established authority. It was as if invading Indians had landed on the coast of England and had then considered rebels any Englishmen who might have risen to throw them out. But such an analogy eluded the colonists; they chose, rather, to think of the proud and defiant Philip as a demon figure who, deep in the dark forests of the wilderness, had schemed hellishly to terminate the order and harmony of Indian-white relations that had existed in New England for more than fifty years.

The idea that such mutual happiness had reigned was also not quite realistic, though the settlers had grown complacent with self-righteousness and had long equated Indian docility with Indian contentment. Philip was heir to peaceful surface relations between the colonists and the natives, but his heritage also included the knowledge of white injustices and pressures which had festered sorely in the hearts of great numbers of Indians, who as yet had made no serious outcry against them. It was almost entirely true, for instance, that wherever white men first appeared in the New World they received friendly welcomes from the natives, and this was also the case in New England. Coastal explorers and traders who had preceded the Pilgrims had received curious and kindly greetings from the natives until the year 1614, when a treacherous captain named Thomas Hunt had destroyed the Indians' trust by kidnaping twenty-four of them and carrying them to Malaga to sell as slaves. Some of them had subsequently been ransomed and given their freedom by sympathetic monks, and one, named Squanto, had been taken by ship to London where, as a curiosity, he had been befriended by an English merchant who had taught him the white man's ways and language. In 1619 Squanto had shipped back to his homeland, only to find that much of the Massachusetts coast had been depopulated by the ravages of a plague. At length he had joined the Wampanoags, an Algonquin-speaking tribe, whose ruling chief, Woosamequin, lived in a village of reed mat lodges on a peninsula near present-day Bristol, Rhode Island, on the eastern side of Narragansett Bay.

Woosamequin, a portly and dignified chieftain of about forty who would later be known to the Pilgrims as Massasoit, was the future father of Philip, and though Philip was not yet born he would eventually hear this first story of white men's treachery as related by Squanto. Nevertheless, though some of the native survivors of the plague along the Cape Cod coast now showed fear of the white visitors who came in big ships, and a group of them even made a token resistance to the landing of the Pilgrims in 1620, Squanto's kindly treatment in London had made him forgiving; and his wondrous accounts of the white men's wealth and power across the seas were not lost on Massasoit, who was quick to perceive that he could use the support of such allies in his efforts to bolster his own prestige and power against the Narraganset Indians who were threatening him from the western side of the Bay.

A native from Maine named Samoset was the first Indian to extend a friendly hand to the Pilgrims. He wandered into the new settlement at Plymouth one day in March 1621 and, using language he had learned from coastal traders, startled the colonists with the words, "Welcome, Englishmen. Welcome, Englishmen." Soon afterward he returned with Squanto, Massasoit, and sixty Wampanoag braves, whom he had led overland from the Rhode Island village. Massasoit was both cautious about the intentions of the settlers and anxious to assure them of his good feelings toward them, and the Pilgrims, who had barely survived their first winter in the harsh wilderness and were in no position to turn down a gesture of friendship, reciprocated. With a trumpet and drum, and a primitive show of diplomatic ceremony, the Pilgrim leaders ushered Massasoit into their newest cabin, whose earthen floor had been laid with a green rug and three or four cushions. Bending over the Indian chief as if he were a European monarch, Governor John Carver kissed his hand; then he offered him a drink of liquor and, with Squanto as interpreter, proceeded to secure the infant colony's immediate safety by concocting a treaty of alliance between the Wampanoags and King James I of England, which Massasoit gravely signed with his mark.

The amicable relations, thus formally launched, were strengthened by Squanto, who stayed with the colonists and during the spring taught them Indian wilderness skills, as well as how to plant corn and fertilize the growths by placing a dead fish at the base of each hillock. Later the English-speaking Indian guided an embassy of Pilgrims across country on a courtesy call to Massasoit's village. The colonists brought the Wampanoag chieftain a gift of a red cotton coat and a necklace of copper beads, and Massasoit, dressed in a squirrel jacket and a mantle of turkey feathers, showed his appreciation by providing the visitors with a feast of dried meat and tautogs—dark-colored fish which the Indians shot with bows and arrows—and by having his guests sleep that night on the same plank bed with himself, his wife, and two of his chiefs.

During their stay at the village the white men had an opportunity to observe Indian life for the first time. The Wampanoag settlement of smoky, grease-stained lodges and longhouses was known as Pokanoket and was situated beneath a prominent, two-hundred-foot hill near the southern end of the peninsula, which the Indians called Montaup, but which the colonists' pronunciation soon changed to Mount Hope. The Wampanoags, whose name meant "Eastern People," had apparently dwelled in the region for a long time, building their settlements on the marshy river banks and in forest clearings between Narragansett Bay and the Atlantic Ocean, and claiming as their own the site of Plymouth where the Pilgrims now lived. That location and many others had been wiped clean of Indians by the plague of a few years before, which had taken the lives of perhaps two thousand of Massasoit's people; but there were still more than a thousand Wampanoags, who formed a confederacy of eight villages on the eastern shore of Narragansett Bay and dominated about thirty other settlements of Sakonnets and Nausets as far east as Cape

Cod. Though not warlike, Massasoit's people were courageous and self-confident, and the men lived vigorously as hunters and fishermen. Except in the semi-starvation time of winter, when they existed on dried meat and other stored provisions, they were abundantly supplied with food. While the squaws tended the garden plots the men stalked deer, dug clams from the mud-banks, netted or shot fish, and treaded the shallows for quahogs and scallops. Berries, nuts, and maple sugar were gathered in season, and meals were varied with cornbread, succotash, and big pots of chowder. The people had no formal religion, but their existence was harmoniously attuned to nature and was guided, they thought, by spiritual forces of good and evil which were responsible for the success or failure of all their undertakings. From legends of their remote past they understood that a good force had created the first man and woman from a stone or a tree, and that somewhere in the warmer lands of the south was a re-gion of a pleasant after-life.

The Pilgrim visit to Pokanoket resulted in a return journey to Plymouth by Massasoit, who joined the colonists in December and supplied four deer to help them give thanks for their first year of survival. Two years later a group of settlers repaid the gesture by traveling again to the Wampanoag capital, this time to help nurse the ailing Massasoit, who the Indians thought was dying. The chief's remarkable recovery, accomplished with the aid of Pilgrim prescriptions of sassafras broth, goose soup, and "a confection of many comfortable conserves" which Edward Winslow brought with him from Plymouth, bound the Wampa-noag sachem even closer to the colonists and established an era that was to prove the undoing of the natives.

To the Pilgrims, Massasoit was an honorable Indian who faith-fully saw that his people remained friendly to the increasing number of English settlers for as long as he lived. During that time the chief, in turn, profited in prestige and wealth. His alli-ance with the whites protected him against the Narragansets, who had previously threatened him, and his influence rose as he

acquired white men's possessions, including guns, horses, and
European manufactured goods. But the newcomers gave nothing without a price, and for his gifts Massasoit had to grant large
cessions of the Wampanoags' ancestral homelands to the expanding English settlements. By the time of the chief's death in 1661
the Indian villages in southeastern Massachusetts and along the
eastern shore of Narragansett Bay were tightly hemmed by the
towns and holdings of white men who were aggressively pressing for still further cessions.

Despite the friendship between Massasoit and the colonial authorities, the years before his death had also seen the beginning of
interracial friction throughout the area. As the settlements pushed
west from the coast, the close proximity of Indians and white men
led to constant quarrels which sometimes ended in violence and
murder. Often the troubles started over land rights and charges of
trespass which the natives could not understand. The Indian had
little comprehension of individual ownership of land, and when
title to large areas of tribal domain passed into English hands the
natives could see no reason why he could no longer hunt or grow
corn on parts of it which the white man was not using. Hauling
him into a colonists' court, where he faced hostile strangers and
received humiliating punishments, only enlarged his resentments.
Sometimes, too, the whites had acquired the land in question by
fraud, and the Indian knew he had been cheated. But under
Massasoit's policy of friendship the individual native always
seemed at a disadvantage in his dealings with the colonists, and he
received little or no backing from his tribal leaders.

The growth of white towns and plantations caused other difficulties. The English settlements provided material attractions
that lured natives to them, and large numbers who went into the
towns to trade stayed to hire themselves out as servants or laborers. Inevitably many of them fell prey to rum, found themselves bound in debt, were abused as savages and inferior people,
or were otherwise subjected to degrading and subservient conditions. Some of them ended in jail, but others made their way

back to their villages, filled with bitterness at the treatment they had received from white men.

The increasing stress was also furthered by the activities of English missionaries who tried to convert the Indians to Christianity. Some of them, such as John Eliot, working among the more northerly Massachuset Indians around Boston, were enormously successful in their labors, and by 1675 there were 1150 converted or "Praying Indians" gathered about the white settlements in fourteen villages that were specially assigned to them. Though he never became a Christian himself, Massasoit was friendly to the missionaries, but other sachems resented the conversions that undermined their authority and divided their people; they became angry at threats of punitive action that were made against them if they interfered with the zealous servants of the white man's god. In 1654 the tolerant Roger Williams at Providence took the natives' side and wrote the governor of Massachusetts to urge that the Indians "not be forced from their religions," for, he reminded the governor, "are not all the English of this land generally a persecuted people from their native land?" Such pleas were usually ignored, and in time the various colonial legislatures went so far as to enact Puritanical codes of conduct for the Indians, even if they were unconverted. Massachusetts decreed the death penalty for both Indians and whites who were guilty of blasphemy, which included the denial of God or the derogation of the Christian religion, and Plymouth forbade all Indian activity, including fishing, hunting, or the carrying of burdens, on the white man's sabbath. Such stern ordinances were difficult to enforce in the Indians' country, but they further incensed the natives and made them more conscious of the curtailment of their ancient liberties.

Massasoit had fathered two girls and three boys, and before his death he asked the General Court in Plymouth to give English names to the two older boys, Wamsutta and Metacom. Being reminded of the two kings of Macedon, the English named the former Alexander and the latter Philip, and on Massasoit's death

Alexander, the older of the two youths, succeeded to the chieftainship of the Wampanoags. His reign, however, was brief. A new generation of colonists had replaced the grateful Pilgrims, and amid the growing bitterness and conflicts of the frontier, they had little of their fathers' patience with the native population that stood in the way of their civilization. On the Indians' side, too, the warmth and friendship of Massasoit were gone, and though there were still many natives who were willing to seek personal favors and advantages by overlooking white pressure and injustices, most of them had grown fearful at what seemed to be their approaching doom, and were angrily counseling the sachems to make a stand and defend their peoples' rights. The situation trapped Alexander, and, though he made no overt move against the English, he tried to assert his leadership before his restless people by becoming bolder and more independent of the colonists than his father had been.

The new truculent attitude of the Indians, under a youthful leader who seemed haughty and unmanageable, irritated the English, and in 1662, less than a year after Alexander had become chief, the authorities at Plymouth summoned him to appear before them to assure them of his loyalty. The order disturbed the Indians, and at first Alexander resisted going. Finally the English sent troops to get him, and the young sachem marched across country in humiliation, accompanied by eighty of his people, including his wife, Weetamoo, who in her own right ruled as squaw sachem over the Wampanoag Pocasset Indians east of Mount Hope. During the stern interrogations to which he was subjected, Alexander became ill with a fever, and, after pleadings in his behalf by Weetamoo, was allowed to leave his two sons as hostages with the Puritans and return to his village. His people started back, carrying him on a litter, but at the Taunton River he suddenly turned worse and died, his head cradled in the lap of his weeping squaw.

The Indians were enraged, some believing that Alexander had died of bitterness over his rude treatment, and others that he had been poisoned by the white men. In their moment of anger and sadness Philip, a more severe and determined man than his brother, donned the wampum mark of chieftainship at Mount Hope. He was only twenty-four years old, but his courage and ability at oratory and statesmanship among the Indians made the English immediately apprehensive of him. There was good reason for their fears. As racially proud as an Indian ever was, he saw clearly what the colonists were doing to his people, and from the beginning recognized them as enemies who would have to be stopped.

There is no contemporary portrait of Philip, and imaginative likenesses of him, made by colonists in later days, are little more than hostile caricatures. Even Paul Revere, who merely copied some engravings of Mohawk Indians and combined them into the crude figure of an Iroquois, showed Philip as an ugly, misshapen chief. More likely, if he was typical of other Wampanoag braves of his age, he was tall, slim, and not unattractive. Like the native youths around him, he had been raised to court danger in the forests, had undergone tests of manhood given him by medicine men and elders of his tribe, and had become experienced and accomplished in the ways of the woods. He could use the bow and arrow, and hatchet and knife, as well as the white men's firearms, though one of his hands was scarred by the explosion of a pistol. To the colonists, who were still used to the terms of European royalty and called him King Philip, he was dignified and impressive enough to personify the menace of natives whom they could not control. Sometimes he was maddeningly indifferent to them, sometimes fiercely sensitive and resentful. In councils he was quick and agile, and often left the English outwitted and furious. Colonial authorities called him sly and calculating, but he was also hot-tempered and quick to respond to an affront. Once, an Indian who was friendly to the English had insulted the name of the dead Massasoit, and Philip in a rage had pursued him across forty miles of water to Nantucket. After he became ruler he was certain that the colonists had killed Alexander, and through long years he burned with determination to avenge his brother's death. Loyal and fanatically devoted to Indian freedom and dignity, he was beyond bribe or compromise, and the growing numbers of colonists who began to see him as a figure of obstinacy and hellishness could not recognize that he understood the situation better than they did. In the settlers' expansion toward the West, there could be no compromise for any of the Indians. Either they submitted and were overwhelmed or, as Philip realized, they stood and forced the colonists back, entirely off the continent if need be.

For thirteen years he kept the settlers on edge, alternately living at peace and giving them little trouble, and then suddenly causing the New England towns to be filled with fears that he was preparing a war against them. On several occasions he was summoned to hearings of white men and, like Alexander before him, was subjected to harsh questioning. He was stronger-willed than his brother, and when confronted with charges of a plot angrily denied it and returned, uncowed, to Mount Hope. In 1671 rumors of a native uprising were more widespread than ever. Settlers and traders rode excitedly to the colonial capitals with stories of having seen Philip's Indians gathering stores of guns and filing through the woods in mysterious armed columns. Again Philip was called to account, and at Taunton in Plymouth Colony he maintained his innocence, but agreed to surrender the guns of his Indians. Some seventy braves who had accompanied him to the hearing gave up their weapons sullenly, but if Philip understood that the agreement also referred to all the Indians under his control he failed to act upon it. When no further arms were turned in to the white authorities, the colonists declared that the Wampanoags had violated the agreement, and prepared to send a punitive expedition against Mount Hope. Hastening to Boston and playing the white man's own game by setting colony against colony, Philip convinced the Massachusetts Bay leaders that the Plymouth officials were being unreasonable to him. The Bostonians, who wanted no Indian war if it could be helped, intervened with

Plymouth and got the expedition called off in return for Philip's signing a new agreement with the English. This time the Wampanoag chief promised to pay one hundred pounds' worth of goods to Plymouth and to obey the government of that colony.

In the light of what was to come, Philip was buying time. There was no doubt that he recognized the inevitability of war, but he was not yet ready for it. The Wampanoags were too few in number to risk conflict alone. In all New England, there were now forty thousand whites. Only five thousand of them were grouped in Puritan settlements around the old, original colony at Plymouth near the Wampanoags, but even closer to the tribe's villages were almost four thousand Quaker and Baptist colonists in Rhode Island, and farther away, but still near enough to come to the aid of Plymouth, were ten thousand settlers in Connecticut and almost twenty thousand in the Massachusetts Bay Colony. Altogether there were only about twenty thousand Indians in southern New England, outnumbered already, two to one. But Philip was sure that by swift and sudden attacks on the white centers he could destroy the enemy and eliminate all the English from the land. The ambitious idea of so huge and devastating an uprising, however, required time for preparation. There was unrest among the tribes throughout the region, but they had to be united under a single war leadership, and their actions had to be carefully coordinated into a general plan, acceptable to all of them.

Philip's task was complicated by all the old fears and rivalries that had divided the natives in the past. Month after month he sent runners through the woods on long diplomatic journeys, or traveled himself to councils in distant villages and argued patiently for concerted action by the Indians before it was too late. In none of the tribes did he find the complete support he was seeking. Many of the braves and younger people listened to him eagerly and nodded approval of the war he preached, but most of the older sachems and wise men resisted him. Some thought the young Wampanoag chief was an upstart and suspected him of trying to gain dominance over their people. Others wondered at his plan and decided that ambition had made him mad. Those who were currying favor from the English told him that the power of the whites was already too strong, and he would be defeated, and even many who were half-heartedly in agreement with him were opposed to playing a secondary role to the Wampanoags. In the face of such hesitation, progress toward unity was slow. The two largest tribes in southern New England—the Narragansets, whose four thousand people lived west of the Rhode Island bay of the same name, and the Nipmucks, whose three thousand members were spread across the forested interior of Massachusetts—at length indicated that they might support the Wampanoags. But the Niantics of the western Rhode Island shorefront, the Mohegans and remaining Pequots of Connecticut, and the Massachuset natives of the north were deeply involved with the whites, who they were sure were too strong to defeat, and even the Sakonnets, a branch of the Wampanoags, who lived south of Mount Hope and were ruled by a matronly squaw sachem named Awashonks, evaded giving Philip any promises.

When the war finally came, Philip was still not ready. He had secured neither alliances nor general support for his plans, and the woods about him were filled with doubters and potential traitors. But the forces of conflict that he had recognized and understood had at last reached their climax, and when a handful of braves finally took to the warpath he had no choice but to go along with them, improvising as he went, and hoping that the storm would rise and sweep the half-hearted into the struggle by his side.

The conflict was precipitated, as it would end, by an incident of treachery to Philip. In January 1675 a Christianized Indian named John Sassamon was found murdered in a pond near Plymouth. Sassamon had been educated by the missionaries and had studied briefly at Harvard, but after a while he had returned to Mount Hope and had become Philip's trusted secretary. A few days before his death Sassamon had shown up in Plymouth and had related to Governor Josiah Winslow everything that Philip was doing, warning him that the Wampanoags were forming a general conspiracy against the English. When Sassamon shortly afterward was found dead, the authorities at once believed it was Philip's work, and in time they rounded up three Wampanoags, including one of Philip's closest counselors. The trial was held in a tense and bitter atmosphere. Public feeling was high against the Wampanoags, and the hostile proceedings of the court in turn aroused Philip and his people, who protested that white men had no right to try Indians for crimes committed against other natives. When the three Indians were found guilty and hanged on June 8, the tribe's anger reached the boiling point. The Wampanoags had suffered the final affront to their self-respect, and the last strands of their restraint snapped.

Almost at once, reports reached Plymouth from the interior country that a crisis was in the making. On June 11 word came from the settlement of Swansea, just north of Mount Hope, that armed Indians were joining Philip from outlying villages, and that the Wampanoags were sending their women to the Narraganset country for safety. Shortly afterward a peppery settler named Benjamin Church, who had acquired land from the Sakonnets and had become friendly with their squaw sachem, Awashonks, attended a native dance at her village and found six of Philip's Indians present, tall, muscular men painted for war and hung with shot bags and rattlesnake skins down their backs. Awashonks, who was fond of Church, paused in her dancing long enough to draw Church aside and "in a foaming sweat" inform him that Philip was urging her to join in a war against the English. Church advised her that it would be a ruinous policy for both of them, and soon afterward he rode into Plymouth to report the incident and to tell the authorities that the squaw had assured him that the Sakonnets, even though they were Wampanoags, would remain at peace.

Despite the warnings, the colonists could not believe that

Philip would actually begin a war. Many times in the past he had threatened to rise up, and each time nothing had happened. But on June 20, 1675, an angry group of young Wampanoags came into Swansea and, after swaggering about belligerently, shot some cattle. The frightened settlers flocked at once to a garrison house, abandoning their homes to the Indians who for the next few days ransacked the village at will. Finally, on June 23, an English youth took a shot at an Indian and wounded him, drawing the first blood of the conflict. The next day the natives retaliated with a vengeance. They swarmed out of Mount Hope, stripped and painted for war, moved north through the countryside, ringed Swansea, and lay in wait behind bushes for victims. One by one, settlers were shot down as they came along the roads or went into their fields. The Indians killed nine men and mortally wounded two others before nightfall.

The news shocked the New England settlements, which had already learned of the siege of Swansea, and had dispatched volunteer companies to its assistance. Unaware of what was occurring on the Indians' side, the colonies assumed that King Philip had now started his war, and from Boston to the Connecticut settlement at New Haven militia units were organized and sent hurrying to the scene of action. By the time the first troops reached Swansea, the Indians had again disappeared south into the peninsula from which they had come, and all was quiet. Though there is no Indian record of Philip's behavior or movements at the time, it is probable that he had not directed his braves in their first impulsive actions, but now that they had killed white men he must have recognized that there could be no turning back, and that he would have to lead the war he had long preached.

The Wampanoags' first problem was to get out of the peninsula before they were trapped. The colonists, too, realized the situation and hastily tried to assemble a fleet of boats to ring the Indians' position. At the same time they made a first cautious move into the peninsula from the north, but were frightened

back by some Indian sentries who fired at them from concealment and mortally wounded their guide. By the time the settlers mustered their courage and moved into the peninsula in
force, Philip and all his people had escaped, crossing eastward to
the swampy mainland and the country of the Wampanoag Pocassets, who were still ruled by Alexander's widow, Weetamoo.

At Mount Hope the colonists dawdled and wondered what to
do next. Some thought that the capture of the Indian stronghold
ended the war, and they went home. Others decided to build a
fort from which to fight Philip in case he tried to return. The
waste of time irritated a few volunteers who thought they should
be pursuing the Indians, and a small group of them, including
Awashonks' friend Benjamin Church, whose knowledge of the
natives had made him something of an authority on the Indians,
and therefore a leader among the whites, boldly crossed to the
mainland and were soon in trouble on the Pocasset shore. Trying to make their way inland, the men first ran into country infested with rattlesnakes, which Church said "the little Company
seem'd more to be afraid of than the black Serpents they were in
quest of," and then were suddenly attacked by a large number
of Indians. Driven back to the beach, the men formed a perimeter among the rocks and sand and held off the natives until
they were rescued by a sloop, which evacuated them under the
Indians' fire and took them back, none the worse for the excitement, to Mount Hope.

From a new headquarters deep in a cedar swamp on the mainland, Philip and the Wampanoags, now joined by Weetamoo's
band of Pocassets, soon showed the nature of the total war that
had begun. With or without allies, the conflict of survival was
under way. In rapid sorties Philip struck savagely against nearby
settlements, burning Rehoboth, Taunton, Dartmouth, and Middleborough, and forcing the latter village, which lay close to
Plymouth town itself, to be abandoned by its frightened inhabitants. In the flames and deaths, panic raced across New England,
and white volunteers poured into the Pocasset country, deter-

mined to eliminate the source of the trouble by finding and killing Philip. On July 19 the settlers moved desperately into the
swamp where Philip lay, pushing through the thick underbrush
and floundering in the mud and tangled growth. Philip's men
fired at them from concealment and kept withdrawing, pulling
the English deeper into the wilderness. By nightfall the colonists
had become confused and were firing indiscriminately at every
sound around them. Realizing the danger of their position in the
darkness, they finally turned about and withdrew, and the next
day decided to change their tactics and lay siege to the swamp.
The task proved impossible. Thinking that Philip might still try
to cross back to Mount Hope, some of the settlers commenced
building a fort between the swamp and the shore. Others attempted to patrol the northern and eastern sides of the swamp.
Ten days later Philip and all his people managed to get past the
patrols and, moving northwestward across the Taunton River,
headed for the vast wilderness of the Nipmuck country in central Massachusetts.

Some Praying Indians from around Boston had already agreed
to join the colonists and try to help the whites bring the trouble-
making Philip to justice. But now the ancient hostilities in the Indians' ranks also became apparent, and from Connecticut came
a well-armed band of Mohegans, who hurried to the scene of
conflict in the hope of getting some Wampanoag scalps and
booty by aiding the whites. Joined by this detachment, the settlers made a determined effort to overtake Philip, and on August
1 they came suddenly on the Wampanoags, who had halted for a
brief rest, thinking that danger was far behind them. After a furious battle the Wampanoags abandoned much of their equipment
and took refuge in another swamp. The whites failed to go after
them, and the next day Philip again escaped. This time he divided
his forces. Weetamoo and her people struck off southward to seek
safety among the Narragansets, and Philip and his warriors continued their flight to the Nipmucks in Massachusetts.

Stirred by the successes of the Wampanoags' initial actions, a majority of the Nipmucks had already decided to join the war as Philip's first important allies. Led by one of their war chiefs, named Matoonas, a group of them had attacked the Massachusetts town of Mendon on July 14, killing several of the settlers and serving notice on the whites that the uprising had spread. The shocked authorities in Boston had at once dispatched a mission to the Nipmucks to try to commit them to peace, but on August 2 the Nipmucks ambushed this group, killed or wounded eight of its members, and drove the survivors into the little frontier settlement of Brookfield, which was immediately besieged for forty-eight hours. When help finally arrived the natives fired the houses and disappeared back into the forest, and the dazed townspeople abandoned the smoking ruins and withdrew to safety farther east.

In early August the Wampanoags joined forces with the Nipmucks. The arrival of Philip among his powerful allies was the signal for an acceleration of all-out warfare in the new theater of hostilities. Up and down the Connecticut River Valley the Indians lashed at white settlers, burning their homes, shooting them down in their fields, and trying to force them from their towns. In succession the natives attacked Northfield, Deerfield, and Hadley, and forced the evacuation of the first two settlements. As volunteer units scurried back and forth, attempting to decide which village to defend next, the Indians caught the whites between towns in bloody ambushes. On September 18 they trapped a provision train and killed sixty-eight colonists, "the very Flower of the County," as one chronicler said. Massachusetts and Connecticut troops hastened into the area to try to protect the villages, but the Indian terror continued. On September 28 natives attacked Northampton, and on October 5 they burned a large part of Springfield. Their last furious assault was launched against Hatfield, where troops finally repulsed them, but all through October they harassed other towns and killed isolated groups of settlers.

The merciless warfare left memories that were to haunt the

colonists for decades. Against the whites the Indians used tactics of fighting that were traditional in the conflicts of New World natives, but were hideous and inhumane to the Europeans. The Indian warrior, with his flaming arrow, bloodstained tomahawk, and barbaric war whoop, erased the benign image of Massasoit and the first hospitable natives. The silent forest became the dread abode of skulking savages no better than wild beasts, and the fierce sieges of frontier settlements provided enduring nightmares of dawn attacks and fiendish atrocities. And yet the English, scarcely emerged from the barbarism of their own Middle Ages in Europe, were quick to accept the no-quarter savagery of absolute racial war, and to retaliate in kind. In England poachers' ears had been cut off, and white men had known serfdom, persecution, and the rack. Now the colonists themselves adopted scalping, offered bounties for enemies' heads, and sold Indian captives into slavery in the Mediterranean and the West Indies. It was war for survival, without compassion on either side.

How much of the fighting in the Connecticut valley Philip actually led is not known. Rumors among the frightened whites had him everywhere, directing his warriors fanatically in each successive strike. Later it appeared that Philip had spent much of the fall hastening back and forth among the different bands and tribes of New England, attempting desperately to forge his confederation and bring wavering chiefs into the war. As he argued and pleaded, his efforts must often have succeeded, for time and again during the fierce struggle native villages which the settlers had considered friendly to them had suddenly risen and turned on unsuspecting white neighbors. The Nipmucks, who were now firmly allied with the Wampanoags, were usually led by their own war chiefs, including old Matoonas, a sachem called Monoco, who was also known as One-Eyed John, another named Shoshanim, whom the whites called Sagamore Sam, and a warrior named Mattaump. Whether Philip directed and coordinated their movements was never discovered, but from natives whom they captured the whites heard repeatedly that the Wampanoag sachem was regarded by all the hostile Indians as the single symbol of their cause.

As winter set in and colonial resistance stiffened, the natives gradually abandoned their attacks and withdrew to safe retreats in the wilderness. Among some of them were first signs of disillusionment. When waging their own wars of the past, the Indians had never conducted combat as a sustained affair. A single attack, usually devastating enough to cripple an opponent, had been viewed as a triumph that settled and, for the time at least, ended a conflict. But this war was different, and not all the natives recognized its nature as Philip did. Victories that produced scalps and loot were not enough. The whites were still there, and apparently were even growing stronger. The Indians had to continue their attacks, Philip argued, until every settlement was destroyed and all the colonists were driven from the land. Under his pleading, opposition faded quickly, and the natives began to plan for a resumption of their raids.

Sometime in December Philip journeyed to the Hudson River, where he established a camp at the site of present-day Schaghticoke, New York, about twenty miles above Albany, and tried to enlist the Mohawk Indians on his side. He parleyed with their chiefs a number of times, but had no success. After Philip's death the colonists spread a report that the Wampanoags had practiced treachery on the Mohawks by causing three of their warriors to be attacked, hoping to be able to place the blame for their deaths on the English, and thus arouse the Iroquoian tribes to join him. According to the story, one of the Mohawks had recovered and informed his people of what had actually happened, and the enraged New York natives had forced Philip to flee back to the Nipmucks. At any rate, the Mohawks, who were traditional enemies of the New England Algonquians, had no desire to help them, and no reason to get into a fight with the British, with whom they were profitably allied in the fur trade in New York, and Philip returned to central Massachusetts without having won them to him.

In southern New England, however, Philip had in the meantime gained the alliance of the strong Narraganset tribe of Rhode Island. The Narragansets were hereditary rivals of the Wampanoags, and had originally resisted joining the conflict. But after hostilities had begun, divisions had split the tribe, and many of the war chiefs and young men had grown impatient to enter the struggle. Their restlessness had disturbed the colonists, and in the middle of July the Massachusetts authorities had forced them to sign a treaty of peace. When the Narragansets provided sanctuary for Weetamoo's people after they had fled from the Pocasset country with Philip, however, the colonists became angered, and in October they summoned the Narraganset sachem, Canonchet, to Boston, and got him to sign another treaty. By it he promised to surrender the Pocasset squaw leader to them within ten days. But the time limit passed, and when Weetamoo was still not surrendered the colonists lost patience and sent a punitive expedition against the Narragansets.

The campaign resulted in a dramatic victory for the English that helped to raise the flagging spirits of the settlements. But it was also a costly one that claimed the lives of many colonists and drove the Narragansets definitely into Philip's ranks. To chastise the Rhode Island natives the United Colonies of Massachusetts, Connecticut, and Plymouth assembled an army of more than a thousand men, the largest force they had ever raised, and in December 1675 the troops rendezvoused on the west side of Narragansett Bay. A few miles to the southwest the Indians, probably more than three thousand strong, had gathered in a heavily fortified village on an island in a wild marsh known as the Great Swamp. Afraid to press into the tangled area, the colonists hesitated until, by luck, they captured an Indian who volunteered to turn traitor and lead the settlers through the swamp on a secret trail that led to the village.

On December 19, a bitterly cold snowy day, the colonists moved into the wilderness behind their Indian guide, and at two in the afternoon, pushing across the iced surface of the marsh.

came suddenly on the fort. It was a huge, walled village on a slight rise, camouflaged by masses of fallen trees and piles of brush that had been heaped in front of the stockade as added protection. Directly in front of the troops was the only gap in the village's walls, and in an instant the colonists charged at their goal, hurtling across the brush and trying to get inside the fort. The Indians, led by a fierce and defiant Canonchet, who now hated the English, met the attackers with a burst of musket fire, and at first drove them back. But more of the settlers came up, and a second charge carried them inside the village, where the Indians and whites fought savagely, hand-to-hand, around the wigwams. As the light of the wintry day faded, the settlers fired the lodges, and the desperate fight swirled wildly through an inferno of flying sparks and flames. Finally the Indians broke off the struggle and, abandoning most of their dead and wounded in the fort, disappeared into the gloom of the swamp.

More than six hundred native men, women, and children perished, "terribly Barbikew'd," according to a later account by the Boston divine, Cotton Mather. But the colonists suffered about fifty casualties of their own, and spent an agonizing night, withdrawing through the dark and frozen marsh with their dead and injured. Canonchet, Weetamoo, and many of the Narragansets and Pocassets had escaped from the fort, but the settlers were in no condition to pursue them. In time the colonial army regrouped and late in January set out again to try to find the surviving Indians. For seventy miles they followed the refugees' trail north toward the Nipmuck country, and then gave it up. The natives had disappeared in the wilderness, and the troops, anxious to be home in time for spring plowing, returned to their respective colonies and disbanded.

Soon afterward the Narragansets and Pocassets reached Philip's forces in central Massachusetts. The arrivals were thirsting for revenge, and were eager to join the new raids that were about to begin. In dozens of camps, war bands of the biggest Indian army that New England had ever known were poised to

strike again. In person and by runner, Philip had given them simple advice: burn the villages and kill the people until all the
whites are dead or driven from the country. Early in February
the first of the war parties began to file off. Others, including
the newcomers, followed, many of the individual bands heading in different directions. The Nipmucks were led by old Matoonas, Monoco, Shoshanim, and Muttaump. The Narraganset
chiefs included village leaders named Pomham, Pessacus, Quinnapin, who had now taken Weetamoo as his wife, another stout-
hearted squaw sachem named Quaiapen, and the proud, fighting
Canonchet. The Wampanoags followed Philip, who was helped
by his uncle, Unkompoin, his chief war captain, Annawon, and
the squaw sachems, Weetamoo and Awashonks; the latter had
finally joined the conflict with her Sakonnets, despite the warning of Benjamin Church.

Rumors of the new Indian movements had scarcely reached
the white authorities before the shocks of devastating raids struck
each of the four English colonies. In Massachusetts, Nipmucks
attacked with such swiftness that town after town had to be abandoned. At widely separated villages the Indians appeared without warning, massacred families at outlying farms, and drove
the townspeople into central garrison houses. Buildings went up
in fire at Sudbury, Groton, and Medfield. More than fifty whites
were slain at Lancaster, and the whole town was evacuated. On
March 26 the important center of Marlborough was partly destroyed. Raids hit Andover, Billerica, Chelmsford, and Woburn,
and south of Boston the Indians struck Braintree, Weymouth, and
Scituate on the coast and brought panic to neighboring towns
that had thought they were safely distant from danger. Far to
the west, other natives once more spread fear along the Connecticut River Valley, attacking Northampton, Longmeadow, and
even Simsbury near Hartford, and in the south, close to the scene
of the disastrous Great Swamp fight, Canonchet and his Narragansets suddenly materialized again and attacked Warwick and
Wickford. At the same time the Wampanoags and their allies,

probably under Philip himself, reappeared in the area where the war had started and fell on unsuspecting towns of Rhode Island and Plymouth Colony. Bridgewater and Rehoboth were both raided, and in Providence eighty houses were burned. On March 26 Indians struck only five miles north of Plymouth itself, killing forty-two whites, and some six weeks later Philip actually entered the capital and burned sixteen houses.

The English colonies of New England were in mortal danger. Out of ninety white settlements in the land, fifty-two had been attacked and twelve completely destroyed. For a moment it seemed that Philip's desperate total war, if continued, might actually achieve its aim and drive every white from the country. But at the height of the Indian offensive disintegrating forces of doubts, fears, and treachery set in, and slowly the momentum fell, and the tide began to turn. For one thing, it was spring, time for planting and fishing, and in their hidden war camps many of the natives were beginning to worry about their food supply. The gardens and fishing places near their old homes were denied to them now, and as yet they had no new ones. The year's fighting, moreover, had wrecked, or lost them, their stores, and during the winter they had used up most of their provisions. Large numbers of natives were already hungry and fearful that their women and children were facing starvation, and some of them began to leave the war parties and turn back to the wilderness to search for fishing sites and to plant new gardens.

Wherever Indian pressure relaxed, the colonists responded desperately with new determination and vigor. Large new units of volunteers were formed and sent rapidly into the field, accompanied by groups of Mohegans, Pequots, Praying Indians, and warriors of Philip who had been captured and won over to the whites. The native auxiliaries knew how to track and fight in the woods and swamps as well as Philip's men, and their appearance as new enemies, more formidable in wilderness warfare than the settlers, dismayed the raiding bands. With the help of these native allies, the colonists were soon finding and cutting up small groups of hostiles who had become detached from the larger bands. In time, their ambushes and sudden attacks caused casualties and set-backs that stunned Philip's people and filled his war parties with doubts. The English settlements had been struck again and again, but the enemy was coming back at them more strongly than ever. In the rear, at the same time, the groups that had left the fighting to seek fishing places and garden plots suddenly found no safety. Indian scouts, loyal to the whites, tracked them wherever they went and led colonial guerrillas in surprise raids on their hidden camps.

Slowly, demoralization set in, as even the big camps and leaders of the war began to be hit. In April some Connecticut volunteers and Indian auxiliaries trapped Canonchet in the Narragansett country and captured him. He was taken to Stonington and sentenced to be shot. Before his death he announced, "I shall die before my heart is soft, or I have said anything unworthy of myself." A Pequot was allowed to shoot him, and as the colonists watched, his corpse was quartered and burned by exultant representatives of the Mohegans, Niantics, and Pequots who had accompanied the Connecticut patrol. In a final gesture the whites themselves sent Canonchet's head to the Connecticut authorities at Hartford.

Canonchet's death depressed Philip. The tide was now turning with increasing swiftness, and the news of other losses soon reached him. Larger numbers of fast, hard-hitting colonial patrols were appearing in the wilderness, and everywhere the Indians were finding themselves forced on the defensive. In the constant fire fights, many bands began to run out of powder and ammunition and, when attacked, could no longer defend themselves on equal terms. Strong bodies of Indians were overwhelmed and wiped out, or shattered and split into wandering remnants that were picked off in mopping-up engagements. As the attrition mounted, the faith and war purpose of the survivors were undermined, and many Indians began to question the wisdom of Philip's war. At the end of June, Awashonks made contact with her old friend Benjamin Church, who had fought through many of the battles of the war, including the Great Swamp fight, and let him know that she wished to sue for peace. When Church visited her to negotiate, one of her chief war leaders bowed to Church and said, "Sir, if you will please to accept of me and my men, and will head us, we will fight for you, and will help you to Philip's head before the Indian corn be ripe."

Church hurried to Plymouth and received permission to lead a volunteer band composed of white settlers and members of Awashonks' band, who were sure they knew where Philip was hiding. He returned to the Indians, organized his unit, and started after the Wampanoag leader. The Sakonnets led him to a swamp near Bridgewater, between Plymouth and Mount Hope, and on July 20 Church fell on Philip's men. The chief escaped, but the colonists and the Sakonnets killed or captured 173 Wampanoags. Among the dead was Philip's uncle and chief advisor, Unkompoin, and among the prisoners were the sachem's wife and son, whom the colonists packed off to slavery in the West Indies for the price of one pound each.

The new episode of treachery was the beginning of the end of Philip's war. Day after day, as he tried to elude Church and his Sakonnet guides, his forces disintegrated. On July 2 one of the largest remaining bands of Narragansets was destroyed in a spruce swamp in northern Rhode Island. More than 170 Indians were captured or killed, and among the dead was the old squaw sachem, Quaiapen. About the same time, another group of 80 Narragansets surrendered at Providence, and near the end of the month Philip learned of the death of the important Narraganset war leader Pomham. Near Dedham, Massachusetts, colonists and Praying Indians had trapped the doughty warrior and his band, who were starving, and had killed almost all of them.

The Nipmucks were faring no better. Many of them, having lost heart, were surrendering at the settlements and were being hanged or sold into slavery. Others were fleeing to the Mohegans in eastern Connecticut, where the sachem, Uncas, welcomed them with the hope that their absorption into his own tribe would bring him increased strength and prestige. It was a false assumption, for after the conclusion of Philip's war the colonists showed small love for any Indians in New England, and neither the Mohegans nor Pequots who had aided them were spared the settlers' crushing envelopment. A few of the Nipmucks thought they had a better chance with the colonial authorities than with Uncas, and on July 27 Boston witnessed one of the most dramatic episodes of the closing days of the war when a Nipmuck chief, Sagamore John, and 180 of his people brazenly marched into town with their brave war leader, Matoonas, and his son securely tied with ropes. The colonists were delighted with their luck; they bound Matoonas to a tree on Boston Common and let Sagamore John shoot his war chief dead.

The defections and deaths failed to crush Philip's spirit, and despite the collapse of his allies and the growing ring of deserters and informers around him he continued to defy his pursuers. On August 6 one of his warriors stole away and offered to lead the English to the Wampanoag hideouts. The colonists followed him to a camp in the wilderness near Taunton. It turned out to belong to Weetamoo, and, though the squaw sachem managed to escape, the raiders rounded up two dozen disheartened prisoners. Later Weetamoo's naked body was found floating in the Taunton River, where she had drowned during her flight. In triumph the colonists took her head to Plymouth and mounted it on a pole.

Few of Philip's friends were now left. With the purpose, perhaps, of a man who prefers to return home to die, he gradually made his way back to his ancestral home at Mount Hope, where the war had started the year before. The peninsula was still a trap, and Philip must have known he would never leave it again alive. Nevertheless, when one of his companions suggested to him that the Indians should now try to make peace with the English, he lost his temper and had the man killed. It set in motion the final act of treason against him. The slain man's brother, an Indian named Alderman. lost no time in deserting to the English and announcing to Benjamin Church that he wished to betray his chief.

Church gathered a troop of eighteen Englishmen and twenty-two Indians, and under cover of night ferried them silently from the mainland to the peninsula. Guided by Alderman, the little band made its way to the Wampanoag camp, where Philip and his war captain, Annawon, lay asleep. There was no sentry posted, and Church deployed his men around the camp without being discovered. At dawn, on August 12, 1676, the silent watchers saw a figure emerge from one of the brush shelters. The native looked around and seemed to stare directly at the hiding place of one of the Englishmen. The latter was sure that he had been seen, and fired. He missed the Indian, who turned and dashed into the woods. In the next instant a volley from the other watchers tore into the Indians' shelters, and more natives emerged in astonishment and raced wildly for safety. Church had foreseen just such a flight, and had set up a more distant ambush into which the frantic Wampanoags were running. Behind many of the trees he had paired Indians and colonists, and had ordered them to hold their fire until the watchers at the camp had driven the Wampanoags toward them. One of the waiting pairs included an Englishman named Caleb Cook and the traitor, Alderman. Suddenly the two saw an Indian running straight toward them. Cook pulled his trigger, but the gun misfired. Alderman's, which had two barrels, worked perfectly. The fleeing native spun and fell on his face in the mud, one of Alderman's bullets in his heart and the other two inches above it.

The two men went forward cautiously and rolled the body over. It was King Philip.

Church's men elsewhere killed more of the Indians, and eventually returned to where a group was gathering around the man whom Alderman had slain. When Church told them who it was, lying twisted in the mud and looking to the colonial leader like "a doleful, great, naked, dirty beast," the men burst into cheers. Annawon and the rest of the Wampanoag stragglers would still have to be mopped up, but the great Indian war leader was dead. Now the settlers could continue their westward expansion in safety.

Exultantly the troops decapitated and quartered the sachem's body and carried his head back to Plymouth, where it was stuck on a pole and remained on public display for twenty-five years. To Alderman, Church gave Philip's scarred hand. It was the Indian's reward for betraying his leader, and for months Alderman made it pay by exhibiting it in a pail of rum "to such gentlemen as would bestow gratuities on him."

III

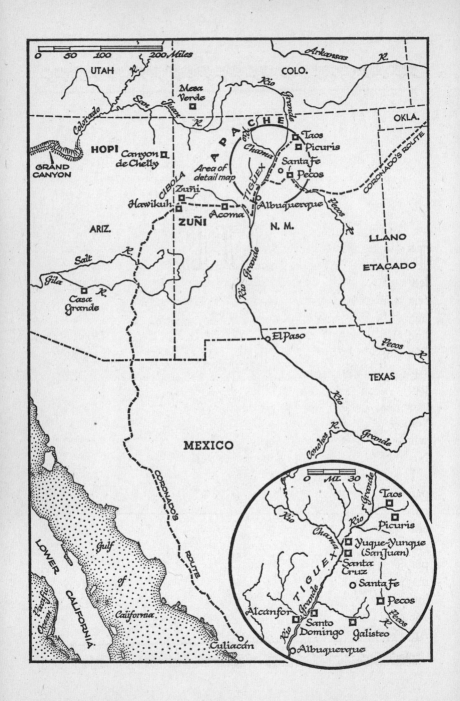

III

POPÉ AND THE
GREAT PUEBLO UPRISING

IN 1598, two decades before the English Pilgrims landed at Plymouth, an expedition of several hundred Spanish colonists, led by Don Juan de Oñate, and complete with eleven Franciscan friars, a herd of seven thousand bawling cattle, a column of helmeted troops in metal and leather armor, and a long, creaking line of supply carts, lumbered north across the burning deserts of Mexico to the fabled Rio Grande. On the banks of that river, on April 30, slightly south of the future town site of El Paso, they paused in a sheltering grove of dusty cottonwoods, and before a cross and the royal standard of the king of Spain took possession "once, twice, and thrice" of all the "lands, pueblos, cities, villas, of whatsoever nature now founded in the kingdom and province of New Mexico . . . and all its native Indians."

For eighty-two years thereafter, in that remote and curtained part of the continent far beyond the horizon of the European colonies being created on the Atlantic seaboard, successive generations of Spanish governors, priests, troops, and settlers extended their reign over a beautiful but harsh wilderness of mesas, plateaus, and river valleys, forcing Indians to submit to the two majesties of church and state, and impressing thousands of them into a cruel *encomienda* system of serfdom. Then, suddenly in 1680, it was all over. In one of the most dramatic uprisings in American Indian history, the oppressed natives struck furiously for their freedom. Streaming from pueblos and cornfields in every part of the province, they slew four hundred Spaniards, drove twenty-five hundred others in shock and terror back to Mexico, and in a few weeks swept their country clean of the white man's rule.

Their stunning triumph, never again matched by natives in the New World, was organized and led by a shadowy Pueblo Indian medicine doctor called Popé, who is still little known to history. To the battered Spaniards, who spent the next twelve years trying to regain the province, defeat was humiliating enough. But it was added gall that an idolatrous medicine man, obviously an agent of the powers of darkness, had been the instrument by which the might and power of the Spanish Crown and the True Faith had been overthrown and chased in ignominious flight from the land.

During their long rule the Spaniards thought they had come to understand the Pueblo people. There were more than sixteen thousand of these Indians, occupying about seventy different sites, some widely separated, on the tops of steep-walled mesas and in the plains and valleys from present-day Arizona to the mountains east of the Rio Grande. Each settlement, originally something of an independent city-state, was gathered around a single communal hive of apartment-like rooms, made of adobe and joined together in a sprawling building that rose several stories high and looked like reddish-brown cubes set back on terraces, one above another. Despite the similarity of their homes, not all the natives were alike in customs, backgrounds, or languages. In the chromatic, rocky desert of the West were Zuñis and Hopis, and along the Rio Grande were Keres, Tewas, and others among whom the Spaniards settled, and whom the white men termed Pueblos for the city-like aspect of their terraced buildings.

All of them, as they sometimes demonstrated, could fight fiercely in defense of their homes, but generally they were a peaceful and mild-natured people, sometimes superstitious and troublesome to their Spanish masters, but more often docile. It was inconceivable to the conquerors that so pacific a subject nation, which had never waged a war of aggression against other Indians, would seriously rise against a colony of Spain, whose armies of conquistadors had crushed the empires of powerful caciques and sun gods everywhere south of the Rio Grande; and even as they fled back to the safety of Mexico after the revolt the refugees from Santa Fe blamed it all on the single satanic instrument, Popé, who in some terrible way had been able to stir up the gentle Pueblos and under his spell "had made them crazy."

Who Popé was in the secret and awesome scheme of native life, and how he had managed to arouse his people in such a sudden and concerted uprising throughout the province, were beyond the comprehension of the desperate Spaniards, who asked every friendly Indian along their escape road, "What was the reason for it?" Even when one old native, whom they dragged from his horse, told them that the Indians resented losing what the Spaniards had taken away from them—their ancestral ways of life and the right to their own beliefs—they thought he was bewitched. Like other white men in generations still to come, they shrugged off as savage stubbornness man's longing to be free, and the patriotic motive behind the hatred and terror of Popé and his wildly screaming Indians eluded them entirely. The uprising was a simple struggle to restore the past, but the Spaniards could not understand it because they could not abide what had been.

Prior to the revolt the Spanish authorities had hardly known Popé. He had been only one of many obscure medicine men who, despite the friars' stern proscriptions of native beliefs, had continued to defy the white men with secret religious practices in the pueblos. After the uprising had occurred, the gulf between the Spaniards and the Indians kept them from learning much more, and when they were finally able to reconquer the New Mexican province Popé was dead and other Indian leaders had taken his place. Under the new Spanish regime the officials were anxious to eradicate the memory of the revolt and the idolator who had led it, and in time even the little that was known about Popé became hazy and uncertain in the white men's chronicles of the province. Today, from the documents of the governors and priests, from contemporary declarations of settlers, soldiers, and witnesses of the events, and from a few frightened narratives of Indians who told the Spanish leaders what had transpired on the native side, we can piece together more about him. But there are still not enough details available about Popé to reveal his complete stature. While his name lives on among the great Indian leaders of America as the genius and symbol of the spectacular revolt, his story gains its fullest perspective only when seen as the climax of the larger and more romantic narrative of his own people. Against their background and early conflicts with the whites, Popé emerges not alone as the precipitant of the revolt, but as the product of the dramatic events and forces that had led to the storm.

The roots of what ultimately occurred in 1680 reached far back to the original forming of the pueblo people's beliefs and civilizations. Their history began in the very dawn of the habitation of the New World by men. In days the Spaniards knew nothing about, the earliest ancestors of the Pueblos had come to the southwest thousands of years ago during the first migrations from the north, hunting mastodons, camels, and outsized bison, with long spear-throwers called *atlatls* that hurled points of flaked stone into the animals. As the ancient beasts had become extinct, the people had gradually learned to gather fruit and roots; to plant corn, beans, and cotton; to weave cloth from fibers; and to settle down in pit houses and grass shelters. Prehistoric, small-sized horses, that had existed on the American continent in earlier years, had also disappeared, but the people had dogs which they trained to carry burdens. In time other migrants and traders from more developed areas in Mexico and elsewhere settled among them and brought them new skills, and by approximately 700 A.D. they had become accomplished potters and basketmakers. After 800 they developed the beginnings of their modern pueblo buildings, fashioning one-storied mud structures of many rooms joined together, and turning their round, cistern-like pit houses into secret ceremonial chambers called kivas.

The first great Pueblo culture reached its peak between 1050 and 1300, when large numbers of people took to living together in many-tiered communal dwellings built in the open or in arched recesses part way up the steep walls of cliffs. In the valleys near the pueblos the Indians tended their fields, practicing both dry-land and irrigation farming, and storing their surplus crops in special rooms against times of drought and famine. All across the high plateau land the people prospered and developed, and in such localities as Mesa Verde in the southwest corner of present-day Colorado they created a golden age of beautiful pottery, turquoise jewelry, and woven cloth.

In one of the great mysteries of prehistoric America this first pueblo era came to a sudden unexplained end late in the thirteenth century. A devastating drought occurred in part of their country from 1276 to 1299, but neither it nor any other reason yet known fully accounts for a wholesale trek by all the Pueblo people, who abruptly abandoned the high plateau sites they had inhabited for centuries. Leaving their towns and buildings standing empty and silent, they moved south and eastward to mesa tops on the desert and to the Rio Grande valley, where they established brand-new settlements in which the Spaniards later found them. There, in a new homeland, they continued their cultural rise, weaving legends and sacred beliefs around fast-receding memories of olden days, and endowing their civilization with endless cycles of colorful and mysterious rituals.

The philosophic base on which they constructed their society was a conviction, permeating all phases of their life, that everything they could possibly comprehend—the rocks and natural forces around them, the ideas in their heads, distances across the land, animals, birds, reptiles, every action, thought, and being in their consciousness—was part of a great living force and con-

tained a spirit that existed everywhere; this spirit behaved alike
in everything in which it dwelled. In their view of their own position in the world, moreover, whatever existed on earth came from
an underworld to which it eventually returned in death. Passage
between the two regions was through the waters of a lake; the
first men had originally emerged in the world, bringing spirit
with them from below, at a mysterious place in the north called
Sipapu. Once on the earth, men thought of everything as radi-
ating from central points of awareness—themselves, a family
group, or an entire pueblo—and all beliefs were bound to Sipapu,
where man had first entered the world, and which each community constructed symbolically within its kiva. Such stone-lined pits
in the center of their round ceremonial chambers were regarded
as the actual passages between the lower world and the earth above,
and the kiva, as a powerful and awesome symbol, was looked upon
by the town as the place where the two worlds joined.

Since the people's welfare and good fortune demanded harmonious attunement to the spirit world around them, Pueblo society was tightly knit and rigidly conformist. Most towns were
headed by a single leader who served for life, and all the people
under him were divided into cults and secret societies, each of
which had its own duties and sacred kiva. Every cult, in turn, had
a head man who was in charge of its ceremonial activities. Only
men were allowed inside the kivas, which were sometimes under-
ground but more often were built above ground like round tow-
ers and entered by ladders which were dropped to the interior
from a hatch in the roof. Inside the chambers the cult leaders
kept their fetishes and other sacred objects, including brilliantly
painted and feathered masks and costumes for kachina dances—
group prayers in which the wearers of the masks believed they
possessed the spirits and powers of the gods they impersonated.

At the times of such dances, the men of a cult disappeared into
their kiva, and when they came crowding back up the ladder and
over the roof, wearing their great masks, the people of the pueblo
participated with them, certain that the gods had come to town

from the sacred lake through the passageway in the kiva. The most important dance was that of the rain gods, the givers of life to the people of the desert, and there was no deception involved in their appearance because everyone, including the portrayers of the gods, understood that the masks actually conveyed their spirits. Nevertheless, the mysteries attending the arrival of the gods inside the kivas could not be witnessed by women or children.

Before the boys of a pueblo were nine years old they were taken into the secret chambers and brought face to face with the masked kachinas, who proceeded to whip them furiously, trying to drive the badness out of them and prepare them for their important future roles. At adolescence they were again given a lashing in the kivas, but this time the kachinas suddenly unmasked in front of them and, threatening quick punishment if they failed to keep the secret, showed them that, after all, they were the real men of the village, who turned miraculously into gods when they put on the masks. After this terrifying initiation the youths received long training in the rituals and secrets of the cult and, when they married, were finally ready to become kachinas themselves.

In addition to the cults, each pueblo's secret societies were charged with specific community functions, such as the prosecution of defensive warfare, the hunting of game, the appointment of non-religious officers, and the training of masked clowns who cavorted in the ceremonial dances and served as town disciplinarians by raffishly ridiculing, censuring, or whipping those who had been guilty of offensive behavior. There were also important curing societies, composed of powerful doctors who kept watch over a pueblo against the evil spirits that brought sickness and death to the people. As recipients of the great knowledge of the medicine men of the spirit world, they were believed able to recognize and do battle with witches that no one else could even see. They used their gifts to unmask the invisible evildoers, and with prayers, chants, and mystic paintings of colored corn meal which they sprinkled on the ground in curative designs, worked hard to charm away the spirits and save their patients. Sometimes the witches refused to leave peacefully, and the doctors had to strip themselves naked, paint their faces black to frighten the witches, and engage in furious and dramatically noisy hand-to-hand struggles with their invisible adversaries. If, after everything, the patient died, it was simply a sign that the witch had been too strong for the doctors, and they were not blamed. When they effected a cure, however, it was proof of their awesome connection with the spirit world and confirmed again their influence over invisible beings. The medicine men, one of whom in later years was Popé, were the people's daily guardians of life and health, and their unique position, constructed on centuries of faith, often gave them influence in political as well as medical matters.

Though possibly past their cultural peak, the people of the pueblos were suddenly faced in the sixteenth century by two developments that threatened their future. From the north there appeared dangerous Ute marauders and wandering bands of fierce Navaho and Apache hunters, who had left their Athapascan relatives in Canada not long before and had migrated to the southwest, where they began to harass the peaceful and productive towns of the Pueblos. The newcomers were non-agricultural nomads, however, who preferred following the game to conquering and occupying a settled site, and their belligerence ebbed and flowed, often disappearing entirely when they approached the pueblos to exchange in peaceful trade their hide and horn products of the buffalo plains and mountains for corn, baskets, and other food and manufactures of the town dwellers. Though their numbers and power gradually increased, the ultimate threat of the Navahos and Apaches was abruptly eclipsed by another invader who appeared without warning from the south, and eventually cut short with finality all chance of further Pueblo development.

The discovery of the Pueblos by the Spaniards, though an inevitable consequence of their conquest of Mexico in 1521, stemmed from a romantic and unplanned adventure that began elsewhere. In 1528 an expedition of four hundred well-armed men under Pánfilo de Narváez had sailed from Cuba to Florida to search for gold. Landing a little north of the present site of St. Petersburg, the group had marched and fought its way through swamps and forests along the Florida Gulf Coast, finding no gold and losing more than a hundred and fifty men to Indian arrows and disease. Ill, weary, and burdened with frustration and fear, the rest of them had built small boats and tried to sail across the Gulf of Mexico to the Spanish town of Panuco near Tampico. In the little vessels thirst, hunger, and the broiling Gulf sun drove many of the men mad, but when they tried to put into harbors for relief, hostile Indians drove them away. Finally a storm hurled them ashore on Galveston Island. Only eighty of the original four hundred were left, starving, unarmed, and without clothes. Conflicts with wild natives along the Texas coast, and an unsuccessful attempt by a large group to make a dash southward by boat reduced this number to five. These men lived as miserable slaves of different bands of Indians for five years. Finally, one of them, named Álvar Cabeza de Vaca, a treasury agent of the King of Spain on the Narváez expedition, and three of the others, including a Moorish slave named Esteban, managed to steal away from their captors and start walking in a generally western direction toward the setting sun, hoping to come on the new frontier settlements which the Spaniards had been building north of Mexico City.

It was a wondrous, overland journey on foot through wilderness and rugged, arid country where no European had yet been, among tribes who knew nothing of the whites, and who marveled at their sudden appearance and treated them as gods. As Cabeza de Vaca and his companions moved westward, they saw many new and thrilling sights, including the first herds of buffalo known to have been viewed by white men, but what excited them most were tales told them by certain of the tribes concerning wealthy and powerful peoples who lived farther north in great cities and opulent countries that were rich in pearls and precious stones. At length, two years after they had begun their journey, the four wanderers emerged from the wild, unknown desert and arrived safely at the northwestern Mexican colonial outpost of Culiacán. Their stories of fabulous new lands that lay just beyond where they had been fired the imaginations of the Spaniards, and in 1539 the first Viceroy of New Spain, Antonio de Mendoza, selected a Franciscan, Fray Marcos de Niza, to reconnoiter the northern territory to discover if it was, indeed, another fabulously rich native kingdom, like Mexico or Peru, worthy of a new expedition of conquest.

Imbued with an enormous imagination of his own, Fray Marcos set off for the distant land, guided by Esteban, the slave, who got out ahead of him and, accompanied by some loyal Indians of northern Mexico, reached an adobe pueblo of Zuñis at the base of a butte in the western desert of what is now New Mexico. Adorned with feathers and bells and taking seriously the character of a god with which the Indians had endowed him during his journey with Cabeza de Vaca, Esteban sent to the Zuñi chief a ceremonial gourd rattle he had picked up during his wanderings three years before. The Zuñi, in a rage, recognized it as belonging to people who had been his enemies, and he apparently ordered Esteban to leave the country. The Moor refused and, instead, sent back glowing reports to Fray Marcos, who was still following hard on his trail, that he had reached a wonderful city of a great and wealthy land called Cibola. It was his last report. Soon afterward the survivors of his party came flying back to Fray Marcos with news that the Zuñis had attacked them and slain the Moor with arrows.

The Franciscan hesitated in fear, then with two Indians stole forward for a swift, secret look at the Zuñi pueblo. From a distance the terraced city seemed to confirm what he wanted to believe, and he hastened back to Culiacán, reporting that everything that Cabeza de Vaca and Esteban had said was true and that with his own eyes he had actually seen "house doors studded with jewels, the streets lined with the shops of silversmiths." Moreover, he said, the Indians with Esteban had told him that this was only the first and smallest of seven cities, which must at last be the seven lost cities of Atlantis, long a part of the shadowy store of medieval myths and legends that were still luring conquistadors on expeditions of discovery throughout the western hemisphere.

The friar's news was what the Viceroy Mendoza was waiting to hear, and the next year, 1540, he dispatched the young, hot-blooded governor of the north Mexican province of New Galicia, Francisco Vásquez de Coronado, not yet thirty years old, with an expedition of 230 mounted troops, 62 foot soldiers, a company of priests and assistants, and almost a thousand friendly Indians to explore and seize the new territory of Cibola. Guided by Fray Marcos, the army of conquistadors followed a rough route northward across waterless deserts, and finally reached the Zuñi pueblo of Hawikuh. The Spaniards were appalled to learn that the miserable-looking mud pile of ladders and adobe walls was Fray Marcos's idea of a sumptuous city of gold and jewels, and the angry Coronado wrote to Mendoza that the priest "has not told the truth in a single thing he said." But the army was starving after its long, wearying march, and at least there were Indian supplies of corn and beans stored in the pueblos.

At first, Coronado's signs of peace were ignored by the frightened inhabitants, who were stunned by the sudden appearance of the strange host and its fantastic animals and equipment. For the first time the Indians were seeing horses, whose long heads and big teeth made the natives certain that they ate people. It was no reassurance to them, either, that the newcomers in shining helmets and suits of armor sat unconcernedly on the snorting beasts, and the alarmed Zuñis made a line of sacred corn meal on the ground, and warned the Spaniards not to cross over it with their animals. When the invaders ignored the warning and started forward, the panicky Indians sounded their war horn and fired a stream of arrows. The sudden answering explosions of Spanish guns and the fierce charge of horses and men with long lances routed the natives, who fled to their pueblo, and the battle was quickly over. While the Spaniards broke into the Zuñis' stores and appeased their hunger, the defeated Indians sent runners to other pueblos with amazing tales of the power of the newcomers, and chiefs from other towns soon arrived with gifts for what the Indians began to suspect were white gods, who ancient legends had dimly suggested would some day appear among them from the south.

That suspicion was soon ended. Hope still breathed in Coronado's breast that he would yet find another Peru, and from his base among the conquered Zuñi he sent off exploring parties in all directions, trusting that somewhere else in this northern country he would turn up a city with glittering walls and golden streets. One of his companies found a new cluster of pueblos in the desert, the homes of the Hopis, with more food but, again, no treasure. A second band of soldiers came on a great gulf in the earth and stared in amazement at the wonder they had discovered, the Grand Canyon of the Colorado River. And a third party, under Captain Hernando de Alvarado, marched eastward past an incredible sky city called Ácoma, built atop a steep-walled mesa some four hundred feet high, and entered the country of the many pueblos along the Rio Grande. The Indians in the area called their homeland Tiguex, and Alvarado adopted the name for the whole region. He explored up and down the river, and found the Indians friendly and peaceful. Once more there was no gold, but the sheltering groves of cottonwoods and willows, the rich, watered fields and pastures, and the numerous settled towns in the vicinity made the location an ideal wintering place for the Spaniards.

Coronado moved his whole army across country to the Rio Grande and established headquarters in the pueblo of Alcanfor, ordering all the Indians to evacuate it and turn its rooms over to his men. His rude command ruffled the feelings of the Pueblos, who were soon further aroused by a stern requisitioning of winter provisions from the meager stores of the towns, and by the insensitivity and rudeness with which the Spaniards began to treat the natives. Abuse of Indian women and brutality toward several chiefs brought matters to a head, and before Christmas revolt flared in some of the settlements, whose outraged inhabitants were now sure that the newcomers were mortals like themselves. For more than three months the Spaniards faced resentment and hostility, and again and again with wild battle cries of "Santiago" launched furious assaults against the walls of defiant cities, cutting down their defenders by the hundreds and burning captured Indians at the stake. Cruelties and atrocities increased on both sides, until at length the chastened Tiguas of the area abandoned their villages and stole away to other pueblos in the north. In the spring, with authority established over the region, the Spaniards re-formed their ranks for another long march and, leaving the silent Tigua towns, headed for the northeastern plains and brand new rumors of a land of gold.

This time Coronado was led by a captive Pawnee Indian whom he had found in one of the pueblos, and whom Alvarado called the Turk because he looked like one. Far out among the buffalo, to the waving grasslands of present-day Kansas, the Turk drew the Spaniards, raving to them of a province called Quivira, whose lord "took his afternoon nap under a great tree on which were hung a number of little gold bells, which put him to sleep as they swung in the air," and where "everyone had their ordinary dishes of wrought plate, and the jugs and bowls were made of gold." It was another will-of-the-wisp, and when Coronado reached Quivira, and found it to be an impoverished settlement of grass huts belonging to Wichita Indians, he had had enough. His men strangled the Turk and the army returned to another bitter and profitless winter in the empty pueblos of Tiguex. In the spring, with all their high hopes of two years before turned to frustration and disillusionment, they abandoned the Rio Grande and straggled gloomily back to Mexico.

Their unhappy reports discouraged further Spanish interest
in the northern country, where it was now proved that there was
neither gold nor other treasure, and for almost forty years the
Pueblos saw no more of white men. Gradually the Indians came
back to their Tiguex settlements, filled with bitter memories of
the invaders. Coronado, however, had had no idea of establishing a colony among them, and the Spaniards had created no lasting damage to the Pueblos' civilization. Once again the Indians
were masters of their homeland, leading the centuries-old lives of
their ancestors, and as time went on the wounds of their first contacts with the Spaniards were overshadowed by a growing desire for the metal tools and other goods of the white man's civilization that Coronado's men had brought among them.

In the South, meanwhile, a new generation of Spaniards began
to talk again of the strange lands and peoples whom Coronado
had visited. There were rumors of rich mines that the conquistadors had missed, and fortunes to be made in Tiguex and in the
mysterious countries that lay beyond the Rio Grande. New Spain
was still filled with adventurers, restless to repeat the glorious
triumphs of Cortes and Pizarro, and by 1580 eager petitioners
were again asking the King of Spain for permission to bring the
northern countries under Spanish domination and convert the
natives who lived in the terraced cities in those regions.

The latter aim, a holy one, though a cover for personal greed,
was more immediately appealing to the authorities, and in July
1581 three Franciscan friars, accompanied by nine soldiers and
sixteen Mexican servants, traveled back to Tiguex along the
newly discovered Conchos River route that led from northern
Mexico to the Rio Grande. The Pueblos received the new white
men without enmity, eyeing their goats and horses and packs
full of trade goods, and allowing them to move freely through
their country. One of the priests resolved to return to Mexico
alone to report what he had seen, and the rest of the party explored east and west, visiting the pueblos and coming again on

the Zuñis. At length, after returning to the Rio Grande, the other two priests and several of the Mexicans decided to settle among the Indians and try to convert them to Christianity; the rest of the group headed back to Mexico.

The following year another missionary party rode north to Tiguex and, arriving among the Pueblos, found to their horror that all three of the priests who had entered the country the previous year were dead. The Indians, it appeared, had slain them for their possessions and trade goods. After fighting several battles with the Pueblos the members of the new group returned to Mexico with romantic tales of what had happened to them, but the stories they told only served to quicken interest in the region. Impatient adventurers, still waiting for permission to lead official expeditions to what was now being called the province of New Mexico, were sure that they could conquer the unruly inhabitants of the north for Cross and Crown, and incidentally find fame and riches for themselves.

Finally, in 1590, one of them, Gaspar Castaño de Sosa, lieutenant governor of the province of Nuevo León, without waiting for word from Spain, organized a colonizing expedition of 170 people, equipped it with two brass cannons and a long train of supply carts, and started off for Tiguex. The group reached the pueblos without serious difficulties and established a camp near an Indian town that was later called Santo Domingo. The Indians watched the new arrivals sullenly, giving them food when they asked for it, but otherwise having little to do with them. After sending a message to the Viceroy in Mexico City announcing his success in establishing a colony, Castaño de Sosa went off exploring the countryside. Soon after his return to the Rio Grande he heard that a party of Spanish troops was marching up the river to Tiguex. Thinking that they were reinforcements for his people, he went out to meet them and was promptly arrested for presuming to establish a colony in New Mexico without royal permission. The soldiers dispersed the settlement and the people gradually straggled back to Mexico. In the capital Castaño was tried, convicted, and exiled to China, where he was later killed in a fight on a Chinese junk.

Other men secretly, and without success, continued after him, trying to steal into the country of the Pueblos, but eight years after Castaño's short-lived colony the Spanish court finally authorized the scion of one of the wealthiest families in Mexico, Don Juan de Oñate, son of a governor and husband of a granddaughter of Cortes, to occupy the land of the Pueblos for the King and establish a permanent frontier settlement in the province. Oñate, a vigorous man in middle life, was a worthy successor to the long line of ambitious conquistadors who had preceded him. Spending a fortune of his own, which he fully expected would be repaid with dividends by the still undiscovered riches of New Mexico, he organized a huge expedition and in 1598 led it north to the Rio Grande. After taking possession of the province "once, twice, and thrice" near the site of El Paso, as already related, he continued through the mountain pass, marched under clear, brilliant skies, and reached the first of the pueblos on June 24. As he moved from one town to another the size of his force awed the natives, and chiefs came forward solemnly to offer friendship and, at the direction of the governor and his host of Franciscan friars, to pledge allegiance to the white man's king and his Christian religion.

At the pueblos of Yuque and Yunque near the juncture of the Chama River and the Rio Grande, Oñate halted and, like Coronado before him, ordered the natives to evacuate one of the towns for his men. The Indians moved out peaceably, and the Spaniards renamed the village San Juan and designated it as the capital of the new colony. Irrigation works were begun, and a church built, and on September 8 the first Mass was sung in the new building. The Spaniards had invited the heads of all the pueblos to witness the colorful ritual of the white man's religion, and the next day Oñate assembled the chiefs again, once more pledged them to be loyal to the Spanish King, whom he represented, and then, through the Father President of the friars, proposed to them that they and their people receive the great joys and benefits of the true faith by accepting the white man's God.

The chiefs were confused, but after discussing it among themselves agreed to allow the newcomers' priests to come and visit them in their pueblos and instruct their people, with the understanding, however, that if the Indians approved of what they learned, they would adopt the white men's teachings, but if they did not like it, they would not be forced to accept what they heard. It was good enough for Oñate and for the friars, who divided the pueblos among themselves and departed for the lonely mission work at the various villages. Meanwhile, with his mind on material rewards, Oñate was restless to find the riches that Coronado had missed, and on October 6 he rode out of San Juan at the head of an exploring party, bound on a great-circle tour of discovery that would take him first to the buffalo plains of Quivira in the east, and then roundabout in the direction of the setting sun and the South Sea, which was rumored to be near, and where he hoped to find pearls.

While he was gone the priests erected crosses at the villages and began their work of telling the natives about Christ and the religion of the white men. Their work was suddenly interrupted by an outbreak of resistance that occurred at the sky city of Ácoma and almost threatened the future of the entire colony. A body of Spanish troops marched westward one day and reached the pueblo perched high above them on the mesa. Faced by a shortage of food, the men followed a path up the steep, rocky cliffs and entered the adobe town. At first the Indians seemed peaceful, and the Spaniards broke into small groups and poked through the apartments. What offense they gave the natives is not known, but suddenly a war cry rose through the village, and angry Indians came pouring out of holes in every rooftop, ready for battle.

The small band of Spaniards tried to gather in one of the streets, but in a moment, a screaming mob of almost a thousand natives, firing arrows and swinging clubs and lances, came at them from every side and cut them off. The wild combat lasted for three hours, and most of the Spaniards were hacked to pieces. Several of them managed to escape down the sides of the mesa, while others jumped to their deaths from the cliffs. Four of the soldiers miraculously survived the four-hundred-foot fall, landing in sand banks at the base of the mesa, and with the other survivors got back to San Juan with news of the catastrophe. Wondering if all the other pueblos would now turn on them, the fearful colonists set a twenty-four-hour watch and dispatched messengers to the isolated priests, warning them to abandon their lonely missions and hasten back to the capital.

Shortly before Christmas, Oñate returned home, disillusioned at having found nothing but a harsh and empty wilderness, and aroused by the sudden threat to the future of his colony. Determined to punish the offending Indians and by a swift and terrible example frighten any other pueblos that might be planning a challenge to his authority, he proclaimed "war by blood and fire" against Ácoma, and sent a force of seventy men, heavily armed with hand weapons and two cannons, against the people of the mesa-top city. The avenging troops divided their forces, a part of them pretending to attack up one side of the cliff, while another stole unobserved up the opposite side.

The battle raged fiercely for three days, and at last the Spaniards got their whole force on top of the mesa and dragged their cannons into position against the pueblo. They loaded the guns with two hundred balls apiece and fired them point-blank into the natives' ranks, piling up masses of Indian dead and wounded. Other soldiers set fire to the pueblos, and in the confusion and smoke of their burning village the Indians gradually gave up the fight, throwing themselves from the cliffs or retreating to their fiery apartments to hang themselves. Almost a thousand Indians perished in the fight, and the Spaniards dragged a host of burned and wounded prisoners back with them to San Juan. Two of the captives managed to cheat their conquerors. In the Spanish capital they fastened nooses around their necks in a gesture that awed the colonists, and scrambling to the top of a tree, cried bitterly to the Spaniards, "Our towns, our things, our lands are yours," and hanged themselves. The other prisoners were not so fortunate. The Spaniards herded them into a mock trial that found them guilty, then cut off the hands and feet of many of the adult male captives, and sentenced the women to "personal service" in the colony, a polite term for slavery.

Soon afterward the Spaniards sacked two more pueblos that made a show of resistance, killing nine hundred Indians in one of them and returning to San Juan with a string of two hundred more captives, whom they tortured or sentenced to slavery. At length the savage destruction of the native villages and the harsh fate of the defenders cowed the rest of the pueblos, as Oñate intended, and peace, enforced by Spanish arms, settled over the Rio Grande valley, lasting uneasily under the oppressor's hand for more than eighty years. During that time the colony that Oñate had established sank roots in the land and extended a stern and alien rule over the Pueblos.

The governors who succeeded Oñate abandoned all hope of finding treasure cities in the province; after establishing a permanent Spanish capital city, which they built of adobes in 1610 and called Santa Fe, they turned their energies to grinding profits from the only source of wealth available to them in the country, the enforced labor of the subjugated natives. To favored men around them the governors granted encomiendas, bodies of land which they seized from the Indians, and to which they bound the native inhabitants as serfs. In addition they ordered every native in each pueblo to pay annual tributes of cloth, maize, and personal labor to the colony. Indians were soon working the white men's fields, tending their goats and cattle, and manufacturing, as slave laborers, cotton shirts and numerous articles of cloth, wood, and hides which the colonists sold for themselves in the markets of Mexico. The most relentless exploiter was the governor himself, who used his autocratic powers to amass a personal fortune before his term in office ended. With the help of a retinue of spies and assistants who encouraged graft and corruption on every hand, he demanded a share of each *encomendero*'s profits, imported goods from Mexico which he forced Indians and colonists alike to buy from him at high prices, and sent back to the South long pack trains of Indian-made products which his agents sold for his personal account.

When they were not working for the governor and settlers, the natives were busy paying tribute in goods and services to the Franciscan friars whom they were forced to accept and support in their pueblos. Guarded by soldiers, the priests had courageously returned to the villages after the Ácoma revolt and had stood with their wooden crosses among the Indians, preaching boldly to them about Christ. Gradually their dedication and bravery stirred the pueblos and gained respect and safety for them, and as the Indians moved closer about them and listened with hushed attention to their dramatic tales and heavenly promises, the friars' faith seized the natives' imaginations. Despite the angry opposition of the medicine doctors, large numbers of Pueblos knelt for conversion in the diamond-clear sunlight, accepting, with more curiosity and expectancy than understanding, the strange ideas and rituals of the white men, and in time grafting them onto their own ancient beliefs and ceremonies in a bizarre mixture of Christianity and spirit worship. As the priest became one with his converts the natives eagerly accepted everything else he taught them, using the new tools he gave them, learning music, crafts, and Spanish methods of agriculture, and feeling strength and pride in their new knowledge and possessions. Eventually, at the edge of each pueblo, they helped the friars rear a village church, fitting for the awesome processions and ceremonies of their new faith and symbolic of the power and wealth of their new life. Altogether, during the first quarter of the seventeenth century, the priests and their charges built fifty churches in New Mexico, all ruled under a strict, provincial hierarchy that was centered in a religious headquarters at the pueblo of Santo Domingo, a short distance southwest of Santa Fe.

With the passage of time, reinforcements from Mexico increased the size of the Spanish colony, and the conquerors' hold over the Indians, aided by the supervisory offices of the friars in the pueblos, gave the conquerors an illusion of security. The entire economy of the valley rested on the exploitation of the natives, who were not allowed to ride horses or use firearms, and the uncomplaining fashion in which the gentle Pueblos responded to demands for labor and tribute made it seem that they, like the Indians of the Caribbean and Mexico, were thoroughly subjugated. From a number of directions, however, disaster was looming for the Spaniards. Many Indians were still unconverted, and even among those who were called Christians the white man's religion had often not penetrated far below the surface. The friars banned the kachina dances wherever they felt strong enough to do so, but it was another thing to drive a centuries-old faith out of people's minds and hearts. In the recesses of the pueblos, the cult leaders kept alive old ways, telling the people that the kachinas were still in the kivas, and even the converted Indians still called on their medicine men, who smoldered with deep resentments over the presence of the friars.

The white men did not help their own cause. An increasing drive for profits led to greater pressures on the Indians, and conflict broke out over policies that would have rushed the natives into total slavery and doomed them to extinction. Many of the Spaniards seriously believed that Indians were animals rather than rational humans, for unlike civilized men they seemed indifferent to the ambitions and desires of thinking persons, had no greed for such things as jewels and gold, and appeared content simply to eat and sleep. Although the friars, too, in their own way, were instruments of native suppression, demanding faith and obedience from the Pueblos and undermining their powers to resist the lay conquerors, they could not, at least, agree that Indians did not possess souls, and their protection of their charges against excessive exploitation brought them into conflict with the lay officials.

Though other factors broadened the struggle, the question of whether the governor or the Franciscans had ultimate authority over the Indians divided the colony into two camps and rocked it with turmoil that grew worse under each succeeding governor. From the adobe palace in Santa Fe the governors issued orders to the Indians, which the priests in the pueblos promptly countermanded. The governors flew into rages of jealousy and pettiness, sometimes spitefully urging the Indians to put on public kachina dances to defy their friars, and at other times sending troops to invade the sanctuary of churches and arrest the priests. The latter retaliated with fury of their own, condemning the governors as corrupt heretics and sending frightened squads of soldiers to seize the rulers for crimes against the Church. One governor was called "a heretic, a Lutheran, and a Jew" and excommunicated. Another was sent back to Mexico for trial by the Inquisition.

Still the Spaniards continued to fight among themselves, and, as the confusion worsened, their authority over the Indians was undermined. Many of the converted Pueblos were appalled by the hostility with which the white rulers treated their own priests, and their respect for the brown-robed friars waned sharply. During the second half of the seventeenth century new difficulties suddenly struck the people of the villages, and for the first time in many years they began to wonder if they had offended their ancient gods. Beginning in 1660 serious droughts settled over the Southwest, bringing famine and disease with them. In one year, it was recorded, starvation was so bad that people were forced to eat hides and cart straps, "preparing them for food by soaking and washing them and roasting them in the fire."

As the Pueblos suffered, their troubles were increased by bands of hungry Apaches, who could find no food on the plains and launched desperate raids against the agricultural settlements for supplies. The Pueblos, fighting hunger and sickness themselves and forced to defend their towns against the fierce attacks, became certain that they had displeased their gods, and in the dark kivas and mud-walled rooms the cult leaders and medicine doctors raised their voices with mounting boldness against the friars and urged their people to return to the ways of their ancestors before it was too late.

At this juncture the fierce and mysterious figure of Popé suddenly appears in the reports of Spanish authorities. Popé was an old but vigorous Tewa medicine doctor in the San Juan pueblo. There is no record of his exact age, but it is apparent that all his life he had resisted the Christian religion and had struggled bitterly to keep alive the traditional Indian beliefs among his people. Again and again the Spaniards had denied him the right to conduct his rituals and finally, as punishment for his stubbornness, had seized and enslaved his older brother. The act had only enraged Popé further, and gradually he had become a symbol of uncompromising hostility to the conquerors.

With the coming of the drought his religious activities began to take on political coloring. He held secret meetings in the pueblo and told the people that the gods were speaking against the friars and that the Spaniards must leave the land of the Indians. In time his audiences grew larger and his influence spread, and soon word of his new activities reached the mayor of Santa Fe, who had him arrested and publicly flogged in the plaza of the capital. After a few days in prison he was allowed to return to his village, but shortly afterward he was again seized, whipped, and released. It did the Spaniards little good. Popé's warnings were already being repeated in pueblos throughout New Mexico, and the flames of the fight for religious liberty that he had started were setting fires in Indian towns everywhere. In alarm, the Spanish governor ordered his troops to visit all the settlements, halt the renewal of Indian dances and rituals, and arrest as many of the medicine doctors as possible. Forty-seven native leaders, including the furious Popé, were seized in the drive and dragged into Santa Fe. They were charged with witchcraft and sorcery. Three of the doctors were hanged as examples, and Popé and the rest were whipped and jailed.

The governor's action made matters worse for the Spaniards.

The people in the pueblos believed that without their doctors they were defenseless against the invisible powers of evil that brought sickness and death to them, and from town to town native runners carried appeals for united action. At length a determined delegation of seventy Christianized Indians from the Tewa pueblos on the Rio Grande marched on the governor in Santa Fe and announced that unless the prisoners were turned over to them by sundown the Indians would rise in revolt throughout the province and kill every Spaniard in New Mexico. The governor consulted his advisers, and after anxious deliberation decided that the natives were in dead earnest, and that the colonists in New Mexico, who numbered about twenty-eight hundred, could not hope to defend themselves for long against some sixteen thousand Indians. Reluctantly he freed the doctors, and the liberated Indians returned to their towns.

Hate and anger had spread everywhere now, and the fact that the governor had shown weakness when threatened with revolt was not lost on the Indians. But Spanish authority was still strong, and most of the people were mortally afraid of the friars and their spies and soldiers, who still demanded obedience and inflicted stern punishments on offenders. In Santa Fe the natives had won an opening skirmish, and the momentum of events was on their side, but if a revolt was to come, it required more than hate in men's hearts. To Popé, the bruised and smoldering medicine man, the time had come for Indian organization, leadership, and a magic spark with which to set the country aflame, and he moved quickly to provide his people with all three.

He traveled to the various pueblos to hold secret meetings with other medicine doctors and chiefs, and soon won their loyalty to his plans. Their first duty, he impressed upon them, was to strengthen the courage of the Indians by cleansing their ranks of informers. As an example, he dramatically announced at one meeting in San Juan that he suspected his own son-in-law, Nicolas Bua, the Spanish-supported Indian governor of the pueblo, of being a spy for the white men. The accusation had its desired result. The next day, Indians stoned Bua to death in a cornfield, and, though Popé had to flee from San Juan and hide in the kiva at the Taos pueblo to evade Spanish questioners, news of the incident spread rapidly among the towns and frightened the natives who had been acting as informers for the priests.

In the Taos kiva Popé continued to meet with other chiefs and prepare plans for a general revolt. In midsummer of 1680 he decided that the time for action had come and summoned his principal followers to him. To battle the Christians he used the mystic powers that he possessed through his close relationship with the spirit world, and before the eyes of his entranced audience conjured up in the gloomy ceremonial chamber the wrathful spirits of three native gods, Caudi, Tilini, and Tleume, who the Indian mind readily imagined had entered the kiva through the passageway that came from the lower world and Sipapu. In feathers and shining paint, the gods breathed fire from every extremity of their bodies and announced that they were working for a revolt of the Pueblos in conjunction with the lieutenant of their war god, Montezuma, in the far-off land of Po-he-yemu. They had been sent to warn the Indians, they said, that the time was ripe for ridding the land of the oppressors, and as the chiefs listened to them in dread silence they commanded Popé to set the date of the uprising, and to send to each pueblo a cord of maguey fibers with a number of knots tied in it to signify the days left before the revolt.

The news of what had transpired in the secret chamber spread wildly among the people, and Popé dispatched his knotted maguey cords to the excited villages, calling for a concerted uprising on August 11, 1680, but slyly sending a later date, August 13, to several Christian chiefs whose loyalty he questioned. As he suspected, informers soon revealed the wrong date to the Spanish friars and notified them that old men in pueblos in the North were plotting a revolt after having received a letter from a lieutenant of Po-he-yemu. The lieutenant, they told the priests, "was very tall, black, and had very large yellow eyes, and everyone feared him greatly." This might have been a description of Popé himself; at any rate, on August 9 priests from three towns sent hurried word to Governor Antonio de Otermín in Santa Fe that "the Christian Indians of this kingdom are convoked, allied, and confederated for the purpose of rebelling, abandoning obedience to the Crown and apostatizing from the Holy Faith. They plan to kill the priests, and all the Spaniards—even women and children—thus to destroy the total population of this kingdom. They are to execute this treason and uprising on the 13th of the current month."

The governor immediately dispatched warnings to the Spanish officials at every pueblo and ordered the arrest of all suspected ring leaders. His warnings were too late. At seven o'clock the next morning a panicked soldier came galloping into Santa Fe with news that the Indians at the nearby Tesuque pueblo had painted themselves for war, had killed the priest and a resident white trader, and were marching to join the natives at San Juan, armed for battle with bows, arrows, lances, and shields. The governor ordered every Spaniard in Santa Fe to gather in the public buildings and sent soldiers scurrying through the countryside to round up whites who were out attending their fields and cattle. He set a guard around the capital, distributed arms to everyone capable of bearing them, and waited for further news. It was not long in coming. During the afternoon, reports came in of uprisings in Taos, Santa Clara, Picuris, Santa Cruz, and other pueblos. Frightened soldiers rode back with tales of dead Spanish ranchers in the fields, smoking buildings, and groups of armed Indians moving across the hills.

For the next three nights there was little sleep in Santa Fe, as the Spaniards waited for an Indian attack on their capital. In the surrounding country the news grew steadily worse. Pecos, Galisteo, San Cristóbal, San Marcos, La Cienega, Popuaque, and other pueblos had joined the revolt, and reconnoitering squads of soldiers reported a growing trail of bloodshed and horror against isolated Spaniards who had been caught in their haciendas and estancias. On August 14 news came that a war party of five hundred Indians was finally marching on Santa Fe, and the next day small groups of them began to be seen moving through the cornfields around the city. More and more of them appeared, and as they pressed closer, filtering into the abandoned homes of Mexican Indians on the edges of the town, they called insultingly across to the defenders and danced defiantly on the rooftops of the flat adobe buildings.

Among the thousand Spaniards gathered in Santa Fe, no more than fifty were regular troops, and most of them were convicts conscripted in Mexico. But every able-bodied man was armed, and the governor was confident that a determined attack by the Spaniards would scatter the Indian host. He tried first to negotiate with the natives, sending an escort of soldiers to provide safe conduct to the palace for one of the Indian leaders whom he recognized. The peace effort failed, and the next morning the soldiers attacked, attempting to dislodge the Indians from their threatening positions. The natives had never been allowed to use guns or own horses, but many of them were now supplied with both, and a furious fight lasted all day. By nightfall, however, the Indians had been pushed out of the fields and were fleeing to the foothills. Their flight was halted by the arrival of large reinforcements from San Juan, Taos, and Picuris, probably under Popé himself, and at dawn the Spanish capital was again under siege.

There was silence for two days as the Indians built up their strength. Then, on August 16, twenty-five hundred natives charged at daybreak, sweeping out of the fields in huge masses that carried across homes and roads and broke the ditch that supplied the Spaniards with water. Groups of Spaniards tried to regain the ditch but failed, and at noon the Indians swarmed around the walls of the palace itself and tried to burn the chapel at one end of the building. The entire garrison poured into the plaza to save the structure, and hand-to-hand fighting raged all afternoon. By darkness the defenders had temporarily pushed the Indians back and barricaded themselves once more in the palace, which was now without water.

The next day the battle began again. The desperate Spaniards, many of whom were wounded, had had a miserable night without water, but they met the attackers fiercely and in a number of sorties tried again to recapture the water ditch. Thrown back under a storm of arrows, stones, and gunshot, they almost lost the brass cannons that guarded the palace gates. They pulled the guns into the building's patio with them, but had to fight off Indians all night, listening to native victory songs and watching the entire city of Santa Fe burn around them. Their anguish was increased by the groans of women and children for water, and at dawn, in a last savage attempt to drive off the natives, the garrison sallied out and took the Indians by surprise. The fighting was as bitter and fanatic as before, but fortune now favored the Spaniards, and after severe battling through the ruined town the Indians finally abandoned the struggle and scattered into the hills, leaving behind three hundred dead and forty-seven prisoners in the Spaniards' hands.

Despite their victory, the shaken defenders were in no mood to remain in Santa Fe. The thirsty people gulped water, executed the Indian prisoners, and on August 21 began an exodus to the south, hoping to find safety in Spanish colonies lower down on the Rio Grande. Their hopes were dashed. Pueblo after pueblo stood emptied of Indians who had joined the revolt, and everywhere were only dead Spaniards and burned ranches. Starving, bedraggled, and hollow-eyed from their nightmare, the long line of refugees, with what small property they had been able to salvage, reached El Paso, where they were finally able to rest in safety among friendly Manso Indians.

Behind them the entire province of New Mexico was again in Pueblo hands. The native reconquest of the country had been complete. Some four hundred Spaniards had been killed, including twenty-one of the thirty-three Franciscan friars in the territory. Popé and his followers moved into the ruins of Santa Fe and after dividing the Spanish spoils ordered the people to forget everything they had learned from the Spaniards and return to the ways of their ancestors. In each pueblo the cult leaders conducted ceremonies in which the Christianized natives were washed clean of their baptisms with yucca suds. Both the Spanish language and Christian names were banned. Every object and relic of the Spanish days was ordered destroyed, and in 1681, the year after the revolt, the atmosphere was so changed that, from reports he received in his place of refuge, Fray Francisco de Ayeta, commissary general of the Franciscan Province of New Mexico, wrote that the Indians "have been found to be so pleased with liberty of conscience and so attached to the belief in the worship of Satan that up to the present not a sign has been visible of their ever having been Christians."

And yet the Pueblo victory soon crumbled from within and turned to ashes. The people's attempt to return to a manner of life that had existed before the coming of the white men proved impossible. With their oppression the Spaniards had brought the material goods and culture of a higher civilization, and the natives could not easily abandon things which now seemed to them useful and desirable. Gradually they began to oppose Popé's stern injunctions, and he retaliated with executions and harsh punishments. Inevitably he turned into a tyrant who even affected the hated ways of the conquerors whom he had ousted.

The records of his reign are scanty and rest almost wholly on testimony given to the Spaniards in later days by reconquered natives. But in the main they each tell the same story. To show his power Popé took to posturing like the Spanish governors before him, demanding that others bow in his presence, using prisoners as servants, and even riding about Santa Fe in the Spanish governor's rattletrap carriage of state. In time, other problems beset the harassed people. Apaches showed up, stronger and more belligerent than ever, and without the Spaniards to help protect them the Pueblos proved no match for the raiders. The Apaches laid siege to the towns, killed the Pueblos in their fields, and finally entered the defenseless villages at will, demanding tribute of maize, cotton cloth, horses, cattle, and Pueblo women. Their seizure of horses led to a revolutionary development among the Indian tribes west of the Mississippi River for up to that time no natives in that part of the continent had possessed horses, and few of them had ever seen one of them. Now the Apaches spread them across the plains and into the Rocky Mountains, and tribe after tribe came into possession of them for the first time and learned to use them in warfare and to hunt the buffalo.

A few years after his triumphal revolt, Popé died. Like many white revolutionists, he had successfully led his people in a popular cause, only to betray them. The despotism of his reign helped to cloud his memory and left to history the image of an autocratic fanatic. But it could not obscure the original patriotic motives of his uprising, nor the fact that for a brief moment he freed his people from the oppression of a foreign conqueror. After his death the lot of the Pueblos continued to deteriorate. The unity among the different cities that Popé had formed collapsed amid rivalries and quarrels. The Apache raids increased, and in 1692, when a Spanish army under Diego de Vargas finally marched north again from El Paso, the country of the Pueblos offered little resistance. With the troops came new governors, friars, and colonists, and in time no sign showed in the hot sun of the arid country that the Pueblos had ever fought for, and won, their right to be free.

IV

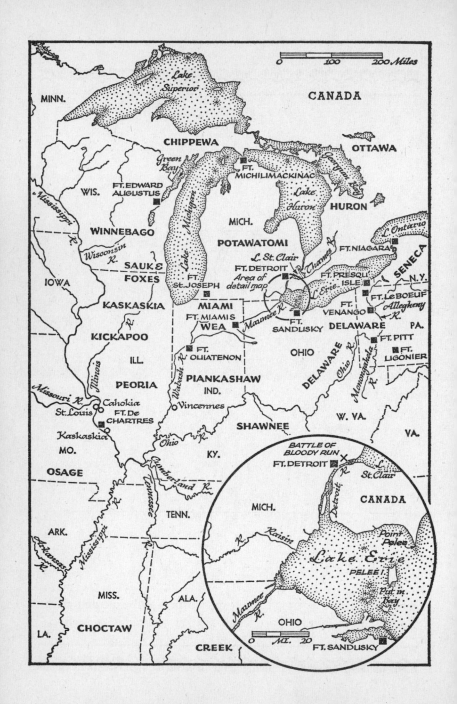

IV

THE WILDERNESS WAR
OF PONTIAC

Sir Jeffery Amherst, commander-in-chief of British forces in North America, had had a glorious military career. As an officer in Germany and the Low Countries during the War of the Austrian Succession he had won honors and fame in battle, and in 1758 he had come to the New World to fight the French. He had reduced Louisburg, captured Crown Point and Ticonderoga, and in 1760, after Wolfe's decisive victory at Quebec, had received the capitulation of the French governor at Montreal. As a military leader Amherst was the model of a successful British general, rigid, proper, and meticulous in every detail. But there was a flaw in his make-up, and three years after the surrender of Montreal, it plunged him into a debacle that tarnished his reputation and clouded the brilliance of his earlier record.

Amherst had an arrogant contempt for Indians. He regarded them as inferior and "wretched" people who were best handled by stern, disciplinarian Indian agents backed by British arms. He had neither understanding of native backgrounds and traditions nor patience with Indians' ideas and needs, and at one time he wrote that "the only true method of treating the savages is to keep them in proper subjection and punish, without exception, the transgressors." In the field his Indian agents were more realistic. But Amherst gave them their orders and expected them to obey him, and in 1763, despite their warnings, which he imperiously ignored, he found himself suddenly enveloped in a catastrophic all-out war with a vast confederacy of powerful tribes, led by a capable and determined Indian leader who refused to be kept "in proper subjection," and who almost proved to be his master.

Amherst's opponent was a tattooed and painted Ottawa war chief named Pontiàc from the Detroit River, deep in the interior of the continent, between Lake Erie and Lake Huron. To white men Pontiac emerged suddenly from obscurity to prominence, and few facts are known concerning his early life. He had been born about 1720, probably in an Ottawa village on the north side of the Detroit River, and it is believed that one of his parents— though it is not sure which one—had been an Ottawa, and the other either a Miami or a Chippewa. What his name meant in the Indian language or how he rose to eminence among his people has never been discovered, but it is clear that by 1763 he enjoyed a formidable reputation among the chiefs and warriors of many tribes besides his own. As a fierce and daring brave he had gained prominence in war parties of Indians who were loyal to the French, and though there is no record of his youth it is probable that he saw steady fighting through the French and Indian War, participating in raids against the British in upstate New York, battling pro-English tribes along the Great Lakes, and finally helping to rout General Braddock, either as a warrior or as the leader of an Ottawa band, in the disastrous defeat of the British column in western Pennsylvania in 1755.

In some ways Pontiac fit the figure of the wilderness savage that Amherst abhorred. He had spent his early manhood as a bitter partisan of the French, and in the desperate struggle between the two European powers in North America had waged war in the traditionally ruthless manner of his own people and their native enemies. Neither the French nor the British had expected their Indian allies to conform to the niceties of civilized conflict, and both had winked at their auxiliaries' ferocity and done little to try to inhibit them. From the imperialistic war of the white men Pontiac emerged as he had entered it, a forest warrior who drank the blood and ate the hearts of brave enemies to acquire their courage, and who was capable of any stratagem or wile to gain his end. At times, when strength was on his side, he could posture with arrogance and boldness, and when the threat of defeat faced him he might, as Amherst contemptuously expected, become abject and docile. But such mercurial behavior was not pointless bullying or cowardice, as Amherst regarded it. To the Indian it was calculated craft, a method of outwitting enemies, and Pontiac, as the British general discovered, was a master at it.

Daring and shrewdness, moreover, were only a part of the Ottawa chief's powerful personality. Indians generally enjoyed good oratory and could sit for hours listening to an accomplished speaker whose dramatic sense of delivery and use of imagery stirred their minds. There were few men anywhere among the Indians whose eloquence could match Pontiac's. In addition, he was a natural-born political leader who might have risen high among white men if he had been born in a civilized society. Unlike most natives, he could think in terms of long-range strategy and could plan and act decisively not for the moment alone but for the achievement of large and distant aims. By the time the English were first aware of him, it was evident that such qualities were already bringing him to the attention of tribes other than his own, and he was receiving the respect and following of peoples who had previously been enemies of the Ottawas. To those natives who welcomed his visits at their council fires, or traveled long distances through the wilderness to listen to his words, he was an unusually self-assured and authoritative figure. His modern biographer, Howard H. Peckham, has pointed out that while some whites who met him called him "proud, vindictive, warlike, and easily offended," others characterized him as "absolute and peremptory," with a "commanding and imperious" bearing. Tall, powerfully built, with beads in his ears, a decorative stone in his nose, and silver trade bracelets on his

arms, he was an outstanding military leader and a canny statesman and orator, who little resembled Amherst's conception of a
capricious and easily controlled savage.

Pontiac's sudden and staggering war against the English,
which saw the capture of eight out of twelve of the British forts
in the Indians' country, the forced abandonment of a ninth, and
prolonged sieges of two others, was an inevitable result of Amherst's short-sighted Indian policies. But the situation he mis-
handled stemmed, in turn, from the long rivalry in North America between France and England, and from the shock and confusion that overwhelmed the natives when the French collapsed
and withdrew from the continent. Along the Atlantic seaboard,
for a full century, Indians had faced the pressures of expanding
settlers who demanded land. Some tribes, like Philip's Wampanoags, had fought to halt the conqueror and had failed. Others,
like the Iroquois, had successfully slowed the settlers either by
their own strength or with the help of white officials and traders
who valued the tribes as war allies and as undisturbed providers
of furs. But in the interior of the continent, beyond the Appalachian range of mountains, where settlers had scarcely yet appeared, the situation had been different, and relations between
white men and Indians had been determined almost entirely by
the rivalries of the imperial powers and the commercial fur trade.

Beginning in the early seventeenth century, far in advance of
the English, Frenchmen had made their way up the St. Lawrence
and Ottawa Rivers and across the Great Lakes, meeting interior
tribes and organizing them in a vast system of trade that almost
annually sent flotillas of canoes, loaded with furs, back down
the waterways to Montreal and Quebec. The French were
at Lake Huron by 1612, eight years before the Pilgrims landed at
Plymouth, and in 1623 one of Champlain's men reached
Lake Superior, deep in the heart of the continent, more than a
thousand miles west of the new Massachusetts colony. Other
explorers and traders from the St. Lawrence pushed down Lake
Michigan and along the water routes through the Illinois coun-

try to the Mississippi, and in time, when Frenchmen from New Orleans came up that wide river, the two fingers of Gallic penetration joined in a great arc of wilderness forts and trading posts that stretched from Quebec to lower Louisiana.

Into the interior with the French traders and soldiers went priests and independent hunters and trappers called *coureurs de bois*, "runners of the woods," who settled peacefully among the different tribes and fathered half-breed families. The Indians generally welcomed the French, who wanted nothing from them but furs and a plot of land on which to build their posts; and the French in return provided them with guns, ammunition, and European trade goods that gave the Indians new strength and power and made life easier for them. With the help of Jesuit "black gowns," whose courage and religious services appealed to the natives' sense of drama, the French drew the Indians closely to them, and tribe after tribe made alliances with the traders and came to depend upon them for manufactured goods that rapidly changed their old ways of life.

On the eastern side of Lake Huron the French had first traded with the Iroquoian Hurons, but beyond them they had come on great numbers of Algonquian-speaking tribes, prominent among whom were peoples known as Ottawas, Potawatomis, and Chippewas (corrupted from their own name, Ojibway). These three tribes had apparently once formed a single nation, living north of the Great Lakes. Before the French met them they had migrated to the Lakes and separated, the Ottawas settling along the northern curve of Lake Huron, the Chippewas moving west to Lake Superior, and the Potawatomis pushing south through the lower peninsula of Michigan. The French had originally met the Ottawas on Georgian Bay in 1615, and found them armed with bows and arrows and war clubs. They were almost naked save for mantles of furs, were fiercely painted and tattooed, and had pierced noses and wore trinkets as decorations on their ears. There were many separate villages of them, each one under its own chief, and the majority of the men were tireless wanderers, used to traveling hundreds of miles on foot or by canoe to trade or make war. Though they planted corn and hunted and fished, they were known principally to the other Algonquians as intertribal traders and barterers who bought corn meal, furs, skins, tobacco, roots, and herbs from one tribe and exchanged them with another, and their name, Ottawa, in the Algonquian tongue meant "to trade."

At first, as the French pushed rapidly to the west beyond them, the Ottawas exercised a minor role in the fur trade, selling their beaver pelts to the "middleman" Hurons, who gave them French goods in return and took their furs down to Montreal themselves to sell for the higher prices in the white men's markets. Soon, however, the entire trade was disrupted, and both the Ottawas and Hurons were enveloped in turmoil that elevated the Ottawas to new importance and almost eliminated the Huron nation. From the south, violent competition had developed for the French. Dutch and British traders, moving up the Hudson River and inland from the Atlantic colonies, had made allies of the powerful Iroquoian tribes and opened trade with them. When the Iroquois ran out of beaver on their own lands, they looked to the north and tried to buy furs from the Hurons. The latter haughtily refused, and the frustrated Iroquois, desperate for pelts to trade for British arms and manufactured goods, began to waylay Huron fur fleets and steal their packs of beaver skins. In retaliation, the Hurons attacked Iroquois villages; at length a huge Iroquois war party struck back and in 1649 invaded the Huron country and all but annihilated the nation.

The remnants of the Hurons fled north and west, spreading panic among neighboring tribes, who scattered westward ahead of them. In the chaos the Ottawas tried to assume the role of middleman that had been vacated by the Hurons, but the Iroquois attacked them also, and the Ottawas fled all the way to the Green Bay region of Wisconsin, where they found shelter with their relatives, the Potawatomis. A few years later they moved even farther west to the Mississippi River, but the Sioux of Minnesota drove them back, and they wandered in small groups along the southern shore of Lake Superior to the Straits of Mackinac. In time many of their bands again played the role of broker to the French, gathering furs from the western tribes and taking them to Montreal by way of the Ottawa River farther north, thus safely by-passing Iroquois war parties that were lying in wait for them on Lake Erie and Lake Ontario. By 1680 the Ottawas were supplying the French with approximately two-thirds of all the beaver they bought, and were becoming strong and wealthy in trade goods. Their new geographical position had brought them into contact with many tribes of the western lakes and the Illinois country, including Menominees, Winnebagos, Sauk, and Foxes in Wisconsin; Miamis, Weas, Kaskaskias, Mascoutens, Piankashaws, and Kickapoos along the rivers of present-day Illinois and Indiana; Shawnees and Delawares in Ohio and western Pennsylvania; as well as their old relatives and friends, the Chippewas, Potawatomis, and Hurons, who were now scattered in villages from the southern shore of Lake Erie to the northern peninsula of Michigan. In the jealousies of the fur trade, brief wars among the various tribes were frequent, but in general most of the natives remained friendly to the French who controlled the country and continued to provide the Indians with guns and trade goods from a number of strategically located posts and forts.

In 1701 the French established a new post on the Detroit River and invited the trading tribes in the Great Lakes country to settle around it. Bands of Ottawas, Chippewas, Hurons, and Potawatomis set up villages near the post, which was first known as Fort Pontchartrain, but was later called Detroit, and in one of them Pontiac was born about 1720. The Ottawas, among whom he was raised, had by now changed materially from the weak and primitive people whom the French had first met a century before at Georgian Bay. The Indians' long relationship with the white men had left its mark on their culture, and though the Ottawas had stubbornly resisted being Christianized by the ever-present Jesuits, they had substituted the ironware and manufactured goods of trade for the tools and implements of their earlier and cruder existence. Instead of stone axes, clay pots, fur mantles, and needles of bone, they now used European hatchets and knives, brass kettles, cloth from France and, awls and needles of steel, and in place of bows and arrows they had come to rely almost entirely on guns and powder both for hunting and to defend themselves against their enemies. Since the French had not tried to appropriate the Indians' lands or coerce them into abandoning their independence, the new and higher material culture had increased the natives' self-respect as well as their power, and in their isolation from the strong urban centers of white civilization along the Atlantic coast proud, young warriors such as Pontiac came to assume that their people enjoyed military equality with the white men.

About 1738, British traders finally began to appear along Lake Erie and in other areas on the west side of the Allegheny Mountains, and the French fur monopoly among the interior tribes ended. The British offered better trade goods for fewer furs, and initiated a new era of bitter competition that drew some Indian villages away from the French. Other natives, however, including Pontiac's band of Ottawas, remained loyal to their traditional allies, and when formal war at last broke out between the two imperial powers those Indians readily joined the conflict on the French side. During fifteen years of struggle the Ottawas remained firmly allied to the commanders and forces of their "father," the French King, and his abrupt capitulation to the Indians' hated enemy, the English, in 1760 came as a frightening shock to the natives. They had committed themselves thoroughly to his side, and some of them refused to believe that he had lost power and would withdraw and leave them to the mercy of their foes.

Nevertheless, late in November 1760 an English force of 275 men, under Major Robert Rogers, the celebrated colonial Ranger leader in the French and Indian War, came sailing up Lake Erie in a fleet of whaleboats to raise the British flag over Fort Detroit. Among the Indian onlookers, as the wilderness post changed hands, was a dismayed party of Ottawas, Hurons, and Potawatomis, and perhaps Pontiac was among them. A few years later, after Pontiac had achieved notoriety, Rogers wrote a dramatic account of having met him at that time. He was the "King or Emperor" of the natives at Detroit, Rogers reported, and added that he possessed "the largest empire and greatest authority of any Indian Chief that has appeared on the continent since our acquaintance with it. He puts on an air of majesty and princely grandeur, and is greatly honoured and revered by his subjects." In similar vein he described how he had told Pontiac of his mission, only to have the native answer him that he would stand in the path the Englishman was walking till morning. This, said Rogers, was "as much as to say I must not march further without his leave." Rogers' account was repeated through the years by most of Pontiac's biographers, but today it is considered fictional. As Peckham revealed, journals of neither Rogers nor his Indian agent, George Croghan, written during their visit to Detroit, mention Pontiac among the other Indian chiefs in the area, and although the future leader might already have begun his rise to power he was still known at that time principally for his fighting ability, and was subordinate in peacetime councils to several older spokesmen for the tribes.

Croghan, an Irish trader who had had much experience as an Indian agent for the English on the Pennsylvania and Virginia frontiers, was a shrewd and capable diplomat, and in a series of conferences with the natives gradually calmed their fears and won them to friendship for the new owners of the post. The Indians received no understanding that the French king had transferred possession of the territory to the British, and were satisfied with Croghan's explanation that the English would do no more than replace the French garrison in the fort and would continue to supply the native peoples with guns and other goods on terms as liberal as those of the French. To such promises the Indians had no objection, and for a while after Croghan and Rogers left them the natives maintained harmonious relations with the members of the new garrison.

But trouble was brewing for them in the East. Croghan, on his return, forwarded a report to Sir William Johnson, British agent in charge of Indian affairs in New York, recommending the continuation of the fair and liberal French methods of treating with the Indians at Detroit, in order to secure their satisfaction and loyalty. Johnson concurred with him and sent the report to General Amherst, noting on his own that "it is very necessary, and will always be expected by the Indians, that the commanding officer of every post have it in his power to supply them in case of necessity with a little clothing, some arms and ammunition to hunt with; also some provisions on their journey homewards, as well as a smith to repair their arms and working utensils, etc."

Amherst bridled at his agents' suggestions. "I do not see why the Crown should be put to that expense," he replied to Johnson. "Services must be rewarded; it has ever been a maxim with me. But as to purchasing the good behavior either of Indians or any others, is what I do not understand. When men of whatsoever race behave ill, they must be punished but not bribed."

His policies, transmitted as orders to the frontier, were eventually felt at wilderness posts. Commanders ceased the traditional French practice of distributing hunting ammunition, provisions, and other small gifts of good will to Indians who called at the forts. Traders who had been used to selling rum for furs were suddenly directed, by British orders, to halt the use of liquor in trade, and when they ignored the directive all trade was prohibited anywhere but at the posts themselves. The changes confused the Indians. For years, when they had run short of powder and lead and needed it for hunting, they had gotten it at the forts, and in times of hunger when game was scarce the French commanders had given them emergency provisions for their families. Now both were denied to them, and the abruptness of the new policies actually caused hardship and distress in many of their villages. The withholding of rum, moreover, irked those who had gotten a taste for it, and still others, who were used to having traders come to their hunting camps wherever they were established in the forests, resented having to make long and inconvenient trips to sell their beaver at the posts.

Still, the Indians were unwilling to risk violence against the new owners of the forts, and when a deputation of New York State Senecas, whom Amherst had also outraged, came to Detroit in the summer of 1761, carrying a red wampum belt that asked the western tribes to join the Iroquois in a general uprising against the English, the Ottawas and their native allies turned them down, and forced the Senecas to abandon their war plans. The Indians' unrest around Detroit, however, was reported to the East, and later in the summer Amherst sent his agents, Croghan and Johnson, to that fort to try to quiet the natives. At the same time he dispatched a large expedition of troops to complete and strengthen the garrisons of the western posts.

Croghan and Johnson might have been spared the trip. Before they reached Detroit they received a letter from Amherst sharply reminding them to hold firm to his Indian policies and not to try "purchasing the good behavior of the Indians by presents." It was much better, he admonished them, "to avoid all presents in the future, since that will oblige them to supply themselves by barter and of course keep them more constantly employed, by means of which they will have less time to concert, or carry into execution, any schemes prejudicial to His Majesty's interests." More disturbing to the agents was a further Amherst reminder to continue to keep the Indians short of ammunition. "Nothing can be so impolitic," he wrote them, "as to furnish them with the means of accomplishing the evil which is so much dreaded."

On September 9 the agents opened a grand council with the assembled tribes at Detroit, but could do little save thank them for their friendship to the British. Neither white man dared to reveal Amherst's policies to the Indians, particularly the order that the natives not be given ammunition, but they could promise nothing positive, and the conference left the Indians more restless than ever. When Johnson returned east, he reported that he thought the western nations would be friendly to the English "unless greatly irritated," but added somewhat as a warning that there were 1180 warriors, including 220 Ottawas, in the Detroit area, and that they were "connected together in an offensive and defensive alliance with the Delawares, Shawnees, Miamies, Weas, Mascoutens, Kickapoos and all the nations of the North."

The records of the conference again failed to mention Pontiac's name, but showed that a chief named Macatepilesis spoke for the Ottawas and delivered a mild and friendly speech. Even if Pontiac had been present, the situation made it unlikely that he would have been chosen on that occasion to speak for his people. From later events it is believed that by now he had become a dedicated enemy of the British and was busy stirring the fears and hatreds of the Indians. But his followers at the time were still in the minority among the natives, and the tribe would not have selected a spokesman who did not represent the views of the majority. With the failure of the British agents to raise the Indians' hopes for improved conditions, however, his prestige began to rise. The natives were "greatly irritated" now, and his fiery orations gave voice to their resentments and increased the number of his followers. To their old complaints he was able to add new ones, equally disturbing to them. For the first time, English traders were pouring through the Indians' country, and they behaved with the arrogance and high-handedness of conquerors who no longer feared French opposition. They charged the Indians high prices, offered them shoddy goods, and on many occasions boldly defrauded them. Though the natives complained about the high prices and the ill treatment they received, the commanders at the posts seemed to support their fellow countrymen's behavior, and further offended the Indians with official brusqueness and indifference.

Throughout the year 1762 conditions grew steadily worse, continuing to play into Pontiac's hands and increase his following among the natives. The tension was heightened by French traders in the region, who were trusted by the Indians, and who seized every opportunity to increase the natives' unrest by assuring them that the French King had merely been "sleeping," but that he was now awakening and preparing to dispatch a new army to the area to rescue his former allies. There was a basis for such talk. The French had surrendered Canada, but the war between the two powers was still in progress elsewhere, and in January 1762 Spain had even entered the conflict as an ally of France. Louisiana and the Mississippi River country, moreover, still belonged to France, and many of the traders actually believed that a combined force of French and Spanish troops might at any time come up from New Orleans to try to retake Canada. Such rumors soon filled the interior wilderness, and on July 3, 1762, the British commander at Detroit wrote east that "the Indians are a good deal elevated on the news of a Spanish war and daily reports spread amongst them that the French and Spaniards are soon to retake Quebec, etc. This goes from one nation to another, and it is impossible to prevent it. I assure you they only want a good opportunity to fall upon us if they had encouragement from an enemy."

In the turmoil Pontiac worked steadily to fan the natives' sentiment against the British. With his keen intelligence and defiant appeals he commanded large audiences, who responded with enthusiasm and carried his messages excitedly from one village to another. In the middle of the summer he apparently presided over a large, secret meeting of all the chiefs of the Ottawas, Chippewas, Hurons, Potawatomis, and other Lake tribes, and afterward sent deputies to the nations on the Wabash River and to the Shawnees on the Ohio. Croghan heard of the meeting from a Detroit Indian, who told him vaguely that he understood that the chiefs were plotting a revolt against the English. Later some Iroquois, who had picked up gossip from the Shawnees, gave him the same information, but when Croghan sent the news to Amherst in New York, the British general dismissed its importance and saw no reason to change his policies or attempt to relieve the causes of the natives' unrest.

During the winter of 1762-1763, Croghan continued to receive disturbing reports. British commanders at each of the posts were turning down Indian requests for ammunition with which to hunt food for their families, and everywhere the natives were showing signs that they at last realized the harshness of Amherst's policies. Fears were rising among them over their future, spurred frequently by new talk of French traders, who were telling them that the British were keeping ammunition out of their hands so that the English could more easily kill them and claim all their lands. As if in proof, British settlers from the eastern colonies were beginning to spread across the mountains into Delaware and Shawnee country in western Pennsylvania and Ohio, and early in December Croghan learned that the Wea Indians on the Wabash had sent the Shawnees a war belt, urging them to join in a war against the British. "If the Senecas, Delawares, and Shawnees should break with us," Croghan wrote Johnson, "it will end in a general war with all the western nations."

The Delawares, whose lands were the first to feel the impact of the newly arrived settlers, were particularly perturbed, and late in 1762 whites in their country began to hear of a strange Indian "prophet" among them, who was having visions and urging the natives to give up the material goods of the white men and return to the ways of their fathers. A few white traders and captives of the Delawares who saw the prophet described him as a revivalist, somewhat under the influence of Christianity, who, "almost constantly crying whilst he was exhorting them," preached that their dependence on the white men's trade goods had placed them in the power of the whites and had destroyed their strength and self-reliance. If they gave up the guns and manufactured articles of the Europeans, he urged, they would regain the strength and independence they had lost, and, uncorrupted by white ties, could speedily drive the settlers from their country. It was a cry for freedom that other Indians had already uttered, and that would continue to find new voices among native peoples for decades to come; its appeal spread rapidly across the Ohio Valley from tribe to tribe, and aroused large groups of Indians who traveled through the wilderness to see and hear the prophet for themselves.

Sometime during the winter, Pontiac either heard the Delaware preach or learned of his message. It made a strong impression on him, and quickened his urge to strike at the English. At the same time his determination was strengthened, both by new reports from French traders that military assistance would be furnished him from Louisiana and by war belts that were again circulated through the Midwest by the Senecas, who indicated that they were ready to fight the British. Gradually Pontiac realized that the time had come to act. Throughout the country the various tribes assured him that they were prepared to join whatever he started, and in the South he was certain that French troops were on hand to support him. As the winter ended he laid careful plans to attack all the British forts in the West in a sudden, concerted uprising, and by the end of April he was ready to move.

On the 27th of that month he summoned a great council of the three Indian villages on the Detroit River. More than four hundred Ottawa, Huron, and Potawatomi chiefs and warriors assembled in a secret meeting place on the banks of the Ecorse River about ten miles below Fort Detroit. Pontiac opened the council with a stirring oration in which he first recited all the wrongs the Indians had suffered since the British had assumed authority over the country, and then played on his listeners' emotions by reminding them of the exciting victories they had won over the English in previous years. As he reawakened their memories of past triumphs he related a version of the message which the Delaware prophet had been preaching to the Indians. The prophet, he told them, had taken a long trip and had met the Master of Life himself, who was unhappy because the natives had allowed themselves to fall victims to the white men. "This

land where ye dwell," Pontiac quoted the Master of Life as telling the prophet, "I have made for you and not for others. Whence
comes it that ye permit the whites upon your lands?" Twisting
the story slightly, he reported that the Master of Life bore no
resentments against the French, who still treated the Indians
fairly, but meant only the English when he referred to the whites.
"Drive them out, and make war upon them," he quoted the Master of Life. "I do not like them at all. They know me not, and are
my enemies, and the enemies of your brothers. Send them back
to the lands which I have created for them and let them stay
there."

Having established divine sanction for his undertaking, he announced to the aroused warriors that he was willing to lead them
against Fort Detroit. They replied that they were ready to follow him, and he at once unfolded his plans to them. While they
returned to their villages and prepared for war, he and some of
his braves would find a pretext for getting inside the fort and spy-
ing out its strength and the best method for an attack. Then they
would convene another council and arrange the assault.

Four days later Pontiac successfully carried out the first step
of his scheme. With some fifty of his warriors he gained admittance to the fort to perform a ceremonial dance for the entertainment of its officers. During the wild leapings and stampings
of the display, some of the Indians managed to steal away unobserved and spy on the interior arrangement of the fort, the
positions of its guns and sentries, and the nature of the buildings
within the walls. When the dance ended, Pontiac told the post
commandant that he would come back in a few days with some
of his people for a good-will council. The Indians trooped off,
and, following Pontiac's plan, held another secret meeting of all
the warriors and chiefs. Once more the Ottawa leader aroused
the natives to a frenzy for battle, and this time told them that on
the second day following he would enter the fort with sixty of
his men for a council with the British. All the other adults of his
Ottawa village would crowd inside the gates after him, and

everyone would carry knives, tomahawks, and sawed-off muskets under their blankets. At a given signal they would throw aside their coverings and fall on the unsuspecting members of the garrison. The Hurons and Potawatomis, meanwhile, would seize every Englishman outside the fort and lie in ambush to capture any British ships that might appear from Lake Erie. At the same time, he told them, he had already sent deputies with war belts to other tribes, including Ottawas and Chippewas in northern Michigan and Canada, and they would soon arrive to join the victory.

Somehow, within the next twenty-four hours, the post's commander, Major Henry Gladwin, learned of Pontiac's design. Gladwin was a cool-headed, unruffled young officer of thirty-four, a veteran of Braddock's defeat of 1755 and of several years' service at the head of British and Colonial troops in the wilderness fighting against the French and their Indian allies. It is not known for certain who informed him of Pontiac's plot, though the Indians blamed a Chippewa squaw named Catherine, who lived in the Potawatomi village on the Detroit River and was a convert to Catholicism. Legend says that she was an attractive young woman who was in love with Gladwin, and that during a furtive visit to the fort to bring him a pair of moccasins she betrayed her people. Contemporary reports, however, indicate that after their final council with Pontiac the excited Indians did little to conceal their war preparations in their villages, and that a number of Frenchmen who enjoyed their trust saw them filing and sawing their muskets to hide beneath their blankets, heard their war songs and dances at night, and caught frightening, fire-lit glimpses of painted warriors brandishing hatchets and knives in rehearsals of combat. After Pontiac's defeat several Frenchmen credited themselves with having carried Pontiac's secret to the fort, and there is evidence that one or another of them might well have done so. But Gladwin never revealed how he received his information, and merely noted in his official report to Amherst that he was "luckily informed."

Unaware that the British officer knew of his plans, Pontiac confidently led his people across the river on the morning of May 7, 1763, and approached the east gate of the post. The fort was the largest and strongest in the west, with a wall of cedar pickets about fifteen feet high and twelve hundred yards in circumference, enclosing what amounted to a small village. Guarded by bastions at three of its corners and by two small, detached blockhouses, the post stood on a slope that ran down to the river, with one of its walls and gates fronting on the water. Inside the fort Gladwin had two six-pound cannons, one three-pounder, and three mortars, as well as a force of approximately one hundred and twenty soldiers and perhaps thirty or forty English traders who could assist in the defense. In the river, also protecting the post, were a two-masted schooner, the *Huron*, of six guns, and a larger sloop, the *Michigan*.

Showing no sign of concern, Gladwin let the entire Indian delegation, numbering some three hundred men and women draped in blankets, push into the fort. Leading the way, Pontiac recognized immediately that the British expected trouble. All the buildings inside the post were locked, the sentinels had been doubled and were at the ready with bayonets, and the rest of the English troops, watching the Indians closely, were drawn up under arms on the parade ground. Pontiac led his chiefs nervously to the council house, where Gladwin and his interpreters awaited him. As he looked around, the Ottawa realized the hopelessness of his situation. He had brought a wampum belt, white on one side, green on the other, to present to Gladwin. The turning of the green side toward the officer was to have been his signal for the attack. But Pontiac withheld the sign. In angry frustration he upbraided Gladwin for the unfriendly appearance of the troops, and complained bitterly that he imagined that "some bad bird has given thee ill news of us." After protesting his innocence he accepted a small gift of clothing, bread, and tobacco from the British officer and stalked out of the fort, followed by his confused people.

Back at the Ottawa village he defended himself against his warriors' criticism for not having given them the expected signal, and argued that the English would have wiped them out. Promising them another opportunity, he returned to the fort the next day, once more protested his innocence to Gladwin, and appealed for another council of friendship between the British leader and the Ottawa people. Gladwin at length agreed to admit the Ottawa chiefs inside the post again on the following day, but said he saw no reason to parley with the younger braves or with other members of the village. Nevertheless, on the morning of May 9 Pontiac led all of his warriors back across the river in a fleet of sixty-five canoes. Outside the post they were halted by Gladwin's interpreters, who told them that only Pontiac and a few of the chiefs could enter the fort. In a rage Pontiac exclaimed that all of his people wanted to smell the smoke of the peace pipe, and that if they could not all come into the fort none would do so, and the Ottawas would throw away their belt of friendship with the English. The message was taken to Gladwin, who in compromise offered to let the Indians enter the fort in small groups. The proposal was unsatisfactory to Pontiac, for he had planned this time to get his braves inside the post and attack the English even if they were on guard against him. As he saw his hopes dashed once more, he turned in silent fury and ordered his followers back to their village again.

On the other side of the river he acted quickly. Forestalling the sure frustration of his braves, he announced that the war would now commence. If they could not get into the fort, they would kill all the Englishmen outside it, keep the post surrounded, and force Gladwin to surrender. He divided his warriors into parties and sent them up and down the river with orders to recross the stream, slay every British subject they came on, and converge in a siege line around the post. At the same time he deployed the Hurons and Potawatomis at a farther distance from the fort, after ordering them to intercept any Englishmen coming toward it, and hurriedly dispatched embassies and war belts to tribes throughout the Ohio valley and the Great Lakes region to proclaim the start of the uprising.

By afternoon the Indians had killed nine persons in the countryside around Fort Detroit and taken several prisoners. Within the walls of the post Gladwin and his men heard the warriors' chilling war whoops and death halloos ringing through the woods, and knew what it meant. Soon afterward groups of braves began to appear on the fort's three land sides. The cannons in the post and on the ships kept them at a distance, where their firing did little harm, but Gladwin did not have the strength to sally out and try to drive them away. The Indians dug in and, under Pontiac's direction, established a watchful circle around the post; the siege continued during the night.

The next day, with diplomatic astuteness not often displayed by an Indian, Pontiac enlisted the aid of some of the leading French residents of the area to help speed the fort's surrender. For ten miles along the river, above and below the post, the shore was lined with the homes and gardens of French traders and artisans who had settled in the district since the fort had been founded. There were more than five hundred such French-speaking *habitants*, and, while they did not wish to become involved in a war between the English and the local Indians, upon both of whom they relied for trade, few of them had much love for the British. On the day of the outbreak Pontiac's braves had scrupulously avoided harming them, and now the Ottawa chief called in their leaders and shrewdly won their support for a scheme to re-establish French authority over the fort. He promised to place one of their number in charge of the post after its surrender and sent three of the Frenchmen to appeal to Gladwin for a council to discuss terms of peace. At the urging of the French emissaries the British leader reluctantly agreed to send two of his officers to meet with Pontiac. The latter instantly seized the Englishmen, held them as hostages, and sent the chagrined French negotiators back to the fort with a demand for its immediate surrender. Gladwin, however, would not be cowed. Outraged, he announced that he would have nothing to do with Pontiac until his two officers were safely returned to him, and vowed to defend the post to the last man.

Pontiac was now faced with the problem of directing a long siege of a white man's fort. Indians had rarely conducted such an operation by themselves, but, though he had no knowledge of siege tactics, Pontiac was determined to force Gladwin to surrender. He tried several attacks, which were driven back by the defenders' fire, and then ordered his people to keep a safe distance but kill any of the garrison who tried to leave the stockade. To assure a supply of ammunition and provisions for his warriors, he also set about to organize a systematic quartermaster arrangement, personally visiting the homes of French habitants along the river, assigning groups of them to keep his individual bands supplied with their needs, and showing his honorable intentions to the French by paying them with promissory notes of birchbark which he signed with the hieroglyph of his totem, the otter. Meanwhile, as his braves kept guard over Gladwin's resolute garrison, he sent armed parties to carry the war against other British forts, and was soon rewarded with news of shattering victories elsewhere in the West.

Even before the first assault on Detroit, Chippewas at nearby Lake St. Claire had responded to Pontiac's call for a general uprising by destroying an English party from the fort that was taking soundings in the lake. Shortly afterward a group of Hurons in the lower Detroit River seized five boats of merchandise bound for Detroit from Niagara. But now the news was more stunning. On May 16 a band of Pontiac's Ottawas and Hurons surprised the English garrison at Fort Sandusky on Lake Erie and captured the post. On May 25, Potawatomis, dispatched from Detroit, overwhelmed Fort St. Joseph in southwestern Michigan and killed or captured all its defenders. Two days later another war party from Detroit, joined by Miami Indians, forced the surrender of Fort Miamis on the site of present-day Fort Wayne, Indiana, while farther east Delawares and Mingoes, responding to Pontiac's summons, left their villages to sweep up Pennsylvania's Monongahela Valley, massacring settlers, firing on Fort Ligonier, and beginning a siege of Fort Pitt.

The Indians' actions had only begun. On May 28, with the entire western wilderness suddenly aflame, Pontiac's warriors trapped a British army supply fleet bound across Lake Erie from Niagara to Detroit. The troops assigned to the fleet had paused for the night at Point Pelee about twenty-five miles from the Detroit River and had pulled their ten bateaux, loaded with 139 barrels of provisions, up on the beach. A little after ten in the evening, the Indians charged into their camp, killed or captured more than fifty of the ninety-six-man complement, and seized eight of the boats and almost all the provisions. Those who escaped fled back across Lake Erie to Niagara, while the victorious Indians sailed the captured bateaux and their prisoners into the Detroit River and past the unhappy defenders of the fort.

Still the native triumphs continued. On June 1, three days after the battle at Point Pelee, the Indians who had previously seized Fort Miamis joined a war party of Kickapoos, Weas, and Mascoutens and forced the surrender of Fort Ouiatenon on the Wabash River at the site of present-day Lafayette, Indiana. The next day, far to the north, Chippewas and Sauk, pretending to play a ball game for the amusement of the British troops at Fort Michilimackinac, turned suddenly on the unsuspecting soldiers and butchered twenty of the thirty-five-member garrison of that strategically located post in the straits between Lake Huron and Lake Superior. In the east the Senecas and Shawnees also entered the war, and on June 16 a party of Senecas attacked Fort Venango, eighty miles north of Fort Pitt, and wiped out its garrison. Two days later they also captured Fort LeBoeuf, a few miles farther north, and the next day, June 19, Senecas, Ottawas, Hurons, and Chippewas joined forces to reduce Fort Presqu' Isle on the present site of Erie, Pennsylvania. With the abandonment on June 21 of the isolated Fort Edward Augustus at Green Bay, Wisconsin, the British in less than two months lost every Ohio Valley and Great Lakes post except Detroit and Fort Pitt, both of which were under siege. The English supply route across Lake Erie to Detroit was no longer safe, and the line of communication from Pittsburgh to Niagara was gone.

In New York, General Amherst had a difficult time realizing what was happening. The first news of the uprising had come to him in frantic dispatches from Fort Pitt, but he had discounted the reports as being "greatly exaggerated" and had written Colonel Henry Bouquet, one of his frontier officers who was then at Philadelphia, that "the post of Fort Pitt, or any of the others commanded by officers, can certainly never be in danger from such a wretched enemy as the Indians are, at this time, if the garrisons do their duty." Gradually, as tidings of disaster continued to reach him, he realized the seriousness of the conflict; he dispatched his aide, Captain James Dalyell, an ambitious and impulsive young officer, to collect an army from garrisons in upstate New York and take it to Detroit if he considered it necessary.

Through the month of June Dalyell made his way to Niagara, gathering a force of 260 men, including a group of provincials under Major Rogers. In Detroit the siege of the fort was continuing. The white defenders behind the pickets had never heard of natives showing such patience and perseverance, and Gladwin daily expected the Indians to grow tired and abandon the profitless venture. But Pontiac held his people together, and as new bands joined him the number of warriors in the siege lines increased. Sometime during the month, word arrived that France and Great Britain had finally signed a treaty of peace, and that war on the continent between the two European powers was completely ended. Pontiac refused to believe it, still preferring to hope that French troops would ultimately appear from the south to help him, but the report unnerved the French *habitants* around the fort and caused some of Pontiac's Indian allies to think that they might have made a mistake in taking up the war hatchet.

On July 28, Captain Dalyell's reinforcements, which had embarked on Lake Erie, pulled up the Detroit River under cover of a heavy fog, and before the Indians could intercept them safely reached the water gate of the beleaguered fort. The members of the garrison cheered the new arrivals, but their joy was short-lived. The self-confident Dalyell told Gladwin that Amherst wanted the upstart Pontiac thrashed, and he would do it himself as quickly as possible. With Gladwin's hesitant approval he gave his men two days' rest, and at two-thirty in the morning of July 31 marched a force of 247 officers and men out of the fort to attack Pontiac's main camp, which he understood was several miles up the river. His plans, however, were known in advance by the Indians. French residents who had been given liberty by both sides to pass freely between their homes and the inside of the fort had overheard rumors of what was going to happen, and had informed the Ottawas. Oblivious of the possibility of ambush, Dalyell hurried his column ahead in the bright moonlight until it reached a narrow bridge that crossed a creek two miles from the fort. There Pontiac caught him. As the soldiers started across the planks a burst of musketry flashed at them, followed by war whoops and yells. In the confusion the column backed on itself, and men began to drop. The Indian fire increased, coming from both sides of the road. Under the shouts of their officers the helpless soldiers poured volleys toward the unseen enemy. As firing also broke out in the rear, Dalyell realized that he was surrounded. Though wounded in the thigh, he hastened back to assess his danger and found the tail elements fighting for their lives. After a moment of indecision he ordered a withdrawal. Slowly the column moved backward, still firing. After a short while the retreat halted, blocked by the heavy flanking fire of a group of Indians who were strongly entrenched behind some cordwood and in a basement excavation for a French habitant's new house. For an hour the British tried vainly to get past them. Finally, in a desperate moment of courage, Dalyell ordered a charge on their position, and led it himself. In the rush he was shot dead, but other troops swept past him, drove the In-

dians away, and cleared the road. Gradually the column's survivors fought their way free of the rest of the natives and got
back to the fort. Dalyell and nineteen of his men had been
killed. Another thirty-four had been wounded, and a number of
soldiers captured. The sortie had accomplished nothing save to
bestow a new name, Bloody Run, on the brook where the British
had been halted.

The victory was only a momentary success for Pontiac. His
over-all position had not improved, for Dalyell's survivors now
gave added strength to Gladwin's forces in the fort. On August
5, moreover, the schooner *Huron* also ran an Indian gantlet on
the river and safely disembarked sixty more men at the fort's
water gate. With the increased complement, Gladwin felt new
assurance, and from time to time even took the initiative and dispatched small striking forces from the fort to hit the besiegers in
limited surprise attacks.

In the East, meanwhile, a murderous border warfare of the
Shawnees, Delawares, Mingoes, and Senecas was spreading panic
among frontier settlements from New York to Virginia. Hundreds of whites were massacred in their cabins among the wooded
valleys and foothills, and thousands of others were sent fleeing
back across the Alleghenies to safety. The terror and bloodshed
stirred both the English government and the colonial adminis-
trations. In London the British ministry, trying to set matters
aright after it was too late, hastily established a line along the crest
of the Appalachians as the westernmost boundary of legal white
settlement, decreeing that the country beyond belonged to His
Majesty's Indian subjects. But the colonial governments, unable
to resist the political pressures of land speculators or to halt westering settlers who chose to push into the wilderness, reacted
differently, and, bowing to a popular clamor for revenge, sent
bands of angry militia against the marauding Indians. As fury
raged all along the frontier both sides were guilty of savage atrocities, and in the fierce struggle, with no quarter given or expected,
the whites began to use contemptuous remarks such as "The

only good Injun is a dead Injun," which generations of western-
moving frontiersmen continued to repeat on other borders
in later years.

In addition to the colonial forces that were being thrown
against the Indians, more British troops began to appear in the
West, underscoring the inevitable hopelessness, from the very
start, of Pontiac's war. Despite the Ottawas' many early victories
the time had long since passed when natives could successfully
hurl back the whites and hold them down. In August a foretaste
of what was to come at Detroit occurred in Pennsylvania when
Colonel Bouquet, fighting his way past desperately resisting
Delawares, Shawnees, Mingoes, and Hurons, pushed a relief
column across the mountains and broke the siege at Fort Pitt.
On September 18 the Indians gained temporary revenge in another part of the theater of war, when more than three hundred
Senecas, probably aided by Ottawas and Chippewas, struck at the
eastern end of the supply line to Detroit and ambushed a wagon
train and a troop of soldiers on the portage road around Niagara
Falls, slaughtering seventy-two officers and men.

Bad news like this continued to enrage Amherst, whose frustration was reflected by the increasing inhumanity of the orders
he sent to his officers. If any of Pontiac's Indians fell into British
hands, he wrote Gladwin at Detroit, they should "immediately
be put to death, their extirpation being the only security for our
future safety." To Bouquet in Pennsylvania he suggested desperately, "Could it not be contrived to send the small pox among
the disaffected tribes of Indians? We must on this occasion use
every stratagem in our power to reduce them." When Bouquet replied that he would try to follow the British general's advice, and added that he would even like to hunt "the vermin"
with dogs, Amherst wrote him again, "You will do well to try
to inoculate the Indians by means of blankets, as well as to try
every other method that can serve to extirpate this execrable
race. I should be very glad your scheme for hunting them down
by dogs could take effect, but England is at too great a distance

to think of that at present." A few weeks later, when he sent a new unit of reinforcements hurrying toward Detroit, the British general ordered their commander to treat the Indians "not as a generous enemy, but as the vilest race of beings that ever infested the earth, and whose riddance from it must be esteemed a meritorious act, for the good of mankind." At the same time, well aware at last of the powerful Ottawa chief who had dared to raise so many native nations against him, he offered a reward of one hundred pounds to the man who should kill Pontiac, and a few weeks later, in a new fit of anger, doubled it.

Such measures ultimately proved unnecessary. As time passed and final victory over the whites seemed no closer, Pontiac's prestige began to diminish among his own people. Week after week the siege of Detroit dragged on without apparent loss of strength or spirit by the garrison. The habitants, who now knew that French troops would never appear from the South, turned away from the natives and, making use of their liberty of movement to bring supplies into the post, tried to prove to the English that they had really always been loyal to the fort's defenders. Their defection, in turn, disturbed many of the native chiefs who had been fighting with Pontiac, and spread doubts among them of the ultimate success of their cause. One by one, bands sought entrance to the fort, announced that they were abandoning the fight, and filed off through the forests to their homelands. Realizing that he was losing his hold, the desperate Ottawa made angry attempts to win small but daring victories that would rally the restless tribes back to his leadership. In a wild attack he sent warriors in canoes against a relief schooner that arrived from Niagara with supplies for the fort. The assault failed, many Indians were killed and wounded, and the schooner successfully unloaded its cargo at the post. The defeat further weakened Pontiac, and a few days later a large band of Potawatomis defected from him and went home.

Throughout September and October dissension spread rapidly across the Indian country. Mississauga Indians arrived from the North with word that they and the Chippewas of that region wanted peace with the English and a resumption of the white man's trade, which they missed. Soon afterward a large band of Miamis appeared on the Detroit River from the South. They too had become half-hearted about the war, and when they found some of Pontiac's camps echoing their feelings, half of them turned back, while their companions waited to see what the other hostiles would decide to do. By the second week of October some of the Chippewas around the post had made up their minds to sue for peace, and had talked many of the Ottawas themselves into joining them. It was getting cold, and the men wanted to hunt before winter set in. Ignoring Pontiac, they entered the fort for a peace council, then went off in canoes to hunting grounds, followed by the last of the Potawatomis.

On October 20, Pontiac called the remainder of his warriors together and made a last, impassioned plea for a continuation of the siege. He was only partly successful. Many of the Indians nodded their willingness to continue the fight, but three days later another group of Chippewas deserted him. That same night Pontiac received a final blow. A French officer arrived from the South, bringing unmistakable confirmation of the news that the Ottawa chief had long refused to believe. Pontiac listened in gloomy silence, as the Frenchman read a letter written to him by the commander of the French Fort de Chartres on the Mississippi River. The great king of the French and the great king of the English had indeed buried the hatchet, the commandant wrote. Halt the war, he begged Pontiac. The hearts of the English and those of the French were now as one. The Indians could no longer strike the one nation without having the other for an enemy also. Bury the hatchet with the English as the French king had. End the war. Live in peace.

The message shattered Pontiac's dream. The next day, grown suddenly humble, he dictated a note to Gladwin, which was carried into the fort. "My Brother," he wrote. "The word which my father has sent me to make peace I have accepted; all my young men have buried their hatchets. I think you will forget the bad things which have taken place for some time past. Likewise I shall forget what you may have done to me, in order to think of nothing but good. I, the Chippewas, the Hurons, we are ready to go speak with you when you ask us. Give us an answer. I am sending this resolution to you in order that you may see it. If you are as kind as I, you will make me a reply. I wish you a good day. Pontiac."

Gladwin was relieved by the collapse of the siege, but he refused to see Pontiac until he had informed Amherst of the turn of events and received the general's reply. Amherst did not get the good news for weeks, and by that time it no longer mattered to him. In early October he had received permission to return to England, and had been succeeded by Major General Thomas Gage. Through with the whole "execrable race" of Indians, Amherst sailed for home on November 17, leaving behind him the mixed reputation of a soldier who had fought well against the French but had been bested by the savage warrior, Pontiac.

In the middle of November, with his force of Indians all but dissolved, the Ottawa chief grew tired of waiting to see Gladwin and left the Detroit River. Accompanied by a group of fellow tribesmen who were still loyal to him, he traveled to the Maumee River in present-day Indiana, where he established a winter camp. In the spring he continued to the French-held Illinois country and the Mississippi River. His heart was still filled with hatred for the English, and among the tribes of the West he saw a chance to revive his war. Back East the Delawares, Shawnees, Senecas, Wabash Indians, and many of the Hurons were still continuing the conflict, and despite the opposition of the French commander at Fort de Chartres, he appealed to the Illinois tribes to join the hostiles. At the same time he sent deputies of warriors down the Mississippi to stir up the Tunicas, Choctaws, and other southern tribes who had already attacked a British force on the river, two hundred and forty miles north of New Orleans, probably in response to one of his earlier appeals.

His attempts to revive the conflict were frustrated. The French frowned on his trouble-making, argued bitterly against him, and refused to give him enough ammunition to wage a serious struggle. In July he acknowledged temporary failure and returned to his village on the Maumee, where he found the tide still turning against him. The Senecas, Menominees, Sauk and Foxes had all made peace with the British, and half of his own Ottawas had given their allegiance to a pro-English chief named Atawang. Everywhere, the natives wished a resumption of the trade in white men's goods. They had forgotten the preachings of the Delaware prophet, and were appealing to the British to send traders back to them.

Still, Pontiac would not give up his cause. Through the fall and winter of 1764 he traveled tirelessly from tribe to tribe, haranguing wilderness villages against the English and attempting to win allies for a new uprising. In the North some of the Chippewa, Miami, and Wabash River bands seemed willing to fight again if another war broke out. Illinois country tribes, including Kaskaskias, Peorias, Cahokias, Osages, Missouris, and Michigameas, all friendly to the French, listened to Pontiac and promised to attack the British if they came onto their lands. In the South British agents heard rumors that Pontiac was scheming with Creeks and Choctaws, and learned that he had even sent war belts to the Arkansas Indians in the Southwest.

But the initiative had now passed into the hands of the British, and their agents and troops were pacifying tribes more quickly than Pontiac could stir them to a new, unified struggle. Late in the summer a huge army of twelve hundred men, under Colonel John Bradstreet, left Niagara for the West. Indian agents moved out ahead of the troops, gathering up tribes with promises of forgiveness and trade, and in September Bradstreet signed many of them to a permanent peace treaty at Detroit. A short time later Colonel Henry Bouquet marched out of Fort Pitt with fifteen hundred men, determined to whip into submission the Indians who were still harassing the Ohio and Pennsylvania frontiers. His show of force caused the capitulation, at last, of the Shawnees,

Delawares, and Mingoes, and their collapse, in turn, took the heart out of the Miamis and Wabash River bands, who also announced their submission.

By the spring of 1765 Pontiac realized that his principal allies were gone. He moved through the Illinois country again, a leader without a following, and on April 18, at the urging of the French, he agreed to meet at Fort de Chartres with an English agent, Lieutenant Alexander Fraser, whom General Gage had sent west to try to win the friendship of the tribes beyond Detroit. Fraser handled Pontiac tactfully and put him at ease by assuring him that, despite his having been their enemy, the British now considered the chief as their brother because the Ottawas had signed a peace for all their people at Detroit. That afternoon Fraser and the French commandant called a council of all the Illinois tribes in the area and told them that both the British and the French were united in desiring all Indians to make peace with the whites and abandon any idea of further war. As the assembled Indians hesitated, trying to decide how to reply, Pontiac arose slowly and, facing the French officer, announced his final capitulation. "My father," he said firmly, as if concealing his emotions so that no one would know his sadness, "you urge me so much to make peace that I can no longer refuse you, and I submit to the wish of the king, my father. I do not desire to oppose him longer and consider from this moment that you have restored peace to all these children. For the future we will regard the English as brothers, since you wish to make us all one."

The Ottawa, from that day, was as good as his word. In July he met the Indian agent George Croghan near the abandoned Fort Ouiatenon on the Wabash River, and accompanied him to Fort Detroit, where he confirmed his desire to make peace. Despite Pontiac's leadership of the war which had been so disastrous to the British, General Gage was far shrewder in Indian affairs than his predecessor, and had decided to undermine, and if possible to end, the Ottawa's still-dangerous influence among the tribes by deliberately playing up to him in order to provoke his followers' jealousy. The policy worked. Rumors spread among the Indians that the man who had urged them to war on the English was now being paid ten shillings a day by his former enemies. and in 1766, when Pontiac traveled under British escort, more like a conqueror than a defeated enemy, to meet with Sir William Johnson in New York, a knowledgeable French trader at Detroit offered to bet that envious Indians would kill the Ottawa "in less than a year."

As it proved, he was almost right. Pontiac returned to the West and settled among his own people on the Maumee River. But his prestige was almost gone. With the return of peace, white injustices against the Indians were reviving. Settlers were flooding once more into the Ohio Valley, the arrogance of the traders and soldiers was increasing, and the fears and resentments of the natives, never thoroughly stilled, were on the rise and causing new threats of war. But Pontiac, the old enemy of the British, was now taking the side of the whites, and counseling peace. In time members of his village began to turn against him, and rumors ran through the forests that his former warriors were administering physical beatings to him, as they would to a squaw. Finally, in May 1768, with the help of a Frenchman Pontiac wrote pathetically to the English at Detroit that his young men had "shamed" him, and that he was being forced to leave his village. With only a small following of relatives and loyal friends he traveled to the Illinois country, but even here there was no longer respect or safety for him. On April 20, 1769, he visited a small trade store in Cahokia, an old French village on the east side of the Mississippi River opposite St. Louis. He was unarmed, and accompanied only by a Peoria Indian who he thought was friendly to him. The Peoria followed him out of the store, and on the street, for some motive that has never been established, suddenly struck Pontiac over the head with his club and then stabbed him. As the Peoria fled, the great war chief, who had once led eighteen powerful tribes from Lake Ontario to the Mississippi in war against the British, sank to the ground and died.

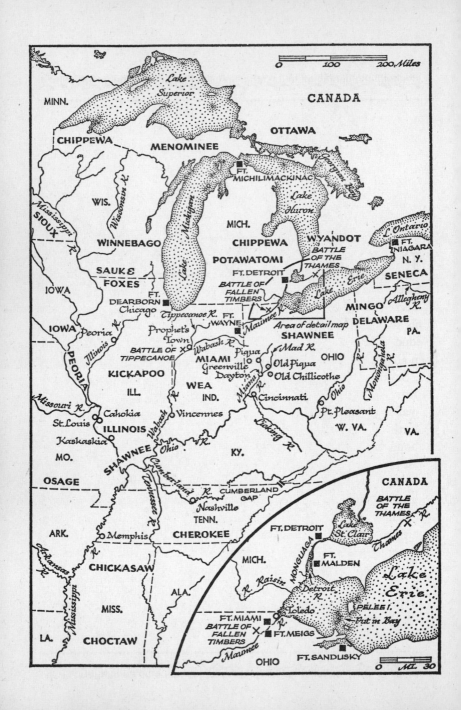

V

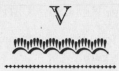

TECUMSEH,
THE GREATEST INDIAN

IN ITS issue of December 2, 1820, the *Indiana Centinel* of Vincennes, Indiana, published a letter praising a late and much-hated enemy. "Every schoolboy in the Union now knows that Tecumseh was a great man," it read. "He was truly great—and his greatness was his own, unassisted by science or the aids of education. As a statesman, a warrior and a patriot, take him all in all, we shall not look upon his like again."

Seven years earlier, frontier communities throughout the territory of the Old Northwest had exulted over the death of the "yaller devil" who had tried to bar white men from the rich lands north of the Ohio River. But with the disappearance of danger thoughtful citizens, such as the *Centinel's* correspondent, had at last begun to realize that a native of soaring greatness had been in their midst. Along the waterways and dirt roads of Ohio and Indiana, settlers who still shuddered with memories of the warfare that had wrested the region from the Indians talked of Tecumseh with admiration and agreed with the verdict of their own hero, General William Henry Harrison, who had led them against the war chief. Tecumseh, Harrison had reported to Washington, was "one of those uncommon geniuses, which spring up occasionally to produce revolutions and overturn the established order of things. If it were not for the vicinity of the United States, he would perhaps be the founder of an Empire that would rival in glory that of Mexico or Peru."

Tecumseh had no opportunity to demonstrate his leadership of Indians in peacetime. He was a product of one of the most critical periods in the history of American Indians, and from birth to death was involved in conflict and war. But by 1846 an American historian, Henry Trumbull, stamped him as "the most extraordinary Indian that has appeared in history," and today, a century and a half after his death, as made clear by Glenn Tucker, his most recent and ablest biographer, he still looms as the greatest native leader in the long and tragic resistance of the Indians of the United States. He was a brilliant orator and warrior and a brave and distinguished patriot of his people. He was learned and wise, and was noted, even among his white enemies, for his integrity and humanity. But his unique greatness lay in the fact that, unlike all previous native leaders, he looked beyond the mere resistance by a tribe or group of tribes to white encroachments. He was a Shawnee, but he considered himself first an Indian, and fought to give all Indians a national rather than a tribal consciousness, and to unite them in defense of a common homeland where they might all continue to dwell under their own laws and leaders. In modern days, world opinion which endorses the right of self-determination of peoples might have supported before the United Nations his dream of a country of, by, and for Indians. But the crisis he faced came too early in history, and he failed. His failure meant considerably more than that the main theater of his struggle, Indiana, originally "the country of Indians," became a white rather than an Indian state. It threw all the tribes back upon their separate resources, as they had been since the beginning of their conflict with white men, and re-established a pattern in which individual tribes or regional confederacies sought hopelessly to cope alone with the invaders. More important, it ended for all time the possibility that an Indian free state or nation might be created within territory won or purchased by the United States from white governments.

The establishment of such a state in Tecumseh's day was not implausible. The United States, which had just won its own independence, had received from Great Britain sovereignty over the vast wilderness of the Northwest Territory. But definition of that sovereignty was in question. France, the first European power to claim possession of the area, had built a few forts and trading posts, but had not otherwise disturbed the Indians' freedom or ownership of the land. The British had followed the French lead, and in 1763, while defending their western forts during the Pontiac uprising, had tried to reassure the Indians by proclaiming native rights to all territory west of the Appalachians. Royal officials had attempted to halt purchases of land west of the mountains and void purchases already made, and until the Revolution they issued numerous edicts designed to stop westward expansion. In 1772 General Thomas Gage, commander-in-chief of British forces in North America, ordered all settlers beyond the Appalachians to "quit those countries instantly and without delay," and the following year Governor John Penn of Pennsylvania announced, "I do hereby prohibit and forbid all His Majesty's Subjects of this, or any other Province or Colony, on any pretence whatsoever, to intrude upon, Settle, or Possess any of the aforesaid unpurchased Lands (beyond the last Pennsylvania purchase), as they will answer the contrary at their Peril."

Many colonial settlers and land speculators, including George Washington, had ignored such proclamations, and despite the efforts of British officials a stream of frontier families had moved into Kentucky and down the Ohio after the collapse of Pontiac. But by the end of the Revolution their inroads had been negligible, and, save for a few small edges where settlers had established themselves, the country north of the Ohio River was still firmly in Indian hands. Furthermore, though the United States assumed possession of the region, it acknowledged that it did not own title to the land. What it owned was simply the exclusive right to treat with the Indians for the land. On June 15, 1789,

Secretary of War Henry Knox confirmed this understanding in a letter to President Washington. "The Indians, being the prior occupants, possess the right of soil," he wrote. "It cannot be taken from them unless by their free consent, or by right of conquest in case of a just war. To dispossess them on any other principle would be a gross violation of the fundamental laws of nature, and of that distributive justice which is the glory of a nation."

This policy, soon ratified by Congress, was later affirmed by the Supreme Court, which held, in addition, that Indian tribes were "distinct, independent, political communities" with which the United States must deal, as it did with all foreign nations, by treaties subject to ratification by the Senate. Thus from the early days of the American Republic it was established that the Indian tribes were separate nations existing on their own lands over which, strangely, the United States government simultaneously exercised sovereignty. For almost a century, as Americans expanded westward, the confusing policy dictated relations between the government and Indian tribes, and until an exasperated Congress finally ended the legal fiction in 1871 it caused endless difficulties and conflicts between the two races. But from the beginning it also offered an obvious opportunity to a determined Indian nationalist: if a tribe possessed the right of soil and, as later acknowledged, an independent status, why did it not also have the right to establish itself as a free nation? In the days immediately after the Revolution time was advantageous for the forcing of the question. The new states had only loose ties to the Indian country of the interior, where there were still few settlers and only a minimum of government. Moreover, the colonists' own struggle for independence and their ideals of liberty and self-government had set burning examples for the natives. The United States had taken the Northwest Territory from Great Britain without either country's having consulted the wishes of the Indian inhabitants. Hailing the fresh words of the Declaration of Independence, public opinion would not have been able to argue with conviction that the idea of a free Indian nation within that region was untenable.

For a number of years after the Revolution, however, the realities of white expansion and the primitive level of native society precluded such a development. Under the leadership of Joseph Brant, who had been educated by the whites, the Iroquois of New York, politically more sophisticated than any other tribe in contact with the Americans, managed to win certain concessions that established United States acknowledgment of Indian rights of possession of soil. But most of the Iroquois had sided with the British during the Revolution and had suffered disastrous defeat in the war, and as beaten enemies they were in no position to proclaim an independent nation in territory claimed by New York.

Elsewhere the possibilities were equally elusive. Even before Yorktown, settlers in the middle Atlantic and southern colonies, guided by Daniel Boone and other frontiersmen, had quickened their move into Indian country, pouring through passes such as the Cumberland Gap that led across the Appalachians, and in 1782 North Carolina had even given western Indian lands to its veterans before bothering to negotiate with the natives for the property. The interior tribes fought hard, alone or in alliance, to drive the invaders from their hunting grounds, but their resistance only brought down upon them the superior fire-power of organized bodies of militia and, eventually, of American troops whose punitive expeditions inevitably became armies of conquest that forced the beaten natives to withdraw from the lands they had been contesting. The Indians had neither the time nor the understanding to set up a free state, and if they had tried to do so they would have lacked a unified force with which to defend their country, as well as the historical setting in which to appeal to world opinion for support. At the same time many chiefs undermined the native position by selling parts of the Indian domain to the invaders. The end of the prosperous days of the fur trade in the trans-mountain region had impoverished them, and in return for trade goods and promises of annuities they signed away lands, whether the areas belonged to them or not, and moved westward toward the Mississippi, allowing a flood of whites to pour across the abandoned regions and engulf tribes that were still trying to resist. As the white tide moved steadily into Kentucky and Tennessee and down the Ohio River, the demand for land increased, and at length in the early years of the nineteenth century the government in Washington embarked on a determined attempt to extinguish Indian title to all territory east of the Mississippi.

For dozens of tribes, numbering thousands of Indians, the moment of both crisis and opportunity had arrived. Defeat would now sweep them all away and unleash an even greater westward surge that no combination of Indians would ever again be able to halt. At the same time the traditional form of resistance, in which individual tribes fought merely to retain their lands, had no better chance of success than in the past. If the Indians were to hold, not for the moment but forever, powerful new ideas were needed, and they had to be political as well as military in nature.

It was the genius of Tecumseh that he, alone among all the natives, saw what was now required. The action of the increasing pressure by whites had finally produced the need for revolutionary reaction. As the greatest Indian nationalist, Tecumseh countered American expansionism with Indian unity, preaching for the first time that Indian land belonged to all the tribes in common, and that no chief could sell any part of it. By rallying natives of every tribe to that policy he would effectively block the American government's attempt to acquire the land by purchase. If the whites tried to seize it by conquest, violating treaties already signed, he would lead an army of every tribe in defense of their common country. The story of how he failed was a tragedy, for in the end it was a white man's war between the United States and Great Britain that obscured his nationalist cause and made the Americans feel that they were fighting merely a military auxiliary of their enemies. The true nature ot his struggle was apparent only after his death, but before that day his courage and energy brought the Indians startlingly close to victory.

Tecumseh's real name was Tecumtha, which in the Shawnee language and allegory could be interpreted as "panther lying in wait." White men pronounced it Tecumseh, however, and understood that it meant "shooting star." He was born in March 1768 in one of the villages that formed a large, straggling settlement of Indian wigwams and bark cabins called Old Piqua on the bluffs above Ohio's Mad River northeast of present-day Dayton. His father, a Shawnee war chief named Puckeshinwa, was a proud, intelligent man who had been born in Florida, and his mother, Methoataske, probably a Creek Indian, was from eastern Alabama. Their birthplace, far from Ohio, reflected the long, nomadic history of the Shawnees, an Algonquian-speaking people, whose restless migrations, tribal divisions, and simultaneous occupancy of areas in widely-separated parts of the frontier made it difficult for white contemporaries to conceive of them as a single nation.

Their original homeland, it is believed, had been in the Ohio River Valley, but French explorers had first found Shawnees living along the Cumberland River in Tennessee and Kentucky; their name meant "southerners." They were a hardy, warlike people, whose hunting bands were already used to ranging long distances along the rivers and forest trails in the hilly Appalachian country, looking for enemies as well as game. In their wanderings the belligerent bands met distant tribes and joined them in warfare, and the attachments led some of them to break away from their own people and establish permanent settlements in their allies' countries. Shortly after 1674 one group of Shawnees migrated to South Carolina, where white men called them Savannahs and gave their name to a river and a colonial settlement. Another band of Shawnees went in the opposite direction, into Pennsylvania, where they settled among the Delaware and other eastern tribes on the Susquehanna, Delaware, Lehigh, and

Schuylkill Rivers. Still other Shawnees remained on the Cumberland, concentrated in the vicinity of present-day Nashville, Tennessee, but hunting in Kentucky and the western country of Virginia and North Carolina. In time the South Carolina group divided, some moving west to settle among the Creeks in Georgia and Alabama, and the rest trekking slowly all the way north to Pennsylvania, where they joined their relatives who were beginning to be pushed west by the colonists. The Shawnees who had stayed on the Cumberland, meanwhile, also began to move. Under pressure from Cherokee and Chickasaw enemies, they migrated in a long circuitous route through Kentucky, and eventually halted in eastern Ohio. Soon most of the Pennsylvania Shawnees, waging rear-guard border warfare against the advancing settlers, joined them, though one band, possibly Puckeshinwa's, migrated at that time all the way from Pennsylvania to Florida. After a while its members again headed north, pausing among friendly Creeks in eastern Alabama, and finally rejoining the main body of their own people, who by then had united in large villages along the Mad River and other streams in western Ohio.

The long, confused wanderings, marked by numerous alliances with other tribes and constant guerrilla warfare against advancing whites, had made the Shawnees more conscious than most natives of the similarity and urgency of the racial struggles being waged against the settlers on many different fronts. To them, the major enemy of all Indians was the English colonist, and from the time of the French and Indian War, when they sided with the French, they were in constant conflict with frontier settlers and with punitive English and colonial expeditions that were sent against them. During the Pontiac war they fought fiercely under Cornstalk and other Shawnee leaders for their lands in western Pennsylvania, and after the defeat of Pontiac they continued to raid and skirmish against the settlers everywhere from Ohio to the mountains of western North Carolina. In Kentucky and Tennessee, where the wooded hills and valleys still provided the

Shawnees with their best hunting grounds, the frontiersmen feared and hated them above all the other tribes, and after the American Revolution their great numbers and continued resistance made them one of the leading native forces in the Ohio Valley and a prime target of the settlers.

Tecumseh's father, like most Shawnee men, was a forest hunter and fighter, constantly involved in violence. Nevertheless, he was at home enough to sire an unusually large Indian family. In eastern Alabama, before he and his wife started north, they had a son. During the long migration to the Mad River, Methoataske, whose name to the Shawnees meant, appropriately, "a turtle laying eggs in the sand," gave birth to two daughters and another son. Tecumseh, born soon after they reached the Mad River, was the fifth child. Later a third daughter and two more sons, including one who was to be known as the Shawnee prophet, were added to the family.

The Pontiac war had only recently ended when Tecumseh was born, but the defeat of the Indians had encouraged settlers to start moving west of the mountains, and soon the Shawnees were engaged in trying to hold their hunting grounds in Kentucky as well as their village sites in Ohio. Border warfare raged steadily in both regions, and in 1774, when Tecumseh was six years old, the skirmishing erupted in a formal conflict, known as Lord Dunmore's War, between the Shawnees and the colonists of Virginia. Some two thousand of the latter, led by Dunmore, their aristocratic and overbearing governor, marched into Kentucky and Ohio. In a fierce battle at the site of Point Pleasant, West Virginia, both sides lost heavily, but the Shawnee commander, Cornstalk, a brave and dignified man, eventually agreed to peace and, to save his people's villages in Ohio, surrendered the Shawnee claim to lands south of the Ohio River and allowed the Virginians to open Kentucky to settlement.

Both Puckeshinwa and Tecumseh's oldest brother, a youth named Cheeseekau, had fought courageously under Cornstalk, and both had survived the war and returned to the family home at Old Piqua. Soon, however, the young Tecumseh experienced two examples of the value of a treaty with white men. Despite the fact that Dunmore had acknowledged Indian right to the country north of the Ohio, frontiersmen continued to invade it, and one day a band of them accosted Puckeshinwa in the woods near Old Piqua and shot him in the breast. That night, when the father failed to return to his family, Methoataske and Tecumseh went in search of him. They found him dying, and learned what had happened. The brutal episode filled Tecumseh with horror and hate, and as his mourning mother urged him to remember the scene he resolved to become a warrior like his father and be "a fire spreading over the hill and valley, consuming the race of dark souls." A few years later white men also treacherously murdered Cornstalk, who had become Tecumseh's idol. The Shawnee war leader had remained at peace under the terms of the Dunmore Treaty, and in friendship had visited an American fort at Point Pleasant. While he was there a mob of soldiers, inflamed by the death of a white man on the Ohio River, had marched on the chief's cabin and shot him down. His death shocked the youthful Tecumseh and again filled him with hatred for white men.

After the death of Puckeshinwa a chief named Blackfish, who ruled the Indian town of Old Chillicothe a few miles from Old Piqua, adopted Tecumseh into his family, and the boy traveled back and forth between the two villages, receiving at both places education in personal conduct, oratory, and tribal lore. The murder of Cornstalk enraged Blackfish, and under his leadership the Shawnees commenced a new war of revenge. In 1778 Blackfish invaded Kentucky, struck at some of the settlements, and captured Daniel Boone and twenty-six other whites. He brought the frontiersman back to Old Chillicothe, where Tecumseh saw him. Later Boone escaped, but the youthful Tecumseh witnessed many other dramatic events at the Indian headquarters, and the fierce border war that raged through Kentucky and Ohio heightened his instincts against the whites. The fighting, a peripheral part of the Revolution, involved the British, who bought American scalps and prisoners from the Indians and at times sent expeditions from the north to help the Indians against the colonists. In the turmoil the natives experienced defeat as well as victory, and at one time a large group of Shawnees, fearful of their future in that part of the country, abandoned the area and the rest of the tribe, and headed westward across Indiana, Illinois, and the Mississippi River and established new homes in what is now the state of Missouri. With them, it is believed, went Tecumseh's mother, who left the youth in Ohio in the care of his older brother, Cheeseekau.

In 1780 an American army under George Rogers Clark drove the natives from both Old Chillicothe and Old Piqua. The two cities were burned, and farther west on the Miami River the defeated Shawnees, Tecumseh with them, built another city, also called Piqua, which meant "town that rises from the ashes." Conflict continued, and two years later Tecumseh, as a youthful observer rather than a warrior, accompanied a group of British and Indians in another invasion of Kentucky. Without taking part in the fighting, he watched the Indians try in vain to capture one of the settlements and then saw them administer a severe drubbing to an army of Kentuckians on the Licking River. Soon afterward, just before the end of the Revolution, he got into his first battle, fighting by the side of Cheeseekau in a small skirmish in Ohio. Cheeseekau was wounded, and Tecumseh was unnerved and fled from the battlefield. That night he upbraided himself for his cowardice. He had finally been tested by fire, and had been found wanting, but it would be the last time anywhere that he would show fear.

With the end of the Revolution, the British withdrew offensive forces from along the Ohio River, and the Indians at last accepted as permanent the loss of their hunting grounds south of the river in Kentucky. But there was still little peace for them. The flood of westward-moving settlers was increasing, and the newcomers now had their eyes on the rich Indian lands that lay north of the river. In the East, many Americans did not agree that sovereignty over the Northwest Territory did not also mean possession of its soil, and land-grabbing syndicates, backed by state laws, made speculative purchases of huge tracts of the Indian country and drummed up profitable sales among innocent settlers and colonizers. The Indians soon felt the pressure of the new arrivals, and once more border warfare blazed.

Tecumseh, still in his middle teens, joined a band of Shawnees that tried to halt the invasion by intercepting settlers' flatboats that came down the Ohio from Pennsylvania. For a while the Indians made the route so hazardous that river traffic almost ceased. With Tecumseh's band at the time was a white youth who had been captured years before and had been adopted into the Shawnee tribe. Though he was almost an Indian, he later returned to civilization and related a significant story concerning this period in Tecumseh's life. After a certain battle on the river the Indians captured a settler and burned him at the stake. Tecumseh, then about fifteen years old, watched the spectacle with horror. Suddenly he leaped to his feet and made an eloquent appeal that shamed the Indians for their inhumanity. Somewhere, despite his deep hostility for the whites, he had gained compassion, and the indignity of the torture revolted him. This revulsion at vengeful cruelty was to be a notable part of his personality throughout his life, and the admiration which white men eventually acquired for him stemmed, in the beginning, from their gratitude for incidents in which he demonstrated his own humane conduct or halted with furious condemnation the excesses of other natives.

In time, as the tide of settlers increased, Tecumseh became the leader of his own band of warriors and waged guerrilla warfare against the whites. In the late 1780s he traveled with his brother, Cheeseekau, to visit his mother in Missouri, pausing for a while with the Miami Indians in Indiana and with Shawnees who were living in southern Illinois. At the latter place, during a buffalo hunt, he suffered a broken thigh when his pony threw him, and spent a year letting the injury heal. In the meanwhile Cheeseekau either took their mother back to her own people among the Creeks or followed her to the South and decided to remain there among Shawnees who were still living in that part of the country.

The border conflict in the Northwest Territory had by now become critical for the settlers, and in 1790 General Josiah Harmar of the United States Army was ordered to give protection to the whites. At the head of fourteen hundred men, he marched into the Ohio and Indiana countries of the Shawnees and Miamis, determined to teach the natives a lesson. At the site of present-day Fort Wayne, a Miami war chief named Little Turtle issued an appeal for all Indians to join him, and Tecumseh, whose injury had now healed, hurried there to participate in the defense of the Indian country. In a series of sharp encounters the natives defeated Harmar and forced him to withdraw, but in the following months other expeditions of regulars and militia continued to harass the natives, and in 1791 General Arthur St. Clair, a hero of the Revolution, led a new and powerful army of more than two thousand men up the Miami River. This time Tecumseh, now a twenty-three-year-old veteran leader of warriors, hung on the Americans' flanks as a scout and raider. In the wilderness Little Turtle, aided by a Shawnee chief named Blue Jacket and a Delaware named Buckongahelos, again waited for the invaders, and at dawn on November 4, 1791, near the headwaters of the Wabash River, they fell on St. Clair and completely destroyed his army. In the disastrous battle, during which Tecumseh stood out as a brave and daring fighter, the Indians killed more than six hundred soldiers and sent the shattered survivors flying back to the Ohio River. It was one of the worst routs ever suffered by an American army, and for a while it spread terror among the whites in the Northwest Territory and halted the flow of new settlers.

Tecumseh followed the victory by leading raids against white frontiersmen in both Ohio and Kentucky. In 1792 he received a request from Cheeseekau to bring a band of Shawnees south to help the Cherokees in their war against the Tennessee settlers. He responded at once, and at the head of twenty or thirty warriors joined Cheeseekau's Shawnees and a large body of Cherokees and Creeks in attacks on settlements near Nashville. In one of the encounters Cheeseekau was killed. Tecumseh buried the body of the brother he had adored, and was then chosen to succeed him as leader of all the Shawnee warriors in the south. For several months he led them in a series of fierce skirmishes and raids against settlers, traveling through large sections of the present states of Tennessee, Mississippi, Alabama, Georgia, and Florida, and winning friendships and renown among the southern tribes. In 1793 he broke off his forays to hurry his followers back north to help defend the Ohio country against an invasion by a new American army, this one commanded by Major General Anthony Wayne.

The native chiefs in the Northwest Territory had deposed Little Turtle, who had begun to preach peace with the whites, and the Shawnee, Blue Jacket, was now in command of the Indian forces. Once more Tecumseh and his followers were assigned as scouts to follow the American army as it moved north. Wayne advanced from Cincinnati in October 1793 with more than thirty-six hundred regulars, marching slowly and building forts at key points in the wilderness. Eighty miles north of Cincinnati he erected a fort at Greenville, Ohio, and paused for the winter. He stayed there during the spring, and in June Tecumseh and a number of Indians routed one of his convoy trains and attacked the fort. They were driven off, and soon afterward Wayne started forward again toward the Maumee River in northwestern Ohio. He had three thousand men with him, but Blue Jacket with fourteen hundred warriors decided to engage him. On August 20, 1794, the two forces met in a large clearing along the Maumee River where a tornado had blown down many big trees. Tecumseh's scouts began the fight by firing on Wayne's advance guard, and in the battle that followed Tecumseh added to his reputation among the Indians by his boldness and courage. Throughout the fight among the fallen trees, he was seen wherever the action was most desperate, and even after his rifle jammed and became unusable he continued to lead and inspire his companions. At the height of the battle another of his brothers was killed, but there was no time for grief. Wayne's sharpshooters kept the Indians pinned down behind the trees, his cavalry thrashed at them, and at length the infantry launched a frenzied bayonet charge across the timbers. It scattered the natives and ended the battle that became known as Fallen Timbers. Leaving their dead behind them, the Indians fled to a British fort lower down on the Maumee, and after being refused admittance retreated toward the site of the present city of Toledo. Wayne destroyed every Indian village he could find, built Fort Wayne at the head of the Maumee in Indiana, and retired for the winter to Greenville.

In the spring he invited the vanquished warriors to a peace meeting. Nearly a thousand of them responded, representing twelve different tribes of the Northwest Territory, and after two months of pressure their chiefs reluctantly signed the Greenville Treaty, which ceded to the United States for sale to settlers almost two-thirds of Ohio, including the Shawnee centers of Old Piqua and Old Chillicothe on the Mad River; a triangular tract in southeastern Indiana; and sixteen strategically located areas in the Northwest, among them the sites of Detroit, Toledo, Peoria, and Chicago. In return the Indians divided among themselves about $20,000 in goods and received the promise of $9500 in annuities.

Tecumseh had refused to attend the council, and after the treaty provisions became known he split with Blue Jacket and announced that he would not accept what the chiefs had done. Nevertheless, as settlers moved into the ceded territory, he recognized the hopelessness of resistance, and withdrew westward with his followers into Indiana. His anger and opposition to the treaty furthered his reputation among both Indians and whites, and as large numbers of disgruntled warriors began to give him their loyalty and call him *their* chief, he became the dominant native leader in the Northwest. He was twenty-seven now, five feet, ten inches tall, a powerful and handsome man with a proud, aggressive bearing. Though there is no definitely established contemporary portrait of him, white men who knew him describe him as hard and fiery, a man who with great authority would announce sternly, "I am Tecumseh," and if challenged would menacingly touch the stem of his tomahawk. At the same time he had a complex personality in which many forces were apparently in conflict, for he could also be tender and sentimental, thoughtful and kind, or even playful and good-humored.

In 1796 he married a half-breed named Manete, who is described as an "old woman." She bore Tecumseh a son, but soon afterward he quarreled with her, and they parted. Toward the end of the century, during a visit to an older sister, Tecumapease, who had remained living near Old Chillicothe in Ohio, he met a sensitive, young white girl named Rebecca Galloway, the daughter of an intelligent pioneer farmer who had once been a hunter for George Rogers Clark. She was blond and beautiful, and he was magnetic and interesting, and a strange, romantic attachment developed between them. In time, as Tecumseh continued to call on her, she taught him to speak better English and read to him from the Bible, Shakespeare, and history. In their conversations she talked earnestly to him about humaneness and love of fellow men, and found him surprisingly tender and understanding. Tecumseh broadened in dramatic fashion under Rebecca's sympathetic teaching. He absorbed the history of Alexander the Great and other leaders of white civilization, pondered over new philosophy from the Bible, and thirsted for even more knowledge that would make him better equipped to understand and deal with the Americans. His regard for the blond, blue-eyed girl also increased, and eventually he asked her father if he might marry her. Mr. Galloway respected Tecumseh and advised him to ask Rebecca. Tecumseh did so, and the girl said that she would be willing if he would agree to give up his Indian ways and live with her as a white man. The decision was painful for Tecumseh, and he took a month to make up his mind. Finally, in sadness, he returned to Rebecca, and told her that he could not abandon his people. He said good-by to her and never saw her again. But the memory of her loveliness and guidance stayed with him, and he never took another wife.

The peace envisioned for the Northwest Territory by Wayne's treaty lasted little more than a decade, and was never more than a truce. As Tecumseh had foreseen, the line established at Greenville between the races could not halt conflict. Though the Indians acknowledged white possession of southern Ohio, many of them continued to live and hunt on their former lands, and they were in constant friction with frontier settlers. Moreover, as whites continued to come down the Ohio River, they began to press for the opening of new Indian lands, and in 1800, as if preparing to slice another large piece from the natives' domain, the government established administrative machinery for a Territory of Indiana, west of Ohio.

During this period another tragedy struck the Indians. Traders and settlers brought liquor into the region in huge quantities, and native bands in close contact with the whites could not resist it. They traded land, possessions, and their services for the alcohol, and almost overnight large segments of once proud and dignified tribes became demoralized in drunkenness and disease. As poverty and death claimed the natives, whole bands disappeared, and the weakened survivors clung together in ragged misery. The Miamis, who in 1791 had helped to destroy St. Clair's army, became, in the view of William Henry Harrison, "a poor, miserable drunken set, diminishing every year." The Piankashaws and Weas, almost extinct, were "the most depraved wretches on earth," and the Chippewas, who had fought nobly under Pontiac, were described as "frightful drunkards." Almost every tribe in the Northwest, including the Potawatomis, Kickapoos, Ottawas, Peorias, Kaskaskias, and Winnebagos, felt the effects of the firewater, and as their bands were reduced to poverty they were forced to steal from the whites to stay alive.

Tribes that remained farthest from contact with the traders, such as the Shawnees, retained their independence and strength. Tecumseh himself refused to drink whisky, and preached angrily against its use by his followers. Nevertheless, the liquor trade continued to threaten his people in Indiana. Despite his opposition, as well as government attempts to stop whisky sales to natives, unscrupulous traders managed to sneak more than six thousand gallons up the Wabash River annually for a trade of no more than six hundred warriors. One of the Shawnees who became most noted among his own people as a depraved drunk was Tecumseh's younger brother, Laulewasika. A loud-mouthed idler and loafer, he had lost an eye in an accident and wore a handkerchief over the empty socket. For years he drank heavily and lived in laziness. Then, suddenly, in 1805, he was influenced by the great religious revival taking place among white settlers on the frontier, and particularly by itinerant Shaker preachers, whose jerking, dancing, and excessive physical activity stirred mystic forces within him.

During a frightening epidemic of sickness among the Shawnees, Laulewasika was overcome by a "deep and awful sense" of his own wickedness, and fell into the first of many trances, during which he thought he met the Indian Master of Life. The latter showed him the horrible torments and sufferings of persons doomed by drink, and then pointed out another path, "beautiful, sweet, and pleasant," reserved for abstainers. Laulewasika's regeneration was instantaneous. He began to preach against the use of liquor, and the intensity of his words drew followers to him. As he continued to have trances and commune with the Master of Life, he changed his name to Tenskwatawa, "the open door," which he took from the saying of Jesus, "I am the door." He allied himself to Tecumseh, and gradually under the war chief's influence broadened his doctrine of abstinence into an anti-white code that urged Indians to return to the ways of their fathers and end intertribal wars. Like other native prophets who had arisen among the Indians in earlier days of crisis, Tenskwatawa soon became a dynamic force for opposition to the whites, but many of his sermons were the words of Tecumseh, who now saw, more than ever before, that the Indians must maintain their self-respect and dignity if they were to have the strength to halt another westward advance by the whites. The two brothers joined forces and moved to Greenville, Ohio, at the very place where the chiefs had signed their treaty with Wayne in 1795; there they built a large frame meeting house and fifty or sixty cabins for their converts.

The Prophet's emotional appeals traveled quickly across the Northwest Territory, and he soon gained followers from almost every tribe. His growing influence and the dangerous concentration of natives around him disturbed General Harrison at his territorial headquarters in Vincennes, and he began to scoff publicly at the Shawnee, hoping that ridicule would undermine the natives' belief in him. He made little progress, however, and in April 1806 he challenged Tenskwatawa to perform a miracle. "If he is really a prophet," he wrote to one group of Indians, "ask him to cause the sun to stand still, the moon to alter its course, the rivers to cease to flow, or the dead to rise from their graves. If he does these things, you may then believe he has been sent from God."

Harrison's challenge was disastrous. From some white source, perhaps from a British agent in the north, the Prophet learned that a total eclipse of the sun would occur on June 16. In a bold and boastful response to Harrison, he proclaimed to the Indians that he would make the sun darken, and on the designated day a huge crowd of natives assembled at Greenville. Moving into their center, Tenskwatawa pointed commandingly at the sun, and at 11:32 in the morning, the moon began to darken the sun's face. The Indians were stricken with awe. As night descended over the gathering the prophet called to the Master of Life to bring back the sun. In a moment light began to reappear. With the return of full daylight the Prophet's reputation and power were assured. Word of the miracle electrified the tribes of the Northwest, and as far away as Minnesota entire bands gave their loyalty to the Shawnee's code. But it was only the beginning.

Miracle begat miracle, and as agents of the Prophet traveled from tribe to tribe, carrying sacred strings of beans to peoples as remote as the Arikaras, Sioux, Mandans, and Blackfeet on the upper Missouri and the plains of central Canada, the Indians accepted any new wonder that was credited to the mystic Shawnee. In the Northwest Territory particularly, the Prophet's preachings inspired the natives with new pride and purpose, and, as Tecumseh hoped, helped to strengthen the feeling of unity among them. Moreover, as Tenskwatawa's personal power increased, he began to stir his followers with demagogic appeals against Christianized Indians and others who weakened the native cause by their friendship for the whites. Violence flared at first against Christian Delawares in Indiana, and soon spread to the Wyandots, Kickapoos, and other tribes, where the Prophet's followers slew natives who were considered bewitched or under the influence of white men. Several hundred Indians were killed before Tecumseh personally stopped the purge. But an idea had been launched, and Tecumseh now continued it by peaceful methods, encouraging and aiding the transfer of power within tribes from weak and venal chiefs who were too friendly to the Americans to young warriors who had promised loyalty to himself and his brother.

Harrison became alarmed as his agents sent reports of the tribes that had deposed their old chiefs and gone over to the Prophet. Tension between Great Britain and the United States, ever-present since the end of the Revolution, had reached a critical point again, and Harrison and most western settlers were certain that the British in Canada were the real troublemakers behind Tenskwatawa. "I really fear that this said Prophet is an engine set to work by the British for some bad purpose," Harrison wrote the Secretary of War on July 11, 1807. As the clouds of international conflict continued to travel across the Appalachians from Washington, the settlers' dread of a new frontier war with the English and Indians heightened, and they looked on the prophet's successes with increasing suspicion and hostility. Gradually Tecumseh felt the growing animosity toward the natives, and recognized its ultimate consequences. In their fear of the British, the Americans would again attack the Indians, and try to drive them out of more of their lands. He saw only one hope—a dream which had been influenced by his knowledge of both the Iroquois League and the formation of the United States, and which he had long nourished for the Indians during his many travels and frontier fights. The unity among the Indians which he and his brothers were beginning to achieve must be broadened and strengthened. All the tribes must be brought together to be ready to fight as a single people in defense of their common lands. To avoid premature conflict he ordered Tenskwatawa to evacuate Greenville, which was too close to settlers in Ohio, and move his center westward to a tract of land that the Potawatomi and Kickapoo Indians had offered him in Indiana. The site lay along the west bank of the Tippecanoe River; its name was an English corruption of a Potawatomi word that meant "great clearing." In May 1808, at the stream's confluence with the Wabash River, Tenskwatawa and the families of eighty of his followers raised the mission house and bark dwellings of a new Prophet's Town. As soon as it was established, Tecumseh and his brother, accompanied by several companions and attendants, set out on horseback to unite the tribes for defense.

Forty-five years before, Pontiac had sent deputies to urge the chiefs and their warriors to war against the English. Now Tecumseh himself, already a war chief of great prestige, appeared at village after village, exciting the people with the presence of the Prophet and himself, and appealing for their support with thrilling patriotic oratory. At many places, chiefs who had signed the Treaty of Greenville and wanted no more war with

the Americans opposed him, and he suffered many rebuffs. Elsewhere, whole tribes responded with enthusiasm to his speeches,
or divided their loyalties between their old chiefs and eager,
young warriors who agreed with Tecumseh's appeals. In Illinois
he won the Potawatomis to him, and rode away with a new
and influential companion, a young Ottawa chief named Shabbona, who had married into the Potawatomi nation. In Wisconsin the civil chiefs of the Sauk and Foxes opposed the mission,
but Tecumseh gained another resolute convert in a war leader
named Black Hawk, who would one day fight his own war
against the Americans. Most of the Menominees and Winnebagos
near Green Bay pledged support, and back in Indiana the Kickapoos and Ottawas also agreed to join if war came. The Missis-
sinewa and Miami Indians, who still looked to Little Turtle for
leadership, had by now degenerated into weak and dissolute
peoples, and Tecumseh made no impression on them. But almost the whole tribe of Wyandots and many villages of Delawares, Weas, Chippewas, Illinois, and Piankashaws, smarting under
the frustrations of debauchery and idleness, found new pride in
the Shawnee's patriotic appeals and promised to take up arms
again in defense of their lands.

After covering the Northwest country, Tecumseh turned
south and west, and in 1809, accompanied by a small band of
followers, visited dozens of tribes, from the Seminoles in Florida
to the Osages in Missouri. He received attention and sympathy,
and made many friends, and among most of the peoples he visited he managed to sow the seeds of future action against the
Americans. Before the end of the year he was back in the north
and heading into New York State, where he tried in vain to enlist the Iroquois tribes in his alliance. After being rebuffed by the
Senecas and Onondagas he returned to Indiana and rejoined the
Prophet on the Tippecanoe River. Despite his tireless journeys,
he still had much work to do to achieve the unity he envisioned.
He had to revisit many of the tribes he had met, make new appeals to those who had turned him down, and secure more bind-

ing agreements with his allies. But he had already made remarkable progress. From Lake Superior to the Gulf of Mexico he had laid the groundwork for the common defense of the Indians' country by the greatest military alliance in native history.

While he had been away the situation had worsened in Indiana. The war scare had abated, but additional pressures were threatening the natives. There were now more than twenty thousand Americans in southern Indiana, and if they were to receive statehood, for which they were clamoring, they would have to secure more Indian land on which to support a larger white population. The politically ambitious Governor Harrison was as aggressive as any of the settlers, and during the summer of 1809 he decided to force the Indians into a new cession. He sent his agents to Little Turtle and a host of the older and weaker chiefs and, armed with maps of central Indiana, met them at Fort Wayne in September. Harrison's letters reveal that he had little conscience in his dealings with the Indians, and that he was not above deceit. He "mellowed" the chiefs with alcohol, and after he had placed considerable pressure on them, they proved obliging. For $7000 in cash and an annuity of $1750, they ceded three million acres of land in Indiana, much of it owned by tribes that were not even present.

The new cession enraged Tecumseh, who heard about it while he was returning from New York. Included in the ceded territory were some of the Shawnees' best hunting grounds. Moreover, while he had been trying to unite the Indians in defense of the country they still owned, Indians behind his back had sold more of it, demonstrating once more that as long as individual tribes and chiefs were allowed to sell land as their own the Americans would find weak and greedy traitors to the native cause. More determined than ever, Tecumseh circulated word that Indian country was the common property of all the tribes, and that he and his allies would refuse to recognize the latest piece of treachery. Angry Indians who agreed with him flocked to the Tippecanoe, and in the spring of 1810 Tecumseh had a force of a thousand warriors at the Prophet's Town, training to repel, if necessary, any attempt by Americans to settle the newly ceded lands.

The hostile preparations disturbed Harrison, and he was further concerned by reports that the Wyandots, Creeks, and Choctaws were in sympathy with the Shawnees, and that a force of eleven hundred Sauk, Foxes, and Winnebagos was marching to the Prophet's Town. Harrison still thought that Tenskwatawa was the main agitator of the native opposition, and in an attempt to calm him he sent a messenger to the Tippecanoe settlement, inviting the prophet to visit the President of the United States in Washington. Early in August he was surprised to learn from his agent that the Prophet's brother Tecumseh was the real leader of the Indians, and that the two men were coming to see him at Vincennes.

On August 11, 1810, the Shawnee brothers, accompanied by several hundred armed and painted warriors, swept down the Wabash River in a fleet of eighty canoes. At Fort Knox, three miles north of Vincennes, an Army captain observed them and reported that, true enough, "they were headed by the brother of the Prophet—Tecumseh—who, perhaps, is one of the finest-looking men I ever saw." Preliminaries and rain delayed the council for several days, but when it began it was tense and dramatic. In a grove near the governor's mansion Tecumseh and Harrison faced one another, both strong, willful leaders of national forces that had met in head-on collision. The two men were proud and suspicious, and as their followers stood nervously in the background, eyeing each other for sign of treachery, the air bristled with hostility. Tecumseh spoke first, beginning slowly, but soon pouring out his words in such swift and passionate flights of oratory that the interpreter had difficulty following him.

The Shawnee first reviewed the history of Indian-white relations in the Ohio Valley, and reminded Harrison of every wrong suffered by the natives at the hands of the Americans. Now, he told the governor, he was trying to unite the Indians, but the American leader was fomenting enmities among them. Tecumseh's words were lofty and eloquent, but we have only the interpreter's stilted translation of his ideas. "You endeavor to make distinctions," the translation of the speech reads. "You endeavor to prevent the Indians from doing what we, their leaders, wish them to do—unite and consider their land the common property. . . . I am a Shawnee. My forefathers were warriors. Their son is a warrior. From them I take only my existence. From my tribe I take nothing. I have made myself what I am. And I would that I could make the red people as great as the conceptions of my mind, when I think of the Great Spirit that rules over all. I would not then come to Governor Harrison to ask him to tear the treaty. But I would say to him, Brother, you have liberty to return to your own country."

Several times Tecumseh turned to his dream of uniting the tribes in order to halt the whites. "The way, the only way to stop this evil," he told Harrison, "is for all the red men to unite in claiming a common and equal right in the land, as it was at first, and should be now—for it never was divided, but belongs to all. No tribe has a right to sell, even to each other, much less to strangers, who demand all, and will take no less. . . . Sell a country! Why not sell the air, the clouds and the great sea, as well as the earth? Did not the Great Spirit make them all for the use of his children?"

Toward the end of his speech, he apparently tried to nettle Harrison. "How can we have confidence in the white people?" he asked him. "When Jesus Christ came upon the earth, you killed Him, and nailed Him to a cross. You thought He was dead, but you were mistaken. You have Shakers among you, and you laugh and make light of their worship." Finally he pointed to the United States as a model for the natives. "The states," he said, "have set the example of forming a union among all the fires

[states]—why should they censure the Indians for following it?"
He ended brusquely. "I shall now be glad to know immediately
what is your determination about the land."

Harrison began his reply by insisting that Tecumseh had no
right to contest the sale of land in Indiana, because the Shawnee
homeland had been in Georgia. The Indian chief stirred angrily,
recognizing the deliberate evasion of his thesis that Indian land
everywhere belonged to all natives. As Harrison went on he
became more impatient, and tension among the onlookers began
to mount. Suddenly Harrison asserted that the United States had
always been fair in its dealings with Indians. Tecumseh leaped to
his feet and shouted, "It is false! He lies!" As he poured his wrath
on Harrison, the governor unsheathed his sword and started forward. Several whites aimed their guns, and the Indians behind
Tecumseh drew their tomahawks. For an instant a fight seemed
imminent. Then Harrison coolly declared the council adjourned
and strode to his house. As the other whites followed him, Tecumseh motioned his warriors back to their camp.

The next morning Tecumseh's temper had subsided, and he
sent his apologies to Harrison. The governor accepted them, and
visited the chief's camp. Tecumseh was in a good mood, and
the two men sat down together on a bench. Gradually the Indian
kept pushing against Harrison, forcing the American to move
closer to one end. Finally, as Harrison was about to be shoved off,
he objected, and Tecumseh laughed, pointing out that that was
what the American settlers were doing to the Indians.

The council reconvened the same day, but accomplished nothing, and Tecumseh and his party soon left Vincennes and returned to the Prophet's Town. Harrison had made no concessions to the natives. He sent the War Department the Indians'
complaint that "the Americans had driven them from the sea-
coast, and would shortly, if not stopped, push them into the
lakes," and though he added, "they were determined to make a
stand where they were," the prospect that such a stand might be
made did not seem to worry him. Six weeks later, alluding to

Northwest Territory lands that the Indians still held, he asked the members of the Indiana legislature, "Is one of the fairest portions of the globe to remain in a state of nature, the haunt of a few wretched savages, when it seems destined, by the Creator, to give support to a large population, and to be the sea of civilization, of science, and true religion?"

The issue was joined. Harrison's attitude served notice that he intended to keep pressing for more Indian land, and Tecumseh knew that to stop him he had to hurry his alliances and strengthen the natives' will to resist. Once more the Shawnee leader made rapid visits to the tribes of Ohio, Indiana, and Michigan, delivering passionate pleas for his confederation. On November 15, 1810, he even crossed to the Canadian side of the Detroit River and at the British post of Fort Malden addressed a council of Potawatomis, Ottawas, Sauk, Foxes, and Winnebagos. Harrison and most of the settlers were confident now that the British were instigating Tecumseh, though this time the reverse was actually the case. Documentary evidence, found in later days, showed clearly that before the War of 1812 the British Government definitely opposed any Indian action that would imperil English relations with the United States or disrupt the lucrative Great Lakes fur trade, and that from Downing Street to Fort Malden British officials were irritated by Tecumseh's activities and tried to discourage his agitation against the Americans. Nevertheless, appearances convinced the settlers that unless something was soon done, the Indians with British assistance would again threaten the entire Ohio Valley. To Harrison the best defense was vigorous offense, and in 1811, he decided that the time had come to smash the Prophet's Town and scatter the leaders of Indian opposition.

All he needed was an overt act by the natives to justify his invasion of the Indians' country, and in July 1811 he gained his excuse when Potawatomis killed some white men in Illinois. Harrison claimed at once that they were followers of the Prophet, and demanded that the Shawnees on the Tippecanoe surrender them to him for justice. In reply, Tecumseh and the Prophet again visited Vincennes for a personal meeting with the American leader. They refused to deliver the Potawatomis, and once more the council ended in an impasse. The Prophet returned to his center on the Tippecanoe, and Tecumseh, accompanied by twenty-four warriors, set off down the Wabash River, bound on a second attempt to unite the southern tribes behind him. As soon as the Indian leader had disappeared, Harrison began preparations for his expedition to the Tippecanoe. "I hope," he wrote the Secretary of War regarding the departed Tecumseh, "before his return that that part of the fabrick which he considered complete will be demolished and even its foundations rooted up."

Tecumseh's second southern journey was an heroic and memorable effort; in six months it took him down the Ohio and Mississippi Rivers to the present site of Memphis, through Tennessee to Mississippi, Alabama, Georgia, and Florida, back north again across Georgia to the Carolinas, through the full length of Tennessee to the Ozark Mountains of Arkansas and Missouri, north into Iowa, and eventually back home. Once more he hurried from village to village, visiting strong interior tribes such as the Choctaws, Chickasaws, Cherokees, Creeks, Osages, and Iowas, and pleading with them for a united war against the Americans. Generally he met with opposition, and was disappointed. Great councils, sometimes numbering more than five thousand natives, gathered to listen to him, and white traders and Indian agents who also managed to be present reported the fervor and eloquence with which the Shawnee spoke.

His words "fell in avalanches from his lips," General Sam Dale said. "His eyes burned with supernatural lustre, and his whole frame trembled with emotion. His voice resounded over the multitude—now sinking in low and musical whispers, now rising to the highest key, hurling out his words like a succession of thunderbolts. . . . I have heard many great orators, but I never saw one with the vocal powers of Tecumseh." Wearing only a breechclout and moccasins, with lines of red war paint beneath his eyes, the Shawnee stood alone with his followers amid the throngs and cried to the Indians to stop their intertribal wars, to unite in a single nation as the states had done, and to fight together for all their land before it was too late. Old chiefs listened to him uneasily, and argued back. They would not unite with old, hereditary enemies. They would not give up their autonomy in a federation that would make them subordinate to strangers. The kind of union that Tecumseh talked about was for white men, not Indians. And besides, it was already too late.

In historic debates with the greatest chiefs of the south, Tecumseh continued to plead his cause, and on several occasions white agents who were present were able to record some of his thoughts, but again in the flowery language of awkward translations: "Where today are the Pequot? Where the Narraganset, the Mohican, the Pokanoket and many other once powerful tribes of our people? They have vanished before the avarice and oppression of the white man, as snow before a summer sun. . . . Will we let ourselves be destroyed in our turn without making an effort worthy of our race? Shall we, without a struggle, give up our homes, our country bequeathed to us by the Great Spirit, the graves of our dead and everything that is dear and sacred to us? I know you will cry with me, Never! Never!" The white observer, writing down the speech, had difficulty translating the Indian's expressions, but as the Shawnee continued the meaning of his words was not lost. "That people," he warned his listeners, "will continue longest in the enjoyment of peace who timely prepare to vindicate themselves and manifest a determination to protect themselves whenever they are wronged."

Again and again young warriors shouted their approval, and small groups promised to strike the Americans when Tecumseh gave them the signal. But the older leaders were wary and afraid. Some of them were receiving annuities and gifts from the Americans, some saw only ruin in Tecumseh's plans, and some thought that their people could do well enough by themselves. Only the Creeks and Seminoles, already smoldering with hatred for the

Americans, provided the Shawnee with hope. To them he gave
bundles of red-painted sticks. When they received word from
him they were to start throwing one stick away each day, and
when all were gone it would be the day on which all the tribes in
every part of the frontier would commence a simultaneous attack on the whites.

Disappointed by his failures in the south, Tecumseh returned
to the Tippecanoe River early in 1812, only to be met by news
of a more stunning setback at home. During the Shawnee leader's
absence, Harrison had finally struck at the Prophet's Town. At
the head of an army of almost a thousand men the American
governor had marched up the Wabash River, and on the night of
November 6, 1811, had camped near the Indian settlement at
the mouth of the Tippecanoe. The ominous arrival of the hostile
force alarmed the Indians; at first, without Tecumseh to direct
them, they were undecided what to do. A band of Winnebagos,
bolder than the others, argued for an immediate attack on the
invading whites, and finally won Tenskwatawa's approval. In the
early hours of morning, some 450 natives crawled through the
darkness toward the Americans. Harrison had placed his men in
an unbroken line around the three sides of his triangular-shaped
camp, and shortly before four o'clock a sentry on the northern
perimeter saw an Indian moving in the gloom and shot him. In
an instant the whooping natives were on their feet, charging toward the whites. The Americans met them with blazing musketry, and only a few of the Indians were able to crash into the
camp, where Harrison's men battled them in hand-to-hand struggles. The rest were chased back, and though they launched a
series of rushes at other sides of the camp they failed to break
through. As the sky lightened they finally withdrew among the
trees, and kept up a desultory fire from cover during the day.
By the second day they had all disappeared, and Harrison moved
his men, unopposed, into the abandoned Prophet's Town. He
fired the buildings and destroyed all the natives' possessions, including their stores of food.

The number of Indian dead in the battle was never known, though it was estimated to be between 25 and 40. Harrison lost 61 killed and 127 wounded, but on his return to the settlements he announced that he had won a great victory and wrote to the Secretary of War that "the Indians have never sustained so severe a defeat since their acquaintance with the white people." The importance of the battle was soon exaggerated beyond reality, and in the flush of excitement many of the western settlers began to think that Harrison had beaten Tecumseh himself. The facts of what had been little more than an inconclusive swipe at a small segment of Tecumseh's followers never fully caught up with the legend of a dramatic triumph, and in 1840 the magic of Tippecanoe's memory still worked well enough to help elect Harrison to the Presidency.

The Americans' aggression, meanwhile, had caused serious repercussions among the natives. By the time Tecumseh returned home the Prophet had moved back into the ruins of the settlement and was sending messengers to all the Northwest tribes, telling them what had happened. Tecumseh reached the Tippecanoe in late February or early March 1812, and seethed with rage as he viewed what had happened behind his back. "I stood upon the ashes of my own home," he said later, "where my own wigwam had sent up its fire to the Great Spirit, and there I summoned the spirits of the braves who had fallen in their vain attempt to protect their homes from the grasping invader, and as I snuffed up the smell of their blood from the ground I swore once more eternal hatred—the hatred of an avenger."

The Shawnee's first anger was directed against his brother for not having prevented the battle. The southern trip had shown Tecumseh that his confederation was far from ready for the united movement he had planned to lead, and the clash on the Tippecanoe would now set off just the kind of a border war he had striven to avoid. Individual tribes would rise by themselves, and once more the Americans would deal with them piecemeal. The Prophet tried lamely to blame the Winnebagos, but Tecum-

seh shook him by the hair, threatened to kill him for his misman-
agement, and finally drove him from the town. The Prophet became a wanderer, still preaching his doctrine, but eventually lost
influence and followers and ended his life in obscurity among
Indians farther west.

The isolated uprisings Tecumseh feared had meanwhile already begun. Irate bands, crying for revenge, fell on settlers in
Indiana and Illinois. They raided independently of one another
and without plan, but the panic they aroused united the Americans against all the natives and strengthened the settlers' conviction that the British and Tecumseh were directing the new attacks. Frontier feelings flamed against both the English and the
Indians, and as frightened settlers abandoned their homes and
fled south to safety, angry militia units built forts and blockhouses north of the Ohio River. In Ohio a large American army
under Brigadier General William Hull began to march north to
Detroit, and in Vincennes Harrison prepared for the full-scale
war of decision for which Tecumseh was not yet ready.

During the spring the tension on the frontier spread to Washington, where it became one of the precipitating factors of the
War of 1812. On June 18 the United States, under the pressure of
Henry Clay and other "War Hawk" legislators from Kentucky
and the West, began the war against Great Britain. Almost immediately both the British and the Americans sent agents among the
tribes, appealing for their help in the struggle. Several of the
older chiefs, who had opposed Tecumseh and maintained their
loyalty to the United States, argued the American case before
their tribesmen. But in a large council called by the Americans
at Fort Wayne Tecumseh defied them. "Here is a chance . . ."
he cried scornfully, "yes, a chance such as will never occur again
—for us Indians of North America to form ourselves into one
great combination and cast our lot with the British in this war.
And should they conquer and again get the mastery of all North
America, our rights to at least a portion of the land of our fathers would be respected by the King. If they should not win

and the whole country should pass into the hands of the Long Knives—we see this plainly—it will not be many years before our last place of abode and our last hunting ground will be taken from us, and the remnants of the different tribes between the Mississippi, the Lakes, and the Ohio River will all be driven toward the setting sun."

His words fired his listeners, and twice he dramatically broke in two the peace pipes which an American envoy handed him. Then, with a large party of Shawnees, Delawares, Kickapoos, and Potawatomis, he marched off to Fort Malden and announced his allegiance to the British. Other bands, remembering his visits and ardent appeals of the past, soon began to join him. Wyandots, Chippewas, and Sioux came from Canada, Michigan, and Minnesota, while his old acquaintance Black Hawk moved across the northern wilderness from Illinois and Wisconsin and arrived with a war party of Sauk, Foxes, and Winnebagos. Elsewhere, Indian runners and British agents carried word that Tecumseh had finally declared war on the Americans, and the response of many tribes showed that the Shawnee's travels had not been entirely in vain. Though they fought without Tecumseh's guiding direction, and not as the united Indian people he had envisioned, bands rose against the Americans on every front, driving United States settlers, traders, and armed forces into retreat in the Northwest, the upper Mississippi, and the deep South. Before the war ended the Americans had stopped them, but the costly months of their hostility were scarred by massacres, the disruption of commerce, and the desolation of settlements from the outskirts of St. Louis to the Creek country of Alabama and Georgia.

On the Detroit River, where Tecumseh soon had a native army that fluctuated between 1000 and 3000 warriors, the American General William Hull established his headquarters at the town of Detroit, and on July 12 launched an invasion of Canada. He crossed the river with 3000 men and prepared to attack the 300-man British garrison at Fort Malden. Hull was an elderly hero of the Revolution, who had become weak and timid with age. His advance guard won a preliminary skirmish with a small, mixed body of Indians and British, but soon afterward Tecumseh and 150 warriors ambushed another of his scouting parties, and Hull pulled up in alarm. While the Americans paused, worried over the size of the Shawnee's Indian force, Tecumseh learned of a United States supply convoy, protected by 230 militiamen under Captain Henry Brush, that was nearing Detroit from Ohio. He slipped a party of Indians across the river and prepared to intercept the column. Brush had already sent a messenger to Hull to ask for troops to help guard the convoy on the final, dangerous portion of its journey, and on August 4 Hull sent 200 men to meet the convoy. Tecumseh trapped the relief column a short distance south of Detroit, killed a large number of soldiers, and sent the rest retreating back to Hull. During the battle he also came into possession of the American general's dispatches, which Hull was sending home, and he forwarded them to the British commander at Malden.

The battle forced Brush to withdraw his convoy to the south and wait behind the River Raisin for help. The news that Tecumseh was behind him and had cut his supply line panicked Hull, and when he further learned that Chippewa allies of Tecumseh had assisted in the British capture of Michilimackinac in northern Michigan and were probably canoeing south to attack Detroit, he hastily abandoned his invasion of Canada and recrossed the river to the American shore. His officers and men were appalled by his cowardice, but the threat of Indian strength now hung heavy over them all. On August 8, Hull sent a new force of 600 men to try to rescue Brush's trapped convoy. By this time some British troops had also crossed the river, and at Monguaga, a few miles south of Detroit, they joined Tecumseh's Indians and helped to intercept the new American relief column. There was a furious battle, during which Tecumseh fought bravely and received a wound in the leg, but the British and Indians were eventually forced to abandon the field and withdraw to the Canadian side of the river. Still, the mauled American troops dared move no farther south, and Brush's supply convoy remained dug in defensively south of the River Raisin.

On August 13 Major General Isaac Brock arrived at Malden with 300 British reinforcements from the east. Brock, the lieutenant governor of Canada, was an able and resolute military leader, well over six feet tall, with a powerful physique and a gentle and considerate nature. He had heard great praise of Tecumseh, and had already formed a high opinion of the Indian chief. On the night he reached Malden he read Hull's dispatches which Tecumseh had captured, and realized from them the extent of the American commander's fears and weaknesses. When Tecumseh came in to be introduced to him, Brock asked the Shawnee leader for his opinion of what they ought to do next. Tecumseh pleased him by urging an immediate attack on Detroit. Only one British officer supported the Indian's view, but at four o'clock in the morning Brock decided to follow Tecumseh's advice, and sent a message across the river, calling on Hull to surrender. The American refused, and as British guns opened fire on Detroit Tecumseh's Indians embarked for the American shore.

At the same time Brock allowed one of his couriers to be captured by the Americans. The courier shattered Hull's nerves by reporting that 5000 Indians were arriving from the upper lakes to join Tecumseh. Hull had still been occupied in trying to rescue Brush's convoy, and had just dispatched a third force of 350 men to bring it in. Tecumseh's men landed between Detroit and the new expedition, and once more the American relief column was brought to a halt when its leaders realized what had happened. As the men wheeled about to march against the Indians in their rear, Tecumseh ranged his warriors around the fort and tried a ruse. He moved them in single file three times out of the woods and across a clearing in full view of the fort's defenders, so that it looked as if the expected Chippewa reinforcements had arrived from the north. The stratagem worked. Brock had just crossed the river with 700 English and Canadian troops and was inspecting the siege lines with Tecumseh, preparing to launch an assault on the fort, when Hull gave up. Without consulting his officers he raised a white flag and surrendered Detroit.

The American commander's ignominious action shocked the United States. His capitulation included even Brush's beleaguered column, but those men, learning what had happened, turned around in fright and raced safely back to the Ohio settlements. The fall of Detroit spread new panic across the frontier, but in the fallen city the helpless members of the garrison soon found themselves turning from contempt for Hull to appreciation for Tecumseh. Though he had fought as an Indian, stripped to leggings and breechclout, the Shawnee chief dressed proudly in white men's clothes for his entrance into Detroit, and like an English staff officer occupied a bedroom and sitting room in the same house with Brock. Many of the Americans had expected to be massacred by the natives, but Tecumseh's absolute control over them and his friendly and dignified conduct gradually won the admiration of the prisoners; later, when they were paroled back to the settlements, they talked of him as a gallant and honorable enemy, and spread a new conception of him as a humane Indian who had treated the captives and inhabitants of the city with consideration.

The dramatic victory, meanwhile, had given the Shawnee leader new hope that he might, after all, achieve his dream of an Indian nation. Additional tribes were entering the war and were striking at other American strongholds. Potawatomis had captured Fort Dearborn and, aided even by a band of Miamis, who had long opposed Tecumseh's appeal for unity, were laying siege to Fort Wayne. If victories continued, the Americans might well be forced to recognize an Indian country. In the fall of 1812 Tecumseh made another tour to the south, principally to see the Creeks, who had promised to support his cause. No white man was present to record his speeches this time, but soon after the Shawnee returned north the powerful Creek Confederation commenced a war across the South that cost the Americans thousands of lives and millions of dollars.

By April 1813 Tecumseh was once again back at Malden. On his way home he picked up 600 recruits from among the Illinois tribes, and now had 3000 natives under his command, one of the largest Indian armies ever assembled. During the Shawnee's absence, General Brock had been killed in action on the Niagara border, and Colonel Henry Procter, a petulant, small-minded officer, had taken command at Malden. He was a fat, haughty man who was disdainful of Indians, and Tecumseh let him know quickly that he considered him a poor substitute for the bold, imaginative Brock. In January, Procter and a force of Indians had gained a notable victory at the River Raisin over an army of 850 Kentuckians, killing or capturing the entire American force. Procter had assured the Americans that he would not allow the Indians to harm the prisoners, but when some of the natives got drunk he looked the other way and did nothing to halt their butchery of all the wounded and defenseless captives. When Tecumseh learned about it he criticized the British commander for weakness in not having controlled the natives. If the Indians were ever to gain recognition of their own state, he told both the British and tribal leaders, they must gain the respect of white men for their humanity and civilized conduct.

The grisly massacre had also aroused the American West to a spirit of no-quarter revenge, and by the time Tecumseh returned from the south his old adversary, General William Henry Harrison, was marching toward Detroit with a new army to avenge the savagery at the River Raisin. On the Maumee River, near the site of Wayne's victory of Fallen Timbers, Harrison paused to build a new post called Fort Meigs, and suddenly on April 25, 1813, found himself besieged by an army of British and Indians, which had come south from Malden under Procter and Tecumseh. A brigade of 1100 Kentuckians made its way through the wilderness to reinforce Harrison's army, and arrived at the river a little more than a week after the siege had begun. In an effort to break through the British lines and get into the fort, the Kentuckians divided their forces and moved down both banks of the river, attempting a complicated plan that included a diversionary fight on the shore opposite the fort. The Americans' scheme miscarried, and the battle that followed engulfed the Kentuckians in another bloody catastrophe. Before they could reach the fort, some 800 troops were surrounded and hacked to pieces by Tecumseh's Indians. Almost 500 Americans were killed and 150 captured.

While Tecumseh remained at the siege lines some of the English and Indians marched the prisoners down-river to Procter's headquarters at the British Fort Miami. Once more the Indians began to murder the captives as they had at the River Raisin, and again Procter did nothing to halt them. This time, however, a native carried word to Tecumseh of what was happening. The Shawnee leader galloped to the British camp and hurled himself into the scene of massacre. The Indians had already killed more than twenty captives, and were tomahawking and scalping others. Tecumseh knocked down one Indian with his sword, grabbed another by the throat, and lunged at the rest. As the natives drew back he shouted at them, "Are there no men here?" The carnage stopped abruptly, and the Shawnee chief hastened to see Procter. When he demanded to know why the natives had again been allowed to kill prisoners, Procter answered lamely, "Your Indians cannot be controlled. They cannot be commanded." His reply filled the Shawnee with contempt. "You are unfit to command," he said to the British leader. "Go and put on petticoats." Then he added, "I conquer to save, and you to murder."

A couple of days later, over Tecumseh's objection, Procter lifted the siege of Fort Meigs. The Indian leader was disgusted, and two months later forced the British commander to surround the post once more. But Procter was weak and indecisive, and soon afterward he again abandoned the attempt to take the

American fort. As opportunities continued to slip away from him, the Indians lost faith in his leadership. Finally, on September 13, disaster struck them all in a naval battle on Lake Erie. At Put in Bay an American fleet under Commodore Oliver Hazard Perry swept the British from the Lake and cut Procter's army in the west from its supply bases in the east. The British commander, aware of his isolation, and fearing Harrison, who was now beginning to move against him with a heavily-reinforced army, decided to abandon the Detroit region and withdraw along the northern shore of Lake Erie to join other English troops on the Niagara frontier. For a while he concealed his plans from Tecumseh, but the Shawnee observed his preparations and realized that the British leader was about to withdraw from the country and leave the Indians to shift for themselves.

Procter's duplicity inflamed Tecumseh. He called his Indians together on the Fort Malden parade ground and humiliated the British commander in front of the other white officers, telling the natives that the English were flying from the enemy. "Listen, Father!" he roared at Procter. "You have the arms and ammunition which our great father sent for his red children. If you have an idea of going away, give them to us, and you may go and welcome. Our lives are in the hands of the Great Spirit. He gave to our ancestors the lands which we possess. We are determined to defend them, and if it is His will, our bones shall whiten on them, but we will never give them up." His speech failed to move Procter, and Tecumseh finally called him "a miserable old squaw."

That same day Procter began his withdrawal, and in time Tecumseh and his Indians were forced to follow him. The Shawnee was crushed. He had managed to wring from the British general a promise to retreat only as far as the Thames River, about fifty miles away, but as the natives trooped off, leaving behind them the country Tecumseh had worked so hard and for so long to save for his people, the chief's spirits flagged, and he was overcome with gloom. "We are now going to follow the British," he told one of his warriors, "and I feel certain that we shall never return."

On September 27 Harrison's army crossed Lake Erie to Canada, and commenced its pursuit of the British. Procter led the retreating army; Tecumseh and the Indians, including a band of Sioux from far-off Minnesota, brought up the rear, holding off advance units of the Americans, and denouncing Procter for refusing to stand and fight. In one sharp skirmish Tecumseh was wounded in the arm. He had decided to try to turn back the Americans without aid from Procter, but after thirteen of his men had been killed and many others wounded, he ordered the natives to continue the withdrawal. On the night of October 4 he went into camp with the British near the present town of Thamesville, a short distance up the Thames River. They had now reached the line which Procter had promised to hold. But that night, as if he had accepted the final defeat of everything he had lived and fought for, Tecumseh had a premonition of death. As he sat by his fire with his closest Indian lieutenants, men who had followed him loyally for years, he said to them calmly, "Brother warriors, we are about to enter an engagement from which I shall not return. My body will remain on the field of battle."

The next morning Procter again wanted to retreat, and Tecumseh had another bitter quarrel with him, this time threatening to shoot him with a rifle. Finally the British commander agreed to honor his promise and make a stand at their present location. But it was Tecumseh, the Indian, who suddenly became the leader of the entire army. While Procter issued faint-hearted orders to his British and Canadian units, Tecumseh selected a defensive position where the main highway ran between the Thames River and a wooded swamp. Organizing the field of combat, the Shawnee placed the British in a line across the highway, with the river and swamp protecting the left and right flanks respectively. On the other side of the swamp he divided the Indians into two groups, putting one of them under his own command as an extension of the British line and placing the other in a larger swamp which paralleled the highway, and from which the warriors could sweep the road with flanking fire.

As the British and Indians took their positions Tecumseh hunted up Procter and, in a forgiving mood, tried to reassure him. "Father," he said, "have a big heart! Tell your young men to be firm and all will be well." Then the Indian moved along the British line, inspecting the positions of the men and pausing to raise their spirits with friendly words. "He pressed the hand of each officer as he passed," a British major related after the battle. "[He] made some remark in Shawnee, which was sufficiently understood by the expressive signs accompanying, and then passed away forever from our view."

At four in the afternoon the Americans appeared down the road. Harrison's force of 3500 troops included 1500 mounted Kentuckians under Colonel Richard Johnson, and two infantry divisions. Against him were 700 British troops and slightly more than 1000 Indians. Harrison had scouted the English positions, and decided to attack with his cavalrymen, sending the infantry after them in close support. As a bugle sounded the charge, Johnson's Kentuckians galloped forward, shouting "Remember the River Raisin." Johnson himself led one battalion against Tecumseh's Indians, and sent the rest of his men toward the British lines which were barring the road. Those horsemen smashed headlong into the English units, and the terrified British gave way at once. Procter, who had been waiting in the rear, jumped in his carriage and fled from the battlefield, abandoning the army and racing for safety in eastern Ontario. His troops, cut to pieces by the Kentuckians and by Harrison's infantrymen, who were now also descending on them, threw up their hands and surrendered in a body.

On the British right flank, meanwhile, Tecumseh's Indians met Johnson's charge with a blaze of musketry that threw the Americans back, and forced the horsemen to dismount and fight from behind trees. At the same time a division of infantry advanced on the run to support the cavalry. They spotted the Indians in the swamp that flanked the road and veered off to attack them. As the Americans pressed into the woods and through the miry underbrush, the battle mounted. Over the din, many men could hear Tecumseh's huge voice, shouting at the Indians to turn back the Americans. "He yelled like a tiger, and urged his braves to the attack," one of the Kentuckians later said. Other men caught glimpses of the Shawnee leader, running among the Indians with a bandage still tied around his injured arm. In the closeness of the combat, the Americans hit him again and again. Blood poured from his mouth and ran down his body but the great warrior staggered desperately among the trees, still crying to his Indians to hold. The dream of an Indian nation was slipping fast, and as twilight came it disappeared entirely. Suddenly the Americans realized that they no longer heard Tecumseh's voice, or saw his reckless figure. As darkness halted the battle the Indians slipped away through the swamp, and the Americans established defensive positions along the road.

In the morning Harrison's men hunted in vain for Tecumseh's body. Somehow, during the night it had vanished, and though several of the Shawnee chieftain's closest followers said later that they had taken it away during the night and buried it secretly, some white men wondered for years whether Tecumseh was still alive. The Americans captured no Indians during the battle, but the struggle on the Thames scattered the warriors and ended further serious resistance in the Northwest. Tecumseh's dream, unrecognized by his enemies, disappeared with his body. No new native leader arose to unite the tribes, and in a few years the advancing tide of civilization completed the demoralization and decay of the proud peoples who had once called the country of the Northwest Territory their home. In time the pitiful survivors, reduced to poverty and sickness, were forcibly dispossessed of what little land remained to them, and were removed to reservations on the west side of the Mississippi River. Many of them, as Tecumseh had foreseen, were moved again and again to make way for new advances of the whites. Today, across the state of Oklahoma, the dispersed descendants of the Shawnee chief's warriors live among other and more numerous tribes, ignored and forgotten by most Americans. To them, however, belongs the pride of knowing that one of their people was the greatest of all the American Indian leaders, a majestic human who might have given all the Indians a nation of their own.

VI

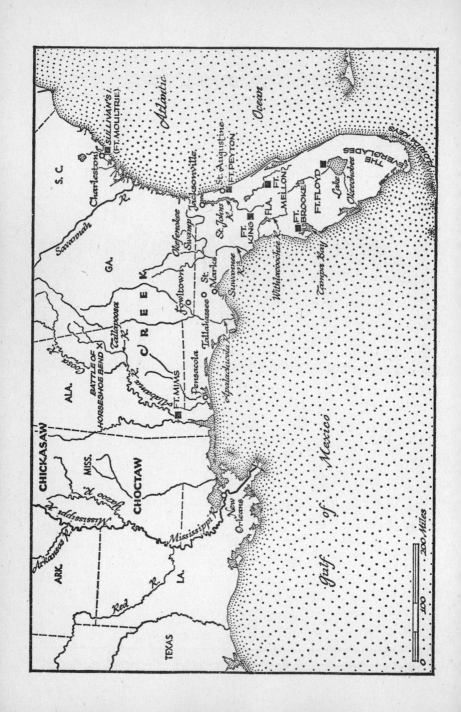

VI

THE DEATH OF OSCEOLA

ON JANUARY 30, 1838, a proud young Florida Indian named Osceola died in a prison fortress on Sullivan's Island in Charleston, South Carolina. Only a few months before, a tired and frustrated United States general, whom Osceola had outwitted in war, had treacherously used a white flag of truce to seize him, and the Indian's "broken-hearted death in chains," after a heroic defense of his homeland, dismayed the American people and focused their attention on the desperate struggle he had been waging against the government in Florida.

From its beginning there had been little about the conflict to furnish Americans with pride. Known to history as the Second Seminole War, it was fought in malarial jungles and swamps, and was marked by deceit and subterfuge on the part of white military and political leaders who were striving to oust the Indians from the Florida peninsula, and by the patriotism of natives who were determined to die for their right to stay. As a war it was, in the words of its fiercest advocate, Andrew Jackson, "disgraceful . . . to the American character," a long and inconclusive succession of debacles and humiliations that lasted for almost eight years, took the lives of more than two thousand officers and men and, failing even to achieve its original purpose, cost the nation between forty and sixty million dollars.

To Jackson and those who prosecuted the war, it had started

as another "Indian outbreak," with Osceola its principal culprit. An obscure and low-ranked Florida warrior, he had seemed to emerge suddenly from the mysterious wilds of the peninsula to disrupt harmonious negotiations with the Seminoles, and to arouse them to an unreasoned defiance of governmental authority. But with his capture and death, such thinking changed. As he and other natives fought back against large American armies, and laid down their lives uncomplainingly rather than surrender, the country at length came to recognize him as the patriot leader of a grievously wronged people. Before the conflict ended, the dead Osceola had become a noble hero in the United States, celebrated even by his former enemies, and memorialized in the names of new American towns and in the works of popular poets and authors.

Osceola's struggle, a by-product of United States expansion after the War of 1812, resulted from an aggressive government policy that was designed to solve quickly the problem of extinguishing Indian title to all land east of the Mississippi River. Years before, the humanitarian Thomas Jefferson had tried to set a moral tone for the conduct of government relations with the natives. "It may be regarded as certain," he wrote in 1786, "that not a foot of land will ever be taken from the Indians without their consent. The sacredness of their rights is felt by all thinking persons in America as much as in Europe." The new Republic's westward expansion had made a mockery of those sentiments, but until the War of 1812 the government had forced the Indians to sign treaties that had at least stamped a semblance of legality, if not of morality, on cessions of tribal homelands. After 1815, when the westward drive began again, few persons paid heed even to the outward forms of legality. The most flagrant violations of Jefferson's ideals were visited upon the natives east of the Mississippi, and particularly on the great Indian confederacies of the South that possessed territory coveted by the people of the Carolinas and Georgia.

As settlers invaded the Indian country of the deep South,

Cherokees, Creeks, Chickasaws, Choctaws, and Seminoles felt the pressure of the newcomers, and when the natives threatened to halt the inroads of the whites, the federal government, led by slave-owning expansionists, provided a solution that ignored the least acknowledgment of "sacred rights." Despite existing treaties, the individual tribes of the South were simply ordered to get out before troops drove them out. Under the Removal Bill, which President Jackson signed into law on May 28, 1830, the southern Indians were offered the privilege of exchanging their ancestral homelands in the Carolinas, Georgia, Florida, Alabama, and Mississippi for territory west of the Mississippi River in the country of present-day Oklahoma, but they were given no alternative other than death to escape the enforced exile.

The infamous policy, removing the Indians to a remote land among wild and strange prairie tribes, desolated tens of thousands of natives, many of whom had white blood, were wholly or partly civilized, and owned homes, farms, livestock, and even slaves, like their white neighbors. It divided the tribes into factions of those who realized they must remove peaceably and those who were determined to resist, turned anguished Indians against one another, and forced some to murderous acts of opposition and others to vain appeals to the law courts and public conscience. A Cherokee Memorial of the times, addressed to Congress and believed to have been drafted for the Indians by John Howard Payne, the author of "Home, Sweet Home," spoke desperately for all the tribes. "We are denationalized!" it cried. "We are deprived of membership in the human family! We have neither land nor home nor resting place that can be called our own. . . . Our cause is your own. It is the cause of liberty and of justice. It is based upon your own principles, which we have learned from yourselves; for we have gloried to count your Washington and your Jefferson our great teachers."

Such appeals failed to move the government, and as the Indians' hopes withered, and troops appeared in their villages to force them on their way, mournful streams of exiles commenced to move westward, swelling in numbers each year. In the winter of 1838 the biggest group, more than fifteen thousand Cherokees who had learned to live like white men and, with the guidance of one of their own educated leaders, Sequoyah, had developed their own written language, trekked sadly along a twelve-hundred-mile "Trail of Tears." Hundreds of people, pushed ahead by the soldiers, died of cold and hunger on the route, but in December President Van Buren announced unfeelingly to Congress that "the measures [for Cherokee removal] authorized by Congress at its last session have had the happiest effects. . . . The Cherokees have emigrated without any apparent reluctance."

Troops and settlers kept the bands of natives moving west, and gradually most of the southeast was cleared of Indians. Only in Florida did the government's plans go awry. There the Seminoles, hounded and bullied like other tribes, had come under the influence of a group of courageous warriors who aroused the natives to armed defense of their country. One of the bravest of them was Osceola, a modest leader of a hunting band, who resisted the removal of his people and at last struck the blow that started the war.

To white men who met him during times of truce or after his capture, Osceola was a strangely mild and unwarlike Indian with a sensitive, almost effeminate, expression. He had noticeably small hands and feet and a round-shouldered posture that made him seem below average height. Despite his frail appearance he had strong emotions and was capable of quick and determined action, and among the natives he was noted as a fearless hunter and warrior and a skillful player of the rugged Indian ball game, the forerunner of the modern-day lacrosse. Actually he was neither a Seminole nor a chief.

He was born about the year 1804 in a village near the Tallapoosa River in Alabama. His people, called Tallassees, were members of the Creek nation of Indians, but there is little known with certainty concerning his immediate family. White and half-breed traders lived in many of the Creek settlements, and Osceola's mother, a pretty Creek woman named Polly Copinger, might have been the daughter of a Creek Indian and a trader named Copinger, while his father is believed to have been a half-breed Scottish-Creek trader named William Powell. Nevertheless, although he had a lighter complexion and less coarse hair than most full-bloods, and though throughout much of his life he was known to white men as Billy Powell, the son of the trader, Osceola in later years insisted that he was a full-blooded Indian.

The Creeks, among whom he spent his boyhood, had been named by early English explorers for the many streams in their wooded lands, and at the time of Osceola's birth they were a large and aggressive confederation of southeastern peoples who lived in a multitude of towns in Alabama and Georgia. From the earliest days of colonial settlement, the Creeks had been involved in affairs in Florida. Originally that more southerly territory had been occupied by a number of fierce and primitive tribes. After the Spanish invasion of the peninsula the whites had subdued and Christianized those peoples, and had built missions for them around the new Spanish towns of St. Marks and St. Augustine. The Florida tribes had learned the arts of civilization and had prospered for a while, but early in the eighteenth century disaster had struck them. Englishmen from the newly settled Carolina coast farther north, aided by powerful armies of Creek allies, invaded the Spanish province, and during several years of savage raiding through the countryside seized thousands of Florida Indians as slaves, and annihilated or dispersed the rest.

By the middle of the century the original tribes of Florida were almost extinct. Some of the Creek raiders found the emptied land warm and inviting, and around 1750 a group of Creeks from Georgia established a new home for themselves in northern Florida. More Creek bands followed them, and as they spread over the land and absorbed remnants of the original Florida inhabitants, together with escaped Negro slaves and assorted stragglers from other southern tribes, they came to be regarded as a new and different Indian people, whom the Creeks in the north called Isty-Semole, which meant wild men, and referred to the fact that they were essentially hunters, "attending but little to agriculture." Later, as they settled down in villages of their own, their name was corrupted to Seminole, and meant simply that they were separatists or runaways from the Creek nation. Their history and that of the Creeks whom they had left continued to be intertwined, but at the time of Osceola's birth they were two different tribes.

In the years before the American Revolution the Creek nation reached the height of its power. The huge inland confederation, still untroubled by white demands for its territory, could muster six thousand warriors from a hundred towns. With the end of the Revolution the tribe's fortunes turned drastically, and the people were forced on the defensive. Land speculators and settlers edged into the Creek country, and repeatedly persuaded the natives to cede strips of their homeland. As the two races came together the angry history of other borders was repeated. In the increasing tension and conflict, white murders of Indians became frequent, and the natives retaliated by raiding the more exposed settlements, killing the inhabitants and carrying off slaves and livestock.

Osceola's earliest years were spent among Indians whose resentments were rising rapidly. On the eve of the War of 1812, Tecumseh visited the Creeks, and Osceola's Tallassees in Alabama listened with favor as the Shawnee visitor from Indiana called on the southern natives to join in a general war against the Americans. British agents also circulated among the Creek towns, and when war finally came the Tallassees were among the Upper Creek "Red Stick" bands who decided to break with the temporizing "White Stick" elements of the nation and enlist in the fight. Osceola was too young to accompany the warriors, but in 1813 he watched the braves of his village leave for battle. On August 30, while the Tallassees helped with diversionary attacks elsewhere, other Upper Creeks overwhelmed the American Fort

Mims near the Alabama River in southern Alabama, savagely massacring 367 people within the stockade. The Indians' excesses brought swift retaliation. Federal troops and militia, aided by large bodies of Indians who had not joined the war, marched against the hostiles from all directions. The hardest blow was struck by General Andrew Jackson, whose army of several thousand Tennessee militia and friendly Cherokee warriors almost wiped out a large force of some thousand Upper Creeks at Horseshoe Bend on March 27, 1814. Other American units sliced through the Upper Creek country, burning the towns and bringing terror to the natives, and one band of Georgia militia attacked the Tallassees' village and scattered Osceola's people into the wilderness.

A few months after Horseshoe Bend, Jackson gathered the friendly "White Stick" Creeks, and as punishment for the hostility of their relatives, forced them to sign a treaty ceding almost eight million acres, or approximately two-thirds of the territory of the entire Creek nation, to the United States. The "Red Sticks," who were dispersed and in hiding, no longer had the power to object to the catastrophic terms of the surrender. In resignation, some thousand of them gradually abandoned their homeland and headed south into Florida, which still belonged to Spain. With them went the Tallassee Indians, including Polly Copinger and her ten-year-old son, Osceola, who still at this time was known as Billy Powell.

Wandering in small bands, the refugee Creeks searched for new places in which to settle. Billy and his mother joined a group of exiles led by a venerable war chief named Peter McQueen, who was Osceola's granduncle. Little is known about Osceola during these years, but McQueen, who still nursed bitter feelings against the Americans, moved the people across west Florida to the protection of a fort which the British had established on the Apalachicola River, despite the fact that it was in Spanish territory. For a while the Creeks hoped for British support in reconquering their homeland, but with the signing of peace between the United States and Great Britain in 1815 the

English abandoned the fort and sailed away, and the refugees continued their wandering. McQueen's people, with the young Billy Powell still in tow, moved eastward toward the head of the Florida peninsula and at last settled among a bitterly anti-American group of Seminoles.

Since they had established their original villages in Florida the Seminoles had made few changes from the ways in which they had lived when they had been Creeks in the north, and the newcomers fitted in easily among them. Living in towns much like the ones that McQueen's people had abandoned in Alabama, they built their houses around central squares, which were used for ceremonies and festivities. In the milder climate of Florida, some of their dwellings were little more than open platforms, elevated above the marshy ground atop log pillars, and covered with thatched roofs. Others were more substantial frame-and-log structures. When more than one clan of people occupied the same town they elected a joint chief called a *mico*, who was advised by a town council of wise men and elders. The council also had the duty of appointing a town war leader, who added to his name the word *tustenuggee*, or "great warrior." He led his people in battle, but did not have the stature or authority in peacetime that was reserved for the mico.

Though they were frequently engaged in warfare, the Seminoles, like the Creeks, were essentially a sedentary people. Most families had private gardens, cleared from the palmetto and underbrush, in which they raised corn, beans, melons, tobacco, and other crops. The luxuriant waters and forests of Florida provided them bountifully with fish and game, including bear, deer, turkeys, and wildfowl, and many of the people owned horses and cattle which they had traded or stolen from white men who lived near the Spanish settlements. From the earliest days, visitors found them living in plenty and often feasting on such native dishes as bear ribs, root jelly, corn cakes, and hominy.

Scattered among the Seminoles, and already a source of constant conflict between the Indians and the Americans north of the Florida line, was a large Negro population, including both slaves and freemen. Many of the Negroes had been legally purchased by the Indians from white owners, and had been taken to live in Seminole villages, where they were treated as dependents rather than slaves. The Indians often took their advice and often intermarried with them, and the children of such marriages were considered free. Some Negroes rose to high advisory positions among the bands, and others established their own mixed or all-Negro villages and became part of the Seminole nation. In addition, through the years, a stream of runaway slaves had entered the country from the north, and seeking sanctuary had settled among the Indian and free Negro villages. In time their white masters had begun to send armed posses across the international border after them, and by the time McQueen's band arrived, large numbers of American slave-catchers were roaming the country, clashing with Indians as well as with free and escaped Negroes, and accusing the Seminoles of harboring and protecting their property.

As the bitterness increased, McQueen's Creeks, still hating the Americans, allied themselves to their new neighbors and helped to stir the border into turmoil. Murders and skirmishing aroused the people of Georgia, and in 1817 General Edmund P. Gaines, commanding American troops on the Florida frontier, sent 250 men across the line to arrest a Seminole chief who had been charged with harboring escaped slaves. In a brief skirmish at the chief's village, which was named Fowltown, five Indians were killed. The rest escaped, and the Americans burned the settlement. The action began the First Seminole War. News of the attack spread throughout the southeast and crystallized the sentiment of the slave-owning population, which had long believed that the United States should seize Florida from a helpless Spain and end the Seminole slave sanctuary by bringing the Indians under control. The United States Indian agent to the Creeks told a Senate investigating committee, "Truth compels me to say, that before the attack on Fowltown, aggressions . . . were as

frequent on the part of the whites as on the part of the Indians."
But Andrew Jackson, back in Tennessee and itching to teach
the Seminoles the same lesson he had taught the Creeks, wrote
to President James Monroe to "let it be signified to me through
any channel that the possession of the Floridas would be desirable to the United States, and in sixty days it will be accomplished." Late in November 1817 some Seminoles retaliated for
the attack on Fowltown by assaulting a party of American soldiers on the Apalachicola River, and two weeks later the United
States government ordered Jackson and General Gaines "to
march across the Florida line" if the Indians refused to make
reparations. The order unleashed the war, and in March 1818
Jackson invaded the Spanish territory with more than two thousand Tennessee and Georgia militia and federal troops.

Jackson's force marched directly through the hostile country,
and again McQueen's Creeks found themselves in desperate battle with Americans. Once more, pro-white Lower Creeks, who
had fought against their own people during the War of 1812,
were with Jackson's army, and on April 12 a group of them
helped a unit of militia to surprise McQueen's band in temporary encampment. McQueen and many of his people escaped,
but the Americans killed 37 Indians and captured 103 others. Osceola was then about fourteen years old, and was later described
by the American militia leader as having been "a lad" among the
captives. An old woman, believed to have been the youth's
grandmother, shortly afterward prevailed upon Jackson to set
the Indian women and children free upon her promise to try to
get McQueen to surrender. Nothing came of her promise, but
Osceola and his mother were freed and began another period of
wandering. They settled first among some other refugees near
the Okefenokee Swamp in northeastern Florida, and later traveled south to the vicinity of Tampa Bay, where they found Peter
McQueen and the survivors of his band established in a new village. Soon afterward they all moved to Peas Creek and built another settlement, where McQueen finally died.

In the meantime Jackson had completed a whirlwind campaign farther north, dispersing troublesome Seminoles, burning their villages, and capturing the cities of St. Marks and Pensacola from the Spaniards, whom he blamed for having failed to exercise authority over the Indians. By the end of the year the war was over, and on February 22, 1819, the humiliated Spaniards ceded Florida to the United States. With Jackson as the territory's first American governor, the new administration turned its attention to the Seminoles, who were now accused of being not only the protectors of runaway slaves but a savage barrier to the peaceful occupation and development of Florida by American citizens. At first many leaders of public opinion, responding to the pressure of slave-owners, demanded that the government root out all the Indians from the new territory and send them somewhere to the trans-Mississippi west, which Army explorers were describing as "a great American desert," of no value to United States farmers and homebuilders. But the Seminoles, whose total numbers were estimated to be more than four thousand, were scattered in widely separated villages, or were wandering "over the whole face of Florida," much of it a wilderness that was still unexplored and teeming with fearsome reptile life, and it was deemed impractical to round them up at that time.

Instead, a group of commissioners gathered all the village chiefs they could find, and at Camp Moultrie in 1823 induced them to sign a treaty which designated as a reservation for all Florida Indians a restricted, inland area in the central part of the peninsula. The reservation was given boundaries fifteen miles inland from the Gulf Coast and at least twenty miles from the Atlantic coast, and the natives were promised annuities, rations, farm implements, livestock, and money for schools and other benefits of civilization as soon as they were all concentrated on the reserve.

The treaty was considered a workable compromise. All land outside the reservation would be opened to white settlement, and the Indians within the reserve would be supervised by a government agent and a police force that would end their protection of escaped slaves. Several years afterward Washington officials questioned the methods by which the commissioners had secured the chiefs' agreement to the treaty, suggesting that coercion and bribery had been used on the Indians. But for the moment, the Seminole will to resist had weakened, and in 1824, under the prodding of the principal chiefs of the nation and of troops and government agents on the peninsula, various bands began to move into the area designated as their new homeland, where, the white officials assured them, the government would protect them forever "against all persons whatsoever."

In the intervening years Osceola had grown to manhood, displaying abilities as a hunter and warrior, and rising to leadership of a small band of Tallassees who came to acknowledge him as their military captain, or tustenuggee. At the same time he had received the Indian name by which he is known to history, and which must have been conferred upon him after he had reached maturity. It was pronounced Asi-Yaholo, and meant "black drink singer," referring to the serving attendant who sang a long, drawn-out cry that accompanied the quaffing of a concoction known as the Black Drink. Among the Muskhogean-speaking peoples of the South, the Black Drink was both an important power, or "medicine," for spiritual purification and a part of the villages' annual thanksgiving "busk" ceremony of green-corn time. The black liquid, made by boiling the roasted leaves of the cassina shrub, and stirring the brew into a froth, acted as a strong purgative, and when taken in large quantities also affected the natives' imaginations making them feel exhilarated and powerful. Village leaders often took the Black Drink before councils to prepare their minds for debate, while warriors used the concoction to cleanse and strengthen their bodies for battle. At such times the drinkers would take long draughts and then force themselves to throw up the liquid, spouting it in streams six to eight feet through the air. Sometimes many drinkers were on their feet at once, spouting simultaneously in every direction, and judging by his name Osceola must have been an important participant in such ceremonies.

Sometime about 1825 he left the Peas Creek town in which he had been living, and at the head of his little group of Tallassee warriors entered the new reservation, settling down as a subordinate tustenuggee. All the Tallassees had come to recognize the leadership of the top Seminole chief, a fat, sluggish man named Micanopy, about forty years old, whose alternating concern for his people and dread of American troops made him waver between enmity and friendship for the whites. At the time of the establishment of the reservation, Micanopy counseled cooperation with the authorities, and after the arrival of Osceola the Seminole chief used him and other young tustenuggees to help police unruly natives and assist the government agent to return trouble-making Indians who had strayed from the reservation.

The peace and control envisioned by the commissioners who had planned the reserve failed to develop. Most of the newly settled Indians had no time in which to establish gardens before winter set in, and many of them in desperation wandered off the reservation and stole supplies from white men. Late in 1825 an Army lieutenant reported that "the major part of the [Seminole] nation are, and have been, suffering for some time in extreme want. Some have died from *starvation*, and many have lived upon the roots of the sweetbriar. . . ." In the following spring it also became clear to the agents that much of the land on which they were penning the Indians was so poor that the natives would have a hard time growing enough food to supply their needs. In February of that year the governor of Florida toured the reserve and sent a horrified report to Washington of land "entirely too wet for cultivation . . . poor, unhealthy . . . wholly unfit . . . sandy . . . under water . . ." The best of the Indian lands, he wrote, "are worth but little; nineteen-twentieths of their whole country within the present boundary is by far the poorest and most miserable region I ever beheld."

Despite these sentiments, the governor was quick to threaten

Indians who left the reserve in forays for food. At the same time he increased the natives' woes by encouraging southern slave-hunters to invade the Indian villages in search of runaways. When the natives insisted that some of the claimed Negroes were their own legitimately purchased property, or even men born to freedom, the governor withheld much-needed rations and annuities from the Indians and warned them angrily that "mighty evils will soon fall on the whole of your nation." As resentments ran through the reservation, quarrels and conflicts again broke out. In time, invading gangs of white men began shooting at the natives; the latter struck back with armed raids and murders of their own, and by the end of the decade relations between the Indians and the whites were again in turmoil.

The agitation for Seminole removal to the west now rose with renewed urgency. Many southern settlers had moved into northern Florida and had established thriving towns close to the Indian reservation. The nearness of the hostile natives, and the shelter that the Seminole villages continued to provide to runaway slaves, were a double menace that frightened and outraged the newcomers, and in Washington their representatives added their voices to those of other Southerners who were demanding the riddance of Indians from the entire Southeast. With the passage of the Removal Bill in 1830 President Jackson's administration received the necessary weapon with which to help the southern settlers, and in 1832, Jackson's Secretary of War, Lewis Cass, was ready to proceed against the Seminoles.

In the spring of that year Cass's agent, Colonel James Gadsden, a young Tallahassee surveyor, met in council at Payne's Landing with delegates from a number of the more friendly and accessible Seminole villages. It is believed that Osceola, who was now in his late twenties, and was still engaged in occasional police work on the reservation for Micanopy and the government agency, was present at the council with a band of some thirty or forty warriors. He was not yet consequential enough among his people to speak for the Indians, and the evidence of his presence suggests that he was there merely as a native policeman to help keep order and to provide protection, if necessary, for the white negotiators.

Though the proceedings of the council were peaceful, its conclusion has ever since been a matter of controversy. In some manner Gadsden induced a few of the chiefs to make their marks to a treaty that committed all the Indians of Florida to peaceful removal. The document they signed was a crafty one. It began with an ambiguously worded preamble, later criticized as being deliberately deceitful, that stated that six of the chiefs, accompanied by two interpreters, including a wily Negro adviser to the Indians named Abraham, would visit the country west of the Mississippi River to which the government was removing the Creek nation, and that if "they" were satisfied with the new Creek land and with the willingness of the Creeks to reunite with the Seminoles, the rest of the articles in the treaty would be binding "on the respective parties." The paragraphs that followed detailed the terms of emigration, promising that after the Indians had emigrated to the Creek lands, the United States would pay them $15,400 for their real improvements in Florida as well as other considerations, and ended with the provision that the Indians would remove "within three years after the ratification of this agreement," certain bands to go west in 1833 and others in 1834 and 1835.

Gadsden also agreed in the treaty to pay the interpreter Abraham $200, and in the light of future events the reason for that payment, a large one by Indian standards, came to be questioned. According to contemporary partisans who were sympathetically attracted to the Indians' cause, Gadsden had known that the chiefs would not have permitted the members of the western delegation to decide alone whether the whole nation would emigrate, nor would they willingly have agreed to all the treaty's other terms, particularly those that called for reunification with their enemies, the powerful Creeks of Georgia, who had aided the Americans against them in two wars, and whose greater numbers would inevitably reduce the Seminoles to an inferior status in the west. Gadsden, it was charged, had offered to pay Abraham the $200 if he got the chiefs to ratify those terms, and to collect his fee the Negro had willingly misinterpreted the document's wording to the Seminoles. Though Gadsden angrily denied the accusation, the chiefs who signed the treaty at Payne's Landing later called it a fraudulent one, and insisted that they understood that the word "they" in the preamble referred to all the chiefs of the nation, not to the members of the delegation that went west to inspect the land.

That group traveled by boat to New Orleans, and up the Mississippi and Arkansas Rivers to Fort Gibson in present-day Oklahoma, where they spent five weeks exploring the part of the new Creek domain that was being offered to them On March 28, 1833, at Fort Gibson, they reluctantly signed crosses to a paper that said that the land was satisfactory to them. The new agreement also included the text of the Payne's Landing treaty, with one important change. In the disputed preamble the government agents now substituted "this delegation" for the word "they."

In Florida the government's interpretation of the delegation's authority stunned the Indians. A few of the villages, including those presided over by two brothers who had been members of the exploring expedition in the West, felt they had suffered enough trials in Florida and were not opposed to moving. Most of the rest of the Seminole towns, including the village of Tallassees in which Osceola lived, accused the government of duplicity, and tried furiously to arouse the entire nation to opposition to removal. Osceola, who was happily settled with two wives, who were reputedly sisters, and had at least two children from these unions, reacted to the government's "forked tongue" with bitterness and hurt. Almost overnight he became an enemy of the Americans and a leader of warriors who were dedicated to resistance.

By the terms of the agreements, Osceola's group was to have been removed in 1833, and in the confusion and expectation of having to flee from their villages few of the people planted gardens that year. But the government failed to ratify the treaty until April 1834, and then it specified that removal would not even begin until 1835. In itself this tardiness violated the time limits written into the treaty and should have made it void. But again in 1834 the worried Indians failed to plant crops; as food supplies dwindled many persons suffered, and once more desperation and resentments sent them on pillaging raids against bordering white settlements. This time neither Micanopy nor the native police helped the reservation agent round up the troublemakers. Osceola and the other tustenuggees were now on the side of their people.

Late in 1834 white men noted for the first time that Osceola was rising to a new position of prestige among the natives. In the crisis of the Seminoles, his bold leadership and uncompromising opposition to removal were winning followers among the nation, and the micos and older men were admitting him to their councils. In October, the government Indian agent, a fifty-two-year-old Georgia militia general named Wiley Thompson, who had served six terms in the House of Representatives and had been a forceful voice for native removal, assembled the Seminole leaders at Fort King, a United States post in the northern interior of the peninsula, and told them that they would have to emigrate to the west by the following spring. On this occasion Osceola not only participated in the discussions, but played a key role in their outcome.

After the agent had delivered his ultimatum to the Indians they asked permission to retire to private deliberations of their own. Thompson managed to plant an informer among them and learned that, as soon as they had met, Osceola had addressed them, urging a united opposition to emigration, and calling for resistance to efforts to force them from their homes. One of the chiefs had then objected to Osceola, counseling the Indians to peaceful compliance with the agent's orders, and Thompson's spy led him to believe that the chief's advice had finally won majority support. When the natives again met with the agent, however, the Indians unanimously told Thompson that the original Camp Moultrie Treaty that had established the reservation, where the natives were to have been protected "against all persons whatsoever," was still in force, that it had seven years more to run, and that the Treaty of Payne's Landing had been obtained from them by deception. Even Micanopy, the head chief of the nation and former friend of the Americans, objected to moving, claiming that his mark on the Payne's Landing treaty was a forgery.

In reply, Thompson brushed off Micanopy with the assertion that the chief had as good as agreed to the treaty because he had touched the pen with which it had been signed. Resistance would be useless, because the President "would compel them to go, even in irons, if necessary." Furthermore, there would be no more payments in Florida of the annuities promised them. At that point Osceola, whom Thompson had noticed whispering advice to Micanopy, rose as spokesman for all the chiefs, and told the agent that the Seminoles had given him their decision. He could keep his annuities, but the Indians would not move. When he was finished talking, the chiefs filed from the council. Thompson wrote an angry letter to the Indian Commissioner, calling Osceola to the attention of Washington officialdom for the first time, and characterizing the Tallasee tustenuggee as a "bold and dashing young chief . . . vehemently opposed to removal."

Soon after the first of the year, and after further futile talks, President Jackson personally sent Thompson a talk from the President to be read to the Indians at still another meeting. This time, Thompson managed to get a large number of native leaders together, and on April 23 at Fort King, in the presence of a business-like commander of American troops, General Duncan Clinch, he read them Jackson's letter, which only repeated what he had already told them. A tall, belligerent chief named Jumper, who had been one of the Upper Creek leaders at the Fort Mims massacre in 1813, and whose oratorical abilities had made him one of Micanopy's most valuable lieutenants, tried to reply for the Indians. When the other chiefs showed that they supported Jumper's words of opposition, General Clinch suddenly cut the Indian short and announced that he was there to enforce the removal and he had enough troops to see that it was done. The meeting broke up. The next day, when the sullen chiefs reconvened with Thompson and Clinch, Micanopy was not among them. The Americans were informed that Micanopy would not recognize the terms of the Treaty of Payne's Landing, and that he did not intend to leave Florida.

The Seminole head chief's defiance brought the situation to a crisis. Thompson had prepared a new document, acknowledging the natives' agreement to emigrate peacefully, and he asked the Indians to sign it. Four of them refused to sign. Thompson immediately struck their names from the roll of chiefs and told them that the Americans would no longer recognize them as leaders of their people. A dramatic story, the truth of which has never been established, adds that Osceola was then asked to make his mark, but instead strode angrily to the treaty table, drew his hunting knife, and drove it through the paper, pinning it to the table. He is said to have nodded at the mutilated treaty and exclaimed, "That's your heart, and my work."

Sixteen other chiefs gradually scratched their crosses on the paper and agreed to assemble their people at Tampa Bay for removal on the following January 15. But Thompson still had the problem of the holdouts. On June 3 he reported that "a few days before, Osceola, one of the most bold, daring and intrepid chiefs in the nation . . . more hostile to emigration, and who has thrown more embarrassments in my way than any other, came to my office and insulted me by some insolent remarks." The affair ended abruptly when Thompson called for a guard to put Osceola under arrest. After a desperate struggle, four soldiers managed to pin him down two hundred yards away, and carried him in irons to the fort. Throughout the night, Osceola raged defiantly at his captors, but the next morning he quieted and sent word to the agent that he would sign the agreement.

Thompson would not release him until several of the Seminole chiefs who had promised to emigrate, and whom Osceola had already condemned as traitors to the Indians, interceded for him and promised to be responsible for his good behavior. Then the agent ordered Osceola to return in five days and, in the presence of the pro-removal chiefs, add his mark to the agreement. The demand humiliated Osceola, but five days later he showed up with seventy-nine of his people, and, surrounded by chiefs for whom he had only bitterness and scorn, signed the paper.

Despite Osceola's acquiescence, Thompson's problems were not ended. In August, some of the chiefs returned to Fort King to raise a new objection—their fear of the treatment they would receive at the hands of their enemies, the Creeks, in their new home. They wanted a government agent specially assigned to protect them in the west. The officers listened sympathetically; but a few weeks later the Seminoles were bluntly informed that Washington had denied their request.

It was a stinging blow to them, and in a secret council on the reservation the anxious natives reconsidered their decision to emigrate. Osceola is not known to have been present, but under the influence of angry leaders who had never agreed to removal, most of the sixteen chiefs who had signed Thompson's agreement changed their minds, voted to adopt resistance as the policy of the Seminole nation, and passed a sentence of death on any Indian who disposed of his property or made other preparations for emigration.

Almost at once, ominous signs filled the Indians' country. Sales of arms and ammunition to the natives rose sharply. Five of the chiefs who were still determined to emigrate fled from the reservation with four or five hundred followers and asked for army protection at Fort Brooke at Tampa Bay. Attacks began on plantations, and by November armed bands of Indians were murdering settlers and looting their homes and stores of weapons and provisions. As the violence increased, Thompson began to worry about his plans for the January removal. Late in November he heard that Osceola and twelve companions had executed one of the cooperating chiefs, who had continued to make preparations to emigrate. The natives had passed sentence of death on him and chosen Osceola to carry it out. The Tallassee had lain in ambush for him, and a short distance from the agency headquarters had shot him dead. The action stamped Osceola as one of the moving spirits of the Indian resistance; Thompson reported to the army that the friendly chief had been "murdered by the treachery" of Osceola and that the consequences "resulting from this murder leave no doubt that actual force must be resorted to for the purpose of effecting removal, as it has produced a general defection."

Thompson soon found that even armed force was too late. Most of the Indians who lived near the agency had already fled to remote towns, and when troops now tried to pursue them the natives disappeared even deeper in the watery wilds of the central part of the peninsula. In time Seminole war parties, bent on fierce hit-and-run raids, and often led by Osceola, began to emerge from their hiding places, striking at plantations and ambushing bodies of soldiers. As terror spread across the frontier, settlers pulled back into hastily erected stockades, and the War Department called frantically for Florida militia to assist the federal troops. By the end of December a second Seminole war was under way, and all hope of the early removal of Indians from Florida had vanished.

During the first months of the outbreak the natives killed several hundred white settlers and a number of soldiers. In one skirmish a band of 80 Seminoles, believed to have been led by Osceola, surprised a military wagon train and drove away its military escort. While the Indians were plundering the wagons, another unit of troops arrived on the scene, and after a sharp fight, the Florida warriors killed eight of the soldiers and forced the rest to flee. Two setbacks of even greater magnitude struck the Americans on December 28. On that afternoon Osceola led a group of his men in a daring raid against the agency headquarters on the reservation; striking from hidden positions near the government buildings, they killed the agent, Wiley Thompson, who had caused Osceola's earlier humiliation, and four other white men. On the same day a larger band of almost 300 Indians, led by Micanopy, Jumper, and a tustenuggee named Alligator, ambushed two companies of troops under Major Francis L. Dade, who were marching from Fort Brooke at Tampa Bay to Fort King. The Indians trapped the soldiers on a road running through palmettos, and at the first volley half of Dade's command fell. The survivors tried to rally behind a pine-log barricade, but after a few hours of fighting were overwhelmed. Only 3 soldiers of the original force of 102 men managed to struggle back to Fort Brooke, and all of them eventually died of their wounds. In the lopsided victory, only 3 Indians were killed and 5 wounded.

Immediately after the events of that day Osceola and his men joined the forces of Micanopy, Jumper, and Alligator in a hiding place in the Wahoo Swamp near the Withlacoochee River. Three days later, while they were still celebrating their exploits, they learned from scouts that a large American army was approaching. Led by General Clinch, the new force included almost 300 regulars and about 500 Florida militia. At noon on December 31 General Clinch reached the Withlacoochee and began ferrying his men across the stream. Some 200 regulars had crossed, when they were suddenly attacked from ambush by 250 warriors under Osceola and Alligator. The soldiers dug in, and while the militia watched helplessly from the opposite bank, unable to cross the stream to help Clinch's men, the Indians and whites fired through the brush at each other for more than an hour, during which time the troops caught occasional glimpses of Osceola fiercely directing the natives' action. Finally General Clinch ordered a bayonet charge that drove the Indians out of their positions. Two more charges with steel temporarily scattered them, but as the afternoon waned Clinch directed the regulars to withdraw across the river, and when the Americans had departed the Seminoles filtered back to their original positions. Clinch, who had lost 4 men killed and 59 wounded, marched his battered troops away, leaving the Indians in possession of the area. Alligator later claimed that only 3 natives had been killed in the battle, but among the wounded was Osceola, who had been struck in the arm by a rifle ball.

The massacre of Dade's command had convinced President Jackson that stern measures were necessary to put down the hostiles, and in February 1836 the War Department dispatched Major General Edmund P. Gaines with a force of 980 regulars and Louisiana militia from New Orleans to Tampa Bay. At the same time, Major General Winfield Scott, a hero of the War of 1812, hastened to Florida to assume over-all command of operations. Neither man was able to accomplish anything. Gaines marched his men north and south through the wet and difficult country, looking for Indians, and was finally surrounded and besieged by a strong force of natives in the wilds bordering the Withlacoochee. He erected a log barricade around his position and slipped a messenger through the Indian lines with an appeal for help to General Clinch. Before aid reached him, the Indians asked for a parley, and Gaines' negotiators met under a flag of truce with Osceola, Jumper, and Alligator. The Indian leaders said that their people were tired of fighting, and wanted Gaines to go away and leave them alone. In the middle of the conference, during which Jumper did most of the talking for the natives, Clinch's relief force arrived and attacked the Indians. Thinking they had been tricked, they scattered into the woods and disappeared.

Scott's activities were equally ineffective. He assembled the largest army yet seen in Florida, composed of regulars as well as militia units that had hastened into the territory from Georgia, Alabama, and South Carolina; divided into three columns, they marched toward the Seminoles' hiding places, hoping to trap the hostiles in a giant pincers operation. But the Indians avoided battle and, slipping around the troops, appeared in Scott's rear, striking suddenly at exposed white posts and settlements, and once more spreading panic among the centers of American population. On April 20 a band of Indians attacked Fort Drane, one of Scott's principal supply headquarters in the north, and for a while the massive concentration of Seminole raiders and Negro spies and sympathizers behind the American armies threatened even the important coastal city of St. Augustine.

After two months of floundering, General Scott was transferred to Alabama, where the Creeks were now in angry resistance against their own removal to the west. General Robert Call, who was governor of Florida as well as leader of that territory's militia, succeeded Scott, and throughout the summer of 1836 tried to do better than his predecessors. Thoug he won several sharp skirmishes against the natives, he failed to come to grips with any of their principal bands. Many of the Indians now looked to the leadership of Osceola, who refused to become entangled in a major engagement and time and again moved his people skillfully around Call's flanks, or into thick stands of marshy undergrowth and trees, called hammocks, where the troops could not get at them. The American soldiers also suffered greatly from the heat and disease in the malarial country, and in July, at the height of the campaign, an epidemic of fever swept through the regular troops at Fort Drane, and forced Call to abandon that principal United States post. Osceola immediately moved his people into its buildings, and Call had to send one of his units back to the fort to drive them out again. After an hour's engagement the natives gave up the post, and withdrew into a nearby hammock where they again eluded their pursuers.

By late fall the Florida governor's campaign had ended in failure, and he was relieved by a new regular army commander, General Thomas S. Jesup, a tough forty-eight-year-old Virginian with a distinguished record of citations won in action in the War of 1812 and against the Creeks in Alabama and Georgia. Jesup arrived in Florida eager to add new laurels to his career by succeeding quickly where others had failed. With a formidable army even larger than Scott's, composed of eight thousand regulars and volunteers from all parts of the southeast, he moved into the Indian country on December 12, pausing to erect strongly fortified posts at the site of the Dade massacre and at the crossing of the Withlacoochee River. His main prey was Osceola, who he understood was now the most influential among the Seminole leaders, but as the army proceeded south the Tallassee war chief stayed one jump ahead of him. In several brushes Jesup captured some of Osceola's people, and learned that his quarry was suffering from malaria, which it is believed he had contracted during his brief occupation of Fort Drane. But Jesup could not establish contact with Osceola himself, and finally, in January 1837, he collided, instead, with a large body of Seminoles led by Micanopy, Jumper, and Alligator, and pursued them into a swamp. Through Negro intermediaries he effected an armistice with the group, and two months later, after protracted councils, managed to meet with the three chiefs and get them to sign an agreement to end hostilities and emigrate peacefully.

As head chief of the Seminoles, Micanopy still exercised authority over the entire nation, and word of his capitulation traveled quickly to all the widely scattered bands on the peninsula. The agreement called for the assembling of all the Seminoles by April 10 at Tampa Bay, and as hostilities gradually ceased and warring groups straggled in submissively, Jesup was certain that the war had ended. On May 8 he reported that all the chiefs had declared their readiness to obey Micanopy's order to emigrate, and that even Osceola and the other most belligerent leaders, at the head of hundreds of their people, had at last given up and were congregating at Fort Mellon on Lake Monroe in the eastern part of the peninsula.

Osceola, looking "care-worn . . . gloomy and thin," had come into that post on May 3, accompanied by the leaders of some twenty-five hundred Seminoles who were reported to be camped in the vicinity. The post commander said that many of the Indians were "literally naked" from their months of fighting and hiding, and he gave them permission to trade for necessities with the fort's sutler. Osceola, he wrote to Jesup, slept in his tent with him one night, and assured him that "it will not be more than a week before they are all on the road to Tampa Bay."

The hopes of the army officers were premature. As the Indians rested in their camps around Fort Mellon, Osceola and the other leaders received disquieting news from the natives at Tampa. Slave-catchers from the north had shown up at Fort Brooke, and were circulating arrogantly among Micanopy's people. The slavers were claiming both Indians and Negroes, and Jesup was giving the Seminoles no protection. Moreover, an epidemic of measles had struck the families who were waiting to emigrate, and rumors were widespread that the army intended to execute some of the Indians before removal began. Many natives in the Tampa camps were in a state of panic, and some were already defying Micanopy and slipping back into the wilderness.

About May 9, the alarming reports moved Osceola to change his mind regarding the wisdom of surrendering. At his request he and the other chiefs at Fort Mellon received permission to visit their villages. They promised to return to the post in a few days, and when they failed to reappear, a messenger was sent to find them. The courier returned with assurances from them that they would leave for Tampa on May 20. The Indians started off as promised, but with a new motive. On the night of June 2 Osceola, leading two hundred warriors, emerged from the wilderness at Tampa Bay, surrounded the camps of Micanopy and Jumper, and ordered those two chiefs to leave with them. At first Micanopy objected, arguing that he had given his word to emigrate, and urging the warriors to kill him. But when they ignored his pleas, he reluctantly mounted a horse and rode off with them. Some seven hundred Indians left their camps to follow Osceola back to the swamps that night, and the next morning Jesup learned that the Tallassee war leader had again thwarted emigration. In angry frustration he laid plans for a renewal of the war against the Seminoles, and wrote bitterly to Washington,

"The country can be rid of them only by exterminating them."

Osceola's daring abduction of Micanopy made his name known throughout the nation and aroused new sympathy for the Seminoles among persons in the Northeast who were opposed to the heartlessness of the government's removal policy. But the young Indian leader's brave will to continue resistance only increased the administration's determination to crush him, and the War Department gave Jesup full support to step up the war. The Americans were unwilling to fight another campaign during the summer heat, however, and hostilities did not begin again until September. In the intervening months Osceola established a village near the St. Johns River in the northeastern part of the peninsula, and waited to see what the whites would do. At Tampa, meanwhile, emigration was not completely balked. A number of pro-removal bands had already been shipped to the Creek lands in the west, and during the summer additional groups of disheartened Seminoles were herded aboard vessels bound for New Orleans and the Mississippi and Arkansas Rivers. Most of the natives suffered miserably during the journey, and some died of disease or starvation along the way, but the survivors reached their destination, and set about establishing the beginnings of the present-day Seminole reservation in Oklahoma.

In September 1837 warfare again commenced in Florida. As Jesup moved inland from the western side of the peninsula a Florida plantation owner named Joseph M. Hernandez, who had been commissioned in the United States Army as a Brigadier General, led a force out of St. Augustine along the eastern side of the St. Johns River. Hernandez soon met with spectacular success, surprising several bands of hostile Indians and capturing them almost without bloodshed. Among his prisoners was the brother-in-law of Micanopy, a sixty-year-old chief known to the whites as King Philip, who indicated to the Americans that the natives were growing tired of being hunted, and that other Indians might be willing to surrender.

At Philip's suggestion Hernandez permitted several captives to circulate through the country, and gradually more of the hostiles gave themselves up. On October 18 two of them came in with word that Osceola himself was near Fort Peyton, just south of St. Augustine, and desired to have a conference with Hernandez. General Jesup, who had crossed the peninsula to St. Augustine, responded cautiously. He had had enough of Osceola's wiliness, and was certain that the Indian was planning once more to humiliate him, this time possibly by an attempt to free King Philip. Two days later another messenger brought Hernandez word that Osceola wished to see him, and Jesup finally directed the Florida commander to agree to the meeting, but to take a strong escort with him. At the same time he gave Hernandez a set of questions to ask Osceola, including an order to "Ascertain the objects of the Indians in coming in at this time. Also their expectations," and ordered him to seize the native leader if the replies were unsatisfactory.

On October 21 Hernandez and his staff, followed at some distance by an escort of about two hundred mounted men, proceeded to Osceola's camp. As they neared the Indians' position, they could see a white flag flying. The Tallassee leader, emaciated and unwell, was standing under the flag of truce with several companions, closely surrounded by the rest of his band. As the Americans dismounted, the Indians greeted them with friendly handshakes and motioned them to join the natives in a council ring. A Seminole chief began to speak for the Indians, and announced that they had invited the general to meet with them at the suggestion of King Philip. They considered the council a truce, he said proudly, and not a surrender. When Hernandez impatiently began to press them with the questions that Jesup had given him, they replied that the Indians wished to make peace, but had not agreed to emigration. Hernandez called the chiefs evasive and told them that the Americans had been deceived long enough, and did not want to be deceived again. As the natives suddenly became uneasy, he announced that it would be necessary for the Indians to come with him. One of the chiefs replied, "We will see about it." The next instant, Hernandez gave a signal, and the mounted men, who had been waiting in concealment, swooped into the camp and surrounded the Indians.

Though they were armed and ready to fight, the natives offered no resistance. According to one of the Americans, Osceola became suddenly "quiet and calm, and not the slightest symptom of emotion could be seen in his countenance, or indeed in that of any of his warriors." The natives were quickly disarmed, and soon after General Jesup arrived on the scene the entire Indian party, numbering twelve important chiefs, seventy-one warriors, six women and four Negroes, was marched off to St. Augustine between a double column of troops. Because he was too ill to walk, Osceola was furnished a mount and allowed to ride.

The manner of Osceola's seizure under a white flag resulted in a storm of protest throughout the country. "We disclaim all participation in the 'glory' of this achievement of American generalship," wrote the *Niles National Register* in an editorial typical of many others. "If practised towards a civilized foe, [it] would be characterized as a violation of all that is noble and generous in war." The outpouring of criticism stung Jesup, who maintained that the Indian leader's earlier treachery had forced him to meet guile with guile. He confined Osceola and the other prisoners in Fort Marion near St. Augustine, and at the end of November public opinion swung somewhat back to him when one of the chiefs, known as Wild Cat, accompanied by nineteen other natives, made a dramatic escape from the fort. The break made it abundantly clear that, despite Osceola's detention, the war was far from ended, and that dangerous Seminole leaders were still at large.

During the month of December, Jesup again used guile to capture more of them. At the government's request, a five-member delegation of Cherokee Indians arrived in Florida to intercede with the Seminole holdouts, and with Jesup's agreement they managed to find Micanopy and persuade him and a number of other chiefs to come into Fort Mellon for a discussion of peace terms. Once more the Indians asserted that they were under a flag of truce, but when they were unable to produce Wild Cat and the other leaders who were still in hiding Jesup angrily arrested Micanopy and his companions and sent them under guard to join Osceola in Fort Marion. The Cherokees regarded the action as another piece of treachery, offensive to themselves as well as the Seminoles, but their protests were unheeded, and they left Florida in humiliation.

Wild Cat's escape from Fort Marion had convinced Jesup that the ancient bastion was too insecure to hold his prisoners, and toward the end of December 1837 he shipped all the captives, including Osceola and Micanopy, to Fort Moultrie on Sullivan's Island at Charleston. The Florida natives, whose brave and prolonged resistance had won the admiration even of their enemies, were received with curiosity in South Carolina, and Osceola particularly was regarded as a celebrity. The Indians were given freedom within the enclosure of the fort, and were allowed to receive visitors; on January 6 Osceola and the other chiefs created a sensation when they were taken to the Charleston theater to attend the performance of a play called *Honey-moon*. An editorial in the *Charleston Courier* set the tone for Osceola's public appearance:

In our humble opinion, he has been to the full, as much sinned against as sinning. Treacherous he may have been, but we cannot forget that he was provoked by treachery, and captured by treachery. We are fairly even with him. We now owe him the respect which the brave ever feel toward the brave; which the victorious cannot violate without brutality towards the vanquished. . . . A tear of forgiveness and generous sympathy is much better due to the once terrible, now stricken warrior of the Seminoles.

The good will of his former enemies had little meaning for Osceola. Still in his early thirties, he was now slowly dying. His chronic malaria had lowered his vitality, and in late January, when the famous artist George Catlin came to Fort Moultrie to paint his portrait, the Indian was suffering from what was diagnosed as an acute attack of quinsy or putrid sore throat. Catlin managed to complete a handsome portrait of him, showing him wearing Seminole finery that included a beaded sash, silver gorgets, and a silk shawl turban, decorated with black and white ostrich plumes, but Osceola was so ill that Catlin did not think he would live through the night. The Indian would not allow the post surgeon, Dr. Frederick Weedon, to treat him, possibly because Weedon was a brother-in-law of the Indian agent, Wiley Thompson, whom Osceola had killed. Instead the native leader insisted on the care of one of his fellow prisoners, an Indian doctor, and, though he lingered longer than Catlin expected, his strength ebbed quickly. His end came on January 30, and was described by Doctor Weedon:

About half an hour before he died, he seemed to be sensible that he was dying; and although he could not speak he signified by signs that he wished me to send for the chiefs and for the officers of the post, whom I called in. He made signs to his wives (of whom he had two, and also two fine little children by his side) to go and bring his full dress, which he wore in time of war; which, having been brought in, he rose up in his bed, which was on the floor, and put on his shirt, his leggings and his moccasins—girded on his war belt—his bullet pouch and powder-horn, and laid his knife by the side of him on the floor. He then called for his red paint, and his looking-glass, which was held before him, when he deliberately painted one-half of his face, his neck and throat—his wrists—the backs of his hands, and the handle of his knife, red with vermillion; a custom practiced when the irrevocable oath of war and destruction is taken. His knife he then placed in its sheath, under his belt and he carefully arranged his turban on his head and his three ostrich plumes that he was accustomed to wearing in it. Being thus prepared in full dress, he laid down a few minutes to recover strength sufficient, when he rose up as before, and with most benignant and pleasing smiles, extended his hand to me and to all the officers and chiefs that were around him; and shook hands with us all in dead silence; and also with his wives and little children; he made a signal for them to lower him down upon his bed, which was done, and he then slowly drew from his war-belt his scalping knife, which he firmly grasped in his right hand, laying it across the other on his breast, and a moment later smiled away his last breath, without a struggle or a groan.

Doctor Weedon did not add a final detail. After the Indian's death, he cut off Osceola's head and kept it as a souvenir in his own home, hanging it occasionally on the bedstead where his sons slept whenever he wished to punish them for their misbehavior. Later he sent it to another doctor in New York, who is believed to have lost it in a fire in 1866.

The death of the Tallassee warrior did not end the Seminole War. The determined chief, Wild Cat, who had escaped from Fort Marion, joined forces with Alligator and others and fought on in hammocks and swamps. Gradually a succession of American military leaders, including Zachary Taylor, drove the Indians farther south into the recesses of the Everglades. Many of the people were captured and shipped to Oklahoma, where they joined Micanopy and the other Seminoles who had already been sent into exile. But a handful of survivors persisted, and in August 1842, when the government finally abandoned the long struggle to root them out, more than three hundred Indians still huddled in refuge in the wilds of the southern portion of the peninsula. As the eastern section of the Seminole nation, their descendants are there even today, fiercely proud in the tradition of Osceola and the patriot warriors who would not give up their homeland.

VII

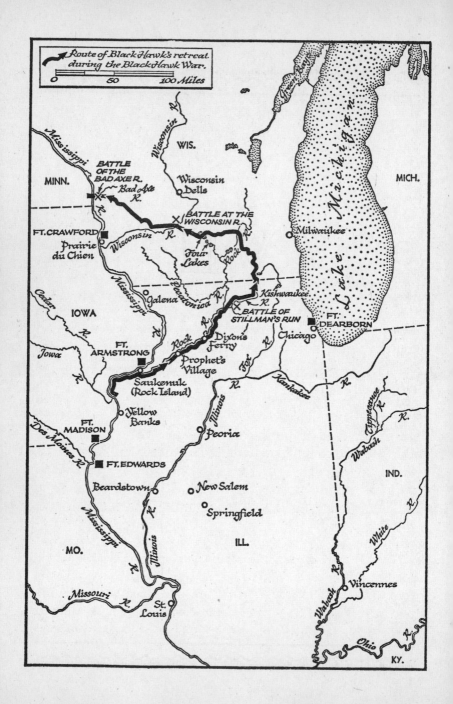

Route of Black Hawk's retreat during the Black Hawk War.

0   50   100 Miles

WIS.

BATTLE OF THE BAD AXE R.

Bad Axe R.

MINN.

Wisconsin Dells

BATTLE AT THE WISCONSIN R.

FT. CRAWFORD

Prairie du Chien

Wisconsin R.

Four Lakes

MICH.

Milwaukee

Lake Michigan

Cedar R.

IOWA

Galena

Pecatonica R.

Kishwaukee R.

BATTLE OF STILLMAN'S RUN

FT. DEARBORN

Iowa R.

FT. ARMSTRONG

Rock R.

Dixon's Ferry

Prophet's Village

Chicago

Saukenuk (Rock Island)

Fox R.

Kankakee R.

Yellow Banks

Illinois R.

Tippecanoe R.

FT. MADISON

Des Moines R.

Peoria

Wabash R.

IND.

FT. EDWARDS

Beardstown

New Salem

Springfield

ILL.

White R.

MO.

Missouri R.

Mississippi R.

Illinois R.

Vincennes

St. Louis

Wabash R.

Ohio R.

KY.

VII

THE RIVALRY OF BLACK HAWK
AND KEOKUK

ONE OF THE most celebrated visitors to the eastern cities of the United States in 1833 was a dour, sixty-six-year-old Sauk Indian warrior from the upper Mississippi Valley named Black Hawk. The year before, American armies had pursued him through the wilds of Illinois and Wisconsin in a short-lived chase which the fearful alarms of frontier settlers and politicians had trumpeted as a major war. Troops and militia had almost annihilated Black Hawk's band of Sauk and Fox Indians, but the proud old warrior had managed to survive with his skin whole, and his captors had sent him east to imprisonment in Fortress Monroe at Old Point Comfort, Virginia. After spending several weeks behind bars he had been released by President Jackson, who had agreed to send him back to his people. But to end any ideas the native leader might still have had of making further trouble, the Chief Executive had approved returning him to the Mississippi by way of some of the large cities in the east, where the Sauk chief could see for himself the power and strength of the American people, who were truly "as many as the leaves on the trees."

Black Hawk's guided sightseeing tour was a personal triumph for him. The headlines of his uprising and capture the year before had made him a notorious figure, and when he appeared in public, a wild and scalping savage from the remote Midwest frontier, the crowds in the sophisticated cities gathered to gape at him. Accompanied by five fellow prisoners, including his two warrior sons, he was escorted from city to city, a hook-nosed, regal-looking patriarch in a red-collared blue coat, with bright baubles on the rims of his ears, a "medicine" skin of a sparrow hawk hanging at his side, and a short tuft on his otherwise cleanly plucked head. His guides showed him railroads, turnpikes, public buildings and government arsenals filled with arms, and wherever he went civic leaders gave him receptions and banquets, and artists came to paint his portrait. At the Norfolk Navy Yard he inspected a seventy-four-gun ship of the line, and in Philadelphia he visited the city prison and went to the theater. In New York he saw a man ascend in a balloon and ventured the opinion that "That man is brave—don't think that he will ever get back." In several cities he vied for attention with President Jackson himself who, somewhat chagrined, found that he had been scheduled to travel the same route at the identical time with the celebrated redskin. Eventually, by way of Buffalo, the Great Lakes, and Detroit, Black Hawk returned to the West, impressed by what he had seen, and filled with gratitude for the warmth with which he had been received. "The tomahawk is buried forever!" he announced to the people of the United States. "We will forget what has past—and may the watchword between the Americans and Sauk and Foxes ever be —Friendship!"

Soon after his arrival home, his glow of satisfaction disappeared. As a war leader, he had fought the Americans and lost, and during his absence in the East the United States had appointed as the new head of the Sauk nation his hated rival, an ambitious younger man named Keokuk, who had led the peace faction of the tribe and had kept many of the Sauk people out of the war. American officials at Fort Armstrong on the Mississippi called Black Hawk into council, broke the news to him, and made him understand that from that time on he was to follow Keokuk's advice "and be governed by his counsel in all things." The solemn-faced war leader was thunderstruck. "The old man rose to speak," reported one of the Americans who was present, "but was so much agitated and embarrassed, that he said but few words, expressive of dissatisfaction, and sat down." Later, indicating his contempt for the younger man whom he had considered a traitor to his people, Black Hawk recalled his feelings of humiliation. "I do not know what object the [American] war chief had in making such a speech," he said, "or whether he intended what he said; but I do know that it was uncalled for, and did not become him. I have addressed many war chiefs, and have listened to their speeches with pleasure—but never had my feelings of pride and honor insulted on any former occasion."

The blow almost destroyed Black Hawk's fighting spirit, but not quite. Shortly afterward he adopted one of the white men's own weapons and asked a government interpreter, Antoine LeClaire, to take down the story of his life. During the months of August and September 1833 he dictated his autobiography to LeClaire, and before the end of the year a young Illinois newspaper editor, John B. Patterson, polished the manuscript and had it published. Though many of the words and phrases were not those of an unlettered native, LeClaire and Patterson both swore that the book was an accurate version of what Black Hawk had related to them, and historical evidence in the reports and writings of other persons have corroborated most of the Indian's account.

It was an interesting document, detailing not only Black Hawk's life but the terrible pressures that had divided the Sauk nation and led it to war. It revealed to white readers the side of the conflict they had not seen, and provided insight into the confusion of a threatened people who, being faced with overwhelming aggression, wavered uncertainly between the decisions of frightened submission and resistance until death. Many Indian tribes, before and after the Black Hawk war, met similar crises and divided into what the aggressors glibly called pro-white and anti-white factions. But few accounts by natives ever related so clearly the contest between a patriot and an appeaser for the loyalty of a tribe. To Black Hawk, fighting a hopeless struggle with an inevitable ending, Keokuk had curried the favor of the white men and had done their bidding for his own advancement and gain. Now he was the head chief of the nation, and it made the old warrior's resentment the greater. "Keokuk has been the cause of my present situation," he cried. The younger man, a persuasive speaker and adroit politician within the tribe, had undermined and betrayed the cause of the fighting Sauk, and it was, Black Hawk complained, "mortifying to my feelings."

The rivalry between the two natives had run like a thread through the events that led to the war, but it had not been its cause. That conflict had stemmed from an earlier act of injustice by white men, and from pressures that had fed the rivalry and provoked Black Hawk into a confused attempt to save the Indians' ancestral village and surrounding cornfields in northwestern Illinois. The United States campaign to smash his defiance had been relatively short and easy, lasting just fifteen weeks and costing the lives of only seventy white persons. But the belligerent spirit of Black Hawk's braves, together with their early victories, had spread alarm through the entire Midwest and had caused thousands of United States troops and volunteers to be rushed to the scene. Among the participants had been many prominent persons who would achieve fame in later years, including Zachary Taylor, Jefferson Davis, Winfield Scott, Albert Sidney Johnston, and Abraham Lincoln, who was captain of a company of Illinois volunteers. Most of them, including Lincoln, saw no combat, but the excitement of the war, the last major conflict with Indians in the Old Northwest Territory, wove a spell of romance about the campaign that lived on in the memories of its veterans.

To Black Hawk, who had brushed aside the temporizing Keokuk in order to fight the war, it had been a defensive struggle, with right and justice on the Indians' side. But time had already passed the natives by, and even so small and pitiful a gesture as the defense of a single village site coveted by white men had been doomed. Ever since the collapse of Tecumseh's great dream of an Indian nation in the War of 1812, no tribe or combination of tribes had been able to stand in the way of white aggrandizement of the Northwest Territory. The opportunity of united native resistance in that part of the continent had vanished, and in the postwar years the helpless, impoverished members of smashed and decaying tribes had watched white settlements spread across Indiana and Illinois "like stains of raccoon grease on a new blanket," as the Indians described it. As the settlers had pushed westward, they had used the policy of Removal to force the tribal survivors across the Mississippi River. Black Hawk's Sauk and Foxes in western Illinois had been among the last of the proud and powerful tribes to feel the pressure, and as the crisis had mounted for them the rivalry between Black Hawk and Keokuk had grown and sharpened.

Black Hawk was about thirteen years the senior of Keokuk. He was born in 1767 in the great village of the Sauk Indians, called Saukenuk, at the junction of the Rock River and the Mississippi, where the city of Rock Island, Illinois, stands today. It was in the center of the country of the Sauk and Fox people, whose busy towns of long, bark-covered lodges and carefully tended gardens of corn, beans, squash, and pumpkins dotted the banks of the Mississippi River from about the mouth of the Wisconsin River in the north to the Des Moines River in the south. The river strip, part of the present-day boundary between Wisconsin and Illinois on the east and Iowa on the west, had long been a principal canoe highway of the fur trade, and the haughty and belligerent Sauk and Foxes were familiar with the French and Spanish traders and officials who paused at their villages and hunting camps on their travels between the Great Lakes and the white settlements on the lower Mississippi.

Though they were treated as a single nation, the Sauk (often spelled as Sac or a variant of it) and the Foxes, both Algonquian-speaking peoples, had originally been separate tribes and had come from different locations. The traditions of the Sauk, a shortening of their own name, Osakiwug, which is believed to have meant "people of the yellow earth," indicated that they had once lived in Canada, perhaps as far east as the St. Lawrence River. The Foxes, whom the French had originally found living on the southern shore of Lake Superior, had had a stormy past. Their own name, Meshkwakihug, meant "red earth people," but the first Frenchmen who saw them had met members of their Fox clan and had fastened that name on the entire tribe. During the Great Lakes wars of the Iroquois and Algonquian peoples in the seventeenth century the Foxes had been forced south to eastern Wisconsin, and when the Sauk had arrived in the same region, driven by the same pressures, the two tribes had formed a confederacy. In the early eighteenth century the Foxes had quarreled with the French and had tried to close their country to the white traders, and after the French had attacked them they had moved in with the neighboring Sauk. Both tribes had given way before the French and, gradually strengthening their alliance, had retreated southwest across Wisconsin and into northern Illinois, claiming the country as their own. Eventually the Foxes had settled around the lower Wisconsin River, and the Sauk had established themselves in villages at the mouth of the Rock River and along the Mississippi.

By the time Black Hawk was born the Sauk and Foxes, still in close alliance, had become strong and prosperous masters of the area. There were perhaps four or five thousand Sauk and sixteen hundred Foxes, all loosely governed in peacetime by venerable civil chiefs and tribal councils composed of the chiefs and adult males. In addition, warriors who proved themselves by valor and expert leadership in battle often gained followings in their villages and, as war chiefs, played influential roles in times of danger. The males of both tribes were divided into large general groups that competed against each other in games and war raids. Neither the Sauk nor Foxes had formal religious beliefs, but understood that the world around them was filled with spirits that could give them help and advice. By fasting and solitary vigils the men would seek the guardianship of a spirit in a dream or vision, and entire villages would frequently appeal to the supernatural by dances and mass ceremonies.

Black Hawk's home village of Saukenuk contained more than a hundred lodges, most of them forty to sixty feet long and occupied by several families. Long sleeping benches, covered with skins and blankets, ran along the insides of the buildings, and flanked a line of cooking fires in the centers of the lodges. The people lived in the villages for only a part of each year. In September, after gathering the harvest, they would leave in canoes or on horses for hunting trips in the wilderness. When cold set in they would establish winter camps wherever they happened to be, and in springtime would move again, hunting, fighting, and trapping. Eventually they would return to the villages in time to plant new crops for the summer.

From the days of their first contacts with the French, the Sauk and Foxes had come to rely on the arms and ironware of the white men, and trapping played a major role in their economy. Once more on friendly terms with the French, whose officials and armies had abandoned their country after the French and Indian War, the two tribes during Black Hawk's youth eagerly hunted beaver, raccoon, and muskrat, and at their villages and hunting camps in the woods welcomed the traders who arrived to exchange guns and manufactured goods for their peltry. British and Spanish traders also competed for their commerce, which in time amounted to more than ten thousand dollars' worth of furs a year, and bands of Sauk and Foxes regularly visited British posts on the Great Lakes as well as the Spanish-governed town of St. Louis on the Mississippi, where officials solicited their trade and loyalty with presents and entertainment.

Early in his life, Black Hawk had taken his name after he had learned in a vision that the sparrow hawk was his guardian spirit. Though he claimed descent from civil chiefs, he was not one himself, and he grew to manhood as a warrior, unprivileged to speak for his people save in matters of war. The principal enemies of the Sauk and Foxes at that time were the Osages, a power-ful Siouan tribe that lived in Missouri, one of the regions where the Sauk went to hunt and perform valorous deeds in battle. At the age of fifteen Black Hawk won distinction by wounding his first enemy, and thereafter, as a brave, he was allowed to paint himself and wear a feather. Soon afterward he joined his father in another raid against the Osages. "It was not long before we met the enemy," he said in his autobiography. "Standing by my father's side, I saw him kill his antagonist, and tear the scalp from his head. Fired with valor and ambition, I rushed furiously upon another, smote him to the earth with my tomahawk—run my lance through his body—took off his scalp, and returned in triumph to my father! He said nothing, but looked pleased. This was the first man I killed!"

In the intertribal savagery of the wilderness he continued to battle and kill, taking the scalps of Osages, Cherokees, and other enemies of the Sauk and Foxes. In one of the conflicts his father was mortally wounded, and Black Hawk took command of the band "and fought desperately, until the enemy commenced re-treating." Thereafter, he recruited war parties of his own and led them in fierce and successful raids that made him one of the Sauk's ablest war chiefs. By the time he was in his thirties he was directing armies of more than five hundred Sauk and Foxes in long campaigns against enemies far from home.

After the American Revolution the two tribes began to meet United States traders and settlers who came down the Ohio River to the Mississippi. Though the land in which Saukenuk and most of their villages lay was now part of the territory of the new re-public, this fact meant little to the Indians, and they continued to give their loyalty and friendship to the Spanish who still ruled in St. Louis and to the numerous British traders who circulated through their country from the Great Lakes. From time to time they heard of American aggressions against the Shawnees and other tribes in Kentucky and Ohio, and both the Spanish and English, who recognized the menace to themselves from the westward-moving Americans, gave the Indians bad accounts of the newcomers. But until 1804 the Americans provided no threat to the natives of the Mississippi River, and the Sauk and Foxes were almost unaware of their presence.

Then suddenly, in that year, they faced calamity. In 1803 the United States had purchased the Louisiana Territory, and in March 1804 a detail of American soldiers reached St. Louis and took formal possession of the region. Shortly afterward a party of Sauk got into a quarrel with American settlers a few miles north of St. Louis and killed three of them. The skirmish frightened other settlers, and rumors spread that the belligerent Sauk were flouting the authority of the new owners of the territory and were trailing American flags from the tails of their warriors' horses as evidence of contempt. The new American commandant in St. Louis demanded that the Sauk surrender the natives who had killed the whites, and at the same time warned his superiors that "The Saucks . . . certainly do not pay that respect to the United States which is entertained by the other Indians."

From his capital at Vincennes, Governor William Henry Harrison of Indiana Territory had already asked Washington to allow him to bring the Sauk and Foxes under some measure of control, as well as define the boundaries of their lands, and on June 27, 1804, Secretary of War Henry Dearborn authorized him to negotiate with the two tribes. "It may not be improper," Dearborn advised Harrison, "to procure from the Sacs, such cessions on both sides of the Illinois, as may entitle them to an annual compensation of five or six hundred dollars."

The suggestion of a land cession from the Sauk coincided with the aims of the Governor, who was already embarked on a policy of extinguishing Indian land claims to the Old Northwest Territory as rapidly as possible. Harrison hurried to St. Louis, and on September 18 had the United States Indian agent in the town send a message to the Sauk and Foxes, summoning their chiefs to a council. The message said nothing about a land cession, and read as follows:

My brothers. The great chief of the seventeen great cities of America, having chosen me to maintain peace and union between all the Red skins and the government of the United States, I have in consequence just received the order from the great Chief of our country, who has just arrived from the post of Vincennes, to send for the chiefs of your villages with some important men, and to bring with them those of you who recently killed his children; I enjoin you to come at once, and if some great reasons prevent you from bringing the murderers with you, this is not to prevent you from obeying the orders which I transmit to you. When you carry them out, you will be treated as chiefs and you will go home after having listened to the word of your Father, and then you can make it understood by your elders and your young people; so open your ears and come at once. You will be treated as friends and allies of the United States.

On receipt of the message the Sauk and Foxes sent a deputation of five chiefs to St. Louis with one of the men who had been involved in the quarrel with the settlers. They directed the members of the mission to surrender the warrior but to follow the established Indian practice of paying goods to "wipe away the tears" of the relatives of the settlers who had been killed, expecting that the Americans, in turn, would then free the man they were surrendering. The deputation did as it was directed, but when its members asked Harrison to release the prisoner, the governor agreed to do so only in return for a cession of Sauk and Fox lands. What transpired during the ensuing negotiations was never fully reported, but evidence that emerged shortly afterward left a disturbing cloud over the entire episode. The governor lavished more than two thousand dollars on the delegation, and a man named Isaac Galland, who knew the natives and was with them in St. Louis, wrote that the money "was spent by them in the grog-shops of St. Louis." The principal Indian, a chief named Quashquame, later told his people that the members of the mission had been drunk most of the time they were in the white man's town. By the time they left St. Louis, at any rate, the Indians had made their marks on a treaty that ceded to the United States all their lands east of the Mississippi, as well as some of their hunting grounds on the west side of the river. Included was all of the present state of Illinois north of the Illinois River, part of Wisconsin, and a section of what is now Missouri. Since settlers were not yet approaching the region, and there was no immediate demand for the tribes' territories, an article in the agreement gave the Indians permission to continue to use the ceded land until the government decided to sell it to white purchasers.

It was one of the cheapest acquisitions of Indian land made by the United States in the Old Northwest Territory, and Galland noted also, regarding the condition of the Indians during the treaty negotiations, that "The writer has no doubt, from his own personal knowledge of Quashquame, that he would have sold to Gov. Harrison, at that time, all the country east of the Rocky Mountains, if it had been required." In return for the cession, the United States paid only $2234.50, the sum that Harrison had already spent on the chiefs in St. Louis, and promised a paltry annuity of $600 for the Sauk nation and $400 for the Foxes, both to be paid in goods. In addition, Harrison applied to President Jefferson for a pardon for the imprisoned warrior, who, it became known, had killed in self-defense, but the native tried to escape from prison before his pardon arrived, and a sentinel killed him with a blast of buckshot in the head.

When the members of the mission returned to their people, they could tell them very little of what had happened. According to Black Hawk they stated that "the American chief told them he wanted land—and they had agreed to give him some on the west side of the Mississippi, and some on the Illinois side. . . . That is all myself or nation knew of the treaty of 1804." It did not overly concern the Indians at the time. The members of their deputation, the natives understood, had made a bargain to free the imprisoned warrior by granting the American chief the right to use some of their hunting grounds. The Indians who had gone to St. Louis had had no authority to do more, and it came as a heavy shock to the people of both tribes the following year to learn that the Americans not only had killed their imprisoned warrior but were now claiming ownership of the heart of the Sauk and Fox homeland, including the site of Saukenuk village itself.

Some hundred and fifty Sauk and Foxes traveled to St. Louis in July 1805 to complain. General James Wilkinson, who had become governor of Upper Louisiana Territory, calmed their fears with promises of more gifts and with assurances that the Americans would not disturb them in their country. Eventually they returned to their villages, but their bitterness toward the Americans did not die. In 1806 a United States Army unit, which visited them from St. Louis, found them in "extreme discontent," murmuring restlessly over the Treaty of 1804, which they blamed on "a few contemptible fellows." British traders, who were still doing business with the Indians, helped keep them aroused, and after 1807 the anti-American preachings of Tecumseh's brother, the Shawnee prophet, and of other more easterly tribesmen who were feeling the pressure of United States settlers, rubbed additional salt in their wounds.

As their hostility continued, the United States determined on a show of force against them, and in September 1808 troops erected Fort Madison on the Mississippi River about fifteen miles above the mouth of the Des Moines River in Sauk country. The action aroused the natives' suspicions, and Black Hawk led a party of warriors to the post to see what the intruders were doing. After a series of councils the Indians became excited and clustered menacingly in front of the gate. "The soldiers, with their arms in their hands, rushed out of their rooms, where they had been concealed," Black Hawk said in his autobiography. "The cannon was hauled in front of the gateway—and a soldier came running with fire in his hand, ready to apply the match. Our braves gave way, and all retired to camp. There was no preconcerted plan to attack the whites at that time—but I am of opinion now, had our party got into the fort, all the whites would have been killed."

More troops arrived to strengthen the fort's garrison, and for a while the Indians left them alone. But the Treaty of 1804 was not forgotten, and relations between the United States and the Sauk and Foxes continued to be marked by distrust and tension. As a leading war chief of the nation, Black Hawk received appeals from Tecumseh to join the confederacy which the Indiana Shawnee was trying to build against the Americans, and, though most of the Sauk and Fox civil chiefs were opposed to becoming enmeshed in a war that might prove disastrous to them, Black Hawk listened to the Shawnee emissaries with enthusiasm, and agreed to join them when Tecumseh gave the signal for an uprising. Meanwhile, the British traders on the upper Mississippi gave him sympathetic counsel, and from time to time he led war and trading bands to the main British posts at Malden and Amherstburg opposite Detroit, where his people were liberally treated with guns and trade goods.

In November 1811 Harrison's victory at Tippecanoe in Indiana smashed the groundwork of Tecumseh's plans for an Indian confederacy. The blow took most of the Northwestern tribes by surprise, but when news of what had happened reached the Sauk country Black Hawk and a small group of angry followers joined a Winnebago war party in another fruitless assault on Fort Madison. The Indians laid siege to the American post for a day and a night, and tried repeatedly to set it on fire with flaming arrows. Each time, the defenders managed to extinguish the blaze. On the second morning Black Hawk "shot in two the cord by which they hoisted their flag, and prevented them from raising it again," but eventually the Indians ran out of ammunition, and "finding that we could not take the fort, returned home."

As the War of 1812 approached, both the British and Americans made determined efforts to win the loyalty of the Northwest tribes. Despite the many difficulties they had experienced with the Sauk and Foxes, United States authorities worked hard to keep them neutral. Early in 1812 American agents escorted a large party of midwestern chiefs, including several Sauk and Foxes, to Washington to meet President James Madison. By the time the Indians reached the capital the war had already begun, and Madison pleaded with them. "I say to you, my children," he entreated, "your father does not ask you to join his warriors. Sit still on your seats and be witnesses that they are able to beat their enemies, and protect their red friends." While he was talking, United States agents in the west were arguing with the chiefs who had stayed home, including Black Hawk. Most of the Sauk and Foxes feared the power of the Americans to destroy their villages, and despite their years of hostility to the United States they took the agents' words soberly.

In the minority among his people, Black Hawk for a while made no move. When he did, he claimed it was because of another act of deception by the Americans. The chiefs returned from Washington, and urged their people to trade thereafter exclusively with the American government factor at Fort Madison. That individual, they reported, had been told by the Great Father in Washington to give the natives their necessities on credit, as the British—and the French before them—had done. It was an important point in the Indians' economy. If they were to sever their relations with the English, as the Americans wished them to do, they would require a substitute market for their furs, but it would have to be one that would continue the traditional system of extending them credit against the returns of their hunts. The chiefs were scarcely home with their advice from Washington before the natives met rebuff. At Fort Madison the government factor informed them bluntly that their leaders had misunderstood what the Great Father had said to them, and that he could not extend them credit. "The news run through our camp like *fire in the prairie*," Black Hawk recalled later. "Our lodges were soon taken down, and all started for Rock Island. Here ended all hopes of our remaining at peace—having been *forced into* WAR *by being* DECEIVED!"

At their home village of Saukenuk, a British trader was waiting for the disillusioned Indians with two boatloads of goods, a keg of rum, a large British flag, and promises of trade on credit. At the urging of the trader, Black Hawk hastily assembled a war party of two hundred Sauk and Foxes who were filled with anti-American feeling, and led them to Green Bay, where they joined Robert Dickson, the chief British agent and trader among the natives of the upper Mississippi country. Dickson appointed Black Hawk the chief of all the Northwest natives who were gathering at Green Bay to help the English, and soon afterward led him and five hundred painted braves to Detroit to join the British troops and their Indian allies under Tecumseh. The Green Bay detachment participated in the defeat of Kentuckian troops at the River Raisin, described earlier. Black Hawk made no mention in his autobiography of his role in the fight, but noted that "the Americans fought well, and drove us with considerable loss! I was surprised at this, as I had been told that the *Americans could not fight!*"

Shortly afterward he and his Sauk and Foxes left Tecumseh's army and, temporarily abandoning the war, returned across country to the Mississippi to take part in the tribe's annual winter hunt. He found his people worried and divided. During his absence both the English and the Americans had continued their pressures on the stay-at-homes, threatening them with ruin if they joined the wrong side. To complicate the situation, the Sauk and Fox homeland lay in a no man's land between the two combatants, and the tribes around them had taken sides and added their own threats to those of the white men. American agents understood their predicament and, seeing the opportunity to win the Sauk and Foxes to neutrality, had invited their hard-pressed villages to move south, away from the British and the pro-British Indians, and accept security within territory that the Americans could defend. A number of the Sauk and Fox bands had responded, and during the early part of 1813 some of their villages had migrated from Illinois and Wisconsin to American-controlled territory on the Des Moines River west of the Mississippi.

The majority of the nation, however, had clung anxiously to their ancestral homes, and Black Hawk and his pro-British war-

riors joined them briefly in a hunt. Early in the spring the British made another appeal to him, and once more he led his band
eastward to engage in the war. Under Tecumseh they cam-
paigned in Indiana and Ohio, and during the summer of 1813
participated in the unsuccessful British sieges of Fort Meigs and
Fort Stephenson. Black Hawk led his warriors in both battles,
but their "success being bad, and having got no plunder," they
became disillusioned with the British leaders and in the fall returned again to Saukenuk.

In his absence, more of the stay-at-homes had crossed the Mississippi to American protection. Black Hawk related what had
occurred.

After I started with my braves and the parties who followed, the
nation was reduced to so small a party of fighting men, that they
would have been unable to defend themselves, if the Americans had
attacked them . . . a council was held, which agreed that Quashquame,
the Lance, and other chiefs, with the old men, women and children,
and such others as chose to accompany them, should descend the
Mississippi and go to St. Louis, and place themselves under the protection of the American chief stationed there. They accordingly
went down to St. Louis, and were received as the friendly band of
our nation—sent up the Missouri, and provided for, whilst their
friends were assisting the British!

The migrating group, according to General William Clark, the
new Governor of Missouri Territory, who was delighted to iso-
late the natives from English influence, was "thought to exceed
1500 souls." He sent them partway up the Missouri River, where
they established new villages and engaged in a winter hunt.

The voluntary removal of so many Sauk and Foxes from the
eastern side of the Mississippi established conditions for increasing American control over those who had accepted United States
protection, and for an eventual division of the nation. But during
Black Hawk's absence the seeds of future dissension had also
been sown among the people who had remained at Saukenuk. On
his return to the village the war leader discovered that the braves
who had stayed in the town had elected a new war chief to lead

them. He was Keokuk, whose name meant "one who moves about alert," a previously-unnoticed member of the tribe, whose mother is believed to have been half-French, and who had been born in Saukenuk about 1780. Already in his early thirties, Keokuk was not known to have possessed any war abilities, and Black Hawk was surprised by the news of his elevation. He asked how Keokuk had become a chief, and the braves told him what had happened.

A short time previously, the village had been frightened by reports that a hostile army of Americans was approaching from the east. The Indians had called a council, and had decided to abandon Saukenuk and move to the west side of the Mississippi River, where the others had already gone. During the council, according to Black Hawk's informants, Keokuk

had been standing at the door of the lodge (not being allowed to enter, having never killed an enemy), where he remained until old Wa-co-me came out. He then told him that he had heard what they had decided upon, and was anxious to be permitted to go in and speak, before the council adjourned! Wa-co-me returned, and asked leave for Keokuk to come in and make a speech. His request was granted. Keokuk entered, and addressed the chiefs. He said, "I have heard with sorrow, that you have determined to leave our village, and cross the Mississippi, merely because you have been told that the Americans were seen coming in this direction! Would you leave our village, desert our homes, and fly, before an enemy approaches? Would you leave all—even the graves of our fathers, to the mercy of an enemy, without *trying to defend them?* Give me charge of your warriors; I'll defend the village, and you may sleep in safety!" The council consented that Keokuk should be a war chief. He marshalled his braves—sent out spies—and advanced with a party himself, on the trail leading to Peoria. They returned without seeing an enemy. The Americans did not come by our village. . . . This is the manner in which, and the cause of, his receiving the appointment.

Black Hawk added that he was "satisfied" with the explanation, but a jealous rivalry had begun that was to grow during the following years and contribute to the distress of the nation.

In 1814 warfare between the British and Americans raged intermittently along the Mississippi past Saukenuk itself, and Black

Hawk and his warriors again aided the English. Early in June, American troops moved boldly up the river into the Sauk and Fox homeland and attempted to build a fort at the old trading town of Prairie du Chien at the mouth of the Wisconsin River. Before the Americans completed the post, a British force drove them away and occupied the site. At the same time Black Hawk's warriors trapped a unit of United States reinforcements trying to get up the river to the fort, and on July 21, in a savage engagement, killed or wounded thirty-four of the Americans, set one of their ships afire, and forced the detachment to flee back down the Mississippi.

Angered by the Indians' interference, the Americans organized a new expedition of four hundred and thirty men under twenty-nine-year-old Major Zachary Taylor, and late in August sent it north to destroy the Sauk villages on the Rock River. News of the punitive force circulated through the Indians' country, and more than one thousand warriors, including Winnebagos, Sioux, and even Sauk and Fox braves from the bands that had recently migrated to American protection on the Missouri, hurried to Saukenuk to help Black Hawk defend the Sauk towns. The British also offered assistance, sending thirty men with a three-pounder gun and two swivels to aid the Sauk leader, and when Taylor's troops hove in sight in eight boats, the combined British and Indian force was waiting for them. Taylor camped for the night on a willow-covered island opposite the mouth of Rock River, and in the pre-dawn darkness Indians swarmed across the stream in canoes and attacked him. The Americans held off the natives until daylight, when the British guns suddenly opened fire on their boats. The accurate shelling splintered the ships and threatened to sink them, and the stunned Taylor ordered a hasty withdrawal. He retreated south all the way to the mouth of the Des Moines River, where he halted and tried to build a post to replace Fort Madison, which had been burned in 1813. Eventually Indian harassments and supply deficiencies forced him to abandon his effort, and in October he returned to St. Louis.

Through all the fighting, Keokuk's activities had been obscure, but Black Hawk had played a leading role and had enlarged his reputation as a formidable enemy of the Americans. His rebuffs to the United States troops had swelled his self-confidence and made him think that, with continued British help, he would soon drive the Americans entirely from the western country and end their threat to the Sauk and Fox lands. The news of the signing of peace between Great Britain and the United States early in 1815 took him by surprise. At the head of some eight hundred warriors he marched on the British at Prairie du Chien and demanded an explanation. The English commander reluctantly read him the terms of the Treaty of Ghent and announced that the British troops would shortly have to retire from the Indians' country. Black Hawk was furious. "I have fought the Big Knives and will continue to fight them till they are off our lands," he announced. "Till then, my father, your red children can not be happy." Turning away from the British, he tried to continue the war by himself, and in May led a bold raiding party of natives against Fort Howard at the mouth of the Cuivre River north of St. Louis. Striking from ambush, the Indians killed four members of the garrison. The rest of the Americans chased the natives from the fort and, after a short pursuit, trapped them in a sinkhole. The two sides fired at each other from cover until nightfall, when Black Hawk managed to get his braves away. The Indians killed eleven soldiers in the sharp fight, and lost at least five of their own number.

The battle ended Black Hawk's hopes of military victory over the Americans. On May 24 the British set fire to their post at Prairie du Chien and evacuated the Mississippi Valley. Soon afterward a number of Fox Indians and the chiefs of the villages that were still on the Missouri River under United States protection met with American officials and, without protest, confirmed their agreement to the Treaty of 1804. In addition, the Sauk and Foxes on the Missouri promised "to remain distinct and separate from the Sacs of Rock River, giving them no aid or assistance whatever

until peace shall also be concluded between the United States
and the said Sacs of Rock River." The defection of the Missouri
villages weakened the position of the Rock River towns, and after
appeals by American agents and a promise of pardons for their
hostility in the War of 1812, a delegation that included both
Black Hawk and Keokuk traveled to St. Louis in May 1816. The
civil chiefs did the talking for the tribe, and in the end reluctantly
made their crosses on a treaty which provided that the Rock
River natives did "unconditionally assent to, recognize, reestab-
lish and confirm" the Treaty of 1804. Black Hawk also agreed to
the document, but might not have understood its significance.
"I touched the goose quill to the treaty," he said later, "not knowing, however, that, by that act, I consented to give away my village. Had that been explained to me, I should have opposed it,
and never would have signed their treaty."

The agreement established an uneasy truce, during which the
natives continued to treat the Americans with resentment and
hostility. As the years passed, the loose, ineffective control over
the unfriendly natives continued to disturb American officials in
Illinois and St. Louis. The Rock River Indians' determination
to retain their homes made them a potential menace behind a
frontier that was moving rapidly westward, and their independent, roving war bands were a constant concern to the settlers.
By 1820 the white newcomers themselves were inadvertently
contributing to the causes of anxiety. As they pushed across
lower Illinois and Missouri they encroached on the natives' hunting grounds, and drove away the game. To avoid starvation, the
Sauk and Foxes turned north and west and invaded the hunting
lands of the Sioux. Their incursions angered those people and
brought on savage, intertribal skirmishing that flared across the
prairie frontier. Inevitably, the Indians embroiled some of the
more isolated settlers in their quarrels, and enraged and frustrated
natives fell on white men and took their scalps.

Governor William Clark, who was also in charge of Indian
affairs at St. Louis, singled out the stubborn Sauk and Foxes of

Rock River as the principal troublemakers, and repeatedly threatened them with war if they refused to halt the outrages. His warnings were wasted, but in 1821 Thomas Forsyth, his agent at Rock Island, managed to establish a sympathetic relationship with Black Hawk's rival, Keokuk. In June of that year Clark demanded that the Sauk and Foxes surrender two of their warriors who had killed a Frenchman the previous year. To his surprise, Forsyth arrived in St. Louis with a deputation of Sauk and Fox leaders, including Keokuk, who brought with them the two murderers. After learning that Keokuk had been responsible for organizing the delegation, Clark met privately with the Indian, and to "enhance the worth and popularity of Keokuk" agreed to acknowledge his importance in the public sessions with the other chiefs. His playing up to Keokuk's vanity had the desired result. The ambitious Sauk, Forsyth told Clark, would undoubtedly be the future head of the nation, and after this visit the Americans could count on him to help bring about better relations "between the Whites and reds."

Keokuk and his companions represented an important breach in the unity of the Rock River natives, and the Americans were happy to encourage their friendship. Before the Indians left St. Louis, Clark showered them with three hundred dollars' worth of presents, including plumes, silk handkerchiefs, and a coat for Keokuk that cost $21.50 alone. Forsyth also purchased gifts for Keokuk's two wives, and shortly after his return to Rock River with the delegation wrote Clark that "if things are well managed in two or three years more his word among the Sauks and foxes will be their law." His hopes were too optimistic, but the Americans' flattery of Keokuk did not escape the notice of other members of the tribe. To the less bold Indians, it indicated that further opposition to the powerful Americans was short-sighted, and even some of the influential leaders saw in his example the promise of presents and favors for themselves. Gradually, with his American patronage, Keokuk's influence increased until he spoke in councils with the authority of a civil chief.

Black Hawk, who was now in his fifties, was not unaware of what was happening. During the next few years, American settlers at last began to build their cabins close to the Sauk and Fox homeland, and United States officials increased their pressure on the Indians to move west of the Mississippi before there was trouble.

Nothing was now talked of but leaving our village [Black Hawk said]. Keokuk had been persuaded to consent to go; and was using all his influence, backed by the war chief at Fort Armstrong, and our agent and trader at Rock Island, to induce others to go with him. He sent the crier through the village to inform our people that it was the wish of our Great Father that we should remove to the west side of the Mississippi—and recommended the Ioway River as a good place for the new village. . . . The party opposed to removing, called upon me for my opinion. I gave it freely—and after questioning Quashquame about the sale of the lands, he assured me that he "never had consented to the sale of our village." I now promised this party to be their leader, and raised the standard of opposition to Keokuk, with a full determination not to leave my village.

Black Hawk also said that he met with Keokuk at this time to see what could be done, and proposed that the Indians offer the Americans another part of their land in return for the right to keep their village sites. Keokuk agreed with him, he claimed, and promised to ask permission to go to Washington to put the matter to the "Great Father." In September 1823 Keokuk applied to Clark to make the trip, and shortly afterward Secretary of War John Calhoun gave his consent. The following June, Keokuk journeyed to Washington, accompanied by one of his wives and nine other Sauk and Fox leaders, but not Black Hawk. The visit did nothing to solve the problem of the villages on the Rock River. Keokuk argued persuasively with the Secretary of War regarding the natives' right to some contested land west of the Mississippi in Missouri, but at length signed away all claim to that area in return for $1000 in cash or merchandise, an additional $500 in annuities to each of the tribes for ten years, and a few other concessions. Then, escorted by Clark, he and the other members of the delegation toured some of the eastern cities. His visits to Baltimore, Philadelphia, and New York pleased Keokuk, and convinced him even more than before of the folly of further opposition to the Americans.

The failure of the trip filled Black Hawk with bitterness. Keokuk returned home, he said, "but his object was to persuade others to follow him to the Ioway. He had accomplished nothing towards making arrangements for us to remain, or to exchange other lands for our village. There was no more friendship existing between us. I looked upon him as a coward, and no brave, to abandon his village to be occupied by strangers."

Black Hawk's enmity did not disturb Keokuk. His ambition was to become the head chief of his nation, and he brushed aside the old warrior's contempt. In the following year, 1825, the Americans called a grand peace council at Prairie du Chien, and Keokuk acted as one of the principal spokesmen for the Sauk and Foxes. Sioux, Chippewas, and other warring tribes of the upper Mississippi country attended the council, and the Americans had them sign treaties of "firm and perpetual peace" among themselves. Black Hawk, who was not present, refused to be bound by the documents, and two years later at the age of sixty roused some of his people for a war against the Sioux. The Americans tried to offer the old man a bribe of seven horses and other presents to drop the campaign, and then sent Keokuk to him with a warning that they would put him in irons and imprison him in St. Louis for the rest of his life if he continued with his scheme. Black Hawk angrily rebuffed Keokuk, but a few weeks later abandoned his plan.

As the Sauk and Foxes divided into camps behind the two leaders, debating whether or not to move, white settlers continued to take up land closer to the Rock River. The proximity of the newcomers at last brought friction. Black Hawk complained that the white men entered Saukenuk with trade whisky, "made our people drunk, and cheated them out of horses, guns and traps." Other whites clashed with Indians on the roads and in the newly cleared fields. "At one time," Black Hawk recounted, "a white man beat one of our women cruelly, for pulling a few suckers of corn out of his field, to suck, when hungry! At another time, one of our young men was beat with clubs by two white men for opening a fence which crossed our road, to take his horse through. His shoulder blade was broken, and his body badly bruised, from which he soon after died!"

The conflicts stirred the resentments of Indians throughout the region, but Keokuk urged them to have patience with the Americans. In 1827 the value of his influence was put to its first test. Winnebagos north of the Sauk and Foxes began to raid nearby settlements, and when the Americans sent troops to the area the Winnebagos called on the Foxes for help. At Clark's suggestion, the American commander appealed directly to Keokuk to do what he could to keep the Sauk and Foxes on the American side. Keokuk scored a notable triumph. Instead of aiding the Winnebagos, large numbers of the tribe acted as spies for the American army, and at the conclusion of the brief campaign, Keokuk was rewarded with a saddle and bridle.

The Winnebago uprising raised a new crisis for Black Hawk's followers. Frightened by the Indian depredations, the governor of Illinois determined that the time had come to insist on the removal of all the Indians to the west side of the Mississippi. On September 4, 1827, he wrote to the Secretary of War, objecting to the natives' continued use of ceded lands and complaining that their presence "has been borne by the people for a few years past with great impatience, and cannot be submitted to much longer." When he failed to receive a satisfactory reply from Washington, he sent an angry letter to Clark in St. Louis, threatening that unless the federal government acted soon "those Indians will be removed, and that very promptly." Clark replied to him with a promise to remove all Indians from Illinois, with the exception of some Kickapoos, by May 25, 1829.

A year ahead of that date, in May 1828, Forsyth met with the

Sauk and Foxes at the Rock River and told them that they would finally have to move by the following spring, whether they wished to or not. Black Hawk and his followers, who had become known as the British Band because of their frequent visits to Malden, still refused to migrate. "We were a divided people," he said, "forming two parties. Keokuk being at the head of one, willing to barter our rights merely for the good opinion of the whites; and cowardly enough to desert our village to them. I was at the head of the other party, and was determined to hold on to my village, although I had been *ordered* to leave it. . . . It was here that I was born—and here lie the bones of many friends and relations. For this spot I felt a sacred reverence, and never could consent to leave it, without being forced therefrom." Nevertheless, "Keokuk," he added, "who has a smooth tongue, and is a great speaker, was busy in persuading my band that I was wrong —and thereby making many of them dissatisfied with me." The meeting with Forsyth broke up, but later in the summer, when the bands rode away for their winter hunts in the north, rumors spread that Keokuk's leadership had finally prevailed and the Indians would never again return to the Rock River.

While the natives were on their hunts, several families of white squatters at last moved into Saukenuk and occupied the Indians' lodges and cornfields. In time the news reached Black Hawk at the hunting grounds, ten days' journey away, and he returned angrily to the village to investigate. To his dismay he found that the settlers had already destroyed some of the Indians' homes, and were building fences and quarreling among themselves over a division of the natives' fields.

I went to my lodge [he said] and saw a family occupying it. I wished to talk with them, but they could not understand me. I then went to Rock Island, and (the agent being absent), told the interpreter what I wanted to say to those people, viz.: "Not to settle on our lands—nor trouble our lodges or fences—that there was plenty of land in the country for them to settle upon—and they must leave our village, as we were coming back to it in the spring." The interpreter wrote me a paper, and I went back to the village, and showed it to the intruders, but could not understand their reply. I expected, however, that they would remove, as I requested them.

In time he returned to the winter camp, and told his people what had happened. The civil chiefs came together to decide what to do, and under the influence of Keokuk agreed to abandon Saukenuk and establish new homes on the Iowa River west of the Mississippi. The decision outraged Black Hawk, and in the spring he assembled a band of loyal followers and led it back to Saukenuk, defying the rest of the nation, who went to the Iowa River. At Saukenuk, Black Hawk found that more whites had come, and that the intruders had enclosed most of the Indians' fields with fences. For a while the situation was explosive. The whites refused to leave; Black Hawk's people finally moved into the lodges that were still empty and tried to plant new gardens. In the tense atmosphere, there were daily conflicts. The settlers refused to put up their cattle at night, and the stock overran the Indians' new cornfields. In retaliation, the natives turned the animals into the settlers' fields. One Indian objected to the plowing of his patch, and the whites beat him with a beanpole. The natives protested repeatedly to Forsyth, but the agent could only remind them of his many warnings to them to leave the area.

Black Hawk finally led his people away for their new hunt; but he threatened to return the following spring. The federal government at last interceded. Clark's May 25th date for removal had passed, and the United States decided that the time had now arrived to take formal possession of the Rock River country. In July 1829 the General Land Office announced that the land around Saukenuk would go on public sale at Springfield, Illinois, in October.

The news that the land had been sold only angered Black Hawk more, and in the spring of 1830 he once again led his followers back to Saukenuk. They stayed for another tense summer, despite the efforts of Forsyth, aided by Keokuk, to get them out, and

Black Hawk told the whites that he would again be back in the spring of 1831.

His warning caused consternation throughout Illinois. There were more than 150,000 whites in the state already. A newly elected governor, John Reynolds, appealed to Washington for action. In St. Louis, Clark was also concerned, and wrote hastily to the Secretary of War for advice on how to proceed. Before a reply reached him spring arrived, and Black Hawk led his British Band of three hundred warriors and their women and children back to Saukenuk.

At first, the Indians seemed anxious to avoid conflict. But they were firm in their determination to reoccupy their lodges and cornfields, and the old clashes soon recurred. The irate Governor Reynolds promptly called out seven hundred members of the militia, to oust the natives from Saukenuk "dead or alive," and informed Clark of what he was doing in the hope that the federal government would remove the Indians peaceably before his militia marched. Clark turned his message over to General Edmund P. Gaines, who was then commander of the Western Department of the army in St. Louis, and Gaines lost no time in leading troops to Rock Island.

As soon as he arrived, the general called Black Hawk, Keokuk, and some of their principal followers to a conference. The old war chief and his men arrived for the meeting in battle regalia, painted for combat and brandishing lances, spears, war clubs, and bows and arrows. "We entered the council house in this warlike appearance," he said, "being desirous to show the [American] war chief that we were not afraid!" Some of the American officers were alarmed, but Gaines was a veteran of the War of 1812 and had already fought under Andrew Jackson against Creeks and Seminoles, and the whooping Sauk did not cow him. Facing Black Hawk sternly, he announced that the government had permitted the natives to remain at Rock River until settlers required the land, but now the whites were claiming it under the terms of the Treaty of 1804, and he and his troops were there to see that the Indians lived up to the agreement they had signed. Black Hawk held his temper, and repeated what he had so often insisted, that he had never sold Saukenuk and would never move from it. His words stung Gaines, who turned to the other Indians and demanded, "Who is Black Hawk? Who is Black Hawk?" Snapping angrily, he told them to stop listening to the old Sauk, and warned them that he had not come to discuss the Treaty of 1804, but to get them to comply with its terms. When some of Black Hawk's followers tried to reply by saying that they were determined to "lay their bones with those of their ancestors" at Saukenuk, he cut them short with a demand that they decide by the next day whether they would leave the east side of the Mississippi peaceably or under the soldiers' bayonets. As the council ended, Black Hawk suddenly drew himself up and, extending his hand to Gaines, said with dignity, "You have asked who is Black Hawk? I am a Sauk. My forefather was a *Sauk!* And all the nations call me a SAUK!"

The atmosphere that night was filled with tension. Keokuk, who was camped with his followers under a large white flag, circulated among Black Hawk's people, reminding them of the Americans' power that he had seen in the East and warning them that they would bring on their own ruin if they did not obey General Gaines. His arguments persuaded nearly fifty families to extinguish their fires in the British Band and move over to the peace faction. The results pleased Gaines, and the next morning he extended his deadline in order to give Keokuk more time to continue luring strength away from the British Band. At the same time, reports reached the Americans' camp that made Gaines feel that he would inevitably have to use force against Black Hawk and his die-hards. The previous fall, the old Sauk had sent a deputation that included his son to the Osages, Cherokees, Creeks, and other southern tribes as far away as Texas to ask their help in a defensive war against the Americans. None of those tribes had responded favorably, but in the north, Gaines now heard, Black Hawk was counting on the assistance of Kickapoos, Potawatomis, and a portion of the Winnebagos, who lived higher up on the Rock River in Illinois, and were under the influence of a bitterly anti-American mystic named White Cloud, who was known to the natives as the Winnebago Prophet. The latter, a tall, heavy-set man in his early forties, had an unkempt and menacing appearance that fitted his reputation for cunning and viciousness. Long a friend and adviser of Black Hawk, he exerted a spiritual hold over the aged war chief, and had promised to aid him if he went to war. Gaines found that the prophet was indeed at Saukenuk, advising Black Hawk. He ordered him angrily to return to his own people, but, fearing that the mystic might rouse other tribes to help the Sauk, he called on Governor Reynolds to send his militia to Saukenuk to reinforce the federal troops.

Gaines made no move against Black Hawk until the militia appeared. On June 25, 1831, some fifteen hundred of them reached the scene, ready for action and bearing "an excess of the *Indian ill-will*, so that it required much gentle persuasion to restrain them from killing, indiscriminately, all the Indians they met." At dawn the next morning, Gaines loosed them against Saukenuk. After a brief bombardment by the federal troops, the volunteers swept into the native village, but found it empty. Black Hawk and his people had evacuated it during the night and stealthily crossed to the west side of the Mississippi. The frustrated militia destroyed everything in sight and leveled the town by fire. The next day Gaines sent messengers across the river to Black Hawk's camp, summoning him to another meeting with the Americans. On June 30 the old war chief and some of his followers appeared, looking chastened and whipped, and agreed to sign "Articles of Agreement and Capitulation," in which they promised never to return to Saukenuk. The document humbled them further, demanding that they cease all communication with the British, submit to the authority of Keokuk, and grant the United States the right to build roads across their

lands in Iowa. At the same time the agreement authorized Keokuk to inform the nearest United States military post if he found
that at any time he was unable to force Black Hawk to observe
the terms of the paper.

To help the members of the British Band avoid starvation during their first year in new homes, Gaines directed the white settlers at Rock River to provide the Indians with a supply of corn
equal to the amount the natives would have harvested from their
fields at Saukenuk. The order displeased the militia, who were
already irritated because they had not been able to exterminate
the offending Indians, and they criticized Gaines and called his
agreement with Black Hawk the "corn treaty." As soon as Gaines
and the federal troops left the area, the militiamen sniped at Indians on the river and destroyed their canoes. Shortly afterward
the volunteers straggled off to their homes, but their belligerent
attitude encouraged the Rock River settlers to send the Indians
only a token amount of corn, and soon many of the natives on
the west side of the Mississippi faced starvation. As their misery
increased, a small group of Sauk tried to steal across the river
and harvest the fields, but the settlers fired on them and drove
them back to their people.

After he had signed the agreement with Gaines, Black Hawk
had decided to abandon further resistance to the whites. He had
resigned himself to live out his last years in quietude, and had
received permission to be buried in the ancestral graveyard of
his people at Saukenuk. But his hostility to the Americans would
not be stilled, and the settlers' violation of Gaines' corn order
stirred him again with resentments. At the same time a new
crisis involved him with the whites. The previous year, a band
of Sioux and Menominees had killed some Fox chiefs, and in
July 1831, a month after Black Hawk had signed his agreement
with Gaines, a large party of Foxes struck back at the Menominees, almost annihilating one of their camps. The assault aroused
the people of Illinois to a new clamor against the Sauk and Foxes,
who, they charged, held "no faith under Treaties, compacts, or

obligations of any sort," and were still a menace. Federal authorities demanded the surrender of the guilty Foxes, who appealed to Black Hawk for advice. The old man was flattered, and, seeing an opportunity to rebuild his following and add to it the support of the Foxes, told them that they deserved praise for having avenged their chiefs, and that the Americans had no right to interfere in intertribal affairs. The Foxes were delighted and, as Black Hawk had hoped, soon joined the members of his British Band.

As American officials continued to demand the surrender of the Foxes, Black Hawk's belligerence flared anew. Retaliatory raids between tribes were part of the Indian way of life, and when no whites were involved intertribal relations were not, in his opinion, the Americans' concern. At the height of the controversy his chief lieutenant, a loud and aggressive warrior named Neapope, or "the Broth," who was about thirty years old, returned from a visit to Canada. The English, Neapope claimed, had maintained that if the Indians had not sold Saukenuk to the Americans, the village still rightfully belonged to the Sauk; and that if United States troops tried to enforce their eviction the British would come to the natives' assistance. On his way home he had stopped also at the prophet's town on the Rock River, and the Winnebago had supplied further good news for Black Hawk. Potawatomis, Chippewas, and Ottawas were ready to assist the Sauk and Foxes, he had announced, and the British had assured the prophet also that they would supply guns, ammunition, and provisions. Furthermore, according to the prophet, if the Indians went to war and were defeated, they could retreat to a haven which the British would provide for them on the Red River in central Canada.

The assurances of Neapope and the Winnebago mystic were distortions and exaggerations of the real situation, but they excited Black Hawk. Despite his agreement with Gaines, the old Indian leader, now almost sixty-five, made up his mind to recruit new followers and return to Saukenuk the following spring. Keokuk learned with alarm of his new plans, and though he argued desperately against him he could not halt him. On the hunting grounds during the winter, Black Hawk ignored his rival, and "conceiving that the peaceable disposition of Keokuk and his people had been, in a great measure, the cause of our having been driven from our village," moved busily among the natives, fanning their resentments and stirring their pride. By the beginning of 1832 his following had swelled to more than six hundred warriors, including bands of hostile Kickapoos, Winnebagos, and Potawatomis. In anger and frustration, Keokuk sent a message to the government agent at Rock Island, warning him that Black Hawk was going back to Saukenuk.

American troops under General Henry Atkinson hurriedly assembled, and on April 8, 1832, a force of two hundred and twenty men embarked on steamboats for Rock Island, hoping to arrive before Black Hawk tried to cross the Mississippi. They were already too late. Three days earlier, Black Hawk and his British Band, now numbering an estimated two thousand warriors, women, and children, had crossed the stream near the mouth of the Iowa River below Saukenuk. The natives trailed slowly toward their old village, and on the way met the Winnebago prophet; he informed them that American soldiers were coming to intercept them. The prophet invited the Sauk and Foxes to come to his village farther up the Rock River and wait there until reinforcements joined them from the other tribes. In the meantime he reassured them that if they acted peaceably the Americans would not interfere with them. The Indians continued toward the Rock River and reached there on April 12, just as Atkinson's men were debarking at Fort Armstrong on Rock Island. To show that they were unafraid of the soldiers, the natives sang loudly and beat their drums, but they rode past Saukenuk and continued on up the Rock River toward the prophet's village.

Atkinson, who feared that his force was not strong enough to risk an engagement with the Indians, paused indecisively at Fort

Armstrong. He wrote to Governor Reynolds of the new threat to the Illinois country, and on April 16 Reynolds again called for volunteers, proclaiming that the settlements were in "eminent danger." Some seventeen hundred men responded to his appeal, and once more the excited frontier communities formed militia companies. Among those who flocked to enlist this time was twenty-three-year-old Abraham Lincoln, a clerk in Denton Offutt's store in New Salem. The volunteers, many of whom looked upon the emergency as an adventurous frolic, rendezvoused at Beardstown on the Illinois River and marched to Yellow Banks on the Mississippi. There they ran into Keokuk and some of the members of his peace faction. Keokuk not only protested his own innocence to the settlers, but offered to join them in their war against Black Hawk. The volunteers refused his services, but watched with amusement as Keokuk and his braves staged a Sauk war dance for their entertainment. Then the whites marched on to Rock Island and joined General Atkinson on May 7.

Black Hawk's people, in the meantime, had reached the prophet's village. Atkinson sent ultimatums after the old chief, demanding that he return to Rock Island, and warning him, "You will be sorry if you do not come back." The messages, Black Hawk said, "roused the spirit of my band, and all were determined to remain with me and contest the ground with the war chief, should he come and attempt to drive us." At the same time Colonel Henry Gratiot, the American agent to the Winnebagos, appeared in the prophet's town with a number of Winnebago chiefs, and told Black Hawk that Atkinson would soon march against him if he did not go back. Black Hawk ignored the warning, but some of the Winnebago chiefs, apparently anxious to be rid of the dangerous Sauk and Foxes and get them into somebody else's country, urged him to continue farther up the river, where he would receive enough reinforcements to help him repel the Americans. Black Hawk gradually realized the discomfort of the Winnebagos, and with some irritation and anger felt that they had deceived Neapope with their promises. He decided to leave them and move farther up the Rock River and told his people that they would visit the country of the Potawatomis to "hear what they say, and see what they will do." Neapope still assured him that British help would come to them, and to encourage his followers Black Hawk told them that he had just received news from Milwaukee that an English force would be there in a few days to assist them.

Accompanied by the prophet, who was still loyal to the Sauk leader, the natives trailed on again to the Kishwaukee River near present-day Rockford, Illinois, where they met a deputation of Potawatomis. Again they were disappointed. The Sauk and Foxes were in urgent need of provisions. The old man tried pleading with the chiefs in a secret meeting late at night, but the Potawatomis wanted no part of his troubles. "I discovered that the Winnebagos and Potawatomis were not disposed to render us any assistance," Black Hawk said. At the same time, he learned that the British had no intention of aiding him, and that the prophet and Neapope had misled him with a string of false promises. In confusion he decided that if Atkinson came after him he would now go back. "It was useless to think of stopping [here] or going on without provisions," he wrote.

Unknown to him, there could no longer be a peaceful turning back. On May 10 Atkinson's army had finally started out after him. In the lead of the pursuit were 1500 mounted militiamen, commanded by General Samuel Whiteside and accompanied by Governor Reynolds and his staff. Zachary Taylor, now a colonel and, after eighteen years, once again moving against Black Hawk, led 340 regulars and 165 militia infantrymen as an escort to the slower-moving boats that carried the army's supplies up the Rock River. Whiteside's horsemen got far out ahead of Taylor's force and swept into the prophet's village. When they found Black Hawk gone, they burned most of the Winnebago settlement. They continued to Dixon's Ferry, where they decided to wait for Taylor and their supplies to catch up with them. Black Hawk, they understood, was only twenty-five miles ahead of them, and the impatient members of one of the battalions, led by Major Isaiah Stillman, itched for action. Confident that they could overtake and whip the natives, they pleaded for permission to continue the chase. As commander-in-chief of the militia, Governor Reynolds authorized them to keep after the Indians "and coerce them into submission," and on the morning of May 14 the small and impetuous force of 275 men started forward again on the trail.

The day before, Black Hawk had had his disheartening interviews with the Potawatomis and had decided to return to Rock River. He was sitting again with some of the Potawatomi chiefs late in the afternoon of May 14 when scouts brought him word that they had sighted Stillman's force about eight miles away. Black Hawk was at some distance from his own camp, and had fewer than fifty of his braves with him. The moment for capitulation had come, he decided, and he immediately sent three of his men with a white flag to the Americans to "conduct them to our camp, that we might hold a council with them, and descend Rock River again." Not certain what the American reception would be, he ordered another party of five warriors to follow the first group and observe what happened to it. His uneasiness was justified. The Americans had already encamped for the night, and the appearance of the three-man Indian delegation threw the volunteers into excitement. As the undisciplined settlers crowded menacingly around the natives, a militiaman sighted the second party of Indians on the prairie. His warning made the Americans decide they were being attacked, and without waiting for orders they leaped on their horses and galloped toward the five warriors. Frightened, the natives turned to flee. In a moment, the settlers were firing. Two of the Indians were overtaken and shot, and the others raced toward Black Hawk's camp, pursued by a cheering throng of Americans. In Stillman's camp a melee occurred as the whites argued over what to do with the members of the first delegation. Several of the unruly settlers suddenly cocked their guns and fired at the natives. One was killed, and in the tumult the other two ran through the crowd and escaped.

The three survivors of the second group reached Black Hawk ahead of the Americans. The old war chief determined to sell his life dearly. He had about forty warriors with him; they went into ambush behind bushes and lay in wait for the settlers. As the American horsemen came up, Black Hawk gave a yell, and his braves charged from their hiding places. In the gathering darkness of early evening the surprise panicked the volunteers. The Indians' shouts and firing stopped them short, and as some men began to fall the others wheeled about and fled back toward Stillman's camp, pursued by about twenty-five of the natives. Their flight frightened others behind them, and the retreat became a rout. A few of the settlers tried to make a stand and were cut down by Black Hawk's frenzied braves. The rest galloped into camp, shouting that a thousand warriors were after them. Their hysteria panicked everyone, and Stillman's entire command lit out for General Whiteside at Dixon's Ferry. The frightened volunteers straggled into Whiteside's camp all night, filled with breathless stories of a terrible massacre. By morning a muster showed that only fifty-two men were missing, and later the figure was lowered to eleven. But the episode unnerved the militia. Atkinson and Zachary Taylor's regulars joined them, and after a futile and frustrating attempt to pursue the Indians most of the settlers, now weary and disgruntled, clamored to go home. Governor Reynolds had already issued a call for two thousand new volunteers, and he managed to keep two hundred and fifty of his original command until the new troops appeared. Among those who agreed to stay was Abraham Lincoln, who had not been involved in Stillman's defeat.

Atkinson's force was now too small to risk engagement with Black Hawk, and while the general waited at Dixon's Ferry for the new volunteers to join him the Sauk war chief moved his band up into present-day Wisconsin. Some friendly Winnebagos helped to guide him to the Four Lakes country of central Wisconsin, where he established his women and children in a hiding place in the marshes. In the meantime several parties of Potawatomis, Winnebagos, and Kickapoos, emboldened by the Sauk's successful defiance of the whites, attacked isolated parties of Americans and raided the cabins of outlying settlers. One group of Potawatomis savagely fell on a settlement at Indian Creek and slew fifteen persons, while a band of Winnebagos murdered the agent at Rock Island, who had been Keokuk's friend. The aggressive spirit of the natives encouraged Black Hawk to send out his own war parties from his hiding place at the Four Lakes; Sauk and Foxes raided the Galena mining district along the western border of Illinois and Wisconsin, and clashed with armed miners and settlers.

The Indians' aggressions spread new panic among the settlements. "The alarm and distress on the frontier cannot be described," wrote one of Atkinson's officers. "It is heart rending to see the women and children in an agony of fear, fleeing from their homes and hearths, to seek what they imagine is but a brief respite from death." In Galena an outraged editor demanded a "war of extermination until there shall be no Indian (*with his scalp on*) left in the north part of Illinois," and a St. Louis newspaper proclaimed that "the lives of a hundred Indians is too small for that of *each* of their fallen victims." The wild fear of the frontier reached Washington, where President Jackson was already fuming over Atkinson's inability to halt Black Hawk. "Some one is to blame in this matter, but upon whom it is to fall, is at present unknown to the Department," the acting Secretary of War wrote Atkinson on June 12, 1832. Three days later Jackson placed Major General Winfield Scott in command of the war against Black Hawk, directing him to assemble an army of eight hundred regulars, six ranger companies, and as many militia as he needed, and march it from Chicago to pin Black Hawk between himself and the troops of General Atkinson.

Before Jackson's orders reached the west, Atkinson had finally received the reinforcements he had been awaiting, and was once more on the move. With a force of three thousand militiamen, a few hundred Indian allies, and four hundred regulars, he marched up the Rock and Kishwaukee Rivers, following Black Hawk's trail. In the swampy country of the Rock River's head-waters he again ran into trouble. His patrols lost the Sauk's trail and his men floundered fruitlessly through the swamps, bat-tling mud and mosquitoes. In time he ran out of provisions and had to halt while he diverted expeditions elsewhere to find food for his army. The sick and hungry volunteers soon had enough of the miserable chase, and when their terms of enlistment ended they went home. This time both Governor Reynolds and Abra-ham Lincoln left the army.

In his hiding place farther west, Black Hawk was also running out of food. In the marshes "there was but little game of any sort to be found—and fish were equally scarce," he said. "We were forced to dig *roots* and *bark trees*, to obtain something to satisfy hunger and keep us alive!" When he heard that Atkinson was again pursuing him, he decided to move west and recross the Mississippi. His attempt to reoccupy Saukenuk had been de-feated, and he was sure that if he rejoined the rest of the Sauk nation in Iowa, and settled down among them again in peace, the Americans would leave him alone. Guided by five Winne-bagos, he started his people toward the setting sun, planning to descend the Wisconsin River to the Mississippi.

Once more his hopes were thwarted. Farther north, also search-ing for the Sauk refugees, was a second American force of Ga-lena miners and volunteers under Colonel Henry Dodge, an ag-gressive leader in the mining district. On July 21 some Winne-bago informers told Dodge that they could direct his men to Black Hawk's hiding place. Joined by one of Atkinson's food-seeking expeditions under General James D. Henry, Dodge set off with the Winnebago guides. When they reached the hiding place they found that Black Hawk had already gone, but some of Dodge's men picked up the Indians' trail, and the American force of about five hundred men started in pursuit. In the late afternoon of July 21 they reached the heights above the Wisconsin River. Black Hawk's people had begun crossing to an island in the center of the river when several of Dodge's scouts discovered them. The Indians chased the scouts back to Dodge's main units, and were then themselves driven back. Dodge's men advanced quickly, moving onto a plain that faced the river. While the Indian women and children continued to cross the stream on rafts and frail canoes made of strips of elm bark, Black Hawk and fifty of his warriors held off the whites, pouring a withering fire on them from a hill that flanked the plain. Eventually the Americans dismounted and moved up the hill, driving the natives down into a ravine that was covered with high grass and underbrush. From this position the Indians held back the Americans, and at darkness Dodge and Henry broke off the action. During the night Black Hawk got the rest of his people across the river, and in the morning the whites, who were short of rations and had no ready means of crossing the river, gave up the chase.

The number of Indian casualties during the battle are unknown. Black Hawk said he lost six men, and Dodge estimated that "from the scalps taken by the Winnebagos as well as those taken by the Whites and Indians carried from the field of Battle we must have killed 40 of them." The Americans lost only one man. During the river crossing some of Black Hawk's people left him and descended the Wisconsin, hoping to cross the Mississippi at the Wisconsin's mouth, according to the Indians' original plan. Black Hawk said he had no objection to their departure, "as my people were all in a desperate condition—being worn out with travelling, and starving from hunger." Eventually many of those who fled down the Wisconsin were intercepted by soldiers from Prairie du Chien and killed; others were drowned or taken prisoner and the rest escaped to the woods where they died of hunger.

Once away from the Wisconsin, Black Hawk tried to hurry

the main band westward across country to the Mississippi, but many of the Indians' horses had given out, and the painful condition of the people who had to walk slowed their progress. Men with wounds from the battle on the Wisconsin became worse and died. As the braves pushed the rest of them along, the natives abandoned their personal possessions, leaving blankets, kettles, and other heavy loads scattered on the trail. In time starvation took its toll, and many of the old men and children perished by the wayside. Still guided by Winnebagos, the natives plodded on across an increasingly rugged and hilly country, heading in a northwesterly direction to the mouth of the Bad Axe River, about forty miles above Prairie du Chien. On August 1, with not more than five hundred of his original band left, Black Hawk reached the Mississippi just below its meeting with the Bad Axe.

The Indians found no canoes in which to cross the broad stream, and the Sauk chief called a council to urge that they head north along the Mississippi and seek shelter among the Chippewas in that direction. The people were too sorely disillusioned by their previous friends to support Black Hawk's proposal, and the other chiefs voted him down. Anxious to get to the west side of the Mississippi, where they thought they would be safe, they started at once to improvise rafts and canoes. A few of the Indians had already managed to make the crossing when the steamboat *Warrior*, with a detachment of troops and a six-pounder artillery piece, came in view on the river. The vessel was returning downstream from Minnesota, where it had gone to urge the Sioux to watch the Mississippi and prevent their enemies, the Sauk and Foxes, from escaping across it. Now the ship pulled toward the Indians and anchored. Black Hawk knew its captain; he raised a white flag and had one of the Winnebagos call out that the natives wished to surrender. The interpreter on the *Warrior* misunderstood what was said, and reported that the Indians wanted those on the boat to come ashore. The troops'

commander refused, and demanded instead that two of the natives come on board the vessel. Black Hawk's people were now
confused, and made no reply. The Americans thought the Indians
were planning an attack; becoming suddenly jittery, they
opened point-blank fire on them with the six-pounder. The shells
caught the natives by surprise and killed many of them. The rest
gained cover and fired back at the ship for about two hours.
Finally the steamboat ran out of fuel, and its captain headed
down-river to Prairie du Chien for more wood.

After the vessel left, Black Hawk again urged his people to
follow him to the Chippewas instead of trying to cross the river.
Only about fifty Indians, including the Winnebago prophet,
agreed to go with him, and that evening he left the main band
and started up the Mississippi. The rest of the Indians prepared
to continue crossing the stream. The engagement with the steamboat had claimed the lives of twenty-three natives, but the delay
in getting to the opposite shore was now to prove more costly
to them.

After Dodge's battle with the Indians on the Wisconsin, Atkinson had again taken up the pursuit. General Scott was in Chicago, unable to move his troops because of a cholera epidemic,
but Atkinson no longer needed his help. Moving at a fast pace
with thirteen hundred regulars and volunteers, Atkinson crossed
the Wisconsin and followed the pathetically clear trail left by
Black Hawk's suffering people. Early in the morning of August
3 his advance units reached the Mississippi and fell savagely on
the Indians, who were again crossing the river. The main elements of the army soon joined the assault, which speedily turned
into a merciless slaughter. Warriors fought back alone and in
small groups, and were overwhelmed. The Americans clubbed
and shot every Indian they saw, killing women and children as
well as braves. Many of the natives tried to swim the river, and
others crossed to islands in the stream and hid in the trees. In the
midst of the battle the *Warrior* reappeared from Prairie du Chien,

and Atkinson loaded it with troops and attacked the islands. As the ship's six-pounder raked the trees, knocking Indians from the branches, the soldiers picked them off on the ground.

More than eight hours after the massacre had begun, it ended. The whites took thirty-nine prisoners, all women and children, and counted about a hundred and fifty Indian bodies. Many others had drowned, or died out of sight. "The Inds. were pushed litterally into the Mississippi, the current of which was at one time perceptibly tinged with the blood of the Indians who were shot on its margin & in the stream," wrote General Joseph M. Street, the Indian agent at Prairie du Chien, to William Clark. "It is impossible to say how many Inds. have been killed, as most of them were shot in the water or drowned in attempting to cross the Mississippi." Those Indians who did get across the river suffered an equally tragic fate. On the west side of the stream, Sioux killed and scalped sixty-eight of them and made prisoners of all the rest.

It was the end of Black Hawk's band, and of his so-called war. The old chief and his party traveled to Winnebago country in the north. The Americans offered a reward of one hundred dollars and twenty horses for his capture, and near the Wisconsin Dells some Winnebagos persuaded the fugitives to return with them to Prairie du Chien. Neither Black Hawk nor the prophet offered objection, and the little party headed south to surrender. The agent at Prairie du Chien turned Black Hawk, his two sons, and the prophet over to Zachary Taylor who, in turn, ordered his future son-in-law, Lieutenant Jefferson Davis, to escort the prisoners to Jefferson Barracks. Earlier, Keokuk had captured Neapope and given him to the Americans. With the three principal trouble-makers behind bars, General Scott and Governor Reynolds met with Keokuk and some of the other peaceful Sauk and Foxes to negotiate a lasting treaty with the nation. To increase Keokuk's influence among the natives the commissioners proclaimed him a civil chief, then wrung from him a new cession of some six million acres of Sauk land running along the Mississippi River in the present state of Iowa. Within the tract the Sauk and Foxes were left with a small reservation.

In time Black Hawk and the other prize prisoners were sent to Washington and Fortress Monroe. With the fight out of them, they made their tour of the eastern cities and returned home to freedom. Black Hawk, after making his final complaint that Keokuk, the man who had opposed and helped to defeat him, was now the white-appointed head chief of his people, subsided into silence. During the following years he watched Keokuk sell more and more of the Sauk and Fox lands in Iowa, and grow wealthy and powerful. In 1836 the artist George Catlin saw Black Hawk at one of Keokuk's transfers of Sauk-owned property. "The poor dethroned monarch, old Black Hawk, was present, and looked an object of pity," Catlin wrote. "With an old frock coat and brown hat on, and a cane in his hand, he stood the whole time outside of the group, and in dumb and dismal silence. . . ."

The old war chief died on October 3, 1838, at the age of seventy-one. Soon afterward his grave was robbed, and his bones were placed on display in the museum of the Geological and Historical Society in Burlington, Iowa, where they remained until a fire destroyed the building in 1855. Keokuk died in 1848 in Kansas, where he had moved after selling the Sauk and Fox lands in Iowa. White men hailed him "in every sense of the word, a great man," and a bronze bust of him was placed in the Capital at Washington.

VIII

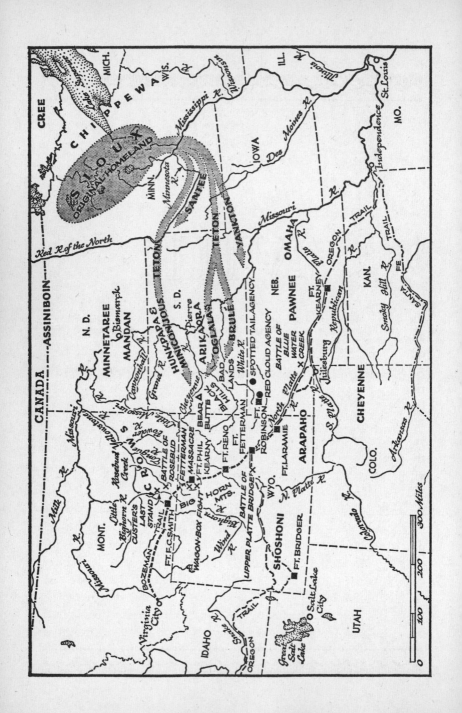

VIII

CRAZY HORSE,
PATRIOT OF THE PLAINS

"BENTEEN. Come on. Big village. Be quick. Bring packs. P.S. Bring pacs."

It was a little before three in the afternoon, June 25, 1876, the centennial year of the United States and the climactic day in the long history of warfare between the North American Indians and the white men. From a grassy ridge overlooking the valley of Montana's Little Bighorn River, Lieutenant Colonel George Armstrong Custer dispatched a hasty message for more ammunition to the pack train that was traveling in his rear. A moment later, confident that Captain Frederick Benteen and the train would follow hard after him, Custer started his five troops of the 7th Cavalry, some two hundred and twenty-five men, down the slope toward a huge encampment of Sioux and Cheyenne villages that lay along the river.

The American commander's impulsive action and the savage resistance of the Indians who swarmed out to meet him ended in a sensational massacre that shocked the nation. It was not the greatest triumph ever scored by Indians; Little Turtle, for instance, had utterly destroyed the army of General Arthur St. Clair and had killed more than six hundred of his men on the headwaters of the Wabash River in 1791. But the victory of the Sioux and their Cheyenne allies came when the industrialized American nation reached from coast to coast, when great armies and great generals had proved the might and power of the United States in a four-year Civil War, and when hostile natives were no longer a menace but a nuisance. The scalped and mutilated bodies on the bluffs above the Little Bighorn shamed and angered the American people. They smarted under the whipping, searched for scapegoats, attacked the Army, the government, and the so-called "peace element" that had pleaded for patience with the Indians, and demanded speedy retribution and a policy that would end further problems with "hostiles."

In their excitement and frustration few persons took time to examine the long train of events on the plains that had led to the massacre. To most Americans it was part of a war that was being waged against "wild Indians" who hated whites and enjoyed killing them. Seventy years before, Lewis and Clark had first publicized the hostility of the Sioux to white men. Their reputation as a fierce and powerful people had increased through the century, and, though westward-surging Americans had been busy fighting other tribes who were closer to them, there was an awareness that some day there would have to be an accounting with the Sioux. Now it had come. There were small pockets of other hostiles still dotting the West, but the Sioux were the biggest and strongest unsubdued nation left in the United States, and the day had arrived to crush them.

In the years that followed the tragedy on the Little Bighorn, victories and pacification of the hostiles led to a clearer perspective on the so-called Sioux troubles. As in many Indian wars, the natives—wild and cruel as they had been made to seem—were not the aggressors. Ringed ever more tightly by growing numbers of white men, they had struggled desperately to maintain their freedom and way of life. Their battles were wild thrashings to escape the whites, to drive them away, and to keep enough of the huge plains country free of civilization for themselves and the herds of buffalo on which they lived.

Nor had they been united in their trials. Like many tribes before them, they had their weaklings and turncoats, great warriors such as Red Cloud, who were undermined and suborned by American power and favor and who gave the Americans aid against their own people. They also had their patriots, men who counseled freedom or death and who died on battlefields or in irons, shouting defiantly, "Come on, Lakotas, it's a good day to die!" American military leaders and war correspondents in the West, seeking a native genius behind the Custer massacre, singled out one of the Sioux for recognition, a stout and scowling combination medicine man and war leader named Sitting Bull, and after the wars Buffalo Bill and others promoted the obliging but still unchastened Sitting Bull as the greatest of all the Sioux warriors. But to the Indians themselves the title was misplaced. In the loneliness of a guardhouse at Fort Robinson, Nebraska, on September 5, 1877, their noblest hero, a shy, brooding young chief named Crazy Horse, only thirty-five years old, fighting wildly to free himself from imprisonment, died under the furious lunges of a sentry's bayonet. An officer who knew his worth called him "one of the great soldiers of his day and generation," and an American correspondent who had accompanied United States troops that he had beaten saluted him as "the bravest of the brave." When Crazy Horse died, tears and a bitter stirring for revenge swept his followers among the Sioux nation, and agency officials feared a new uprising. Today, on the Sioux reservations of the West, his name is enshrined in the memories of his people, who are proud of their relationship to him. He never signed a treaty with white men, and resisted them all his life. To the Sioux he is the greatest of all their leaders.

Americans met Crazy Horse at Platte Bridge, Fort Phil Kearny, the Rosebud, the Little Bighorn, and many other battles on the plains. But few of them knew anything about him during his lifetime because he stayed away from their posts and agencies and, except in conflict, had little to do with them. After his death his companions and friends told their great stories about him to white questioners, and gradually the transcripts of their interviews increased in number until years later Mari

Sandoz and other writers and historians who were interested in the Sioux were able to measure his true stature for the American people who had been his enemies. But what they unfolded was more than a narrative of a man's life. A leader is also the product of his time and people, and Crazy Horse's story, as reflected by the testimony of his contemporaries, is also the epic of the Sioux nation's gallant and desperate fight to remain free.

Crazy Horse was born about 1842 on Rapid Creek near present-day Rapid City, South Dakota, on the eastern side of the most treasured part of the Sioux domain, the tall and beautiful Black Hills, which the natives held to be sacred medicine grounds and called *Pa Sapa*. It was ten years after Black Hawk's vain attempt to save his home in Illinois, and the Sauk and other tribes east of the Mississippi had been crushed and demoralized and were being resettled on western reservations from Nebraska to Oklahoma.

Crazy Horse's people were foreigners to the western country also, but they had arrived there years earlier and under different circumstances. The Sioux are believed to have lived originally, before the white man reached North America, in the Southeast of the present-day United States, members of a widely dispersed Siouan-speaking family. During the sixteenth century they settled in villages around the lakes and headwaters of the Mississippi River. They were forest Indians, hunting in the woods, growing corn and gathering wild rice from the marshes around their towns. When they traveled, it was on foot or in bark canoes. A numerous and aggressive people, they carried on constant warfare against their Algonquian-speaking neighbors.

The coming of the French and British favored the Algonquians, who dealt with them and used their new guns and metal weapons, and gradually, with their superiority in arms, Chippewas and others pushed the Sioux westward. The Sioux were never a united people, but were separated into many factions and bands. Encompassing all of them were three great families, the Santees, Yanktons, and Tetons, who called themselves the same name

meaning "allies": the Santees pronounced it Dakota, the Yanktons said Nakota, and the Tetons called it Lakota. It is with the
Teton or western Sioux that this chronicle of Crazy Horse is
chiefly concerned. Within that group, which had seven great divisions, his own Oglalas and the Brulés (or Burnt Thighs) were
known as the southern Lakotas; the Hunkpapas and four other
tribes (Miniconjous, Two Kettles, No Bows, and Blackfeet
Sioux) made up a northern group.

Each group in turn was composed of separate bands with other
names, endlessly confusing to the white man. Both Crazy Horse
and Sitting Bull, for instance, were Tetons or, as they called themselves, Lakotas; but Crazy Horse was a Hunkpatila of the
Oglalas, while Sitting Bull was a Hunkpapa of the north. The two
men were raised and lived in different parts of the plains country
and came together as allies only in the last days of resistance to
the whites.

During the late seventeenth and early eighteenth centuries the
Tetons began to break away from the eastern Sioux, who remained in Minnesota as woodland tribes. The Tetons moved
gradually west, still afoot, emerging on the plains and learning to
hunt buffalo, and at length they reached the Missouri River,
where a new force entered their lives—the horse.

According to the best evidence, no Indians on the plains had
horses prior to 1680. In that year, when the Pueblo Indians of
New Mexico rose up against the Spaniards and drove them back
to Mexico, the whites left many of their horse herds behind. The
town-dwelling Pueblos had no use for the animals, and in trades
and raids Apaches and Utes made off with many of them. Gradually the increasing numbers of animals moved north from
tribe to tribe. Friendly peoples, and sometimes prisoners of war
from tribes that owned horses, taught one another to ride. As
soon as men lost their fear of the animals they wanted more of
them, and horses became a principal object of intertribal trading
and raiding. It took each tribe about a generation to become
mounted, since the older people were generally content to let

the youths master the animals while they kept their traditional ways of life and walked. As the horses spread north the tribes gained greater mobility in both hunting buffalo and making war. Loads were shifted from dogs to horses, the tipis became larger because the lodge poles that horses could drag along the plains, as the people moved from one location to another after game, could be cut longer than the ones that had been tied to the backs of dogs. Life became easier, more varied and adventurous. Stealing horses became a part of life, another test of manhood like counting coup—touching a live enemy and getting away unharmed to boast about it.

The Sioux, as they moved westward, found horses among some of the tribes who were there ahead of them and whom they gradually displaced. For a time the Tetons stayed along the Missouri and learned the use of the horse; then, beginning in 1772, some of them crossed the river and headed up toward the western part of South Dakota. They moved across dry, windy country and through fearful eroded badlands, and in 1775 or 1776 an Oglala war party arrived at the Black Hills. The Indians gazed in awe at the beautiful parks and dark stands of trees rising from the brown land. It became to them a storied island of peace and mystery, and though it was claimed by the Crows the Tetons decided to make it their own.

Still, the majority of the Tetons had not migrated into the plains. They remained on both sides of the Missouri in South Dakota, in touch with their source of white men's supplies in the trade centers behind them. In the 1790s traders from St. Louis began pushing up the higher Missouri in keelboats and pirogues. They did some business with the Sioux, but when they tried to get past their villages the Tetons harassed them, exacted tribute from them, and often frightened them back. Lewis and Clark found the Tetons the terrors of the river in 1804, and almost had a battle with them. By refusing to let the Tetons cow them, the captains won their respect, and the Tetons afterward established a friendly, though still haughty, relationship with American traders and allowed them to move in freedom up the river.

The new traders provided the Tetons with more guns, and gradually Sioux excursions to the west increased. During the first quarter of the nineteenth century the Teton bands extended dominion over most of South Dakota between the Missouri River and the Black Hills. In this time and region were born two Sioux who later became well known to the whites, Man-Afraid-of-His-Horse and Red Cloud. Man-Afraid was born about 1815, and Red Cloud in September 1821.

After the War of 1812, American troops tried to make the middle stretches of the Missouri safe for traders. In 1825 the Sioux signed a treaty of peace and friendship on the river with the United States, and soon afterward a few enterprising traders moved west across Dakota to establish outpost trading centers for the Oglalas, who brought in robes and the furs of small animals. The trade expanded, and as rival American groups broadened their spheres of activity from the Missouri River to the Rocky Mountains competition among the white men increased, and traders fought for exclusive dealings with individual tribes.

By the early 1830s the Sioux in the Dakotas and along the Missouri River were trading almost entirely with agents of the powerful American Fur Company, which had built strong posts at Pierre and other points on the Missouri. The rival Rocky Mountain Fur Company, an aggressive group of mountain men who had been trapping and trading along the Continental Divide, had tried to establish a competitive post on the Missouri and cut into some of the American Fur Company's trade, but had failed. Suddenly in 1834, two of the leaders in the Rocky Mountain trade, William Sublette and Robert Campbell, built a trading post of their own near the mouth of Laramie Creek on the North Platte River in eastern Wyoming, and Campbell traveled to the Sioux to urge them to move south and trade at the new post.

Campbell's appeal began a new era for the Sioux. The new post, which was first called Fort William but later, when replaced by a more substantial building, became better known as Fort

Laramie, was almost in the geographical center of the plains, lying directly at the crossroad of the principal east-west and north-south Indian routes in the Nebraska and Wyoming country. Native war and hunting parties, as well as white travelers, including trappers, soldiers, and emigrants to Oregon and California, used the Platte River route from the Missouri to the Rocky Mountains. And the fort, only slightly southwest of the Black Hills region of South Dakota, was on an avenue that could connect the Sioux and Cheyennes of the north with the Arapaho and other tribes of the southern plains.

Sioux bands almost at once accepted Campbell's invitation to come south. In 1834 the most powerful Oglala chief, a man named Bull Bear, led a hundred lodges of his people to the new post. The following year the rest of the Oglalas, some two thousand people, trekked down to the Platte. It was a permanent move. The Oglalas turned their backs on the upper Missouri River and began to hunt and fight in the country between the Platte River and the Black Hills. In 1840 the Brulés also moved south and joined them, and gradually the newcomers, now battling Pawnees, Snakes, and Crows, roamed as conquerors across the entire central plains from mid-Nebraska to Wyoming's Wind River Mountains and from the Platte River to the Yellowstone in Montana.

Fort Laramie, grown big and busy, became a permanent source of white men's arms and supplies for the Sioux, and some of the natives pitched their tipis near the fort and took to living there almost the year round. Rival traders erected other posts and supply houses nearby and in the stiff competition used liquor to win the Indians' favor. The unscrupulousness of the whites impoverished many of the natives, who traded horses, clothing, and whatever they owned for whisky, and it almost demoralized whole bands. In 1841 a rivalry broke out among the Oglalas between the Bear people, who were followers of Bull Bear, and the partisans of another chief named Smoke. Quarreling, helped along by liquor, ended in a fight between the two factions, and the young Red Cloud and other followers of Smoke killed Bull Bear.

The murder caused greater bitterness among the two factions, and they separated; but a moral regeneration swept many of their leaders, and they tried to persuade their young people and warriors not to take the white man's liquor, which undermined their manliness and would in time destroy their tribe. The counseling proved effective, and eventually the danger of complete demoralization of the Oglalas by liquor disappeared. The nomadic bands avoided liquor and too close an association with all whites save a few favored traders, and scornfully gave the name Loafers-about-the-Fort to the weaker Indians who continued to hang around the posts and beg for white men's supplies and whisky.

The Brulés and the Smoke faction of the Oglalas still wintered in their old haunts on the east side of the Black Hills, and there about 1842 Crazy Horse was born. His mother was a Brulé woman, the sister of Spotted Tail, who was to become a celebrated Brulé chief, and his father, known as Crazy Horse at the time, was a respected Oglala holy or medicine man, who could see things of the future, and whom members of his band consulted for wisdom and advice. About a year later a brother was born, and there was also a sister in the family. When Crazy Horse was still young his mother died, and his father took her sister to live with him in his tipi and raise his children as a step-mother.

As a boy Crazy Horse was considered unusual and somewhat strange. Other Indians remembered him as serious and thoughtful, scarcely ever participating in the boisterous games and races of the tipi camps, but usually standing quietly in the shadows around the adults. He was, moreover, very light-skinned for an Indian and had hair so soft and pale that he was known as the Light-Haired Boy, and also as Curly. When he accompanied his people to Fort Laramie, emigrant women who paused at the post on their way to Oregon thought he was a captive white youth.

His father, it was said, brooded often about the plight of the Sioux people, worrying that the white men and their liquor would soon destroy the Indians unless a strong leader arose from one of the camps to end the quarreling, unite the Sioux, and inspire them to throw off the white men's influences in their daily lives. Undoubtedly, his counsel and influence were strong on his sons, and he spoke to them often of the weaknesses of the divided bands.

During his early years Curly saw the demoralizing influence of the white men at close range. Each year he went down to Fort Laramie with his people and watched the trade. Too many of the Indians still took the white men's liquor, and there were frequent knifings and drunken quarrels around the tipis. Sometimes they would become roaring fights that would embroil a whole village. An old woman in her cups would fancy a slight or accuse an imaginary tormentor. A drunken man, taking her side, would shoot the object of her accusations, and the victim's friends and relatives would strike back vengefully. By the time order returned, five or six Indians might be dead, and the whole camp would mourn.

The Sioux had honorable societies of braves, called *akicitas*, named for animals such as the fox and bear, that policed the camps and kept order among the people. They enforced the authority of the chiefs, both in battle and in daily village life, and at Fort Laramie the akicitas often dealt roughly with Loafers and weaklings who took the white men's liquor and caused fights. Sometimes they even drove troublemakers from the camps, and condemned them to wander alone in the plains or find a home with another band or tribe.

But the principal object of scorn of the akicitas and of many of the proud, young warriors was the white man himself. Each year the stream of emigrants traveling past Fort Laramie on the Oregon Trail grew larger, and each year the white men and their women seemed more arrogant and offensive to the Indians. Along the trail, the great need for food for the long line of covered wagon parties depleted the buffalo herds and made game scarce and hunting poor in that part of the Indians' country. The white people did not stop, but their passage caused hard times for the natives and made them wonder fearfully what would happen when some of the travelers did begin to halt and settle on the hunting grounds. Many of the older men who had had contacts with more easterly tribes knew of the disasters that had been visited on the Indians east of the Missouri River, wherever white men had moved in and claimed the land. They were aware of smashed and degenerate peoples who had been dispossessed and relocated, and at night they told those stories to the younger men and children. Gradually the fears of the people increased, and the warriors began to think of preventing the whites from continuing to come through their country.

But the lure of trade was still too strong, and the chiefs who were in command did not want to drive away the supply houses around Fort Laramie that were their source of guns and other supplies of the white men. Some of the warrior bands made threatening attempts to halt covered wagon trains on the upper Platte, but each time so-called trade chiefs such as Conquering Bear and old Smoke stopped them and apologized to the whites for their unruliness.

As a young boy through the 1840s Crazy Horse saw all this and was aware of the growing conflict between the pro-white trade chiefs and the men whose fear and hatred of the whites was increasing. His father and his father's warrior friends were in the latter camp, and he felt their influence. But his own anti-white feelings were also molded and inflamed by what he could see for himself at Fort Laramie: the high-handedness of whites toward the Indians, the fears and snobbery of emigrant women, and the cheating, robbery, and bad treatment of the natives by too many of the rough frontier settlers with the covered wagon trains who did not conceal their opinion that the only good Indians were dead ones.

As native fears and hostility increased, the government responded to appeals for protection for the travelers using the Oregon Trail; in 1849 the United States purchased Fort Laramie from its fur-company owners, converted it into a major military post, and sent troops to garrison it. The arrival of the soldiers only intensified the restlessness of the Sioux and the other tribes who hunted in the western country, and the next year Indian agents of the government proposed a council with all the nations of the upper Platte to try to quiet them.

The gathering occurred in September 1851, at Horse Creek near Fort Laramie, and some ten thousand Indians, summoned by agents, traders, and Indian and half-breed messengers, came in from all parts of the plains. Friends and foes camped near one another, and it was a tumultuous session in which several of the tribes almost came to blows. The commissioners at the council were headed by David Mitchell, the Superintendent of Indian Affairs, who had come from Washington; they had two principal purposes: to secure guarantees of safety for the whites who used the Oregon Trail, and to try to establish a maximum of safety for white people throughout the plains by ending warfare among the tribes. To achieve the latter goal, Mitchell established boundaries, based on vague ideas of tribal homelands, within which each nation would have the exclusive right to hunt. The idea of dividing the plains among long-time foes was impractical, and it was never taken seriously by the Indians, whose self-respect rested on valorous horse raids and battle deeds against enemies, and whose needs drove them after buffalo herds wherever they were.

In return for the free transit of whites along the Oregon Trail and for permission to erect certain forts to protect the emigrants, Mitchell offered the Sioux government annuities for fifty-five years. He also pledged that soldiers would be used to safeguard the rights of Indians against the whites. The Sioux held long councils over his proposals. Many of the natives were against them. Finally most of the natives agreed to the terms, but they were displeased when Mitchell demanded that the Sioux name a single head chief to be responsible for all of them. They argued that there could be no head chief over all the tribes and bands of the Lakotas, the westering Tetons, but Mitchell insisted, and finally, with impatience, selected the amenable trade chief, Conquering Bear of the Brulés, and announced that he would now be the head of all the Sioux.

The action meant little to the Indians. Conquering Bear signed the treaty, and for the next few years the Brulés and Oglalas abided by its terms, trekking to Fort Laramie each year to collect their annuities in return for not molesting the whites who passed through their country, and calling the Oregon Trail "the holy road," because the whites on it could not be touched. But the northern Sioux returned to their country, knowing that Conquering Bear could never speak or act for them; and while the Oglalas, who had not touched the pen at the 1851 Council, were content to let Conquering Bear be the principal spokesman when dealing with the whites, they continued to look on their own chiefs as their real leaders.

Meanwhile, with the army in control at Fort Laramie, the worst excesses of the whisky trade disappeared. The Brulé and Oglala bands of the old Smoke faction spent much of their time far from white influences, hunting north of the Platte and, despite the strainings of the warriors, living up to the terms of the treaty in refraining from making war against other tribes. Though only about ten years old, Crazy Horse, still known as Curly, attached himself to one of his village's ablest warriors, a man called Hump, who adopted him as his protégé, made bows and war clubs for him, and trained him in the thousand skills of an expert Sioux warrior. Crazy Horse's father, still hoping for a great leader for his people, encouraged both his sons to emulate the tribe's bravest hunters and warriors, and before he was twelve the youthful Curly killed a buffalo and held his seat on a newly captured wild horse. At village ceremonies in which youths received new titles to honor their exploits he was re-named His Horse Looking, and his brother was called Little Hawk.

In 1854 the peace on the Platte River was shattered. That August some four thousand Sioux had made their annual trip to Fort Laramie for the distribution of the blankets, provisions, and other goods that made up the annuities. While the Indians waited for the arrival of the government supply wagons from the East, a party of Mormon emigrants traveled past their villages on the Oregon Trail. A cow belonging to one of the Mormons broke away from the man driving it and ran into a Brulé camp. Its owner chased it to the edge of the village, became frightened by the large crowd of natives, and went on to Fort Laramie; he told the officer in charge there that the Indians had stolen the animal from him.

Traders nearby knew the real story, but they could not help the Indians; an Indian from another tribe, visiting in the Brulé camp, had shot the cow after the Mormon had left, and the natives had butchered it. The commander at Laramie summoned Conquering Bear to the fort, and the chief offered to pay the Mormon more for the animal than it was worth. But through faulty translation by a drunken interpreter the episode was made to seem an aggressive act against the whites by the Brulés, and an impatient officer, Second Lieutenant J. L. Grattan, fresh from West Point and anxious to "crack it to the Sioux," took twenty-nine men and two howitzers to the Brulé camp to seize the killer of the cow. His conduct was unjustified as well as rash. At the Indian village, the interpreter, now roaring drunk and hurling insults and threats at the startled Indians, demanded the surrender of the visitor. Both Conquering Bear and Man-Afraid arrived to try to ease the situation, but when they were unable to get the frightened warrior to submit to arrest Grattan lost patience and abruptly ordered his men to open fire on the village. The first blast from the two howitzers struck Conquering Bear, the friendly trade chief, and he fell mortally wounded. In an instant, Indians swarmed over the whites from all sides. Grattan and most of his men were cut down before they could run. The rest were hacked to pieces as they tried to retreat. Only one man, fatally wounded, crawled away and after hiding at a trader's home got back to Fort Laramie, where he died.

The entire Sioux camp pulled up stakes and headed north in flight across the plains, carrying the wounded Conquering Bear with them. Young Crazy Horse and his family traveled with his step-mother's band of Brulés. The sudden fight and the sight of the dying Conquering Bear, the whites' own choice for head chief of all the Sioux, were shattering experiences for the youth. When the Brulés paused in a temporary hiding place, he rode alone far out of camp, hobbled his horse, and lay down on a high hill. It was the custom of a plains Indian youth, when he reached adolescence, to be sent alone to a wild place, where in solitude and reverence he might seek out a guardian spirit or medicine vision that would guide and protect him through the rest of his life. Hunger, thirst, loneliness, and sometimes terror, protracted over several days, would quicken his imagination or induce hallucinations, and during storms or in dreams he would suddenly recognize with a start what he had come to find, the vision of a guardian spirit, moving across the ground or through the air, vivid and apparently real—a single image such as a howling yellow wolf, or a complicated tableau such as a man riding a lame buffalo across a black sky streaked with lightning flashes. Eventually, after the youth returned proudly to his camp, there would be a dance celebrating the attainment of his manhood, at which he would sing of his newly acquired guardian spirit and announce hints of its nature to the people. Then he would take a new name for what he had seen in his vision, collect some items that were relevant to his protector and that would become sacred to himself, carry them always in a personal medicine bundle, and ever afterward fashion his conduct according to the promptings, signs, or feelings communicated to him by his guardian. The spirit, like Macbeth's witches, might move him to feel that no other Indian would ever kill him, and with that knowledge he would awe his companions by his recklessness and daring in raids and battles. But he might also learn that if it was raining when he entered a certain battle his medicine would not work, and he might die. Then nothing, perhaps, could get him into that particular battle if it rained.

The quest for a vision was a serious and important step in the life of a plains boy, and usually his father and a medicine man or other elders in his camp would prepare and instruct him for his ordeal and see him leave on his lonely vigil. But in the case of young Crazy Horse it was related that he went off by himself, shaken by the Grattan battle, and kept secret for several years the nature of the vision that came to him. He finally revealed to his father and friends that he had stayed on the hill for three days, thinking over the fight that had struck down Conquering Bear, and growing hungry and sick. He had put stones between his toes and under his back to keep from falling asleep, but he had seen nothing. Finally, so weak that he could hardly stand, he gave up and tried to reach his horse. But his head reeled, and he sat down in the shade of a tree. Suddenly his horse came toward him, but out of a strange and unreal world, carrying a rider with long, brown hair hanging unplaited below his waist. The man wore no paint and showed no signs of having taken scalps, but had a small, smooth stone tied behind his ear. As the rider kept coming, bullets and arrows began to streak at him, but they dropped away silently before they touched him. Then people, apparently his own, emerged all around the rider and clutched at him, trying to hold him back, and as he rode through them, shaking them off, a storm enfolded them, and the man seemed to be a part of the storm. A little zigzag lightning streak was on his cheek, and hailspots dotted his body. Then the storm faded, and a small, red-backed hawk flew over the man's head, but still the people grabbed at the rider, trying to hold him back, and still did not succeed.

When Crazy Horse awoke, he knew he had seen his vision. But he did not tell anyone about it until he was sixteen and anxious to become a warrior. Then his father recognized that in his distress and turmoil over the Grattan attack the boy had received an exciting and powerful medicine that could help him become the great leader of the Sioux for whom the Oglala holy man had long hoped. If the youth trusted his vision and followed the example of the rider he had seen, he could not be struck by enemy arrows or bullets. But he must be first among his people in battle, and though there would be darkness and opposition all around him, with others among the Sioux trying to stop him, he must move ahead, unafraid. The holy man made a medicine bundle for his son and got him a red-backed hawk to wear in his hair and a smooth brown stone to tie behind his ear. When the youth finally went into a fight, with a small lightning streak painted on his cheek and hailstone dots on his body, his vision seemed to come true. He astounded his companions by his courage and daring, but took two scalps, against the advice of his guardian spirit, and was wounded in the leg. The medicine, his father told him, was strong indeed, and the next day the holy man at last bestowed his own name, Crazy Horse, on his son, taking a new name, Worm, for himself, and crying to the Oglala village that the people had another Crazy Horse, a great warrior with a powerful medicine.

Meanwhile, after the Grattan massacre the wounded Conquering Bear named Man-Afraid as his successor and died. The soldiers' attack also killed the Treaty of 1851, as far as the Indians were concerned, and many of the chiefs and warriors burned with a spirit of revenge. In November 1854, three months after the fight, Spotted Tail and other Brulés left the bands hiding in the north and returned in war paint to the North Platte River, where they satisfied their anger by attacking a mail coach on the Oregon Trail. The next year the Brulés also threw off the inhibitions of the 1851 Treaty that had kept them at peace with other Indians, and once again launched raids against old enemies. Curly, who had not yet revealed his vision to his father, accompanied a Brulé band, led by Spotted Tail, to the country of the Pawnees and Omahas in eastern Nebraska. Though he was an observer rather than a warrior he witnessed combat, and in the excitement fired an arrow at an Indian who was hiding in the brush. He was sickened when he discovered that he had killed an Omaha woman.

After the excursion he returned to the Sioux country with Spotted Tail, and he was still with the Brulés when they were struck by a new blow. In the late summer of 1855 an army under General W. S. Harney marched west along the Oregon Trail to reinforce Fort Laramie and punish the Indians for the Grattan massacre. On September 3, at the Blue Water Creek, just off the North Platte east of Fort Laramie, Harney came on the Brulé camp in which Curly was living with Spotted Tail's people. Curly was away that day, chasing a horse on the plains, and missed the trouble. After accusing the chiefs of responsibility in the Grattan affair, Harney fell suddenly on their village, killing nearly a hundred of the people, capturing a great number of women and children, and scattering Spotted Tail and the rest of the Brulés in flight. Curly returned soon after the struggle and found several wounded natives in hiding. Their frightened stories, together with the sight of the many dead Indians and destroyed tipis and village possessions, filled him with a bitterness toward the whites that lasted all his life.

At Fort Laramie, where Harney imprisoned his captives, the American general demanded the surrender of the Indians who had attacked the mail coach the previous year. The Oglalas under Man-Afraid had already come down to the post to show that they did not want war, and Spotted Tail and the Brulés who had raided the coach now gave themselves up to try to effect the release of the prisoners and secure the safety of the rest of the people. Harney sent Spotted Tail and his companions to Fort Leavenworth on the lower Platte, where they were imprisoned for two years and became so impressed with the strength of the Americans that the other warriors regarded them, after their return, as men who had been won over to the whites and could no longer lead them in the defense of their country.

Harney, however, was still not finished. In a show of strength he marched from Fort Laramie directly through the Sioux country, looking for hostiles but not finding any, and finally reached Fort Pierre on the Missouri River, where he wintered. In the spring of 1856 he called the various Sioux tribes to Fort Pierre from the plains and forced them to sign a new treaty in which they promised to remain at peace. To succeed the dead Conquering Bear he appointed a chief of the Hunkpapas named Bear Ribs to be the new head of all the Lakotas, but the Indians again did not take it seriously. Man-Afraid, who attended the council for the Oglalas, did not even sign the new treaty.

In the months that followed, Curly went on living part of the time with the Brulés and part with the Oglalas. When he was with the Oglalas he stayed close to his mentor, Hump, who continued to train him as a hunter and warrior. In the summer of 1857, when Curly was about fifteen, he accompanied Man-Afraid's son, known as Young-Man-Afraid-of-His-Horse, and a party of Oglalas on a visit to the Cheyenne Indians on the Solomon River in Kansas. The Sioux youth was impressed by the unity among the Cheyenne people, and compared it unhappily with the disunity among the stronger and more populous Sioux, which his father had pointed out to him. But the Cheyennes were also having trouble with whites, who were trying to extend governmental authority over their country, and after troops suddenly attacked a village in which Curly was living, and again scattered the Indians, including himself, he left the Cheyennes and rode back north to his own people. He joined them late in the summer, and traveled with the Oglalas to a great council of all the Tetons at Bear Butte on the eastern side of the Black Hills. The seven tribes were there, living in huge tipi camps that were pitched in a great sacred circle. Each camp was made up of the villages of its individual bands. The Hunkpatilas, Curly's band of Oglalas, meant those who camp at the horn, because its place among the Oglalas was at the opening of the big village circle, where it stood guard. Altogether, thousands of Lakotas were gathered for the council, and the vast assemblage of chiefs and

braves who had come in from every part of the plains made Curly
agree with his father that it would be good for all the Sioux if
they could remain united in this fashion against the whites.

But the huge horse herds of such a large camp quickly depleted the grass for miles around, and the people could feed
themselves best when they hunted buffalo in smaller bands.
When the council ended, and the chiefs had decided that they
must all resist movements into their land by the white men, the
tribes divided again and went their separate ways. The Oglalas
heard of good hunting grounds along the headwaters of Powder River west of the Black Hills, and they moved into that central part of Wyoming, far north of the Platte. It brought them
into Crow territory, and once more Oglala bands clashed with
Crows, and with others farther west. It was in 1858, when he was
sixteen years old, that Curly rode for the first time as a full-
fledged member of a war party, wearing the small polished stone
behind his ear and the red-backed hawk in his hair, and showing
such power of his medicine in battle that his father gave him
his own name, Crazy Horse.

After that, the young warrior participated in constant raids
and fights, and his skill, courage, and coolness lifted him high
among his admiring band. They were good days for the Oglalas.
The plains were filled with buffalo, and the white men, who
were becoming involved in their own Civil War, paid little
attention to the Indian country north of the Platte River. But
rivalries still troubled the Sioux; during this period the maturing
Crazy Horse himself aroused jealousies among some of the young
men of another band of Oglalas, whose leading warrior was the
powerful Red Cloud. They were called Bad Faces because of the
quarrelsome nature of their original chief. About 1860 in the
Powder River country, Crazy Horse courted Red Cloud's niece,
a Bad Face maiden known as Black Buffalo Woman. But while
Crazy Horse was off on a raid a Bad Face warrior named No
Water, apparently with the connivance of Red Cloud and other
Bad Faces, returned from the war party claiming he had a tooth-

ache, and took Black Buffalo Woman as his wife. Crazy Horse smothered his resentment of the trick, but the episode caused ill will between the partisans of the two men and had serious consequences later.

The Oglalas north of the Platte lived in freedom from the white man's interference until 1862. In that year, suddenly, their relatives who still dwelled in Minnesota were goaded into an uprising by the settlers swarming in around them, and after a fierce war some of them were driven into Canada and others across Dakota and the Missouri River to the Teton bands, who gave them shelter. The Minnesota War spread alarm throughout the West among settlers and miners, who now feared trouble from all the plains tribes; in response to their pleas that the Civil War had left them without adequate military protection, the government authorized the raising of volunteers and rushed them up the Missouri, Platte, and Arkansas Rivers. The Indian-hating militia, filled with the usual fears and prejudices of the frontier, were anxious for a fight, and news of their threats and boasts made the Oglalas and other Tetons uneasy.

Conflict occurred first between the Platte and Arkansas Rivers. That area was hemmed by increasing white traffic on the Oregon Trail on its northern border and the Santa Fe Trail on its southern flank, and was pierced by new routes between the settlements in eastern Kansas and Nebraska and the new mining towns of Colorado. In 1864 violence flared between the whites and Indians in that region, and raids and retaliations occurred throughout the summer and fall. In October the Indians gave signs of wanting peace, and two Cheyenne leaders, who had tried to halt their warriors, managed to effect an armistice with the whites. The latter told them to set up a peaceful camp and remain quiet, and the Indians did this even raising an American flag to show their friendly intentions. But on November 29 a hotheaded unit of Colorado volunteers under Colonel J. M. Chivington roared into their camp in a surprise raid at dawn and slaughtered men, women, and children. The survivors fled to other

Cheyennes, and in December dispatched angry war pipes to all the Indians between the Platte and the Arkansas.

The natives' revenge was terrible. They struck at white settlements and posts all along the South Platte River, plundering ranches and stage stations, looting wagon trains and government stockades, destroying telegraph poles and attacking Julesburg twice and burning the town. Northern Oglalas, with Crazy Horse among them, came riding south to join the warriors, and they participated in the second raid against Julesburg. Then, with Crazy Horse and the northern Sioux showing the way, the entire Indian force of some nine hundred lodges—six thousand people in all—trailed out of the devastated southern country, across western Nebraska to the South Dakota Black Hills. Spotted Tail's Brulés left them there, and the rest went west to Powder River in Wyoming where they pitched their camps near those of the Oglalas.

Chivington's raid started something that was not easy to stop. The blow against the Cheyennes reminded the nervous Sioux of Harney's massacre of their own people on the Blue Water, and convinced them that the whites were planning new assaults of the same kind against all the Indians, including themselves. After the South Platte depredations the actions of the outraged military leaders, who were determined to punish the natives, only provided support for the Indians' fears. The Civil War was ending; troops freed from service in the East were being rushed to the plains, and at Fort Laramie a large punitive expedition was being prepared to invade the Powder River country and destroy the hostiles. In April and May 1865, small Indian raiding parties that included Crazy Horse and other Oglala braves scouted the whites along the North Platte, and saw the build-up of army strength. The Indians returned to the northern country, and planned a new war expedition to strike the North Platte in July.

Before they could act they were temporarily diverted by a

sudden appeal for help from their relatives, the Loafer Sioux who had been living around Fort Laramie. The tipi villages of those people, whom the whites referred to as "friendlies," had grown large, and the arrival of new troops who were quick to think of all Indians as hostile had resulted in a number of misunderstandings and serious incidents, including the hanging of two friendly chiefs. The military leaders, preparing for action against the hostiles in the north, finally decided to clear the Laramie region of the troublesome Loafers, and on July 11 began to march them under military guard down the Platte River to Fort Kearny in the east. The Indians, who numbered between fifteen hundred and two thousand, realized they were being sent into the country of their dreaded enemies, the Pawnees, and in panic managed to dispatch messengers to the Oglala bands in the north. Despite their contemptuous feelings for the Loafers, Crazy Horse and a large party of warriors at once hurried south and struck the column at Horse Creek east of Fort Laramie, killing the American commander, driving the troops into a defensive corral, and freeing most of the natives. Some of the Loafers, who feared their northern kinsmen more than exile at Fort Kearny, fought their own people, and a number of Indians were killed. But the majority got away, and trailed north to the Oglala camps.

Soon afterward the big native expedition against the North Platte got under way. Some three thousand warriors of several tribes, led by Red Cloud, Hump, and other war chiefs of the Sioux. moved south and on July 24 reached the hills above an army garrison west of Fort Laramie. That night Crazy Horse received his first important recognition as a warrior. Because of his daring and skill in battle, he was chosen by the war chiefs as one of a party of twenty decoys who would try to lure the whites into an ambush the next day. The plan, however, miscarried. Crazy Horse and his companions rode down to the post and taunted the members of the garrison to come out and fight them. But the soldiers pursued them only a short distance, and when the great mass of braves who had been hiding in the hills impatiently burst forth the troops withdrew to their stockade, and the chiefs called off the fight.

The same scheme was tried again the next day, and this time Crazy Horse and the other decoys were more successful. An unsuspecting wagon train was coming up the trail to the post, and a troop of cavalry swooped out of the stockade to warn the train and give it protection. The Indians overwhelmed both the cavalry and the wagon train, and after a wild fight in which they killed many of the whites the chiefs ended the attack. The Indians withdrew, and, satisfied with their victory, held scalp dances and headed back to their people at Powder River for a hunt.

But the American punitive expedition was now ready. The troops came in three columns, led by Sioux-hating Pawnee scouts wearing army coats. The men in the ranks, however, had little taste for the war in the wild, unmapped country, and for a month they marched erratically around, threatening mutiny and clashing inconclusively with bands of Indians. The major villages managed to elude them, and finally the troops returned to the Platte River, harassed by Indians who raided their camps and stole their horses. The expedition had been worse than a failure; it left the Indians more determined than ever to keep the whites out of the country north of the Platte.

In the hit-and-run fighting, Crazy Horse had again distinguished himself by his command of other warriors, and the war chiefs now gave him a second honor. To make the people stronger in the struggles that seemed to lie ahead, the Oglalas selected a member of each of the bands to be a "shirt-wearer," or protector of the people. The men chosen were the most valiant and reliable of the younger warriors. They were given special leather shirts made from big-horn skins, fringed with hair locks that celebrated the brave deeds of each man. Crazy Horse, who had earned the right to wear more than two hundred of the locks for coups counted, horses captured, enemies killed, and other proud accomplishments, was selected from the Hunkpatilas;

he was charged with leading the other Hunkpatila warriors in camp and on the march, and with supervising the enforcement of order and justice among all the people. It was a significant honor for him; all the other young men chosen were the sons of the chiefs of the bands. Only Crazy Horse was a "commoner," the son of a holy man, and considered strange because he was still more quiet and brooding than the rest of the warriors, and because his powerful medicine had told him to take no scalps.

The frustration of the 1865 punitive expedition brought a crisis in the relations between the Americans and the plains hostiles. With the end of the Civil War, white men were pushing west in swelling numbers, and the government was under pressure to open new lines of communication across the plains. The most urgent task was to keep Indians away from the Platte, where the nation was building the first transcontinental railroad. But the busy settlements around the new gold mines in western Montana were appealing for a north-south road to connect them with the Platte highway, and the most direct one would have to cut straight through the Sioux hunting lands in the Powder River country. A pioneer trailbreaker named John Bozeman had already tried to open this route, but the Indians had chased him away, and few white men were willing to risk traveling Bozeman's trail without military protection.

Since the army had failed to pacify the Indians by war, peace advocates now came west, hoping to induce the hostiles to abandon fighting and sign treaties that would allow the government to build guardian forts in the natives' country and proceed unhampered with its road and railroad building. With the promise of new gifts and annuities, the negotiators got some of the friendly Sioux around the forts on the upper Missouri to sign their treaties, but Sitting Bull's Hunkpapas and the other northern hostiles stayed far away from them on the plains and refused to have anything to do with them. Farther south, the commissioners went up the Platte to Fort Laramie and tried to coax the Oglalas and Brulés to come in and sign. Some of the Brulés, including

Spotted Tail, who again had had enough of war, finally appeared and touched the pen, but the Oglala bands were more wary.

At last, in June 1866, the Oglalas, led by Old-Man-Afraid, their peace chief, and Red Cloud, who was now head of all the warriors, came down from Powder River to see what the white men wanted. Apparently the commissioners tried deception. They wanted to open the Bozeman Road through the Powder River country and build forts to protect it, but they seem to have pretended in their councils with the Indians that they were referring to another location farther west where a road was already opened. On June 13 the cat was suddenly let out of the bag. A large column of infantry under Colonel Henry B. Carrington marched into Fort Laramie from the east and guilelessly revealed to the Indians that they were on their way to Powder River to build posts and guard the road that Bozeman had pioneered through the Sioux lands. The angry chiefs accused the commissioners of deceit. Red Cloud muttered that "in two moons the command would not have a hoof left," and left Fort Laramie; the Oglalas broke camp and followed him back to Powder River, determined to guard their country.

Carrington started north on June 16, leading some seven hundred men, including the 18th Infantry and scouts and woodchoppers. When he reached the head of Powder River he enlarged a post that already existed there and renamed it Fort Reno, then marched on to Piney Fork south of present-day Sheridan, Wyoming, where he built Fort Phil Kearny. Crazy Horse and other warriors hung on his flanks, watching him all the way, and sending word of his activities to the Oglalas, who were holding their annual Sun Dances on the Tongue River. When the dances were finished, more warriors streamed over to see what they could do. But Red Cloud himself was indecisive. He seemed unwilling to risk a large battle and told his people that they would fight the invaders after the fall hunts.

Meanwhile, Carrington sent men to the Bighorn River in Montana to construct a third post, Fort C. F. Smith, and announced that wagon trains could now travel the Bozeman Road in safety. His optimism was premature. Despite Red Cloud's hesitancy, the restless warriors began to raid all along the trail, attacking wagon trains and messengers and closing in on the forts themselves to run off stock and ambush members of the garrisons who ventured outside the stockades. The road was soon as unsafe as it had ever been, and Carrington's forts were isolated and in a state of siege.

In December, with the fall hunts ended, Red Cloud was ready for war. More than a thousand lodges moved near Fort Phil Kearny. Red Cloud launched his attack on December 6, sending a party of decoys to lure the soldiers into a prepared ambush. The troops refused to follow the decoys, and the plan failed. But the Sioux harassments and the frustrations of the siege had irritated some of Carrington's officers, and they now chafed to conduct offensive operations of their own. Carrington restrained them until December 21. On that day, which was cold and clear, with recently fallen snow covering the hillsides, the Indians struck again. This time Crazy Horse's mentor, Hump, began the battle by sending a party of braves against a train of woodcutters near the fort. When the whites made a corral and signaled to the post for aid, Captain William J. Fetterman, an impetuous officer who had contempt for the fighting qualities of the Indians and regarded Carrington as a coward, hastened out to the rescue with eighty men. Hump immediately withdrew his braves and sent Crazy Horse galloping forward at the head of a group of decoys. It was a great day for Crazy Horse. Against Carrington's order, Fetterman and his men decided to carry the fight to the Sioux, and pursued the taunting decoys over a ridge and out of sight of the fort. There Hump's entire force emerged from hiding and screamed down on the soldiers. They charged directly into the troops, raced back and forth among them, shooting arrows and swinging their war clubs, and cut them into small groups. As the men went down, the Indians attacked them savagely, bashing in their heads and mutilating their bodies. In a short time Fetterman's whole command was wiped out.

Biting winter weather set in almost immediately and saved the frightened remnants of the fort's garrison. The Indians divided into small bands and left the area, looking for warmer camp sites and game. But when the cold eased, they were back along the trail, attacking every white man who ventured to travel it and renewing their sieges around the forts. New efforts were made at Laramie to talk peace with the hostiles, and in June some of the Oglala and Brulé chiefs, including Old-Man-Afraid and Red Cloud, went down for another talk. Old-Man-Afraid did all the speaking for the Oglalas, and demanded that the whites would have to evacuate the forts and get out of the Powder River country before there could be peace. As a result of Red Cloud's silence a suspicion apparently grew among some of the warriors that their war chief was beginning to soften toward the whites, and a number of the young Oglalas for the first time began to look upon Crazy Horse as the man who might someday have to lead all of them.

But the chiefs went back north, still at war with the whites, and in August launched two new attacks against the forts. At the Big Horn, several hundred Indians, mostly Cheyennes, surprised a haying detail and an escort of soldiers in a field outside Fort C. F. Smith, but were driven off by a determined defense. The battle added to the misery and fears of that long-isolated outpost, but accomplished little else. At Fort Phil Kearny, on August 2, 1867, some one thousand Oglalas and other Sioux again attacked a party of woodchoppers, guarded this time by a detachment of soldiers armed with new fifty-caliber, breech-loading Springfield rifles. Hump once more led the warriors, while Red Cloud and the older war chiefs watched through field glasses from the top of a ridge. But the battle developed without plan, and the braves rushed out of hiding before Hump's decoys could do their work.

The whites, under command of a doughty Civil War veteran, Captain James W. Powell, had established a corral of fourteen wagon boxes, removed from their wheels and arranged in a large oval, to hold their stock at night, and when the Indians charged, most of the men got safely into the boxes. Crazy Horse led part of the warriors in an attack against the woodcutters' camp outside the corral, while Hump directed the assault against the wagon beds. It was a fiercely fought and dramatic fight. Crazy Horse swept the woodcutters out of their camp, then joined Hump, whose warriors were being held off by the white men's fast-firing breech-loaders. The Indians circled the corral, screaming and whooping, firing arrows and bullets and hurling lances at the wagon boxes, but were unable to close in. They withdrew, dismounted and tried to charge in a wedge-shaped formation on foot, but were again driven back by the rifle fire. Finally, after another mounted attack, the chiefs sighted a relief column of soldiers hurrying from the fort, six miles away, and signaled an end of the battle. The Indians withdrew, driving many American horses and mules with them. They had lost six men killed and six wounded, and the whites had suffered slightly higher casualties.

Despite the fact that it had been a rebuff to the Indians, the spectacular wagon-box fight dramatized the strength and stubborn determination of the Powder River hostiles, and the government again made efforts to restore peace. A new treaty was devised with a host of catch-all promises designed to attract the good will of as many bands as possible, and lavish presents, including guns and ammunition, were offered to the natives if they signed. One by one, chiefs of friendly as well as hostile bands were lured in from all parts of the plains; they touched the pen to the new agreement and returned to their people with their new gifts. But Red Cloud, the war leader most wanted by the whites, held out; finally, in full capitulation to him, the government ordered the abandonment of the Bozeman Trail and the evacuation of the three ill-starred forts that had tried to protect it. When the soldiers marched out, grimly remembering the sacrifices and suffering that had been in vain, the Cheyennes set fire to Fort Phil Kearny, and Red Cloud's exultant warriors burned Fort C. F.

Smith. Then, on November 6, 1868, after a special Oglala council had granted him the right to speak to the whites with the authority of a peace chief, Red Cloud rode down to Fort Laramie and signed the treaty.

Most of the natives who signed the agreement that year, including Red Cloud, later insisted that the whites did not tell them truthfully what was in the document. Both north and south of the Platte River, the bands maintained that they understood that the treaty promised to keep troops and other white men out of their countries, to leave the Indians at peace, and to allow them to re-open trade for white men's goods at the posts along the Platte River. This was far from the actual terms of the treaty, which acknowledged that the Powder River and Bighorn country was unceded Indian land in which the Sioux and Cheyenne could continue to hunt without white interference, but at the same time established all South Dakota west of the Missouri River as a reservation and provided that the Indians must go to live at agencies within the reservation on the west side of the Missouri River. Regarding their right to trade at the Platte River posts— which the Indians earnestly desired after the years of interrupted trade and their consequent shortages of white men's goods—the government was misleading. It gave both the Indians and the traders reason to believe that such traffic would be allowed. But in reality the most pressing reason for the entire attempt to re-store peace with the Indians was to secure the Platte Valley highway and transcontinental railroad route from native molestation, and the first thing the government did after the hostiles signed was to ban all trade on the Platte and drive all Indians north of that river.

It led at once to new turmoil. Armies south of the Platte ordered bands of Cheyennes, Brulés, and southern Oglalas to the new agencies on the Missouri, and when they refused to go the troops harried the natives, encouraged the slaughter of the buffalo that was their food supply, and finally sent most of the Indians hastening in fear into the country north of the Platte. Other bands that tried to trade along the river were rounded up and marched off to the agencies along the Missouri in a country they regarded as alien.

Once again the most troublesome holdouts were the northern Tetons and their northern Cheyenne allies, who claimed they knew nothing about a reservation and refused to leave the Powder River country and go to the Missouri agencies. The situation reached a new crisis in 1870, when white men along the Platte got the idea that the Big Horn Mountains were filled with gold and once more pressured the government to open that area to them. In an attempt to avert another war, officials induced Red Cloud of the Oglalas and Spotted Tail of the Brulés to come to Washington to see the President and negotiate. Many of the Oglalas, including Crazy Horse, were now openly suspicious of Red Cloud, who had signed the 1868 Treaty that provided for a reservation and agencies, and they wondered uneasily what more the chief would agree to in the white man's city. But Red Cloud's trip was something of a triumph for the hostiles' cause. The warrior and his entourage met President Grant, toured Washington in carriages, and inspected cannons and other evidences of American military strength. But they conducted themselves proudly, and when they were told to take their people to the new agencies Red Cloud stoutly refused, and insisted that he had come to Washington only to secure the right of the Indians to trade peaceably on the Platte. The full text of the treaty was read to the natives; so much in it was apparently new to them that Red Cloud became infuriated by what he heard, and one of the other chiefs tried to kill himself in shame.

Red Cloud went on to New York and, at the invitation of easterners who thought that the army and the government were responsible for all the Indian troubles in the West, delivered a stirring defense of his people, charging the whites with a long list of betrayals and deceptions of the Sioux. His speech at Cooper Institute caused a sensation, and the ensuing clamor for justice to the Indians at last forced a chagrined reversal of government policy. Red Cloud went home with permission to trade at Fort Laramie, and in 1871, despite angry opposition from the anti-Indian white population in the West, a new "peace" commission established a special agency for Red Cloud's Oglalas on the North Platte River just thirty-two miles east of Fort Laramie. Another agency was also built for Spotted Tail's Brulés; it was located on the White River north of the Platte in northwestern Nebraska.

Meanwhile, during the negotiations, a serious division had occurred in the Powder River country between Red Cloud's Bad Faces and Crazy Horse's Hunkpatilas. Ill will had developed gradually as the Hunkpatilas had grown more wary of Red Cloud's talks with the whites. But a private affair of Crazy Horse's had much to do with it. He had never lost interest in the Bad Face maiden, Black Buffalo Woman, who had been taken from him by a trick. She had apparently also maintained her admiration for Crazy Horse, and the couple had indulged in an open courtship that on several occasions had aroused the anger of the woman's husband, No Water, and his Bad Face friends. One night in 1870, when No Water and many of the Bad Faces had gone down to the Platte to await the return of Red Cloud from the East, Black Buffalo Woman, who now had three children, rode away from the Bad Face camp with Crazy Horse. Some of the Bad Faces sent word to No Water, and he returned in a jealous rage and shot Crazy Horse in the jaw with a revolver. The Hunkpatila recovered and, admitting that he had done a foolish thing, sent Black Buffalo Woman back to her people and restrained his followers from taking revenge on No Water.

But the episode widened the breach between the two bands of Oglalas. Many of the Bad Faces, who had regarded Crazy Horse's many war honors with envy, now came to hate him, and found satisfaction in giving greater loyalty to their own war chief, Red Cloud, whom the Hunkpatilas were calling two-faced. The final rupture came with the establishment of Red Cloud's agency. Confirming the Hunkpatila fears, it meant that the Bad Face leader had at last given up the fight for freedom, and had sold out to the white men for their gifts and favor. Most of the Bad Faces moved to the new agency with Red Cloud, and even Old-Man-Afraid and members of some of the other bands, grown weary of fighting, joined them. But the Hunkpatilas, drawing around them all the other Oglalas and their northern allies who would still have nothing to do with the white men, remained in the north and looked for new leadership from their own strong man, the uncompromising warrior, Crazy Horse.

In 1871 he was almost thirty years old, still slender and boyish-looking, with long brown hair and deep, intent eyes. His father, the holy man Worm, and his step-mother, the Brulé, were still alive, but Little Hawk, the brother he adored, had been killed by white men in the western country, and his teacher, the valiant Hump, had lost his life in a battle against the Shoshonis. After the unhappy episode with Black Buffalo Woman, the Bad Face had apparently given birth to a daughter by Crazy Horse, and No Water's people were raising the child. The Hunkpatila had looked to his own village and taken another woman, Black Shawl, to live with him in his lodge, and she too gave birth to a daughter. Crazy Horse named her They Are Afraid of Her, but several years later the little girl caught a sickness and died, and he was thrown into grief.

During the winter of 1870-1871 the Hunkpatilas and the other Powder River hostiles camped in a new area, farther north in Crow Indian territory on the Rosebud tributary of the Yellowstone River in Montana. The more northerly Tetons, including Sitting Bull's tough Hunkpapas, often hunted there, and Crazy Horse's people met them and felt strong again in knowing that they still had powerful allies. In 1872 the Hunkpatilas held a great Sun Dance with the northerners, and later in the summer Crazy Horse and his war chiefs coordinated attacks with Sitting Bull against a body of troops escorting a Northern Pacific railroad survey party through the Indians' country, and forced them to abandon their work.

That year, tales of the winter handouts and easy life around the agencies reached the Powder River bands, and when cold weather arrived many of Crazy Horse's people went south to visit those who were living with Red Cloud. Their stories, in turn, excited many of the natives around the agencies who missed the wild, free life of the hunting bands, and with the return of warm weather they joined Crazy Horse's people and trooped back north to swell the size of the hostiles' camps. The back-and-forth movement became an annual affair, participated in by an increasing number of Indians, who thus managed to enjoy freedom in the summer and live off the government in the winter. It irritated the agency officials, who already chafed because Crazy Horse and his followers had not come in originally with Red Cloud, and who now recognized that those who went north in the summer only supported his defiance. But they were unable to interfere with the natives' movements, and in fact had a more immediate problem with Red Cloud himself.

The government still wanted the Platte Valley cleared, and the agents were under orders to try to persuade Red Cloud to allow his agency to be moved to the White River north of the Platte, where Spotted Tail's Brulé agency was located. Red Cloud resisted for a long time, even going to Washington again in 1872 to argue against the move; but in the summer of 1873, while the Bad Face leader was hunting south of the Platte, some of the other chiefs at the agency agreed to the move. Red Cloud returned to find the transferral under way. He was angry, but mostly because he had not been the one to give the assent, and he soon acquiesced and quieted down at the new site.

The shift to the north infuriated the Powder River hostiles, who considered it a dangerous withdrawal toward their Black Hills and South Dakota hunting grounds. In a short time whites poured into the abandoned region between the Platte and White Rivers, and confirmed their fears. But a more menacing invasion soon threatened them from another direction. During that same summer of 1873 Northern Pacific railroad survey parties returned to the Yellowstone, escorted this year by a more formidable body of troops, the veteran Indian-fighting 7th Cavalry, led by Lieutenant Colonel George Armstrong Custer.

Ever since the Civil War, in which he had had a gallant record, Custer had been a publicized hero. He had come west after the war, looking for more glory, and had led the 7th Cavalry in cruel and unreasonable warfare against southern Cheyennes and other tribes in Kansas and on the southern plains. He was an irascible, unstable man who treated his own troops so badly that they often went A.W.O.L. When he caught them he shot them without trial, and then on one occasion went A.W.O.L. himself. In 1867 he was court-martialed for his behavior, but was soon back in command of the 7th Cavalry, and in 1868, seeking headlines again, he savagely slaughtered Black Kettle's unfortunate southern Cheyennes in an unjustified attack on the Washita River. Some of the survivors fled north and joined the Powder River hostiles; and in 1873, transferred from the south, the 7th Cavalry and Custer, whom the Indians called Long Hair, faced the Sioux.

Early in August, Crazy Horse and his warriors fought a series of sharp battles with Custer in the Yellowstone Valley, but the troops drove the Indians away each time, and the survey party which Custer was guarding was able to complete its work. It was only the beginning of the natives' troubles with Custer, and the start of a continuous conflict with him that was to end at the Little Bighorn. In 1874 he was back in their country again. This time, in an even more flagrant violation of the Treaty of 1868, he led an expedition of twelve hundred men, including the 7th Cavalry, two companies of infantry with Gatling guns and artillery, sixty Indian scouts, newspaper correspondents, and scientists, to explore the Sioux' sacred *Pa Sapa*, the Black Hills, and gather military and scientific information about the region. The group had originally been ordered by General Philip H. Sheridan, commander of the Division of the Missouri, to make a reconnaissance preparatory to constructing a fort in the Black Hills to guard the building of the Northern Pacific railroad. But all through the winter, rumors had been encouraged by Custer that there was gold in the Black Hills, and President Grant had received word that the flamboyant officer was "inciting the public" to form prospecting parties to accompany the expedition.

Custer's invasion was as deliberate an incitement to trouble with Indians as was ever committed. When he left Fort Abraham Lincoln at Bismarck, North Dakota, he was accompanied by civilian gold hunters. Less than sixty days later the expedition had returned to the post, having already sent back excited messages that gold had been found in the Black Hills "from the grass roots down." If the military wanted a reason for a war with the northern hostiles who had so far refused to go to agencies, it had now provided one. Prospectors poured into the Black Hills, pushing aside the troops who made feeble and belated efforts to keep them out of what was still Indian country. By 1875 it was too late to halt the stampede.

Crazy Horse had not been near the Black Hills during the time of the expedition, and when the Hunkpatila leader learned about it Custer had already departed. The news stirred all the Lakotas, and they called Custer "the Chief of all the Thieves" and his route to the Black Hills "the Thieves' Trail." When the miners began to appear, Crazy Horse led a war party to the Black Hills and harried the prospectors until cold weather arrived. But he could not stop them, and he returned to his camp for the winter, wondering what to do.

In the spring the government made the first move. Red Cloud and a number of the agency chiefs were summoned again to Washington and told that the United States wished to buy the Black Hills from the Indians. The chiefs were bullied and threatened, but could not agree on what to do. A minor scandal occurred when Red Cloud even presented the government with a bill erroneously given to him by a shady person who had been hired to entertain the chief at "bad houses" while he was in Washington. Finally, when the Indians decided that they would have to consult their people, the government announced that it would send a special commission to the Red Cloud Agency in the fall to negotiate with all the Sioux for the purchase.

The chiefs returned home to find the country in an uproar. Whites were flooding into the Black Hills, and the government had even sent an official expedition, headed by Professor W. P. Jenney of the New York School of Mines, to be sure that the Hills were indeed worth purchasing. When Red Cloud and his companions reported that a commission was coming in the fall to buy the area, a new quarrel broke out. All through the Sioux country the chiefs and warriors argued whether to sell the holy *Pa Sapa*. Some of the Indians who had been living at the agencies saw the great crisis that was building for the Sioux and rode away to the north to join Crazy Horse and pledge to fight with him to the end.

On September 4 the commission reached the Red Cloud Agency and two weeks later began negotiations. Some twenty thousand Indians were present, mostly from the Red Cloud and Spotted Tail reservations. But other delegations had also come in, and, though Crazy Horse was not there, some of his warriors had arrived to watch. The chiefs were in a quandary. No one man could be the spokesman, and none of them wished to take the lead in front of all the people. After three days of arguing among themselves the chiefs were abashed when a young warrior from Crazy Horse's band pushed his way forward with a Winchester and a fistful of cartridges and announced that he was going to kill the commissioners. Some Oglalas seized him, but in the excitement many of the mounted warriors began to circle menacingly as if preparing to charge at the white men. They were halted by Young-Man-Afraid-of-His-Horse, who ordered them to disperse and go to their camps. The meeting broke up without a fight, and the next day the chiefs told the commissioners that they would sell the Black Hills if the government would pay the price they asked and feed and clothe the Sioux for seven generations to come. The chiefs were not agreed on the price, but Red Cloud asked for $600,000,000. The commissioners countered by offering $6,000,000, which the chiefs refused, and the council ended without accomplishing anything.

When they returned to the East, the frustrated commissioners reported that the government would be unable to make progress with the Sioux until those people had been taught a lesson. Furthermore, they maintained, the Indians and not the whites had originally violated the Treaty of 1868, because the natives had not gone to the Missouri River agencies or taken up farming, as that document (which, they forgot to add, had probably not even been read to the Sioux) had stipulated. Their angry report ended the government's efforts to buy the Black Hills peaceably, and in November 1875, at the instigation of President Grant, the Indian Office ordered all the hostile Indians to come into the Sioux agencies by the following January 31, or be driven in by troops. Back of the order lay the hope that once the bands were cowed they could be induced to give up the Black Hills, the Big Horns, and the Powder River country for a reasonable price.

Apparently few persons expected that the northern hostiles would risk a war with the formidable forces that would be thrown against them. But January 31 came and went; the bands in the north either would not or could not come in on such short notice in mid-winter, and early in February the Indian Office turned the situation over to the military, estimating that the hostiles numbered about three thousand people, including only a few hundred warriors. The guess might not have been far wrong, but it overlooked the fact that shortly afterward, when winter began to ease, thousands of armed natives, as was their habit, began to ride off from the agencies to join the bands in the north. For the most part, they went this time in sullen determination, knowing that they were heading for a war in defense of the Sioux lands.

Crazy Horse and his Oglala band had been in camp on the Tongue River, but when they received the order to come in they had moved to Powder River near the villages of Sitting Bull and the more northerly warriors. Early in March, runners brought them word that soldiers were coming north against them. They were ten companies of cavalry and two of infantry that had left the North Platte River on March 1 under General George Crook. As the soldiers came closer, a band of northern Cheyennes under Two Moons that was camped near the mouth of the Little Powder, not far from Crazy Horse, decided to obey the white men's orders and go in. Some of Crazy Horse's people agreed that it would be the wisest thing for themselves also, and they moved to the Cheyenne camp to accompany those people to the agencies. Almost at once, disaster struck them. Crook's scouts saw the Cheyenne camp, and at dawn on March 17, 1876, six companies of Crook's cavalry under Colonel J. J. Reynolds launched a furious charge on the village that took the natives by surprise. The Indians fled up a steep hillside, leaving dead and wounded behind. But when they got their women and children safely started toward Crazy Horse's camp, the warriors came back down the hill, counter-attacking with such fury that the troops gave way. Reynolds ordered the village burned, and beat a rapid retreat up Powder River to Crook's main force.

The destruction of the Indian camp, in which Crook had hoped to base his men for further operations, forced the American commander to abandon his entire campaign. It was still bitter winter weather; Reynolds had many wounded men, the troops were without shelter or adequate supplies, and angry Indians were buzzing at the soldiers, stealing their horses and the few beef cattle they had left. Unhappily, Crook turned his men around and returned to the Platte.

Two Moons and his Cheyennes now joined Crazy Horse, determined to fight to the end with the Sioux. The Hunkpatilas who had started to go to the agencies were back also, and soon after the battle all the Oglalas met in an unprecedented council and named Crazy Horse the supreme chief of their tribe, for both war and peace. They sent messengers racing south to the Oglalas wintering at the Spotted Tail and Red Cloud agencies, telling them that Crazy Horse now led them all, and urging them to come north with guns to fight the whites.

As the people began to leave the agencies for the war, the northern camps crossed to the Rosebud to hunt buffalo and make dried meat for the summer. Newcomers reached them each day, swelling the circles of hostile tipi villages. They were from all the Teton tribes, and from other Sioux tribes newly come from Minnesota. From the southern agencies even "friendlies" and Bad Faces showed up, including Red Cloud's son, carrying a silver-mounted rifle that had been given to his father in Washington. The year of crisis had come for the Sioux nation, and at last it was almost united. Only Red Cloud and the other chiefs and natives who had become used to staying year-round at the agencies, and who were afraid of the "big trouble" up north, were absent.

Early in June the Hunkpapas held their Sun Dance; word went round that Sitting Bull had had fifty little pieces of skin cut from each of his arms with an awl, and had then made the sun-gazing dance, staring at the sun until he fell as if dead and had had a vision: many soldiers falling into camp. The people knew that it meant that troops were coming, and soon word arrived that it was true. Crook was back on the Rosebud, marching north again with some thirteen hundred men, including Crow and Shoshoni scouts. The Sioux had moved west to the Little Bighorn River after the Hunkpapa Sun Dance, but now a thousand warriors, including the Oglalas under Crazy Horse, returned to the Rosebud to try to stop the new invasion.

On the morning of June 17 the Indians ran into some Crow scouts on a ridge above Crook's camp, which lay in a valley on the west side of the Rosebud just south of a brush-filled canyon. Crook had been informed that the hostiles' village was on the stream north of the canyon, and he had been about to break camp and launch a surprise attack on the Indian settlement when the Crows came galloping down the slope, shouting, "Lakotas! Lakotas!" On the Indians' left flank the Sioux apparently chased the Crows into the valley, colliding in a wild fight with Crook's cavalry. On the right the Indians under Crazy Horse seem to have tried some sort of decoy. They withdrew slowly as Crook's infantry came at them, then suddenly halted and launched a charge of their own. The battle broke into hand-to-hand fights, with charges and counter-charges all over the valley. In the melee Crazy Horse was a figure of furious action, with his hair hanging long and unbraided, the polished stone of his vision at his ear, and a red calfskin cape flying out behind him with white spots on it like the hailstones of his medicine dream.

As the fighting grew more intense, Crook ordered part of his forces into the canyon to attack the village which he thought lay at its northern end. The Crows refused to go into what they believed was an ambush, and shortly afterward, when the Sioux seemed on the verge of overwhelming the troops still in the valley, Crook called back the men in the canyon. Those troops appeared suddenly in the rear of the hostiles, who were now running out of ammunition. The fighting swirled a few minutes longer, and then the Sioux broke off the engagement and rode away.

The Indians said later that they lost eleven men killed and five wounded in the action. Crook had nine white men killed and twenty-one wounded, and also lost many of his native scouts. The next day he was forced to abandon his offensive again, and withdrew once more to a base camp in the south, where he remained for six weeks waiting for reinforcements. He claimed a victory because he had driven off the Indians; but if it was a triumph, it was a disruptive one. His offensive had been part of a carefully planned three-pronged campaign, designed to ensnare and destroy the northern hostiles, and the other two prongs were even then on the move, unaware of Crook's withdrawal. One of them, under Colonel John Gibbon, was approaching from western Montana. The other, commanded by General Alfred Terry, had been making its way westward from the Missouri. On July 21, four days after the Battle of the Rosebud, Gibbon and Terry joined forces at the mouth of that stream on the Yellowstone.

With no third prong left to drive the Indians against them, the plan had to be revised. Losing no time, Terry ordered Gibbon to go back to the Bighorn and march south along it to the Little Bighorn. Custer and the 7th Cavalry, who were with Terry, would go along the Rosebud parallel with Gibbon and catch the Indians between them. Terry expected that Custer would make a leisurely march and not start across toward the Little Bighorn until the evening of June 25, when Gibbon would have had time to arrive opposite him for a joint attack on June 26. The commanders separated, and at noon on June 22, Custer started up the Rosebud with about six hundred soldiers, forty-four Indian scouts, some twenty packers and guides, and a civilian newspaper correspondent.

The Sioux and Cheyenne warriors, meanwhile, had gone back from the Rosebud to their camps on the Little Bighorn, and for several days the bands mourned their dead in the Crook fight and danced over the scalps they had taken. Their villages, set up in five large circles of tipis and several smaller ones, extended about three miles along the west bank of the river. On the north was the camp circle of the Cheyennes, and at the south were Sitting Bull's Hunkpapas. Between them were the villages of the Oglalas and the other Sioux. Altogether, between twelve thousand and fifteen thousand Indians were present, including perhaps as many as five thousand warriors, already aroused by the excitement of the battle with Crook.

On June 25, the seventh day after the fight on the Rosebud, a native on a ridge above the camp saw a bank of dust rising across the plains, and many men moving beneath it. It was Custer, already on his way from the Rosebud, hurrying toward the Little Bighorn a day ahead of time. He had planned to rest in the hills until the 26th, he told his officers, but scouts had informed him that the Indians had learned of his presence, and he must now attack them before they got away. A few miles short of the river, he paused and ordered Major Marcus Reno and three companies, together with some Indian scouts, to move straight to the Little Bighorn, cross the stream and attack the southern end of the village. He would take five companies himself north along the east side of the river, cross lower down, and attack the northern end of the camp. Captain Frederick Benteen with three companies would come up as reinforcements, along with another company that was protecting the pack train.

Custer had no idea how large an Indian village lay in front of him. And the natives were ready. As Reno's troops splashed across the river and charged at the Hunkpapa tipis on the camp's southern end, a swarm of warriors came out against them, led by Sitting Bull, Gall, and Black Moon. At the Hunkpatila village, Crazy Horse painted a lightning streak on his face and hailstone dots on his body, put the red-backed hawk of his medicine vision in his hair and the polished stone behind his ear, mounted his yellow pinto, and called for the Oglalas to follow him. "Come on, Lakotas! It's a good day to die," he yelled, as they gathered behind him.

The strong Hunkpapa stand had meanwhile frightened the scouts into flight, and forced Reno to come to an abrupt halt. He dismounted his men and tried to form them into a skirmish line, but the Indians surged forward and pushed them back, and they finally mounted again and withdrew in disorder to the cover of the trees along the river. When it looked as if they would be overrun in the timber thicket, Reno ordered a retreat to the bluffs across the stream. The troopers broke into wild flight, with every man for himself, and the Indians whooped and howled after them, cutting them down as they would a herd of fleeing buffalo. A third of Reno's command was lost in the panic, and the rest reached the top of the bluffs and formed defensively for the fight of their lives just as Benteen's three companies arrived. The men dug in together, but at that moment most of the Indians turned suddenly away from them and galloped north along the river.

The diversion was caused by Custer's five companies that had appeared on a ridge above the river opposite the northern part of the camp. The American commander had finally realized the immense size of the hostile village, but he was still bent on a fight. When he saw women and children running from the south end of the camp, he was sure that Reno was chasing them, and his men cheered the sight of the Indians "skedaddling." After sending his excited message to Benteen for more ammunition packs, Custer started down to the ford to launch his own attack.

It was said that four brave Cheyenne Indians crossed to meet Custer and for a moment held him up. At any rate, the warning ran through the camp to the south end, and the warriors came charging back to meet the new threat. Gall led the Hunkpapas along the eastern bank, and Crazy Horse went through the village, sweeping up more braves to follow him. While Sitting Bull stopped in the camp with the older chiefs to take care of the women and children, Crazy Horse went on, leading his warriors across the stream and up a ravine to get at Custer from the north. Other Indians had now joined the four Cheyennes and were driving Custer away from the ford. Dividing his troops into two columns, the American leader turned anxiously to the north and hurried along the slope above the river, apparently looking for another place to cross. But the Indians were closing in, and the men had to fight as they moved. Troopers dropped, and the peril of both columns increased. Suddenly Gall and his Hunkpapas appeared from the south. They rode savagely at the troops, isolated several of the companies, and in a few moments overwhelmed them and cut them to pieces. In the face of disaster, Custer backed up to a high ridge with the rest of his men and prepared to make a stand. As he reached a knoll, he was hit from the rear. Out of a ravine came Crazy Horse at the head of a mass of warriors who surged behind him in a wedge formation. The Oglalas charged into the troops, broke their ranks, and fought wildly, man against man. Then they galloped off, circling around the soldiers, who formed a ring. More Indians arrived every minute, and the throng around the troops became more dense. Many of the natives were on foot, firing from hiding places in the ravines. Some of those who were on horses dismounted and drew back to wait. Others, still on their horses, rode round and round, charging in boldly every so often for a shot, and then darting away. Crazy Horse was in the thick of it, taunting the soldiers and exhorting his warriors. His medicine was strong, and no bullets reached him. The Cheyenne veterans of the Washita had recognized Custer, and they exulted in revenge. The squaw killer, as they called him, would not get away today. No one knows how long the soldiers fought. It might have been an hour. Their casualties mounted, and their ammunition dwindled. The Indians could see the end coming. Finally one warrior charged boldly into the weakened circle and out the other side. Others followed him, and then others, and at last it was over.

The Indians were firing at the soldiers' bodies to be sure they were dead when one of the natives saw more troops on a distant ridge. They were the companies of Reno and Benteen, who had heard the sounds of the Custer battle and had finally left their own defensive position to come and see what was happening. With wild whoops the Indians charged at the new arrivals, and again Reno and Benteen went on the defensive and were surrounded. They managed to hold off the natives until dark, and during the night they strengthened their position. At dawn the Indians resumed the fight, and continued it until late in the afternoon. Then a Sioux scout arrived with word that more soldiers, the troops of Terry and Gibbon, were coming up the river. While some of the warriors kept up the siege, the rest of the natives withdrew and fired the grass on the plains. Behind the dense clouds of smoke the entire Sioux and Cheyenne camp packed up and trailed south.

Reno's men knew they had been fighting Hunkpapas, and at first it seemed that Sitting Bull had been the principal architect of the Indian victory. But there was no single hero. Gall had fought tremendously against both Reno and Custer, and Crazy Horse had inspired the circle of Indians that finally overran Custer. But the proudest moment in Sioux history was also the signal for the beginning of the end, and sad days were about to mark Crazy Horse alone as the Sioux's great man.

More than 250 whites were killed and 44 were wounded at the

Little Bighorn. But the Indians had many losses also—no one ever knew how many—and though they probably now could also have whipped Terry and Gibbon, they were not fighting an all-out war in the sense that the army viewed it, and they had no inclination for another battle. They withdrew southward to the base of the Big Horn Mountains and danced and celebrated in safety. During the summer Crazy Horse led several raids against the miners and settlers in the Black Hills, but it was clear to him that the Indians had lost that region to the whites forever. Moreover, there would never again be peace for the hostiles. The Americans were shocked and shamed by the Custer massacre, and soldiers would come and come again until they had made the natives pay for what had happened on the Little Bighorn.

Late in the summer the Indians went back to Powder River and learned that the first punitive expeditions were starting after them. Both Crook and Terry were back in the field with reinforcements. The tribes at last split up, evaded the soldiers who were looking for them, and went their separate ways. Some of the Indians followed Crazy Horse to Bear Butte, and others went with Sitting Bull to the lower Yellowstone. As fall approached, the many natives who had been used to wintering at the agencies left the camps of the hostiles and, as if nothing had changed, started back to the white men's headquarters. At Slim Buttes north of the Black Hills, on September 9, a group of forty lodges under Iron Plume was discovered and attacked by a detachment of Crook's cavalry. Iron Plume sent a hurried call for help to Crazy Horse, but by the time the Oglala arrived with some six hundred warriors Crook had already come up with his main force, Iron Plume with a grievous wound had surrendered, and the troops had occupied the Indians' camp. Crazy Horse's braves fired on the soldiers from bluffs around the village, but they were short of ammunition and lacked a war spirit, and the troops finally drove them off.

The situation of the Sioux now began to deteriorate rapidly.

Army troops had occupied all the agencies after the Little Bighorn battle, and in the fall word reached the northern bands that new commissioners had threatened to withhold further rations from the peaceful chiefs and their people if they did not sign an agreement in the name of the whole Sioux nation, surrendering not only the Black Hills but all the unceded country west of it, including the Powder River country and the Big Horn Mountains. A provision of the 1868 Treaty had said that no new treaty could be made with the Sioux without the approval of three-fourths of the adult males, but the commissioners had overlooked that provision, and the fearful chiefs had signed the new agreement in two days. In addition, the agency natives had been given the choice of being transferred to new homes on the Missouri River or of going into exile in the Indian Territory of Oklahoma. Red Cloud had been humiliated. He had pleaded that he had had nothing to do with the war, and, when he had run off from his agency in a huff, hated Pawnee scouts had pursued him, taken away his arms and horses, and hauled him back to General Crook, who had disgraced him further by ordering him deposed as head chief and naming in his place his rival, Spotted Tail.

The impatience of the Americans at the agencies was matched by their determination in the field. They now owned the country they had wanted, and they would soon move the Sioux to the Missouri River, which the chiefs had indicated they preferred to Oklahoma. But first the army had to bring in all the hostiles, particularly the dangerous bands of Crazy Horse and Sitting Bull. From a base at the mouth of the Tongue River on the Yellowstone a new army under Colonel Nelson A. Miles went after Sitting Bull. In October Miles found the Hunkpapas and had a council with the tough medicine man. It ended in a fight, but the Hunkpapas got away. Later, when winter overtook them, many of the people grew weary of being chased, and gradually came in and surrendered at the agencies. Sitting Bull and Gall held out, and in February, the two men led 109 of their lodges across the border into Canada, where Sitting Bull remained in exile until 1881. He returned to the United States long after hostilities had ended.

Meanwhile, Crazy Horse had learned of the surrender of the Sioux lands, and his people smoldered with anger at the agency peace chiefs who had betrayed them. But the northern country was dangerous now, full of troops, and there was little time to think of anything save keeping out of the soldiers' way. Crazy Horse moved the Oglalas back to the Tongue River, and in November heard that Crook was marching toward him again from the Platte. Before the Americans reached the Oglalas, however, they ran into Dull Knife's Cheyennes in a canyon on the head of Powder River, and on November 25 some of Crook's cavalry under Colonel Ranald Mackenzie attacked their village, killed many of the people, and drove the survivors in flight to Crazy Horse's camp. The destruction of the Cheyennes frightened some of the Oglalas, and they struck their tipis and started off for the agencies, but the rest of them, together with the Cheyenne refugees, moved to the north, out of Crook's way.

The days were shortening now, and with the advancing cold the Indians felt the fears and loneliness of the hunted. Runners kept coming to them from the agencies with messages of peace and rations if they would give up and come in. At the Tongue River, Miles was anxious for the glory of taking Crazy Horse, who was becoming notorious among the whites as the most powerful of the hostile holdouts, and he too sent messages to the Oglala chief. In December, Crazy Horse recognized the pessimism and weariness of his people, and sent nine men carrying a white cloth on a lance to Miles' post to test the officer's intentions. As the Sioux emissaries neared the fort, some of the Americans' Crow scouts charged out, firing at them. They killed five of the Sioux, and the rest got away. Crazy Horse abandoned the idea of giving up, and led his people back to the Tongue. It was a desperately cold winter, and the Oglalas huddled dispiritedly in the warmest sites they could find. Food was scarce, but troops, now in heavy fur coats, were still marching, and few of the natives dared to wander far for game. Native messengers who found the hiding places kept arriving from the agencies, telling them that everyone was thinking and talking of Crazy Horse's continued defiance, but they urged them at the same time to give up the foolishness and come in to where there was warm shelter and food. Many of the people wavered, and some stole away. But the warriors were firm, and most of them stayed with Crazy Horse.

In January, Miles with some five hundred infantrymen found their hiding place. The warriors held off the soldiers while the camp moved safely away. But the troops had their trail now, and kept coming. Again and again Miles attacked them, and each time Crazy Horse and the warriors fought them back in cold and fog and snow until the people had gotten away. On January 8 they fought for five hours. The Indians at last ran out of ammunition and swung their empty rifles like clubs at the soldiers. But the camp had moved safely off again, and Miles gave up the chase. The Indians crossed to the Little Bighorn, starving now, and suffering intensely from the bitter cold.

At the agencies, meanwhile, the Americans redoubled their efforts to talk Crazy Horse into surrendering. The longer he held out, the higher his prestige rose among those who had already come in, and if he were still at large in the summer he might lure many of the natives back to him and again became dangerous. Large groups of emissaries, including one headed by Spotted Tail himself, were sent looking for him with packloads of food, tobacco, and other presents. The messengers had success with one band after another, and they trooped into the agencies in a series. But Crazy Horse listened to the emissaries and sent them back, and soon he and his people were almost alone in the northern country.

But at last the iron will of defiance snapped. He saw the suffering of his people, and the sorrow coming into the faces of the older men around him; in May, as the country warmed, word came to him that Crook had finally promised that if he came in the Americans would give his people an agency of their own in the Powder River country where they could hunt in peace. He started the Oglalas south. They would go to see Crook at the Red Cloud Agency.

The hostiles marched in on May 5, 1877, and all the thousands of Indians at the agency gathered to witness the arrival of the last of the fighters. It was a proud procession, almost a triumphal parade, with Crazy Horse and his war leaders riding abreast in the lead, the warriors behind them in columns in feathers and paint, carrying rifles, shields, and lances, and the whole village trailing after them in the rear. Altogether they were more than 800 people, 145 lodges, with 1700 ponies, a procession two miles long. Red Cloud had ridden up-country to meet them, and he and agency police led them to the soldier camp at Fort Robinson near the agency. The Oglalas had ridden in silence, but as they neared the fort they began to sing their war songs. One officer, it is said, remarked, "By God! This is a triumphal march, not a surrender!" Crook was waiting for them, and had their guns and horses taken from them. It was a day of victory for him. The courageous and iron-willed Crazy Horse, whom he had not been able to beat in battle, had come in.

The Oglala chief tried to talk to Crook about the agency that had been promised for him in the north. But Crook evaded a discussion of it and offered, instead, to try to get the Oglalas permission to make a hunt in the northern country. Even this fell through. The Nez Percés of Idaho had gone to war and had come into Montana, and it was no time to let the Sioux return to that country and perhaps join the Nez Percés. Crazy Horse brooded unhappily at the agency, and soon there were rumors that he was planning to break out with his warriors. The old ill-will between the Hunkpatilas and Red Cloud's Bad Faces came to the surface again, and it appears that Red Cloud and his followers became intensely jealous of the attention being paid to Crazy Horse. Soon there was intrigue. No Water, the husband of Black Buffalo Woman, was at the agency, and his friends stirred trouble for their old enemy by whispering to the whites that Crazy Horse was scheming to return to the north.

Agency officials now watched Crazy Horse closely. Spies were set on him, and tales and rumors multiplied. At a council between army officers and the Indians the worst seemed to be confirmed. One of the officers asked Crazy Horse if he would agree to lead Oglala scouts north to help the army fight the Nez Percés. Crazy Horse objected at first, then agreed and said he would go north and fight until not a Nez Percé was left. The interpreter translated Crazy Horse's words to say that he would fight until not a white man was left. The officers were angry, and they refused to believe the correct translation when it was given to them later. Instead, they informed their superiors that Crazy Horse had indeed become dangerous again, and Crook returned to the agency to see for himself. He started for the camp of Crazy Horse a few miles from the agency headquarters, but was stopped by one of No Water's friends, who told him that Crazy Horse had threatened to kill the general. Crook believed the story; he returned to his camp and summoned all the chiefs, including Crazy Horse, to a council. Crazy Horse refused to come, and some of the agency chiefs who showed up told Crook that the Hunkpatila was a desperate man, and it would be best to kill him. Crook refused to agree with them, but he compromised and ordered the chiefs to help the troops arrest Crazy Horse and bring him to Fort Robinson near the agency headquarters.

The government still planned to move the Sioux from all the agencies to the Missouri. But such a transfer, it now seemed, would be accompanied by trouble unless Crazy Horse were first removed from the scene. To Crook, the war leader's arrest had become necessary, and apparently there were plans to send him to a prison in the Dry Tortugas. They were never carried out.

On September 4, eight companies of cavalry and four hundred Indians, led by Red Cloud and other friendly chiefs, left Fort Robinson to arrest Crazy Horse. The Oglala saw them coming and fled with his family to the Spotted Tail Agency. His pursuers overtook him there, and after a parley Crazy Horse agreed to go back with them to talk to the army officers. The following day the party returned to Fort Robinson. Crazy Horse was led into a guard room. When he saw that he was being imprisoned, he pulled a knife from under his blanket. An Indian jumped on his back and grasped his arms, and in the commotion Crazy Horse tried to struggle free while Red Cloud shouted, "Shoot in the middle. Shoot to kill!" As Crazy Horse twisted and struck at the man holding him, other Indians tried to wrestle him down, and the officer of the day went at him with his sword, yelling, "Kill the son of a bitch!" A guard lunged with his bayonet and hit a door instead, pulled the blade free, and thrust again, deep into Crazy Horse's body. The young chief wrenched once and sagged, looking up at the men still holding him. "Let me go, my friends," he pleaded. "You have hurt me enough."

They laid him on the floor in his blood and sent for the post surgeon, and the word went round all the camps by signal fires that the great Lakota was dying. Suddenly a hush came over the whole agency, and it was as if everyone suddenly realized that it was his own son, his own brother or father, who was dying. The Hunkpatilas gathered at the guardhouse to be near their war leader, and the chiefs who had been in battles with him, and had allowed jealousies to turn them against him, waited in shame. In the night, the old holy man of the Oglalas, Worm, the father of Crazy Horse, came and sat by his son. Crazy Horse saw him. "Ahh-h, my father," he is said to have whispered. "I am badly hurt. Tell the people it is no use to depend on me any more now." A few moments later the thirty-five-year-old chief, the warrior of the lightning streak and hailstones, died.

On October 27, 1877, the Sioux from the Red Cloud and Spotted Tail Agencies began their exodus to the Missouri River. They streamed eastward in two long processions, thousands of Indians guarded by troops of cavalry. In one of the columns were Crazy Horse's people. Some seventy-five miles east of the agency there was a sudden excitement, and Crazy Horse's people turned out of line. Some two thousand Indians who had fought with the great Hunkpatila leader swung to the north and raced suddenly for the Canadian border and freedom. The cavalry were too few to try to stop them. As they watched them go, bound for the camp of the exiled Sitting Bull, they could not see that they carried with them the spirit of Crazy Horse, all that was left to the once-powerful Sioux nation.

IX

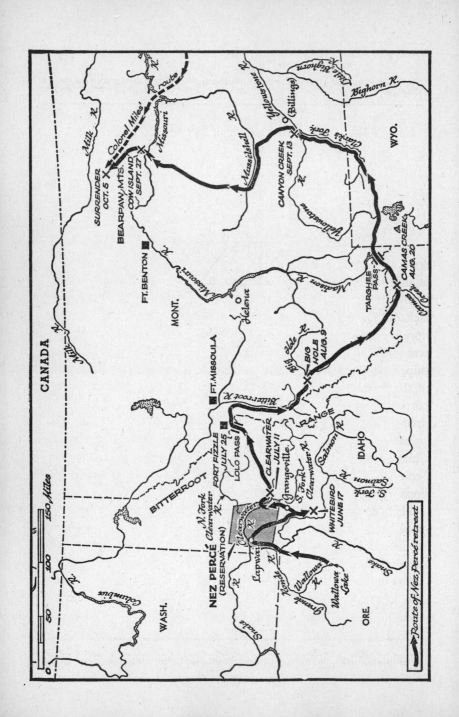

IX

THE LAST STAND OF CHIEF JOSEPH

IN JUNE 1877, just one year after the Custer debacle, an unexpected Indian outbreak flared in the West. To an American public wearied and disgusted with a governmental policy, or lack of policy, that seemed to breed Indian wars, this one, an uprising by formerly peaceful Nez Percés of Oregon and Idaho, was dramatized by what appeared to be superb Indian generalship. One army detachment after another, officered by veterans of the Civil War, floundered in battle with the hostiles. Western correspondents telegraphed the progress of a great thirteen-hundred-mile fighting retreat by the Indians, swaying popular imagination in behalf of the valiant Nez Percés and their leader, Chief Joseph, who, as handsome and noble in appearance as a Fenimore Cooper Indian, became something of a combined national hero and military genius.

The government received no laurels, either, as the long trail of bitter injustices that had originally driven the Nez Percés to hostility became known. The war, like most Indian troubles, had stemmed from a conflict over land. For centuries the Nez Percés had occupied the high, grassy hills and canyon-scarred plateau land where Washington, Oregon, and Idaho come together. A strong and intelligent people, they had lived in peace with the whites since the coming of Lewis and Clark in 1805, and it was their proud boast that no member of the tribe had ever killed a white man.

Joseph was the leader of only one of the Nez Percé bands, a group of some sixty males and perhaps twice that number of women and children, who lived in the Wallowa Valley in the northeastern corner of Oregon. Isolated on all sides by natural barriers of high mountain ranges and some of the deepest gorges on the continent, the valley's lush grasslands provided some of the best grazing ground in the Northwest, and settlers were particularly anxious to possess it. But Joseph's band of Nez Percés had lived there in security and peace for generations, and just before he died in 1871 Joseph's father, a prominent chief named Wellamotkin, known familiarly to the whites as Old Joseph, had fearfully counseled his son: "When I am gone, think of your country. You are the chief of these people. They look to you to guide them. Always remember that your father never sold the country. You must stop your ears whenever you are asked to sign a treaty selling your home. A few years more, and the white man will be all around you. They have their eyes on this land. My son, never forget my dying words. This country holds your father's body. Never sell the bones of your father and your mother."

The crisis came for Joseph almost immediately after his father's death. He was thirty-one years old, a tall and powerfully built man with the philosophical bent and strong and logical mind of a civil, rather than a war, chief. Like most members of his band he had had many friendly contacts with white men, and he did not fit the typical picture of a hostile Indian who had grown to manhood hating the Americans. Though he had come to believe that the Indians and whites did not mix well, he had a humanitarianism that transcended national loyalty and an understanding of conflicting forces that was rare in either Indians or whites.

He had been born in the spring of 1840, probably near the juncture of Joseph Creek and the Grande Ronde River in the deep, sheltered warmth of the Joseph Canyon, where his father's people and their herds waited out the winter till chinook winds told them that they could ascend to the high, greening meadows and fast-running streams of the nearby Wallowa Valley. At the time there were some four to six thousand Nez Percés; most of them lived in small fishing villages that dotted the banks of the Clearwater and Salmon Rivers and the middle stretches of the Snake and its tributaries, and were widely spread over a vast expanse of territory. Each village or small concentration of them lived under the leadership of its own chief, and during his youth Joseph visited most of the settlements with his father, learning the tribal lore that held them all together as a single nation. It was a colorful past, filled with dramatic events that spoke of many lands and tribes other than their own.

From their earliest days, the Nez Percés were known to be a traveling people, and at various periods of the year journeyed far and wide from their home settlements. War parties constantly ranged southward through Idaho and Oregon against the Shoshonis, who were the Nez Percés' traditional enemies. Others traveled to northern Idaho and Washington to visit Spokans and Coeur d'Alênes, with whom they sometimes fought and were sometimes friendly, and still others made long excursions across the rugged Bitterroot Mountains to join Flathead Indians on buffalo hunts in western Montana. All the Nez Percés, at one time or another, traveled down the Columbia River to the Dalles to trade with Chinook people who came up from the Pacific Coast, and until the middle of the eighteenth century the western Indians exercised a dominant influence on the culture of the Nez Percés, whose way of life more closely resembled that of the fish-eating Columbia River tribes than the buffalo-hunting plains Indians of Montana.

Sometime about 1730 the Nez Percés first saw horses in the camps of their Shoshoni enemies in the south. The animals had come overland from the Spanish settlements in New Mexico, via Apaches and Utes, and by trading and raiding the Nez Percés soon had herds of their own. With the animals they began to cross the Bitterroots in larger numbers and move farther east

across the plains, assimilating to a greater degree than before the
ways of the plains Indians with whom they traded and fought.
At the same time a remarkable event occurred in their own homeland. Perhaps alone among all the Indian tribes on the continent,
the Nez Percés learned to practice selective breeding and developed a strong and beautiful type of spotted horse that became
known for its speed and endurance. The Nez Percés were already fashioning the most prized bow on the plains, one made
from the horn of a mountain sheep, and now they appeared with
the handsomest war horse, a spotted and painted pony, which
they festooned with feathers. Known today as the Appaloosa
(from "a Palouse," the name of a portion of the original Nez
Percé country), the horse is still a favorite of cowmen in the
rugged plateau country of the Northwest.

By the end of the eighteenth century many of the Nez Percés
had become essentially plains Indians, though they continued
to return regularly to their home villages on the Columbia River
tributaries, where fish and roots still constituted a major part of
their diet. But their journeys took them into strange and faraway
lands, and they were already in contact with tribes who lived
along the upper Missouri River in the Dakotas. From them they
heard of white men, and in their camps they saw trade guns and
other goods that made the strangers with beards seem worth
meeting. They had already learned of white men from the coastal
tribes at the Dalles, who showed them metal goods left along the
Northwest Coast. But unlike the Missouri River whites the sea
traders on the Pacific did not give guns to the Indians, and firearms were already becoming a necessity in the hunts and wars
on the plains. In the spring of 1805 the Nez Percés sent three of
their young men to the Missouri River villages of the Minnitaree
Indians in present-day North Dakota to try to purchase guns,
and they returned with six of them.

In the fall of that same year, the members of the Lewis and
Clark Expedition, bound for the mouth of the Columbia River,
struggled through the Bitterroot Mountains and emerged in the

Nez Percé country. It was an exciting event for the villagers, who had never seen whites before. The explorers were starving after their ordeal in the mountains, and the Indians welcomed them into their settlements and gave them food. But the natives' kindly feelings for the Americans increased when the captains promised to send them traders who would provide them with more guns and white men's goods. The expedition leaders could not live up to their promise, and the first known white man to arrive within trading distance of the Nez Percés was David Thompson, a member of the Canadian North West Company, who crossed the Canadian Rockies and circulated through the country of the upper Columbia River and its tributaries between 1807 and 1812. There are indications in Thompson's journals that a mysterious group of Americans was also in contact with the Nez Percés during part of the same time, but history knows nothing else about them, and for a number of years the Nez Percés did most, if not all, of their trading with Thompson and his colleagues.

Thompson called the Nez Percés Shahaptians, which was a Flathead word for them and referred to the geographic location of their homeland, south and west of the Flatheads. But from the Columbia River tribes some of the Nez Percés copied the habit of wearing small pieces of shell in their noses as adornments. They abandoned the custom entirely soon after the arrival of white men in their country, but Thompson's French-Canadian *engagés* saw their pierced noses and found that Nez Percé was easier to say than Shahaptian, so that name soon took hold for all of the tribe.

In 1812, American traders of John Jacob Astor's company finally reached the Northwest and opened trade of their own in competition with the Canadians. The American stay was of short duration. The War of 1812 forced the sale of Astoria, and the Americans abandoned the country to Canadian monopoly. The Nor'Westers built inland posts and pursued a vigorous trade through much of Idaho, and the Nez Percés received a growing supply of guns and trade goods. In the early 1820s the North

West Company merged with the Hudson's Bay Company, and factors and traders of the big British firm brought new wealth to their Indian clients.

With their horses and guns, the Nez Percés continued to roam eastward, and in the late 1820s their buffalo-hunting parties began to meet American trappers and mountain men as far east as Wyoming's Green River Valley. The Indians liked the wild, free fur men, who helped them fight their mutual enemies the Blackfeet, and who lived with them in their camps as equals and gave them higher prices than the British for their pelts. The Nez Percés whooped and sported with the Americans at the trappers' annual rendezvous, and some of the mountain men took Nez Percé women as their wives.

During the 1820s, also, another influence of the white men entered the Nez Percés' lives. Hudson's Bay men began taking Northwest Indian youths to an Anglican mission school at Red River in central Canada, and when the youths returned to their villages they stirred an interest in Christianity among their people. Earlier, many of the Nez Percés and Flatheads had learned some of the rudiments of the white men's religion from Iroquois Indians, who had been reared as Roman Catholics in eastern Canada and had followed the Nor'Westers as engagés and free trappers into the Oregon country. Now, both the Nez Percés and the Flatheads desired to have the religion for themselves, regarding it as a power like their own medicine that would endow them with added wisdom and strength. In 1831 they began to send emissaries to St. Louis with returning mountain men, hoping to enlist teachers who would come to live with them.

In the American city they met both Roman Catholics and Protestants, and missionaries from various churches were soon racing one another to Oregon to save the Indians' souls. In 1836 the Reverend Henry H. Spalding and his wife opened a Presbyterian mission at Lapwai in the heart of the Nez Percés' country near present-day Lewiston, Idaho. At first the Indians were overjoyed to have teachers among them, and they attended the mission classes with enthusiasm. The Spaldings taught them reading, writing, and farming as well as religion, and many of the Nez Percés abandoned their trips to the buffalo plains and settled down to raise grains, vegetables, and herds of the white man's cows. A few of the leading men were converted as examples for the rest, and among them was Old Joseph of the Wallowa band, who became a fast friend of the Spaldings. On November 17, 1839, Spalding recorded that he "lawfully" married Joseph and his wife "Asenoth," and on April 12, 1840, he noted that he baptized Joseph's new son "Ephraim," who was undoubtedly the future young Joseph.

All did not go well at the mission, however, and in time many of the natives became disillusioned with the white man's medicine, which did not seem to give them the new power in war and hunting that they expected. Other Indians, who had somehow thought that the missionaries would be like the "big-hearted" trappers and would be a new source of white men's goods at cheap prices, began to quarrel with the Spaldings and urged them to leave their country. By the late 1840s, when settlers began to stream into Oregon, the situation at the mission had become dangerous. Many of the natives now accused the Spaldings of having brought the white men to steal their country, and when the neighboring Cayuse Indians, with similar fears, heightened by the panic of a measles epidemic, turned on their own missionaries, the Marcus Whitmans, and massacred them in 1847, the Spaldings fled from Lapwai.

Some of the Nez Percés, including a chief named Lawyer, who lived on the upper Clearwater River, were loyal to the missionaries and were sorry to see them go. Old Joseph probably also regretted their departure, though Spalding believed that Joseph had turned against him. At any rate, Joseph and his people retired to the isolation of the Wallowa Valley and, like the rest of the Nez Percés, avoided becoming involved in a punitive war which the Americans waged against the Cayuse who had killed the Whitmans.

In 1855, after peace had returned to the country, Joseph and the other Nez Percé leaders signed a treaty that defined a large reservation for the tribe. According to Americans at the treaty council, the Wallowa chief still carried a Bible and spoke warmly of the Spaldings. His friendship for the whites had apparently not waned, and shortly afterward, when the Yakimas and other Northwest tribes, who had been traditional allies of the Nez Percés, rose up against the Americans, Joseph approved of aid that some of the members of the Nez Percé nation gave to the United States troops. But in 1860, when white trespassers found gold on Nez Percé land and miners overran part of the reservation, his good feeling came to an end. White men cheated, bullied, and murdered Nez Percés in their own country, and there was no redress. New towns sprang up, crowding Indian villages out of existence, and in 1863 commissioners arrived from the East to try to end the turmoil by gathering the Indians into a new and smaller reservation. For a while the Nez Percé chiefs at the council were united in opposition to the Americans' proposal, but finally, after secret night meetings with individual chiefs, in which the commissioners apparently gave promises of private favors, some of the leaders, headed by Lawyer, agreed to accept the new reservation.

The agreement reduced the Indians' land to less than one-fourth of its previous size, and all the chiefs who signed represented bands whose homes already lay within the boundaries of the new reservation. The Wallowa Valley was part of the huge area being ceded, and Joseph, along with some two-thirds of the tribal leaders, refused to sign the document. Neither Joseph nor his son were regularly practising Christians at this time, but the aging chief is said to have returned to the Wallowa in anger from the council and to have torn up the Bible the missionaries had given him, exclaiming that he wanted nothing more to do with the white men or their civilization.

From then on, Lawyer and the other Indians on the new reservation lived in close and unhappy relationship with the white settlements that mushroomed about them, while Joseph's people continued their old way of life, unmolested by the Americans, who made no move immediately to claim the Wallowa. But as the settlers edged toward the routes into the valley, the Indians sensed the approaching conflict, and the old chief knew that a crisis was inevitable.

In 1871 young Joseph buried his father in the beloved Wallowa and assumed leadership of the band. Almost at once the emergency arrived. Settlers from Oregon's Grande Ronde found a pass into the valley and moved in, claiming the Indians' land. The new chieftain protested to the Indian agent on the reservation, and an investigation was undertaken by the Bureau of Indian Affairs to determine whether the Treaty of 1863 affected Joseph's band, which had not agreed to it. The inquiry resulted in a decision that the Wallowa still belonged legally to the Indians, and on June 16, 1873, President Grant formally set aside the Wallowa "as a reservation for the roaming Nez Percé Indians" and ordered the white intruders to withdraw.

Recognition of their rights brought satisfaction and relief to the Indians, but it was short-lived. The settlers, refusing to move, threatened to exterminate Joseph's people if they did not leave the valley. In defiance of the presidential order, more whites rolled in by the wagonload. As friction increased, Oregon's governor, Lafayette P. Grover, attacked Washington officials for having abandoned the government's position of 1863 and forced the Administration to reverse itself. In 1875 a new and confusing presidential edict reopened the Wallowa to white homesteaders.

The Nez Percés were dismayed. Young Joseph, called by the Indians Heinmot Tooyalakekt, meaning "thunder traveling to loftier mountain heights," counseled patience. He moved the Indian camps from the neighborhood of the settlers and again appealed to the federal authorities. The assistant adjutant general of the Military Department of the Columbia, Major H. Clay Wood, was assigned to make a survey of the conflicting claims. and in his report, forwarded to Washington by his commanding officer, O. O. Howard, the one-armed "Christian" general of the Civil War, stated, "In my opinion, the non-treaty Nez Percés cannot in law be regarded as bound by the treaty of 1863, and insofar as it attempts to deprive them of a right to occupancy of any land, its provisions are null and void. The extinguishment of their title of occupancy contemplated by this treaty is imperfect and incomplete."

At first the government took no action, but as harassment of the Indians continued and the threat increased that they might retaliate with violence, a new commission of five members was appointed to meet with the Nez Percés in November 1876 with authority to make a final settlement of the matter for "the welfare of both whites and Indians."

The commissioners—Howard, Wood, and three eastern civilians—found Joseph a disquieting figure. Thirty-six years old now, straight and towering, he seemed strangely amicable and gentle; yet he bore himself with the quiet strength and dignity of one who stood in awe of no man. And when he spoke, it was with an eloquent logic that nettled the whites, who found themselves resenting their inability to dominate him.

Why, they asked him, did he refuse to give up the Wallowa? He answered by referring to the land as the Mother of the Indians, something that could not be sold or given away. "We love the land," he said. "It is our home."

But, they insisted, Lawyer had signed it away in 1863.

Joseph had a ready reply that embarrassed them. "I believe the old treaty has never been correctly reported," he said. "If we ever owned the land we own it still, for we never sold it. In the treaty councils the commissioners have claimed that our country has been sold to the government. Suppose a white man should come to me and say, 'Joseph, I like your horses, and I want to buy them.' I say to him, 'No, my horses suit me, I will not sell them.' Then he goes to my neighbor, and says to him, 'Joseph has some good horses. I want to buy them but he refuses to sell.' My neighbor answers, 'Pay me the money, and I will sell you Joseph's horses.' The white man returns to me and says, 'Joseph, I have bought your horses and you must let me have them.' If we sold our lands to the government, this is the way they were bought."

To all their arguments, Joseph replied with an uncompromising "No" and the exasperated commissioners made no progress with him. But events were moving against the Indians. The situation in the Wallowa had grown perilous, and the commission was under political pressure. Two excited white men had killed an Indian youth after mistakenly accusing him of stealing their horses. Joseph had had all he could do to keep his people calm, and the settlers, fearing an uprising, were arming and calling for military protection.

To the commissioners, despite the fact that it was unjust and there was no legal basis for it, there could be only one decision, and before they left the reservation headquarters at Lapwai they rendered it: Unless, within a reasonable time, all the non-treaty Nez Percés (the other bands that had not signed in 1863, as well as Joseph's people in the Wallowa) voluntarily came onto the reservation, they should be placed there by force. General Howard, symbolizing the force that would be used, signed the report along with the three easterners. Only Major Wood's name was absent; it is believed that he submitted a minority report, though it has never been found.

Immediately after the decision the Indian Bureau defined the "reasonable time" and ordered the Indians to come onto the reservation by April 1, 1877. It was almost an exact repetition of the order of a year before that had started the hostilities with the Sioux. Unable to move their herds and villages across the rugged canyons in the dead of winter, the Nez Percés appealed for another conference, and as April 1 came and went General Howard agreed to one last meeting with all the non-treaty chiefs at Lapwai. It did no good. The die had been cast, and Howard adamantly refused to discuss the commission's decision. As the Indians pleaded in proud but pitiable terms to be allowed to remain in the lands where their fathers were buried, the general finally lost patience and threw one of the most respected old chiefs, a deeply religious war leader and tribal orator named Toohoolhoolzote, into the guardhouse. It broke the spirit of the others. To gain Toohoolhoolzote's release they capitulated with bitterness and agreed to have their bands on the reservation in thirty days.

All Joseph's skill as a diplomat had to be called into play when he returned to his people. He had abandoned his father's counsel and trust, and there were cries to ignore him and go to war rather than to move to the reservation. When Joseph argued that the white man's power was too great for them to resist and that it was "better to live at peace than to begin a war and lie dead," they called him a coward. But he received strong assistance from his younger brother, Ollokot, a daring and courageous buffalo hunter and warrior who had won many tribal honors and held the respect of the more belligerent younger element. Eventually the two brothers won agreement to the capitulation from the band's council, and the Indians prepared to round up their stock and move.

A half year's work was crowded into less than thirty days as the people combed the mountains and forests for their animals and drove them down the steep draws to the Snake. The river was in flood, and hundreds of head of stock were swept away and drowned during the tumultuous crossing. Other portions of the herds, left behind on the bluffs and plateau, were driven away by whites, who attacked the guards and harassed the withdrawing Indians. By June 2, with twelve days of grace remaining, the people reached an ancient tribal rendezvous area just outside the border of the reservation. Here they joined the other non-treaty bands and lingered for a last bit of freedom.

It was a fatal pause. On June 12 the Indians staged a parade through the camp, and one of the young men named Wahlitits, whose father had been murdered by a white man two years before, was taunted by an old warrior for having allowed the slaying to go unavenged. The next morning, his honor as a man impugned, Wahlitits stole away with two companions. By nightfall, in an outpouring of long-suppressed hatred, the youths had killed four white men along the Salmon River and wounded another one, all notorious for their hostility to the Nez Percés. The young men returned to the camp, announced what they had done, and raised a bigger party that continued the raids during the next two days, killing fourteen or fifteen additional whites and striking terror among the settlers and miners of central Idaho.

Both Joseph and Ollokot had been absent from the camp during the first raid, butchering cattle on the opposite side of the Salmon River. They returned to find the camp in confusion and the older people crying with fear and striking their tipis, intending to scatter to hiding places. Most of the Indians were certain that there would now be war, but Joseph still hoped to avert it. He tried to calm his people, assuring them that General Howard would not blame the whole tribe for the irresponsible actions of a few of its young hotheads, and urged them to remain where they were and await the troops, with whom he would make a settlement. The situation, however, had gone too far. The warriors rode around the camp, crying out that they would now give General Howard the fight that he had wanted, and the people would not listen to Joseph. One by one the bands departed to a hiding place farther south, in White Bird Canyon, leaving behind only Joseph, Ollokot, and a few of the Wallowa Indians.

Joseph's wife had given birth to a daughter while he had been across the Salmon, and he lingered with her now in their tipi. Several warriors were detailed to watch him and Ollokot, lest these leaders who had so often pleaded for peace would desert the non-treaties and move onto the reservation. But though he had vigorously opposed war Joseph would not abandon his people; two days later he and Ollokot, resolved to fight now that hostilities seemed unavoidable, joined the non-treaties in the new camp at White Bird.

Back at Lapwai Howard was stunned by news of the Salmon
River outbreaks. He had planned all winter against trouble in the
Wallowa, and when Joseph had moved out peacefully he had
thought that all danger was past. At the news of the outbreaks
he hastily ordered two troops of the 1st Cavalry that had been
stationed at Lapwai, ninety troopers and four officers under Captain David Perry and Captain Joel Trimble, to round up the hostiles and force them onto the reservation. Eleven civilian volunteers and twelve treaty Nez Percés accompanied the troops, and
after a rapid two days' march of almost eighty miles they
learned of the Nez Percé camp in White Bird Canyon and prepared to attack it early the following morning.

Alert Indian spies warned the Nez Percés of the troops' ap-
proach. The soldiers would have to descend a long draw of tree-
less, rolling land, flanked by ridges and hills, to reach the Nez
Percé village, which lay behind two buttes at the bottom of
the slope. The chiefs were uncertain whether to resist and detailed six men to take a flag of truce forward and try to arrange a
peaceful meeting with the officers. At the same time the old men,
women, and children were ordered to drive in the camp's stock,
while the warriors stripped for action, mounted their ponies,
and sought hiding places to the right and left of the draw to
await events. The total manpower of the Indian bands was about
a hundred and fifty, but many of the men that morning were
lying in camp, drunk on whisky seized during the raids and unable to fight. Others had no weapons or were too old, sick, or
frightened to use them. Altogether not more than forty-five or
fifty Indians—armed with bows and arrows, shotguns, old muz-
zle-loading fur-trade muskets, and a few modern rifles—rode
out to defend the village.

The nature of the terrain, offering a multitude of hiding places
for flanking attacks, should have put the troopers on their
guard. Instead they trotted confidently down the draw, ready
for a thundering surprise charge. As they rounded a small hill
the Indian truce team appeared directly ahead of them. Behind

the men with the white flag were other Nez Percés, sitting on their horses waiting to see what would happen. There was an instant of surprise. Then a volunteer raised his rifle and shot at the truce team. The Indians backed away, unharmed; a Nez Percé behind them fired in return, killing one of Perry's two trumpeters, and the fight was on. As Indians began shooting from all directions, Perry hastily deployed his men in a line across the draw, placing the volunteers on a high, rocky knoll to his left. The company in the center dismounted, letting men in the rear hold their horses, and the company on the right remained mounted.

The battle, fought without plan by the Indians, lasted only a few moments. On the left a small body of Nez Percés swept from behind a hill and galloped straight at the volunteers, sending them flying in panic back up the draw and exposing Perry's whole line. At the same time Ollokot, leading a large number of warriors, emerged from cover on the right and, firing as he came, charged into Perry's mounted troop, frightening the horses and disorganizing the soldiers. The men in the center, seeing Indians and confusion all around them, gave way and made a sudden rush for their horses. In a few minutes the entire command was cut into small groups fighting desperately for their lives. Nineteen men under Lieutenant Edward Theller tried to make a stand but were driven against a rocky wall and wiped out. The rest of the troop disintegrated into a fleeing rabble and got away, leaving behind them a total of thirty-four dead, a third of Perry's command. The Indians had only two men wounded and none killed; equally important for the future, they retrieved from the battlefield sixty-three rifles and a large number of pistols.

Perry's defeat spread alarm throughout the settlements of the Northwest and angered the rest of the nation, to whom the Custer massacre was still fresh. Howard was shocked; fearing that the uprising would spread to the treaty Nez Percés as well as other Northwest tribes, he called for troop reinforcements from all over the West. Men were started inland from Portland and San Francisco, artillerymen returning from Alaska were diverted up the Columbia, and from as far away as Atlanta, Georgia, infantry units were entrained for the scene of the new Indian outbreak.

Within a week Howard himself took the field. With a force of two hundred and twenty-seven hastily assembled troops, twenty civilians, and a large group of packers and guides, he marched hurriedly out from Lapwai, intending to punish the hostiles. The Indians, reinforced by a small band that had just returned from the Montana buffalo plains under the leadership of two redoubtable warriors, Five Wounds and Rainbow, had withdrawn from White Bird and, when Howard caught up with them, had crossed with all their equipment and pony herds to the relative safety of the south bank of the Salmon. For a while the two groups faced each other from opposite sides of the wilderness river while Howard planned how to get the troops across the turbulent stream and catch the Indians before they could retreat into the rocky wilds of central Idaho. From his rear he received false information from excited settlers that a large band of hitherto peaceful Nez Percés, under a famous tribal war chief named Looking Glass, was planning to leave the reservation and join the hostiles. Accepting the information as true, he divided his forces and sent Captain Stephen Whipple with two troops of cavalry to intercept Looking Glass.

It was a disastrous move. As Whipple departed, Howard received boats and started across the river, only to see the Indians move off into the wilderness ahead of him. For several days he was led on a wearying, frustrating chase through mud and driving rain, up and down steep hills and mountain slopes, and across some of the most rugged terrain in the West. Meanwhile Whipple reached Looking Glass's village on the reservation and, although he found it peaceful, launched a vicious assault upon it. The startled Indians, struck without warning, fled across a river to the shelter of some trees, where they were rallied by their outraged chief. Rumors now came to Whipple that the main band of Indians had somehow evaded General Howard, had recrossed the Salmon, and were between him and the general, threatening his own rear, Howard's supply lines, and all the settlements on the Camas Prairie, which he was supposed to be protecting.

The rumors this time were true. With Howard's troops floundering in the wilds, the non-treaties had managed to cross again to the north side of the Salmon. Howard tried to follow them, couldn't get his men and equipment across the river, and had to go back over the entire dreadful mountain trail to the place of his original crossing, where he had left his boats. Meanwhile Whipple, forgetting Looking Glass in the face of the full Nez Percé force, sent out a reconnoitering party of ten men under Lieutenant S. M. Rains, and dug in for an expected attack. The Indians wiped out Rains' party to a man, cut up another group of scouts and several hastily formed bodies of civilian volunteers, and finally, bypassing Whipple and the terrified settlers barricaded in Cottonwood and Grangeville, moved to another hiding place on the South Fork of the Clearwater River. Here they were joined by Looking Glass's infuriated band. It gave the Indians another forty fighting men but also raised the number of women and children, who would have to be carried along and protected from the soldiers, to a peak figure of five hundred and fifty.

From the beginning it had been assumed by the whites that Joseph, spokesman for the non-treaties in peacetime, had also been leading them in war. Howard had credited him with skillfully contriving the ambush of Perry at White Bird. Now Joseph was being given grudging praise for the masterful way in which the Indians had evaded Howard in the wilderness and doubled back to get between him and Whipple. In addition, the Nez Percés had been conducting themselves in an unusual manner for Indians "on the warpath," refraining from scalping or mutilating bodies, treating white women and noncombatants with humanity and even friendliness, and otherwise adhering to what was considered the white man's code of war. This too was credited to Joseph, whose dignity and decency at prewar councils were recalled by Howard and the Indian agents.

The truth was that Nez Percé successes were resulting from a combination of overconfidence and mistakes on the part of the whites, the rugged terrain that made pursuit difficult, and, to a very great extent, the Indians' intense courage and patriotic determination to fight for their rights and protect their people. Indian strategy and tactics had also played a role, but at each step of the way these were agreed upon in councils of all the chiefs and were carried out on the field by the younger war leaders and their warriors. Joseph sat in the councils, but since he had never been a war chief his advice carried less weight than that of such men as Five Wounds, Toohoolhoolzote, and Rainbow. On the march and in battle Joseph took charge of the old men, women, and children, an assignment of vital importance and sacred trust, while Ollokot and the experienced war chiefs led the young men on guard duty or in combat. The whites had no way of knowing this, and, as events continued to unfold, the legend that Nez Percé strategy was planned and executed by one man, Joseph, was spread far and wide by the hapless army officers opposing him and accepted without question by correspondents and the United States public.

On July 11, with a reinforced army of four hundred soldiers and a hundred and eighty scouts, packers, and teamsters, Howard was back in pursuit of the Nez Percés. Suddenly he sighted their camp lying below him on the opposite side of the Clearwater River, opened fire with a four-inch howitzer and two Gatling guns, and prepared to launch an attack. The Nez Percés were taken by surprise, but old Toohoolhoolzote and twenty-four warriors raced across the river, scaled a bluff to the level of the soldiers, and, taking shelter behind boulders, engaged the troopers with a fierce and accurate fire that held them up until more Indians could come across and get into the fight. The firing was sharp on both sides, but as increasing numbers of mounted

Nez Percés began appearing over the top of the bluff to circle the troops' rear and flanks, Howard hastened his men into a square and ordered them to dig in on the open, rocky ground with their trowel bayonets.

The fighting raged all day and continued in the same spot the next morning, an almost unprecedented length of time for Indians to maintain battle in one location. The Nez Percés, outnumbered almost six to one and occasionally under artillery fire, kept the troopers pinned down and on the defensive with marksmanship that Howard's adjutant, Major C. E. S. Wood, described as "terribly accurate and very fatal." Several times small groups of Indians darted forward to engage the soldiers in hand-to-hand fights, and once they almost captured Howard's supply train. In addition, the Nez Percés held the only spring in the area and controlled access to the river; under the blazing July sun the soldiers suffered terribly from thirst.

By noon of the second day the chiefs had decided that there had been enough fighting without decision. Many of the warriors had become restless and tired and wanted to leave. Holding the line long enough for Joseph to get the families packed and safely away with the herds, the Indians, one by one, ceased fighting and withdrew down the bluff. Howard's troops followed the last of them across the river and through the abandoned camp. It was an anticlimactic and hollow finish to a battle that had cost the army thirteen killed and twenty-seven wounded, two of them fatally. Howard could count four Indians killed and six wounded, but the hostiles had escaped from him again.

The Nez Percés crossed the Clearwater north of the troops and paused at an old meeting ground on the Weippe Prairie to decide what to do next. They had had enough of Howard and thought that if they left Idaho and went somewhere else the general would be satisfied and would leave them alone. Looking Glass, who many times had hunted buffalo and fought with the Crows in Montana, urged that they cross the mountains and join that tribe. They could then hunt on the plains in peace, he told them, and the war would be over. It was a harsh proposal, for it meant the final abandonment of their homeland, but with the people's safety weighing heavily on them Joseph and the other chiefs reluctantly agreed to the exodus. On July 16, having named Looking Glass as supreme war chief for the trek to the Crows, the bands set off on the arduous Lolo Trail across the wild and precipitous heights of the Bitterroot Mountains.

Smarting under increasing criticism from Washington, as well as from the press and public, Howard once more took after the Indians, doggedly following their trail up through the thick and tangled forest growth of mountain slopes to the high, ridge-top route that led from Idaho to Montana. It was a painful and grueling trip for both pursuers and pursued. The Indian families, stumbling along over steep and rocky trails, guarded by the warriors and driving some two thousand horses with them, managed to keep well ahead of the troops, who, with their guns and camp equipment, found the going even rougher. In the meantime word of the Indian flight had been telegraphed ahead to Montana, and from Missoula Captain Charles C. Rawn, with thirty-five men of the 7th Infantry and two hundred citizen volunteers from the Bitterroot Valley, hastened to the eastern end of the Lolo Trail and threw up a log fort from which to block the hostiles' passage until Howard could catch up to them from the rear.

On July 25, after nine days in the mountains, the Nez Percés appeared above Rawn's fort, and Joseph, Looking Glass, and an elderly chief named White Bird came down for a parley. Explaining that they were on their way to the Crows, the Indians promised to move peacefully through the Bitterroot Valley, respecting the settlements and paying for any supplies they needed. It satisfied the volunteers, who, having no stomach for an Indian fight, deserted Rawn and stole back to their homes. As a federal officer, Rawn was obliged to continue his posture of resistance, but fortunately for his depleted garrison the Indians shrewdly bypassed his fort and, making a noisy feint in front of him, quietly filed around him on another mountain trail that led them into the Bitterroot Valley. The embarrassed Captain withdrew to Missoula, and his log bastion was promptly dubbed Fort Fizzle by the many wags who were beginning to root for Joseph and the apparently unconquerable Nez Percés.

Moving through the heavily settled valley, the Indians scrupulously maintained their promise to commit no hostile act. At Stevensville they paused to buy coffee, flour, sugar, and tobacco and paid the merchants with gold dust and currency. The friendly treatment they received from the Montana citizens made the Indians believe that, now that they were out of Idaho, the war was over and they were safe. They moved leisurely south to the Big Hole Valley and, on an open meadow beside the willow-lined Big Hole River, pitched camp to rest.

Howard was still far back in the Bitterroots, temporarily out of the picture. But, unknown to the Nez Percés, a new force of 163 army regulars and 35 volunteers under Colonel John Gibbon was hurrying across country from Fort Shaw, on the Sun River, by forced marches to attack them. On the night of August 8 Gibbon gained a wooded hill above the unsuspecting Nez Percé camp and, the next morning at dawn, launched a surprise attack. Firing volleys into the sleeping village, the soldiers charged down the hill in a long line, forded the shallow river, and swept into the camp, shooting and clubbing men, women, and children. Some of the Nez Percés were able to seize their weapons and ammunition belts and escape to the shelter of the willows. There they were rallied by the aged White Bird, who cried at them, "Why are we retreating? Since the world was made, brave men have fought for their women and children! Fight! Shoot them down! We can shoot as well as any of these soldiers!"

Gibbon's commanding officer on the left had been killed during the opening charge and without a leader that part of the line faltered as Indians stood their ground and fought back desperately from the tipis. The troopers were forced toward the right, allowing the Nez Percés in that sector to erect a firing line against them. This brought confusion to the main part of the camp, where Gibbon's men, in complete control, were unsuccessfully trying to set the leather tipis afire. With his milling troops being pushed together and soldiers being struck both by the Indians on the left and by White Bird's snipers on the right, Gibbon, who had been wounded in the leg, ordered a withdrawal across the river to the protection of the wooded knoll from which the attack had been launched. To his chagrin the Nez Percés swarmed after him, and in a few moments he found himself on the defensive, fighting fiercely, his position encircled by well-concealed Indian sharpshooters.

As the soldiers pulled out of the village, the old men, women, and children, directed by Joseph, hurried back in, picked up their dead and wounded, struck the tipis, and, driving their pack strings and pony herds ahead of them, moved off toward the south. The warriors remained behind, continuing the siege on the hill throughout the day and into the night, pinning down Gibbon's men in shallow holes and behind fallen trees, and picking off anyone who showed himself. Cut off and without prospect of relief, the soldiers found their position rapidly becoming desperate. The men ran out of water, and cries from the unattended wounded filled the air. Gibbon's howitzer, ordered to come up after the initial attack, arrived on the scene and was immediately captured by a group of wild-charging Nez Percés, who rolled it over a steep bluff. Another body of Indians seized a packload of two thousand rounds of Gibbon's ammunition. By eleven that night, with their camp safely away, the warriors mercifully decided to break off the engagement and spare the surviving troopers. Backing off slowly to guard against pursuit, they took the trail after Joseph.

Gibbon's men, cut up and dazed, were in no condition to follow. Thirty-three soldiers were dead and thirty-eight wounded; fourteen of the seventeen officers were casualties. Howard's men, coming up hurriedly the next day, found the troops still in a state of shock, burying the dead and trying to care for the groaning wounded.

The Indians' losses at the Big Hole had also been high. Between sixty and ninety Nez Percés had lost their lives, including Rainbow, Five Wounds, and some of the tribe's ablest warriors. Many of the casualties had been women and children, slain during the initial attack on the tipis. Joseph's wife had been among the seriously wounded, and Joseph had been seen fighting his way through the early part of the battle sheltering his new baby in his arms.

The Nez Percés now quickened their retreat across southwestern Montana. Gone were illusions that the whites would let them be. In their desperation to escape, only one haven seemed left to them. Like Sitting Bull, they would go to Canada and seek refuge among the tribes in the country of Queen Victoria. Canada was hundreds of miles away, but they would get there somehow. Looking Glass, blamed for the false sense of security that had led to so many deaths at the Big Hole, was relieved of command, and a tough fighter named Lean Elk, whom the whites had known as Poker Joe, was elevated to supreme war chief. The column headed eastward toward Targhee Pass, which would lead the refugees over the Continental Divide to the Yellowstone, where they could turn north to Canada. West of the pass, rear-guard scouts brought word that Howard was catching up and pressing close behind them again. In a bold night attack, twenty-eight warriors led by Ollokot and three other chiefs stole back to Howard's camp and ran off the general's entire pack string. Howard came to a dead halt, forced to scour the settlements for more animals, and the Indians hurried on, unhampered, across the Divide and into the area which five years before had become Yellowstone National Park.

A sight-seeing party, of which General William Tecumseh Sherman was a member, had just left the area, but the Nez Percés swooped up two other groups of campers and took them along.

The chiefs insisted on humane treatment for the frightened tourists, who included a number of women. In time, as the Indians continued across the park, past geysers and bubbling mudpots, the sight-seers were allowed to escape. On the eastern side of the park the Indians found themselves harassed by new bodies of troops, coming at them from posts on the Montana plains. One force of the 7th Cavalry under Colonel Samuel Sturgis tried to set a trap for the Indians in the upper Yellowstone Valley, but the Nez Percés fought their way skillfully through a mountain wilderness where the whites thought passage would be impossible and emerged on the Clark's Fork River in Sturgis's rear. Realizing he had been tricked, Sturgis gave chase with three hundred men, following the Indians across the Yellowstone River and down its northern bank past present-day Billings, Montana.

On and on the Indians hurried. Near Canyon Creek they passed a stage station and captured a stagecoach. The warriors let its occupants escape into some nearby willows and had a day of great fun, driving the incongruous-looking coach along in the rear of the column. The sport ended abruptly. At Canyon Creek the bands turned north, and here, on September 13, Sturgis's hard-riding cavalry overtook them. There was a furious fight. A rear guard of Indians, hiding behind rocks and in gullies, held off the troopers while the Nez Percé women and children drove the pack strings and herds to the protection of a narrow canyon that cut north through rimrock country. Sturgis ordered his men to dismount, an error that allowed the Indians to escape into the canyon. Later the cavalry tried to follow the Nez Percés in a running fight up the canyon, but the Indians succeeded in making pursuit difficult by blocking the canyon floor behind them with boulders and brush. At darkness, weary and running out of ammunition and rations, Sturgis gave up the chase. Three of his men had been killed and eleven wounded. The Indians counted three wounded, but the long pursuit was beginning to tell heavily on them. They too were becoming tired and dispirited, and they were losing horses. Many of the animals were going lame from the difficult trek and had to be abandoned. Others were being lost in the hurry to keep moving.

Beyond Canyon Creek their old allies the Crows, now in service as scouts for the army, began to attack them. The Nez Percés fought them off in running engagements and continued across the Musselshell to the Missouri River, helping themselves to army stores at a military depot on Cow Island while a frightened sergeant and twelve men looked on helplessly from behind an earthwork. Just across the Missouri the Indians fought off a half-hearted attack by a small force from Fort Benton and hastened on across badlands and open, rolling plains to the Bear Paw Mountains. About thirty miles short of the Canadian line, exhausted by the long flight, they paused to rest, confident that they had outdistanced all pursuers.

Once more they were wrong, outflanked again by the telegraph, and this time the pause would end in their last stand. From Fort Keogh in the east, Colonel Nelson Miles, with nearly six hundred men that included the 2nd and 7th Cavalry, the mounted 5th Infantry, and a body of Cheyenne warriors, was hastening obliquely across Montana, hoping to intercept the hostiles before they crossed the border. On the cold, blustery morning of September 30, Miles' Cheyenne scouts sighted the Nez Percé tipis in a deep hollow on the plains close to Snake Creek on the northern edge of the Bear Paw Mountains. Miles ordered an immediate attack, and the Cheyennes and 7th Cavalry, supported by the 5th Infantry, charged across the open ground toward the village.

The assault caught the Nez Percés in three groups. Some, including women and children, were on the distant side of the camp and were able to mount and flee to the north, where they scattered on the broken plains, to die from hunger and exposure or eventually to reach Canada in small, pitiful groups. Others, including Joseph, were trapped with the horses at some distance from the camp. A third group, at the village, found protection behind a low-lying ridge. These warriors, hidden behind rocks, opened a deadly fire on the attackers, inflicting heavy casualties and sending the troopers reeling back short of the camp. Two officers and twenty-two soldiers were killed in the assault and four officers and thirty-eight enlisted men wounded.

The 2nd Cavalry, meanwhile, had been sent around the camp to capture the Nez Percé horse herd and try to cut off escape. This unit had better luck. The troopers charged into the herd, stampeding the horses and splitting the Indians into small groups that fought back hand-to-hand or sought cover in gullies or behind rocks. A few of the Indians got away on ponies and disappeared to the north. Others, among them Joseph, crawled or fought their way back to the main body of Nez Percés and reached the camp under cover of darkness. The troopers drove off at least a third of the horses, however, and killed most of the Nez Percés' remaining war leaders, including the brave Ollokot and Toohoolhoolzote.

The heavy casualties Miles had sustained deterred him from ordering another charge, and he decided to lay siege to the camp. He made one attempt to cut off the Indians from their water supply by establishing a line between the village and the river, but the troops detailed to the task were driven back by fierce Indian resistance. As the siege settled down, both sides dug in, continuing a desultory sharpshooting fire between the lines. The weather turned bitterly cold, and the next morning five inches of snow covered the unretrieved bodies of the dead. The Indians, wounded, hungry, and cold, suffered intensely. Using hooks, knives, and pans, the people tried to dig crude shelters in the sides of the hollows. One dugout was caved in by a hit from Miles' howitzer that had been tilted back for use as a mortar, and a woman and child were buried alive.

As the siege continued, Miles grew concerned. There were rumors that Sitting Bull, with a band of Sioux, was coming to the Nez Percés' rescue from Canada. And, even if they did not show up, Howard was getting closer, and Miles wanted the glory of Joseph's end for himself. Hoping to hurry the surrender, he hoisted a white flag over his trenches and, after negotiations with a Nez Percé who could speak English, lured Joseph across the lines. The two men parleyed amicably for a few moments, but when Joseph began to detail terms for an honorable surrender, Miles had him seized and made prisoner. The same day, however, the Nez Percés captured one of Miles' officers. The next morning an exchange was agreed to, and Joseph was returned to his camp.

The siege went on amid cold and snow flurries, and on October 4 Howard reached the battlefield with a small advance party that included two treaty Nez Percés. The appearance of their old enemy, heralding the arrival of reinforcements for Miles, finally took the heart out of the suffering Nez Percés. The next morning the two treaty Nez Percés crossed the lines and told the chiefs that if they surrendered they would be honorably treated and sent back to Lapwai. The chiefs held a final council. White Bird and Looking Glass still opposed surrender. Joseph pointed to the starving women and children in the shelter pits and to the babies that were crying around them. "For myself I do not care," he said. "It is for them I am going to surrender."

As the council broke up, Looking Glass was suddenly struck in the forehead by a stray bullet and killed. As the surviving warriors gathered around the slain chief, Joseph mounted a horse and, followed by several men on foot, rode slowly up the hill from the camp and across to the army lines where Howard and Miles awaited him. As he reached the officers, he dismounted and handed Miles his rifle. Then he stepped back and adjusted his blanket to leave his right arm free; addressing Miles, he began one of the most touching and beautiful speeches of surrender ever made.

"Tell General Howard I know his heart," he said. "What he told me before I have in my heart. I am tired of fighting. Our chiefs are killed. Looking Glass is dead. Toohoolhoolzote is dead. The old men are all dead. It is the young men who say yes or no. He who led the young men is dead. It is cold and we have no blankets. The little children are freezing to death. My people, some of them, have run away to the hills, and have no blankets, no food; no one knows where they are—perhaps freezing to death. I want to have time to look for my children and see how many I can find. Maybe I shall find them among the dead. Hear me, my chiefs. I am tired; my heart is sick and sad. From where the sun now stands, I will fight no more forever."

The fact that neither Joseph nor any other individual chief had been responsible for the outstanding strategy and masterful success of the campaign is irrelevant. The surrender speech, taken down by Howard's adjutant and published soon afterward, confirmed Joseph in the public's mind as the symbol of the Nez Percés' heroic, fighting retreat. Although the government failed to honor Miles' promise to send the Indians back to Lapwai, sympathy was aroused throughout the nation for Joseph's people. At first the Indians were shipped by flatboats and boxcars to unfamiliar, hot country in the Indian Territory, where many of them sickened and died. But friendly whites and sympathetic societies in the East continued to work for them, and public sentiment finally forced approval of their return to the Northwest. In 1885 Joseph and most of his band were sent to the Colville Reservation in Washington. Joseph made many attempts to be allowed to resettle in the Wallowa but each time was rebuffed. In 1904 he died, broken-hearted, an exile from the beautiful valley he still considered home.

EPILOGUE

THE SURRENDER of Joseph's Nez Percés in 1877 almost completed the military conquest of the American Indian. What remained was pacification rather than conquest, and it dragged on for thirteen more years as the government penned western natives on reservations and showed them with the grim use of arms that it meant to keep them there.

The wild spirits of tribesmen who would be free refused to stay penned; these men died and starved by hundreds as they broke away, again and again, trying like hunted animals to find safety from their tormentors. In 1878 elusive Bannocks were chased through the wilds of the Idaho mountains. The same year the northern Cheyennes, who had been exiled to a barren, malarial reservation in Oklahoma, burst out in an epic attempt to return to Montana's Powder River. Under Dull Knife and Little Wolf a starving, bedraggled column of men, women, and children plodded north through the central plains, pushing almost blindly over what had become the white man's country, across rivers, railroads, highways, cattle ranches, and settlers' farms, fighting off armies that tried to halt them. When some of them were finally captured and herded into another agency, the government withheld food and water from them and put some of their leaders in irons. Still they refused to give up. They broke out again, and hurried stubbornly on once more toward their old hunting grounds; this time, when overtaken by troops, they were mowed down and all but annihilated.

The next year rebellious Ute warriors were pacified in Colorado, and in the 1880s it was the turn of the fierce Apaches in New Mexico and Arizona. It took several expeditions and years of pursuit, hard fighting, and protracted councils in the mountain fastnesses of the Southwest, including Mexico, to convince Geronimo and a handful of his followers that they could no longer roam in freedom. By 1886 they too were in hand and on their way to exile in Florida.

As Indian resistance finally withered, dreams took the place of guns. History, harking back to the days of the visionary prophets of Pontiac, Tecumseh, and Black Hawk, was repeated. The crushed and demoralized western tribesmen sat in their blankets on the reservations, wondering what to do next, and in time word came to them from the distant Nevada desert of a new Indian prophet, a humble Paiute Indian named Wovoka who had received revelations from the Great Spirit. Again, Christianity and Indian aspirations came together in a new form. At his home on the Walker River reservation, Wovoka, a portly and peaceable man who had been raised in the home of a devoutly religious white family, began to work "miracles." They were the tricks of a charlatan, but he soon began to believe in his powers and the messages he received in trances. As his reputation spread among the tribes, pilgrims came to see him from all the defeated nations of the West.

His advice to them was to perform a special dance, accompanied by a chant, which eventually would restore the Indians' world as it had been before the white men had come. The soldiers, the agents, the settlers—all the conquerors—would disappear, the dead Indian heroes would come back to life, and the plains once more would be filled with buffalo. To the dispirited warriors it was an exciting prospect, and Wovoka's message traveled from tribe to tribe, igniting new hopes and dreams. Within months, Arapaho in Wyoming, Bannocks and Shoshonis in

Idaho, and Sioux in the Dakotas were all shuffling in weird circles, chanting and stiffening in frenzied trances, calling back the olden days and waiting with outstretched arms for the disappearance of the whites and the return of the buffalo.

It was bound to end in tragedy, and it did in 1890. Wovoka's movement was a peaceful one, but its mystery and hold on the minds of the desperate natives unnerved the reservation agents and military leaders, who termed it "the Ghost Dance." At the Sioux' Standing Rock Agency in the Dakotas, Sitting Bull, who had returned from Canadian exile in 1881, was narrowly watched. When his people began to dance, and even to wear sacred "ghost shirts" which they believed would protect them from white men's guns and bullets, the old medicine man was ordered arrested. Like Crazy Horse, the great Hunkpapa resisted his captors and was killed in a scuffle. Other Sioux broke out at once, racing wildly for freedom. They were pursued in the snow, and at the so-called massacre of Wounded Knee in December 1890 some three hundred Indian men, women, and children were slaughtered by the raking fire of Hotchkiss guns.

The long conquest of the American Indian was ended. With the failure of Wovoka's dance and the sacred protection of the "ghost shirts," the movement collapsed. There was no more fighting. The army became garrison troops, and the problem of the surviving tribesmen settled into the hands of the civil agencies of the government.

The history of the Indians did not end in 1890, and it is not ended today. As the natives ceased to become a menace, and were herded out of sight and mind on remote and unwanted reservations, non-Indian Americans tended to forget about them. Only those who lived near the reservations knew anything about the Indians, and in general they looked down upon them, and treated them as inferior people. They had little patience with the defeated ones, and from generation to generation very little, if anything, changed in the relations between whites and Indians.

Today, more than a century after Wounded Knee, the United States government still has not established a mutually satisfactory relationship with the tribes, and most non-Indian Americans still know almost nothing about the Indian population. The image of the "vanishing American" is no more. The Indian population is fast increasing, and it is estimated that there are now more than two million persons who can be called Indians in the United States. In 1990, the U.S. Census Bureau counted almost 400,000 of them still living on reservations. But there are still Indians and Indians. They speak more than a hundred different tribal languages. They are in all states of economic condition (from extreme poverty and near-starvation to affluence), range across many levels of acculturation (some have accepted few of the white men's ways of life and some are completely assimilated and indistinguishable from white men), and present a bewildering number of local, regional, and even national concerns and problems that cannot be discussed or dismissed with brief generalizations (in dealing with Indian affairs, the government must still be prepared to cope with thousands of treaties, statutes, and individual legal decisions of the past, as well as the history that the tribes have not forgotten).

On the whole, the Indians are still a proud and dignified people. But they are still a conquered people who lost their sovereignty, and many of them continue to stand in confusion and helplessness between two worlds. Their old standards and ways of life are smashed and gone, but it is not possible—even in a hundred years—for a once free and independent people to entirely abandon and forget what once was. From their military defeat until 1934 the Indians were denied freedom of religion and were often severely punished for trying to practice their religion. Now, with that freedom restored, many of them reveal that, like Popé's Pueblos in the seventeenth century, they remain true to the sacred beliefs, values, and practices of their ancestors.

They need—and most of them welcome—the material benefits of modern-day mainstream American culture: its education, medicine, technology, and science, and readily use whatever is helpful to them, both in their individual lives and in the planning and development of tribal resources. The lack of interest of most of the non-Indian population in the Indians since 1890 has been partly to blame for the continuance of what some call the "Indian problem." Congress has annually voted large appropriations for Indian affairs, but policies have been erratic and confusing, well-meant programs have been ill-designed and underfunded, and government administration of Indian affairs has too often been stupid or criminal. Agents have cheated and stolen from Indians, and have left a black record in their failure to protect whole tribes from exploitation, robbery, and other injustices by aggrandizing elements of the white population.

In the course of years, an increasing number of Indians have become educated (some at tribally-owned colleges), a few have become wealthy, and many have become a productive part of American society. But many are still poorly educated, impoverished, and discriminated against as Indians. It is unthinking to characterize them—as some still do—as "drunks," or "people who won't work." These, and similar contemptuous generalizations, usually stemming from stereotypical thinking, are the images of a people who do not yet have a productive place in American life; who drink, like the Indians of Tecumseh's day in the Old Northwest, to forget their fate and achieve an escape; who, like King Philip's Indians in New England, do not work because the conditions of work for them are colored by humiliations and racism.

Most Indians, even those who live in cities, are still enrolled on reservations, which are not concentration camps but rather the only property that has been left to the tribes. A reservation is the Indians' land base, their place of security, a home from which young men or women can journey to a city in search of employment, and to which they can return to revisit family, take part in ceremonies, or find friends and comfort if the city did not work out. At the same time, many reservations are so barren that they cannot possibly support their populations. Others inevitably catch the eye of white men (for minerals, natural gas, timber, and other natural resources), and there is constant pressure to separate the Indians from their lands. Deceptive arguments ("free the Indians") and un-American policies (the arbitrary ending, or "termination" of federal-Indian relations without the agreement of the Indians, leading inevitably to the unprotected exploitation of the Native Americans by whites and the dissolution of certain reservations) made headlines in the 1950s. The "termination" policy, bringing new hardships to many tribes, was deemed a failure and was followed by a period of militancy, mostly by young Indians, and a succession of new government policies and programs designed half-heartedly to answer the Indians' demands for self-determination and the right to manage and control their own affairs.

During the last quarter of the twentieth century, most Indians finally found that they no longer had to face an "either-or" choice—either continue to be an Indian and die off on a reservation, or become a white and enjoy all the benefits of the white man's world. Regaining a sense of pride in their own tribal traditions and heritage, as well as in their Indianness, they discovered that their new self-esteem helped them to be comfortable in the world of the dominant culture. By the 1980s, numerous Indians were enrolled in colleges and graduate schools, entering professions, and becoming known nationally and internationally for their work.

On the reservations, meanwhile, all the old problems of poverty, high unemployment, ill housing, and poor health remain, reflecting the fact that the "Indian problem," really the problem of the white man's making, is still far from solved today.

Its solution requires the interest and knowledge of non-Indians, whom the Native Americans need to understand and support the tribes, but who up to now have known almost nothing about Indians. From 1890 almost until the end of the twentieth century, Indians to a large extent could have been said to have been almost exclusively the "possession" of government agents, certain sympathetic church and charitable groups, museum keepers, and students of anthropology, ethnology, and sociology. In a way, they dehumanized the Indian, but it did not matter to them, because the rest of the population was too busy to care. What was left was the dusty and almost meaningless arrowhead in a museum display box, the television image of what Indians were never like, and assorted prejudices and impatient demands from Congress and newspaper editorial writers for the Indians to "hurry up and get assimilated, damn it."

So the issue is still joined. The forces in American life that want Indians to get off the reservations and be like all other Americans may someday have their way. But the Indians will resist patiently for decades still to come, and it will not happen easily or soon. When and if it does occur, much of the greatness and majesty and wonder of the United States will have disappeared. Indian culture and Indian thinking, untreasured by the unknowing, will be gone, and only the history books will be able to tell us of it and make us wonder why we did not enfold it and make a place for it in our national life.

BIBLIOGRAPHY

Chapter 1. THE REAL HIAWATHA

Champlain, Samuel de. *The Works of Samuel de Champlain*, ed. by Henry P. Biggar. Toronto, 1922-1936.

Charlevoix, Pierre F. X. de. *History and General Description of New France*. New York, 1866-1872.

Colden, Cadwallader. *The History of the Five Nations of Canada* (1727). Ithaca, N.Y., 1958.

Fenton, William N. *Roll Call of Iroquois Chiefs*. Washington, D.C., 1950.

Henry, Thomas R. *Wilderness Messiah*. New York, 1955.

Hewitt, J. N. B. *A Constitutional League of Peace in the Stone Age of America*. Washington, D.C., 1918.

——. *Legend of the Founding of the Iroquois League*. Washington, D.C., 1892.

——. *Iroquois Cosmology*. Washington, D.C., 1903.

——. Iroquoian contributions to *Handbook of American Indians North of Mexico*, ed. by F. W. Hodge. Washington, D.C., 1907.

Hunt, George D. *The Wars of the Iroquois*. Madison, Wis., 1940.

Morgan, Lewis H. *League of the Ho-De-No-Sau-Nee*. Rochester, N.Y., 1851.

Parkman, Francis. *The Jesuits in North America in the Seventeenth Century*. Boston, 1867. *The Old Regime in Canada*. Boston, 1874. *Count Frontenac and New France Under Louis XIV*. Boston, 1877.

Schoolcraft, Henry R. *Notes on the Iroquois*, Albany, 1847. *The Indian Tribes of the United States*, Parts I-VI. Philadelphia, 1851-1857.

Thwaites, Reuben Gold, ed. *The Jesuit Relations*. Cleveland, 1896-1901.

Wilson, Edmund. *Apologies to the Iroquois*. New York, 1959.

CHAPTER II. THE BETRAYAL OF KING PHILIP

Church, Thomas. *Entertaining Passages Relating to Philip's War.* Boston, 1716.

Collier, John. *The Indians of the Americas.* New York, 1947.

Drake, Samuel G. *The History of King Philip's War.* Boston, 1829.

Ellis, George W., and Morris, John E. *King Philip's War.* New York, 1906.

Howe, George. "The Tragedy of King Philip." *American Heritage Magazine,* New York, December 1958.

Hubbard, William. *A Narrative of the Troubles with the Indians in New England.* Boston, 1677.

Leach, Douglas Edward. *Flintlock and Tomahawk.* New York, 1959.

Lincoln, Charles H., ed. *Narratives of the Indian Wars.* New York, 1913.

Mather, Increase. *A Brief History of the War with the Indians in New England.* Boston, 1676.

Underhill, Ruth M. *Red Man's America.* Chicago, 1953.

CHAPTER III. POPÉ AND THE GREAT PUEBLO UPRISING

Bancroft, Hubert H. *History of Arizona and New Mexico, 1530-1888,* San Francisco, 1889.

Hackett, Charles Wilson, *Revolt of the Pueblo Indians of New Mexico.* Albuquerque, 1942.

Hallenbeck, Cleve. *Alvar Nuñez Cabeza de Vaca.* Glendale, Calif. 1940.

———. *Land of the Conquistadores.* Caldwell, Idaho, 1950.

Hammond, George P., and Agapito, Rey. *Narratives of the Coronado Expedition, 1540-1542.* Albuquerque, 1940.

Horgan, Paul. *Great River.* New York, 1954.

Stanley, F., *Ciudad Santa Fe, 1610-1821.* Denver, 1958.

Twitchell, Ralph E. *The Leading Facts of New Mexican History.* Cedar Rapids, 1911.

Winship, George P. *The Coronado Expedition.* Washington, D.C., 1896.

CHAPTER IV. THE WILDERNESS WAR OF PONTIAC

Blackbird, Andrew J. *History of the Ottawa and Chippewa Indians of Michigan.* Ypsilanti, Mich., 1887.

Carver, Jonathan. *Travels through the Interior Parts of North America . . .* London, 1778.

Jenness, Diamond. *The Indians of Canada.* Ottawa, 1934.

Long, J. C. *Lord Jeffery Amherst.* New York, 1933.

Parkman, Francis. *History of the Conspiracy of Pontiac.* Boston, 1868.

Peckham, Howard H. *Pontiac and the Indian Uprising.* Princeton, 1947.

Quaife, M. M. *The Siege of Detroit in 1763, Including the Journal of Pontiac's Conspiracy and John Rutherfurd's Narrative.* Chicago, 1958.

Rogers, Robert. *A Concise Account of North America.* London, 1765.

CHAPTER V. TECUMSEH, THE GREATEST INDIAN

Arnow, Harriette S. *Seedtime on the Cumberland.* New York, 1960.

Bakeless, John. *Daniel Boone.* New York, 1938.

Beard, Reed. *The Battle of Tippecanoe.* Chicago, 1889.

Blumenthal, Walter Hart. *American Indians Dispossessed.* Philadelphia, 1955.

Bodley, Temple. *History of Kentucky.* Chicago, 1928.

Brady, Cyrus T. *Border Fights and Fighters.* New York, 1902.

Britt, Albert. *Great Indian Chiefs.* New York, 1938.

Carter, Clarence E. *The Territorial Papers of the United States,* VII, VIII (Indiana, 1800-1810 and 1810-1816). Washington, 1939.

Catlin, George. *Manners, Customs and Condition of the North American Indians.* New York, 1842.

Cleaves, Freeman. *Old Tippecanoe: William Henry Harrison and His Time.* New York, 1939.

Drake, Benjamin. *The Life of Tecumseh and His Brother the Prophet.* Cincinnati, 1841.

Eggleston, Edward, and Seelye, Lillie Eggleston. *Tecumseh and the Shawnee Prophet.* New York, 1878.

Esarey, Logan, ed. *Messages and Letters of William Henry Harrison.* Indianapolis, 1922.

Fey, Harold E., and McNickle, D'Arcy. *Indians and Other Americans.* New York, 1959.

Gray, Elma E. *Wilderness Christians.* Ithaca, N.Y., 1956.

Gurd, Norman S. *The Story of Tecumseh*. Toronto, 1912.

Hodge, Frederick W. *Handbook of American Indians North of Mexico*. Washington, 1907.

Lossing, Benson J. *The Pictorial Field Book of the War of 1812*. New York, 1869.

MacLean, J. P. "The Shaker Mission to the Shawnee Indians." *Ohio Archeological and Historical Society Proceedings*, XI, 1903.

McKenney, Thomas L., and Hall, James. *The Indian Tribes of North America*, ed. by Frederick W. Hodge. Edinburgh, 1933.

Mooney, James. *The Ghost Dance Religion*. Washington, D.C., 1896.

Oskinson, John M. *Tecumseh and His Times*. New York, 1938.

Royce, Charles C. *Indian Land Cessions in the United States*. Washington, D.C., 1899.

Swanton, John R. *The Indian Tribes of North America*. Washington, 1952.

Trumbull, Henry. *History of Indian Wars*. Boston, 1846.

Tucker, Glenn. *Tecumseh, Vision of Glory*. Indianapolis, 1956.

Underhill, Ruth M. *Red Man's America*. Chicago, 1953.

Witherell, B. F. H. "Reminiscences of the Northwest." *Wisconsin State Historical Collections*, III, 1857.

Wood, Norman B. *Lives of Famous Indian Chiefs*. Chicago, 1906.

Wood, William. *Select British Documents on the War of 1812*. Toronto, 1928.

CHAPTER VI. THE DEATH OF OSCEOLA

Blumenthal, Walter Hart. *American Indians Dispossessed*. Philadelphia, 1955.

Boyd, Mark F. "Asi-Yaholo or Osceola." *Florida Historical Quarterly*, Vol. XXXIII, Nos. 3, 4, January and April 1955, Gainesville, Fla.

Catlin, George. *Manners, Customs and Condition of the North American Indians*. New York, 1842.

Coe, Charles H. "The Parentage of Osceola," *Florida Historical Quarterly*, Vol. XXXIII, Nos. 3, 4, January and April 1955, Gainesville, Fla.

———. *Red Patriots: The Story of the Seminoles*. Cincinnati, 1898.

Debo, Angie. *The Road to Disappearance*. Norman, Okla., 1941.

Foreman, Grant. *Indian Removal: The Emigration of the Five Civilized Tribes of Indians*. Norman, Okla., 1932.

Giddings, Joshua R. *The Exiles of Florida*. Columbus, Ohio, 1858.

MacCauley, Clay. *The Seminole Indians of Florida*. Washington, D.C., 1887.

McKenney, Thomas L., and Hall, James. *The Indian Tribes of North America*, ed. by F. W. Hodge. Edinburgh, 1933.

McReynolds, Edwin C. *The Seminoles*. Norman, Okla., 1957.

Motte, Jacob Rhett. *Journey into Wilderness*, ed. by James F. Sunderman. Gainesville, Fla., 1953.

Smith, W. W. *Sketch of the Seminole War, and Sketches During a Campaign, by a Lieutenant of the Left Wing*. Charleston, 1836.

Ward, May McNeer. "The Disappearance of the Head of Osceola." *Florida Historical Quarterly*, Vol. XXXIII, Nos. 3, 4, January and April 1955, Gainesville, Fla.

CHAPTER VII. THE RIVALRY OF BLACK HAWK AND KEOKUK

Black Hawk. *Black Hawk, an Autobiography*, ed. by Donald Jackson. Urbana, Ill., 1955.

Coues, Elliott, ed. *The Expeditions of Zebulon Montgomery Pike*. New York, 1895.

Drake, Benjamin F. *The Life and Adventures of Black Hawk*. Cincinnati, 1838.

Hagan, William T. *The Sac and Fox Indians*. Norman, Okla., 1958.

Hodge, Frederick W. *Handbook of American Indians North of Mexico*. Washington, 1907.

Jones, William. *Ethnography of the Fox Indians*. Washington, 1939.

McKenney, Thomas L., and Hall, James. *The Indian Tribes of North America*, ed. by F. W. Hodge. Edinburgh, 1933.

Reynolds, John. *My Own Times: Embracing Also the History of My Life*. Chicago, 1879.

Stevens, Frank E. *The Black Hawk War* . . . Chicago, 1903.

Swanton, John R. *The Indian Tribes of North America*. Washington, 1952.

Thwaites, Reuben Gold. *The Story of the Black Hawk War*. Madison, Wis., 1892.

Wakefield, John A. *History of the War Between the United States and the Sac and Fox Nations*. . . . Jacksonville, Ill., 1834.

CHAPTER VIII. CRAZY HORSE, PATRIOT OF THE PLAINS

Boller, Henry A. *Among the Indians*. Chicago, 1959.

Bourke, Captain John G. *On the Border with Crook*. New York, 1892.

Brininstool, E. A. *Crazy Horse*. Los Angeles, 1949.

Brown, Joseph Epes. *The Sacred Pipe*. Norman, Okla., 1953.

Carrington, Margaret. *Ab-Sa-Ra-Ka, Land of Massacre*. Philadelphia, 1869.

Chittenden, H. M. *The American Fur Trade of the Far West*. New York, 1902.

Custer, Elizabeth. *Boots and Saddles*. New York, 1885.

DeVoto, Bernard. *The Year of Decision: 1846*. Boston, 1943.

Downey, Fairfax. *Indian-Fighting Army*. New York, 1944.

Dunn, J. P. *Massacres of the Mountains*. New York, 1958.

Finerty, John F. *War-Path and Bivouac*. Chicago, 1955.

Grinnell, George Bird. *The Fighting Cheyennes*. Norman, Okla., 1956.

Hafen, LeRoy and Young, F. M. *Fort Laramie*. Glendale, Calif., 1938.

Haines, Francis. *The Appaloosa Horse*. Lewiston, Idaho, n.d.

Hebard, Grace R., and Brininstool, E. A. *The Bozeman Trail*. Glendale, Calif., 1960.

Hieb, David L. *Fort Laramie*. Washington, D.C., 1954.

Hyde, George E. *Red Cloud's Folk*. Norman, Okla., 1937.

———. *A Sioux Chronicle*. Norman, Okla., 1956.

King, Charles. *Campaigning with Crook*. New York, 1890.

Lavender, David. *Bent's Fort*. New York, 1954.

Lowie, Robert H. *Indians of the Plains*. New York, 1954.

Luce, Edward S., and Evelyn S. *Custer Battlefield*. Washington, D.C., 1952.

Mattes, Merrill J. *Indians, Infants and Infantry*. Denver, 1960.

Oehler, C. M. *The Great Sioux Uprising*. New York, 1959.

Parkman, Francis. *The Oregon Trail*. New York, 1918.

Robinson, Doane. *A History of the Dakota or Sioux Indians*. Minneapolis, 1956.

Roe, Frank Gilbert. *The Indian and the Horse*. Norman, Okla., 1955.

Ruby, Robert H. *The Oglala Sioux*. New York, 1955.

Sandoz, Mari. *Crazy Horse*. New York, 1942.

Schmitt, Martin F., and Brown, Dee. *Fighting Indians of the West*. New York, 1948.

Stuart, Granville. *Forty Years on the Frontier*. Glendale, Calif., 1957.

Vestal, Stanley. *Warpath and Council Fire*. New York, 1948.

———. *Sitting Bull*. Boston, 1932.

Ware, Eugene F. *The Indian War of 1864*. New York, 1960.

Wellman, Paul I. *The Indian Wars of the West*. New York, 1954.

Wissler, Clark. *The American Indian*. New York, 1931.

Chapter IX. THE LAST STAND OF CHIEF JOSEPH

Allen, A. J. *Ten Years in Oregon*. Ithaca, N.Y., 1950.

Bancroft, Hubert H. *History of Oregon*, I, 1834-48. San Francisco, 1886.

———. *History of Washington, Idaho and Montana*. San Francisco, 1890.

Cox, Ross. *Adventures on the Columbia River*. London, 1831.

DeVoto, Bernard. *Across the Wide Missouri*. Cambridge, Mass., 1947.

Drury, Clifford M. *Henry Harmon Spalding*. Caldwell, Idaho, 1936.

———. *The Diaries and Letters of H. H. Spalding and A. B. Smith, 1838-42*. Glendale, Calif., 1958.

Elsensohn, Sister M. Alfreda. *Pioneer Days in Idaho County*, I, II. Caldwell, Idaho, 1947, 1951.

Fee, Chester. *Chief Joseph: The Biography of a Great Indian*. New York, 1936.

Ferris, Warren A. *Life in the Rocky Mountains, 1830-35*. Salt Lake City, 1940.

Haines, Francis. "Where Did the Plains Indians Get Their Horses?" and "The Northward Spread of Horses among the Plains Indians." *American Anthropologist*, January-September 1938.

Horner, J. H., and Pfister, Grace. *Wallowa, the Land of Winding Waters*. Joseph, Ore., 1950.

Howard, Helen A., and McGrath, Dan L. *War Chief Joseph*. Caldwell, Idaho, 1952.

Howard, O. O. *Nez Percé Joseph*. Boston, 1881.

Irving, Washington. *Astoria*. Philadelphia., 1836.

Jackson, Helen Hunt. *A Century of Dishonor*. Boston, 1887.

Jessett, Thomas E. *Chief Spokan Garry*. Minneapolis, 1960.

Josephy, Alvin M., Jr. "The Naming of the Nez Percés." *Montana Magazine of Western History*, Vol. V, No. 4, Helena, Mont., 1955.

Kip, Lawrence. *The Indian Council at Walla Walla*. Eugene, Ore., 1897.

McWhorter, Lucullus V. *Hear Me, My Chiefs!* Caldwell, Idaho, 1952.

———. *Yellow Wolf*. Caldwell, Idaho, 1948.

Merk, Frederick. *Fur Trade and Empire*. Cambridge, Mass., 1931.

Morgan, Dale. *Jedediah Smith and the Opening of the West*. New York, 1953.

Parker, Samuel. *Journal of an Exploring Tour beyond the Rocky Mountains*. Ithaca, N.Y., 1838.

Rollins, Philip A. *The Discovery of the Oregon Trail*. New York, 1935.

Spinden, H. J. "The Nez Percé Indians." *Memoirs of the American Anthropological Association*, Vol. II, Part 3, Lancaster, Pa., 1903.

Splawn, A. J. *Kamiakin*. Portland, 1944.

Stevens, Hazard. *Isaac I. Stevens*. Boston, 1900.

Teit, James A. *The Salishan Tribes of the Western Plateaus*. Washington, D.C., 1930.

Thwaites, Reuben G. *The Original Journals of Lewis and Clark*. New York, 1904-1905.

White, M. Catherine. *David Thompson's Journals Relating to Montana and Adjacent Regions, 1808-12*. Missoula, Montana, 1950.

Wood, H. Clay. *The Status of Young Joseph and His Band of Nez Percé Indians*. Portland, Ore., 1876.

INDEX

Abraham, 191
Acoma (pueblo), 76, 81
Alabama River, 183
Alcanfor (pueblo), 76
Alderman, 60-62
Alexander, *see* Wamsutta
Algonquian Indians, 5, 27, 53, 216, 260
Alligator, 198, 201, 208
Alvarado, Capt. Hernando de, 76
American Fur Company, 263
Amherst, Sir Jeffery, 97, 106-10, 119-23
Amherstburg (Canada), 223
Andover (Mass.), 56
Annawon, 56, 61
Apache Indians, 34, 72, 86, 93-94, 261, 315, 342
Apalachicola River, 183
Arapaho Indians, 264, 342
Arkansas Indians, 126, 150
Arkansas River, 192, 203, 277
Astoria (Ore.), 317
Atawang, 126
Athapascan Indians, 34
Atkinson, Gen. Henry, 242-47, 251-252
Atlanta (Ga.), 328
Atlantis, 34, 75
Atotarho, 16-17, 20-22
Awashonks, 46, 47, 56, 58, 60
Ayeta, Fray Francisco de, 93
Aztec Indians, 6, 9, 12, 35

Bad Axe River, 250
Bannock Indians, 341, 342
Bear Paw Mountains, 337
Bear Ribs, 275
Beardstown (Ill.), 243

Benteen, Capt. Frederick, 257, 299-301
Big Hole River, 333-35
Big Horn Mountains, 287, 302-303
Bighorn River, 282, 284, 286
Billerica (Mass.), 56
Bismarck (N. Dak.), 292
Bitterroot Mountains, 315-16, 332-33
Black Buffalo Woman, 276-77, 288-289, 306
Black Hawk, 152, 163, 211-253, 260, 342
Black Hills, 260, 262-64, 265, 275, 290, 291-94, 302-303
Black Kettle, 291
Black Moon, 299
Blackfeet Sioux Indians, 150, 261, 318
Blackfish, 140
Bloody Run, 121
Blue Jacket, 143
Boone, Daniel, 135
Boston (Mass.), 41, 44, 50-51, 60
Bouquet, Col. Henry, 119, 122
Bozeman Road, 282-85
Bradstreet, Col. John, 126
Braintree (Mass.), 56
Brant, Joseph, 135
Brantford (Ontario), 29
Braddock, Gen. Edward, 98
Brock, Gen. Isaac, 165-67
Bridgewater (Mass.), 59
Bristol (R. I.), 37
Brookfield (Mass.), 51
Brulé Sioux Indians, 261, 264-65, 269-275, 278, 281, 284, 286-88, 290
Brush, Capt. Henry, 164
Bua, Nicholas, 88
Buckongahelos, 143
Bull Bear, 264-65
Burlington (Iowa), 253

357

Cabeza de Vaca, Alvar, 73-74
Cahokia (Ill.), 128
Cahokia Indians, 126
Calhoun, John, 232
Call, Gen. Robert, 200
Camas Prairie, 329
Camp Moultrie (Fla.), 187, 206-207
Campbell, Robert, 263-64
Canadian North West Company,
 317-18
Canonchet, 54-56, 58
Canyon Creek, 336-37
Cape Cod, 37, 39
Carrington, Col. Henry B., 282-83
Carver, John, 37
Cass, Lewis, 190
Catherine, 113
Catlin, George, 207, 253
Cayuga Indians, 8, 14
Cayuse Indians, 319
Cazenovia (N. Y.), 24
Chama River, 80
Champlain, Samuel de, 5
Charleston (S. C.), 177, 206
Cheeseekau, 139, 141-44, 204
Chelmsford (Mass.), 56
Cherokee Indians, 12, 25, 138, 144,
 158, 179, 180, 218, 238
Cherry Valley Massacre, 6
Cheyenne Indians, 257, 264, 275, 277-
 278, 284-87, 291, 298, 300-301, 304,
 337, 341
Chicago (Ill.), 145, 251
Chickasaw Indians, 138, 158, 179
Chinook Indians, 315
Chippewa Indians, 101-103, 109, 113,
 117-18, 123-26, 147, 152, 163-65, 235,
 251, 260
Chivington, Col. J. M., 277-78
Choctaw Indians, 125, 158, 179
Church, Benjamin, 47, 59, 61
Cibola, 74-75
Cincinnati (Ohio), 144
Clark, George Rogers, 141, 146
Clark, Gov. William, 226, 230-31,
 234, 237, 252
Clark's Fork River, 336
Clay, Henry, 162
Clearwater River, 315, 319, 329-31
Clinch, Gen. Duncan, 194, 198-99

Coeur d'Alêne Indians, 315
Colden, Cadwallader, 7-9
Columbia River, 315-17
Columbus, Christopher, 34
Colville Reservation, 340
Conchos River, 78
Conestoga Indians, 13
Connecticut River, 51, 56
Conquering Bear, 267-73
Cook, Caleb, 61
Cooper Union, 287
Copinger, Polly, 181
Coronado, Francisco Vásquez de, 75-
 77
Cortes, Hernando, 35, 78
Cottonwood (Ida.), 329
Cow Island, 337
Crazy Horse (Curly), 259-309, 343
Creek Indians, 126, 138, 144, 158-59,
 166, 179, 181-86, 191, 196, 203, 237
Croghan, George, 105-107, 109-10
Crook, Gen. George, 295-98, 302-304,
 306-307
Crow Indians, 262, 264, 276, 289, 296,
 304, 331-32, 337
Crown Point (N. Y.), 97
Cuivre River, 229
Culiacán (Mexico), 74
Cumberland Gap, 135
Cumberland River, 137
Custer, Lt. Col. George Armstrong,
 257, 259, 291-92, 298-302, 327

Dade, Maj. Francis L., 198
Dalles, The, 315, 316
Dalyell, Capt. James, 119, 120, 121
Dartmouth (Mass.), 49
Davis, Jefferson, 214
Dayton (Ohio), 137
Dearborn, Henry, 219
Declaration of Independence, 134
Dedham (Mass.), 59
Deerfield (Conn.), 51
Deganawidah, 17-23
Delaware Indians, 26, 28, 108, 110,
 117, 121-22, 125, 127, 152, 162-63
Delaware River, 13
Des Moines River, 215, 222, 225, 228
Detroit (Mich.), 105, 109, 163, 165-
 166, 212

Detroit River, 98, 103, 163
Dickson, Robert, 225
Dixon's Ferry (Ill.), 244, 246
Djigosasee, 18
Dodge, Col. Henry, 248-49
Dull Knife, 304, 341

Ecorse River, 111
Eliot, John, 41
El Paso (Tex.), 65, 92, 94
Erie Indians, 13
Esteban, 73-74

Fallen Timbers, Battle of, 145, 164
Fenton, Dr. William N., 11
Fetterman, Capt. William J., 283
Five Nations, League of, 22-29
Five Wounds, 328, 330, 335
Flathead Indians, 315, 317, 318
Forsyth, Thomas, 231, 234
Fort Abraham Lincoln, 292
Fort Armstrong, 212, 232, 242
Fort Benton, 337
Fort Brooke, 196, 202
Fort C. F. Smith, 282-86
Fort Dearborn, 166
Fort de Chartres, 124
Fort Drane, 199
Fort Edward Augustus, 118
Fort Gibson, 192
Fort Kearney (Nebr.), 279
Fort Keogh, 337
Fort King, 194, 196
Fort Knox, 153
Fort Laramie, 263-70, 274, 275, 278-
    279, 281, 288
Fort Le Bouef, 118
Fort Leavenworth, 274
Fort Ligonier, 118
Fort Malden, 157, 163, 169, 223, 235
Fort Madison, 222
Fort Marion, 204
Fort Meigs, 164, 168, 226
Fort Mellon, 201-204
Fort Miami, 168
Fort Miamis, 117
Fort Michilimackinac, 118, 164
Fort Mims, 194
Fort Monroe, 211
Fort Ouiatenon, 118

Fort Peyton, 204
Fort Phil Kearny (Wyo.), 259, 282-
    285
Fort Pierre, *see* Pierre (S. Dak.)
Fort Pitt, 118
Fort Pontchartrain, 103
Fort Presqu' Isle, 118
Fort Reno, 282
Fort Robinson, 259, 306-308
Fort St. Joseph, 117
Fort Sandusky, 117
Fort Shaw, 333
Fort Vinango, 118
Fort Wayne, 117, 143, 153, 162
Fox Indians, *see* Sauk and Fox Indi-
    ans
Franciscan Friars, 65
Franklin, Benjamin, 9
French and Indian War, 98, 217

Gadsden, Col. James, 190
Gage, Gen. Thomas, 125, 133
Gaines, Gen. Edmund P., 185, 199,
    237, 238-39
Galena (Ill.), 247
Galisteo (pueblo), 90
Gall, 299-301, 303
Galland, Isaac, 220
Galloway, Rebecca, 146
Galveston (Tex.), 73
Georgian Bay (Ontario), 3, 101-103
Geronimo, 342
"Ghost Dance," 343
Gibbon, Col. John, 297-98, 301-302,
    333-34
Gladwin, Maj. Henry, 113-17, 119-25
Grand Canyon, 76
Grangeville (Idaho), 329
Grant, Ulysses S., 287, 292, 294, 321
Gratiot, Col. Henry, 243
Grattan, Lt. J. L. 270, 272-74
Great Swamp, 54-56, 59
Green Bay (Wis.), 102, 225
Green River, 318
Greenville (Ohio), 144-45
Groton (Mass.), 56
Grover, Lafayette P., 321

Hadley (Conn.), 51
Harmar, Gen. Josiah, 143

Harney, Gen. W. S., 274-75, 278
Harrison, Gen. William Henry, 131, 147, 149, 159-60, 163-64, 169-70, 219, 223
Hatfield (Mass.), 51
Hawikuh (pueblo), 75
Henry, William, 219
Hewitt, J. N. B., 11, 15
Hiawatha, 3-29
Hopi Indians, 66, 76
Horse Creek, 268, 279
Howard, Gen. O. O., 322-23, 325-34, 338-39
Hudson River, 13
Hudson's Bay Company, 318
Hull, Gen. William, 163-65
Hump, 269, 275, 283-85, 289
Hunkpapa Sioux Indians, 261, 275, 281, 298-301, 303
Hunt, Capt. Thomas, 36
Huron (schooner), 114
Huron Indians, 3-5, 13, 25, 101-103, 105, 109-15, 117-18, 122, 125

Illinois River, 243
Inca Indians, 6, 12
Indian Creek, 247
Inquisition, 86
Iowa Indians, 158
Iowa River, 232, 236, 242
Iron Plume, 302
Iroquois Indians, 3-29, 102-103, 107, 109, 135, 151-52, 216, 318

Jackson, Andrew, 177, 183-89, 212, 237, 247
James, Gen. Henry, 248
James I, King, 38
Jefferson, Thomas, 178, 221
Jefferson Barracks (Mo.), 178, 221
Jenney, Prof. W. P., 293
Jesuit *Relations*, 4
Jesup, Gen. Thomas, 200-204
Johnson, Col. Richard, 171
Johnson, Sir William, 106
Johnston, Albert Sidney, 214
Joseph, Chief, 313, 319-26, 329-40
Joseph Canyon, 314
Julesburg (Colo.), 278

Kaskaskia Indians, 103, 126, 147
Keokuk, Chief, 212-15, 227, 231-43, 253
Kere Indians, 66
Kickapoo Indians, 103, 108, 118, 147, 150-52, 162-63, 234, 239, 242, 247
King Philip's War, 33-62
Kiskaukee River, 248
Knox, Henry, 134
Kurile Islands, 33

La Cienega (N. Mex.), 90
Lafayette (Ind.), 118
Lake Champlain, 13
Lake Erie, 98, 169-70
Lake Huron, 98
Lake Monroe, 201
Lake St. Claire, 117
Lake Superior, 26, 103, 153, 216
Lakota Sioux Indians, *see* Teton Sioux Indians
Lancaster (Mass.), 56
Lapwai (Idaho), 318, 319, 326, 328, 329, 340
Laramie Creek, 263
Laulewasika, *see* Tenskwatawa
Lawyer, Chief, 319, 320, 322
Lean Elk, 335
Lewis and Clark Expedition, 258, 262, 313, 316-17
Lewiston (Idaho), 318
Licking River, 141
Lincoln, Abraham, 214, 239, 246, 248
Little Bighorn River, 257-59, 291, 298-302
Little Hawk, 269, 289
Little Turtle, 143, 153, 257
Little Wolf, 341
Lolo Trail, 332
London (England), 36
Long Knives, 163
Long Island, 28, 35
Longfellow, Henry Wadsworth, 3, 11
Longmeadow (Conn.), 56
Looking Glass, 328-29, 331-32, 335, 338
Lord Dunmore's War, 139-40

Macatepilesis, 108
Mackenzie, Col. Ranald, 304

Mackenzie River, 33
McQueen, Peter, 183-86
Mad River, 137
Madison, James, 223-24
Man-Afraid-of-His-Horse, 263, 270, 273-75, 282, 284, 289
Mandan Indians, 150
Manete, 146
Manso Indians, 92
Marlborough (Mass.), 56
Mascouten Indians, 103, 108, 118
Massachuset Indians, 41, 46
Massasoit (Woosamequin), 36-41, 52
Matoonas, 51, 56, 60
Mattaump 52, 56
Maumee River, 125, 128, 144
Medfield (Mass.), 56
Memphis (Tenn.), 158
Mendon (Mass.), 51
Mendoza, Antonio de, 74-75
Menominee Indians, 103, 126, 152, 240
Mesa Verde, 69
Metacom, *see* Philip, King
Methoataske, 137
Mexico City (Mex.), 73
Miami Indians, 26, 103, 108, 117, 124, 126-27, 142-43, 147, 152, 166
Miami River, 143
Micanopy, 189-90, 193-94, 198, 201-203, 206, 208
Michigan (sloop), 114
Mico, 184
Middleborough (Mass.), 49
Miles, Col. Nelson A., 303-305, 337-340
Milwaukee (Wis.), 244
Mingo Indians, 117, 121-22, 127
Miniconjou Sioux Indians, 261
Minnesota War, 277
Minnitaree Indians, 316
Mississauga Indians, 123
Mississippi River, 12, 94, 100, 102, 163, 178, 211, 215, 218-21, 225, 229, 232, 236, 242, 249-51, 260
Missoula (Mont.), 333
Missouri River, 228-29, 261-63, 277, 316, 337
Mitchell, David, 268-69
Mohawk Indians, 8, 14, 53

Mohegan (Mohican) Indians, 57-60 159
Monguaya, 164
Monoco, 52, 56
Monongahela Valley, 118
Montagnais Indians, 5
Montaup (Mount Hope), 38
Montezuma, 89
Montreal (Canada), 97, 100
Mount Hope, 38, 44, 46-49, 50, 60

Nanticoke Indians, 28
Narraganset Indians, 37, 39, 46, 50, 54-56, 59, 159
Narragansett Bay, 37, 38, 54
Narváez Pánfilo de, 73
Nashville (Tenn.), 138
Nauset Indians, 38
Navaho Indians, 34, 72
Neapope, 241, 244, 252
New Amsterdam, 12
New Haven (Conn.), 48
New Orleans (La.), 101, 109, 203
New York City, 212, 233, 287
Nez Percé Indians, 306-307, 313-40
Niantic Indians, 46, 58
Nipmuck Indians, 46, 50-56, 59-60
Niza, Fray Marco de, 74
No Bow Sioux Indians, 261
No Water, 276, 288, 306
Norfolk (Va.), 212
Northampton (Mass.), 51, 56
Northern Pacific Railroad, 289-91
Northfield (Conn.), 51

Oglala Sioux Indians, 261, 262-65, 269, 273-309
Ohio River, 12, 131, 136, 163
Okefenokee Swamp, 186
Old Chillicothe (Ohio), 140
Old Joseph, 314, 319-21
Old Piqua (Ohio), 137, 140
Old Point Comfort (Va.), 211
Ollokot, 324-25, 327, 330, 335, 338
Omaha Indians, 273-74
Onandaga Indians, 8, 14, 152
Oñate, Don Juan de, 65, 80-83
Oneida Indians, 8, 14
Ongwanonsionni Indians, 13
Oregon Trail, 266-70, 274, 277

Osage Indians, 126, 152, 158, 218
Osceola, 177-208
Otermín, Antonio de, 90
Ottawa Indians, 98-128, 147, 152, 157
Ottawa River, 100, 103
Ozark Mountains, 158

Paiute Indians, 342
Panuco (Mexico), 73
Parkman, Francis, 6
Patterson, John B., 213
Pawnee Indians, 264, 273, 274, 279-280, 303
Payne, John Howard, 179
Payne's Landing (Fla.), 190, 192, 194, 195
Peas Creek (Fla.), 186
Peckham, Howard H., 99
Pecos River, 90
Pensacola (Fla.), 187
Pequot Indians, 35, 46, 57-60, 159
Perry, Commodore Oliver Hazard, 169
Perry, Capt. David, 326
Pessacus, 56
Philadelphia (Pa.), 212
Philip, King (Metacom), 33-62, 100
Philip, King (brother-in-law of Micanopy), 203-204
Piankashaw Indians, 103, 147, 152
Picuris, 90-91
Pierre (S. Dak.), 263, 275
Piscataway Indians, 28
Platte Bridge, 259
Platte River, 263-64, 267, 270, 273-74, 277-81, 286, 288, 290
Plymouth (Mass.), 41, 44-45, 54, 59-62, 100
Pocasset Indians, 49, 54, 55
Po-he-yemu, 89
Point Pelee, 118
Point Pleasant (W. Va.), 139
Pokanoket, 38, 159
Pomham, 56, 59
Pontiac, 97-128, 138, 151, 211, 342
Popé, 65-94, 344
Portland (Ore.), 328
Potawatomi Indians, 27, 101, 105, 109, 111-17, 123, 147, 151, 152, 157-58, 162-63, 166, 239, 241, 245, 247

Powder River, 276, 278, 280-91, 294-295, 302-303, 306, 341
Powell, Capt. James W., 284
Powell, William, 181
Powhatan Indians, 35
Prairie du Chien (Wis.), 228-29, 250, 252
"Praying Indians," 41, 50, 57
Procter, Col. Henry, 167-70
Prophet, the, see Tenskwatawa
Prophet's Town, 151, 154, 160
Providence (R. I.), 41, 59
Puckeshinwa, 137, 139
Pueblo Indians, 65-94, 261, 344
Put in Bay, 169

Quaiapen, 56
Quashquame, 220
Quebec (Canada), 3, 100
Quinnapin, 56, 59
Quivira, 77

Rainbow (warrior), 328, 330, 335
Rains, Lt. S. M., 329
Rapid City (S. Dak.), 260
Rawn, Capt. Charles C., 332
Red Cloud, 259, 263, 270, 279, 282-290, 292-93, 295-96, 303, 306-308
Red River, 242, 318
Regnault, Cristophe, 3, 4
Rehoboth, 49
Removal Act (1830), 179
Reno, Maj. Marcus, 298-99, 301
Revere, Paul, 43
Reynolds, Col. J. J., 295
Reynolds, John, 237-52
Rio Grande, 65, 76-80, 92
River Raisin, 164, 167, 168, 225
Rock Island (Ill.), 215, 235-37, 247
Rock River, 215-16, 228, 230, 235, 240-44, 248
Rocky Mountain Fur Company, 263
Rogers, Maj. Robert, 104
Rosebud River, 259, 296-98

Sac Indians, see Sauk and Fox Indians
Sagamore, John, 60
St. Augustine, 200, 204
St. Clair, Gen. Arthur, 143, 257

St. Lawrence River, 5, 12, 216
St. Louis (Mo.), 128, 163, 217, 221, 222, 228-29, 230, 237, 247, 262, 318
St. Marks (Fla.), 187
St. Petersburg (Fla.), 73
Sakonnet Indians, 38, 46, 47, 56, 59
Salmon River, 315, 325, 328-29
Samoset, 37
San Cristóbal, 90
San Juan (P. R.), 80-83, 91
Sandoz, Mari, 259-60
Santa Clara (pueblo), 90
Santa Cruz (pueblo), 90
Sante Fe (N. M.), 85-92
Sante Fe Trail, 277
Santee Sioux Indians, 260-61
Santo Domingo, 79
Saponis, 28
Sauk and Fox Indians, 103, 118, 126, 152, 154, 157, 163, 211-53, 260
Schaghticoke (N. Y.), 53
Schoolcraft, Henry R., 10
Schuykill River, 138
Scituate (Mass.), 56
Scott, Gen. Winfield, 199, 214, 247, 251-52
Seminole Indians, 152, 159, 177-208, 237
Seneca Indians, 8, 14, 107, 110-11, 118, 121, 125-26, 152
Shabbona, 152
Shawnees, 26, 103, 108-109, 118, 121-122, 125-26, 137-73, 222
Sheridan (Wyo.), 282
Sheridan, Gen. Philip H., 291
Sherman, Gen. William Tecumseh, 335
Shoshanin (Sagamore Sam), 52, 56
Shoshoni Indians, 289, 296, 315, 342
Simsbury (Conn.), 56
Sioux Indians, 102, 150, 162-63, 228, 233, 240, 250, 257-309, 338, 343
Sipapu, 70
Sitting Bull, 259, 281, 294, 296, 298-304, 309, 335, 338, 343
Smoke, 264-65, 269
Snake River, 315, 324
Solomon River, 275
Sosa, Gaspar Castaño de, 79-80
Spalding, Rev. Henry H., 318-20

Spokan Indians, 315
Spotted Tail, 265, 273-74, 278, 287-90, 295, 303, 307-308
Springfield (Mass.), 51
Squanto, 36
Standing Rock Agency, 343
Stevensville (Mont.), 333
Stonington (Conn.), 58
Straits of Mackinac, 103
Sturgis, Col. Samuel, 336
Sublette, William, 263
Sudbury (Mass.), 56
Swansea (Mass.), 47

Tallapoosa River, 180
Tallassee Indians, 180, 182, 188-89, 192, 201-202
Tampa (Fla.), 186, 201-202
Tampico (Mexico), 73
Taos (N. M.), 89-91
Targhee Pass, 335
Taunton (Mass.), 44, 49, 60
Taylor, Zachary, 208, 214, 228, 244, 246, 252
Tecumapease, 146
Tecumseh, 131-73, 182, 214, 222-26, 342
Teharonhiawagon, 10, 15, 16
Tenskwatawa, 148-51
Terry, Gen. Alfred, 297-98, 301-302
Tesuque (pueblo), 90
Teton Sioux Indians, 260-63, 269, 275-277, 287, 296
Tewa Indians, 66
Thames River, 169-70
Theller, Lt. Edward, 327
Thompson, David, 317
Thompson, Gen. Wiley, 193-97, 207
Ticonderoga, 97
Tiguex, 76-79
Tippecanoe River, 151, 160, 223
Tlaxcalan Indians, 35
Toledo (Ohio), 145
Tongue River, 282, 294, 303-304
Toohoolhoolzote, 324, 330, 338-39
Trimble, Capt. Joel, 326
Trumbull, 132
Tucker, Glenn, 132
Tunica Indians, 125
Tuscarora Indians, 11, 28

Tutelo Indians, 28
Two Kettle Sioux Indians, 261
Two Moons, 295

Uncas, 59
Unkompoin, 56, 59
Ute Indians, 72, 261, 315, 342

Van Buren, Pres. Martin, 180
Vargas, Diego de, 94
Vincennes (Ind.), 131, 219

Wabash Indians, 125-27
Wabash River, 160, 257
Wa-co-me, 227
Wahlitits, 324-25
Wahoo Swamp, 198
Walker River reservation, 342
Wallowa Valley, 314-15, 319-23, 326, 340
Wampanoag Indians, 33-62
Wamsutta (Alexander), 41-42
Warrior (steamboat), 250
Warwick (Conn.), 50
Washington (D. C.), 202, 219, 223, 232, 247, 253, 287, 292
Washington, Pres. George, 134
Washita River, 291, 301
Wayne, Gen. Anthony, 144
Wea Indians, 103, 110, 118, 147, 152
Weetamoo, 42, 49-50, 55-56, 60
Weippe Prairie, 331
Wellamotkin, *see* Old Joseph
Weston, Dr. Frederick, 207
Weymouth (Mass.), 56
Whipple, Capt. Stephen, 328-29
White Bird, 332-34, 339
White Bird Canyon, 325-29

White Cloud, 239
White River, 290
Whiteside, Gen. Samuel, 244-46
Whitman, Marcus, 319
Wichita Indians, 77
Wickford (Conn.), 56
Wildcat, 204
Wilkinson, Gen. James, 222
Williams, Roger, 41
Wind River Mountains, 264
Winnebago Indians, 103, 147, 152, 154, 157, 160, 162, 223, 228, 234, 239, 241-44, 246-49, 250-52
Winslow, Edward, 39
Winslow, Gov. Josiah, 47
Wisconsin River, 228, 248-51
Withlacoochee River, 198, 201
Wood, Maj. C. E. S., 331
Wood, Maj. H. Clay, 321-23
Worm, 273, 289, 308
Wounded Knee, 343-44
Wovoka, 342-43
Wyandot Indians, 25, 150, 163
Wyoming Valley Massacre, 6

Yakima Indians, 320
Yankton Sioux Indians, 260-61
Yellow Banks, 243
Yellowstone National Park, 335-36
Yellowstone River, 264, 290-91, 302-303, 335-36
Young-Man-Afraid-of-His-Horse, 275, 293
Yukon River, 33
Yunque and Yuque (pueblos), 80

Zuñi Indians, 66, 79

FOR THE BEST IN PAPERBACKS, LOOK FOR THE

In every corner of the world, on every subject under the sun, Penguin represents quality and variety—the very best in publishing today.

For complete information about books available from Penguin—including Puffins, Penguin Classics, and Arkana—and how to order them, write to us at the appropriate address below. Please note that for copyright reasons the selection of books varies from country to country.

In the United Kingdom: Please write to *Dept. JC, Penguin Books Ltd, FREEPOST, West Drayton, Middlesex UB7 0BR*.

If you have any difficulty in obtaining a title, please send your order with the correct money, plus ten percent for postage and packaging, to *P.O. Box No. 11, West Drayton, Middlesex UB7 0BR*

In the United States: Please write to *Consumer Sales, Penguin USA, P.O. Box 999, Dept. 17109, Bergenfield, New Jersey 07621-0120*. VISA and MasterCard holders call 1-800-253-6476 to order all Penguin titles

In Canada: Please write to *Penguin Books Canada Ltd, 10 Alcorn Avenue, Suite 300, Toronto, Ontario M4V 3B2*

In Australia: Please write to *Penguin Books Australia Ltd, P.O. Box 257, Ringwood, Victoria 3134*

In New Zealand: Please write to *Penguin Books (NZ) Ltd, Private Bag 102902, North Shore Mail Centre, Auckland 10*

In India: Please write to *Penguin Books India Pvt Ltd, 706 Eros Apartments, 56 Nehru Place, New Delhi 110 019*

In the Netherlands: Please write to *Penguin Books Netherlands bv, Postbus 3507, NL-1001 AH Amsterdam*

In Germany: Please write to *Penguin Books Deutschland GmbH, Metzlerstrasse 26, 60594 Frankfurt am Main*

In Spain: Please write to *Penguin Books S. A., Bravo Murillo 19, 1° B, 28015 Madrid*

In Italy: Please write to *Penguin Italia s.r.l., Via Felice Casati 20, I-20124 Milano*

In France: Please write to *Penguin France S. A., 17 rue Lejeune, F-31000 Toulouse*

In Japan: Please write to *Penguin Books Japan, Ishikiribashi Building, 2-5-4, Suido, Bunkyo-ku, Tokyo 112*

In Greece: Please write to *Penguin Hellas Ltd, Dimocritou 3, GR-106 71 Athens*

In South Africa: Please write to *Longman Penguin Southern Africa (Pty) Ltd, Private Bag X08, Bertsham 2013*